Blackstone's
Handbook for the Special Constabulary

Edited by
Dr Bryn Caless

Contributors
Jerry Bownas, Mark Simpson,
Barry Spruce, and Robert Underwood

OXFORD
UNIVERSITY PRESS

OXFORD
UNIVERSITY PRESS

Great Clarendon Street, Oxford OX2 6DP

Oxford University Press is a department of the University of Oxford.
It furthers the University's objective of excellence in research, scholarship,
and education by publishing worldwide in

Oxford New York

Auckland Cape Town Dar es Salaam Hong Kong Karachi
Kuala Lumpur Madrid Melbourne Mexico City Nairobi
New Delhi Shanghai Taipei Toronto

With offices in

Argentina Austria Brazil Chile Czech Republic France Greece
Guatemala Hungary Italy Japan Poland Portugal Singapore
South Korea Switzerland Thailand Turkey Ukraine Vietnam

Oxford is a registered trade mark of Oxford University Press
in the UK and in certain other countries

Published in the United States
by Oxford University Press Inc., New York

© Oxford University Press 2010

The moral rights of the authors have been asserted
Database right Oxford University Press (maker)

Crown copyright material is reproduced under Class Licence
Number C01P0000148 with the permission of OPSI
and the Queen's Printer for Scotland

First published 2010

British Library Cataloguing in Publication Data

Data available

Library of Congress Cataloging-in-Publication Data

Blackstone's handbook for the special constabulary / edited by Bryn Caless;
authors, Jerry Bownas ... [et al.].
    p. cm.
    Includes bibliographical references and index.
    ISBN 978-0-19-959257-9 (pbk. : alk. paper)
        1. Police—Great Britain—Handbooks, manuals, etc.   2. Constables—
Great Britain—Handbooks, manuals, etc.   3. Volunteers—Great Britain—
Handbooks, manuals, etc.   I. Bownas, Jerry.   II. Caless, Bryn.
    HV8195.A2B63 2010
    363.20941—dc22

                                                              2010016761

Typeset by MPS Limited, A Macmillan Company
Printed in Italy on acid-free paper by
L.E.G.O. S.p.A.

ISBN 978-0-19-959257-9

10 9 8 7 6 5 4 3 2 1

Forewords

The Special Constabulary is fundamental to British policing. When Sir Robert Peel started the Metropolitan Police in 1829 he was clear that this was to be founded upon locally appointed ordinary citizens working with the consent of local people. The principles set down by his first commissioners included the line that the police are the public and the public are the police. This concept of a locally appointed, locally accountable police force is in our DNA but is very different from models in other countries where there are national forces seen as the arm of state power.

For many centuries people have volunteered to help keep order in their local area and the Special Constabulary merely follows that tradition. It is not policing on the cheap, it is the most powerful form of public engagement. The fact that ordinary people can come forward and take on all the powers and expectations of a regular officer adds so much to the openness of policing.

A few years ago the Irish government was thinking of setting up a volunteer police body and I was contacted by an Irish radio station to explain how it worked here. The presenter found it difficult to understand how a volunteer sworn in as a police officer off duty and on duty could be trusted with that degree of power and would be able to cope with the demands of the role. When I thought about it, yes, it is remarkable and hard for outsiders to understand, but it works and it works very well.

The Special Constabulary has come a long way over the last ten years. There was a time when it looked like Specials would wither on the vine: numbers were declining and the forthcoming introduction of Police Community Support Officers looked like a real threat. Through the interest of John Denham MP, then Police Minister, and a small but dedicated group of Specials chief officers, the decline was reversed. It is difficult to summarize all the work which then went on to create the National Strategy for the Special Constabulary. The best thing to say is that Specials are now embedded as a key element of Neighbourhood Policing and numbers continue to increase. More importantly, the credibility of the Special Constabulary has never been higher, driven by the professionalism and dedication of its members.

One of the challenges that the Special Constabulary faces is the growing complexity of policing and how we train volunteers to cope with the full range of duties. We have had to be realistic on this. The core role of any police officer is in local patrol and reassurance. This is also the role the public value the most. By being clear on this point we have been able to design training and induction packages around this core role and through that set a clear image in the public mind. This is not to say that Specials cannot do other things to broaden their experience, but we build upon this core role.

I am sure that this book will be a valuable resource for all Special Constables and further increase their professionalism. Policing is about relationships and building them to create trust with the public to solve problems and gain intelligence and information. I think the Special Constabulary is one of the most wonderful examples of volunteering you can think of. It strengthens that relationship with the public, and its members through their self-sacrifice and their dedication are an inspiration.

Peter Fahy
Chief Constable
Greater Manchester Police
and
ACPO Lead for Workforce Development

The Special Constabulary have a long and distinguished history and an important future in British policing. The idea of voluntary community policing goes back long before Sir Robert Peel created the modern police force in 1829. Constables drawn from their peers and supporting the Justice of the Peace were part of the fabric of an English local government that delivered the local peace for centuries. With the creation of the 'employed' police, the 'special' constabulary gradually shifted in their role. However, they played a crucial role in bolstering the regular police in 1848 at the time of the Chartist unrest and were critical in both World Wars.

As the role of the modern police force has expanded in the age of technology, the Special Constabulary has gone through its most dramatic shift since the Second World War. From an ill defined role—helping out on busy evenings, manning front counters, and looking after local fetes and events—the Specials have rapidly professionalized and become a volunteer reserve, the major gateway to the regular force, and a major part of the national Neighbourhood Policing approach.

This book is, therefore, very timely. It provides the most comprehensive survey of the role and challenges facing Special Constables. It takes the reader from an application to join to an understanding of the range of powers and duties that a Special will be asked to undertake. For a volunteer public service that is professionalizing, this is a much needed professional manual.

Peter Neyroud QPM
Chief Constable and Chief Executive of the
National Policing Improvement Agency

Acknowledgements

The Editor wishes particularly to thank:

Chris Booty, Chief Inspector in Devon and Cornwall Constabulary, for his help and deep knowledge in our discussions about the Special Constabulary, and for introducing me to key players;

Robin and **Sarah Bryant** for permission to adapt material from their definitive *Blackstone's Student Police Officer Handbook* (Oxford University Press), and for friendship over many years;

Graham Cline (Enquiries) and **Patricia Hughes** (Assistant Librarian), both of the National Police Library (Bramshill; through the courtesy of The Chief Executive Officer of the National Police Improvement Agency (NPIA), Chief Constable **Peter Neyroud**): especially for chasing down obscure and long-out-of-print material on the Special Constabulary;

Peter Daniell, Law Commissioning Editor of Oxford University Press—always encouraging, always cheerful, always ready with difficult deadlines; and **Lucy Alexander** for chasing me to complete on time;

Lesley Douglas-Kerbes for her researches in New Zealand and friendship for longer than either of us needs to remember;

my colleague **Kevin Lawton-Barratt** whose expertise in teaching forensic science is matched by his relishably dry wit, and I thank him for looking over the sections of this *Handbook* that we have written on *his* speciality;

David Llewellyn of Gwent Police for his comprehensive information on the Special Constabulary in Wales and for his photographs;

Fay Patey for her comments on the Canadian versions of the Special Constable and for *never* replying to my e-mails;

Chief Inspector **John Pavett** of Gwent Police for many conversations and insights into both regular and Special constables;

Ian Pointon of the Police Federation, for his usual robust approach to policing and his humour and care;

Acknowledgements

The Office of Public Service Information (opsi) for permission to quote extensively from government documents under Class Licence Number C2007000322;

the **anonymous reviewers** who kept us waiting for their thoughts, and for whom no effort on our part was enough;

Nathan de Thabrew, Special Constable and student, for his interest and comments;

Inspector **Andrew Turner** of Devon and Cornwall Constabulary for illuminating discussions on Specials in roads policing.

Special thanks to **Jerry Bownas**, **Mark Simpson**, **Barry Spruce**, and **Bob Underwood** for all their hard work in meeting impossible deadlines (and not sighing too audibly when my e-mails had no attachments . . .) and for being a knowledgeable and productive writing team.

Love and huge thanks to **Clare**, my forbearing and photocopying wife, and **Maddy**, my youngest daughter; for all they had to put up with when deadlines loomed, and for all their love; and to the rest of the family too: **Helen** and **Wez**, **Sally** and **Johnny**, and **Kit** and **Meghna**; for stimulating conversations and amused affection for their too-often preoccupied and occasionally grumpy parent.

Robert (Bob) Underwood: My thanks go to **Robin** and **Sarah Bryant** and fellow contributors to the *Blackstone's Student Police Officer Handbook* (Oxford University Press) for permitting me to adapt material from that publication. Without their support, my contribution to this book would have been so much more difficult. I would also like to thank my family for their ongoing and continued support for this and other writing projects and for remaining so incredibly patient whilst I hide away from them to work endlessly on my beleaguered laptop.

Barry Spruce would like to thank all his colleagues in the Extended Policing Family department at Kent Police, as well as those in the wider Operations Directorate, including those within the Special Constabulary. Special thanks must go to **Emma**, **Phoebe**, **Joseph**, and **Ethan**.

Mark Simpson particularly wishes to thank Dr **Steve Tong** and the Department of Law and Criminal Justice Studies at Canterbury Christ Church University, PC **Paul Gasson** of Kent Police for his continued guidance and his Special Constabulary and regular officer colleagues in Kent Police. Special thanks go to my parents **Colin** and **Skye**, my sister **Catherine**, and to **Emma** for all her patience and affection.

Contents

Contents

List of Figures

List of Figures

List of Abbreviations

ABH	actual bodily harm
ACPO	Association of Chief Police Officers
ANPR	automatic number-plate recognition
APA	Association of Police Authorities
ASB	anti-social behaviour
ASBO	Anti-social Behaviour Order
ASCC	Area Special Constabulary Coordinator
ASP	Armament Systems and Procedures (manufacturer's name)
BCS	British Crime Surveys
BCU	Basic Command Unit
CAP	common approach path (to crime scene)
CBL	computer-based learning
CBT	motorcyclist's Compulsory Basic Training course
CCTV	closed-circuit television
CDRP	Crime and Disorder Reduction Partnership
CHIS	Covert Human Intelligence Source
CJPOA	Criminal Justice and Public Order Act 1994
CJS	criminal justice system
CPIA	Criminal Procedures and Investigation Act 1996
CPR	cardiopulmonary resuscitation
CPS	*see* PPS below
CSAS	Community Safety Accreditation Scheme
CSI	crime scene investigators
CSP	Community Safety Partnership; Welsh name for CDRP, above
CT	counter terrorism
DNA	deoxyribonucleic acid
DPP	Director of Public Prosecutions
DVLA	Driver and Vehicle Licensing Agency
EFPN	endorsable fixed-penalty notices
ELC	experiential learning cycle
ESP	Employer-Supported Policing
ESV	Employer-Supported Volunteering
EVA	Environmental Visual Audit
FILA	free and independent legal advice

List of Abbreviations

FIS	local Force Intelligence Systems
FOA	first officer attending (scene of possible crime)
FPN	Fixed Penalty Notices
FTE	full-time equivalent
GBH	grievous bodily harm
GPMS	Government Protective Marking Scheme
HMIC	Her Majesty's Inspectorate of Constabulary
HSE	Health and Safety Executive
IDENT1	UK-wide automated fingerprint analysis system
IPCC	Independent Police Complaints Commission
IR	infrared
JP	Justice of the Peace, lay magistrate
LCN	Low Copy Number DNA analysis
MAPPA	Multi-Agency Public Protection Arrangements
MO	*modus operandi*, the way it was done
MOPI	Management of Police Information
NADC	National ANPR Data Centre
NCALT	NPIA's National Centre for Applied Learning Technologies
NDC	New Deal for Communities
NDNAD	National DNA Database
NEFPN	non-endorsable fixed-penalty notice
NIM	National Intelligence Model
NIP	Notice of Intended Prosecution
NOMS	National Offender Management Service
NOS	National Occupational Standards
NPIA	National Policing Improvement Agency
NPT	Neighbourhood Policing Team
NRD	number-plate reading device
NTT	Neighbourhood Task Team
OCR	Optical Character Recognition software
OIC	officer in charge
OST/PST	Officer/Personal Safety Training
OSU	Operational Support Unit
PAC	Police Action Checklist
PACE Act 1984	Police and Criminal Evidence Act 1984
PACT	Partners and Communities Together
PAVA	synthetic pepper spray
PCSO	Police Community Support Officer
PDP	Personal Development Profile
PNB	Pocket Notebook

PNC	Police National Computer
PND	Penalty Notice for Disorder
PNLD	Police National Legal Database
POH	*Police Operational Handbook*, Bridges, I (ed.) (2006)
PPE	personal protective equipment
PPS	Public Prosecution Service (formerly CPS, Crown Prosecution Service)
PR	personal radio
PSV	Police Support Volunteers
PTSD	post-traumatic stress disorder
QC	Queen's Counsel, a senior barrister
RJ	Restorative Justice
ROA	Rehabilitation of Offenders Act 1974
ROTI	recording of a taped interview
ROVI	recording of a videotaped interview
RPU	Roads Policing Unit
RV	rendezvous point (outside crime scene)
SC	Special Constable(s)
SDN	short descriptive note on a case file
SNTT	Special Neighbourhood Task Team
SOCA	Serious and Organized Crime Agency
SOCO	Scenes of Crime Officer; now mostly called CSI (see above)
STR	Short Tandem Repeat DNA profiling
TRiM	Trauma Risk Management
TWOC	taking [a conveyance] without the owner's consent
UDT	unarmed defence training
VDRS	Vehicle Defect Rectification Scheme
VEL	vehicle excise licence
VOSA	Vehicle & Operator Services Agency
VRM	vehicle registration marks

Introduction

This Handbook is designed primarily for the Special Constable and nearly all the case studies, tasks, and examples used in it are related to or drawn from the experiences of being a volunteer police officer. That is not to say that it cannot be read with profit by others in the policing family such as Police Community Support Officers (PCSOs), wardens and other members of local partnerships, neighbourhood policing teams, and regular police officers. Indeed, the book has much to offer the student of policing whether or not s/he is actually engaged in the practice. It aspires to be as up-to-date as possible, subject to the continuous flux and change that surrounds modern policing in England and Wales. Actually, it is the peripheries that change; policing itself changes very little.

Sir Richard Mayne, the first Commissioner of the 'New Police' for the metropolis of London wrote this in 1829:

> The primary object of an efficient police is the prevention of crime: the next that of detection and punishment of offenders if crime is committed. To these ends all the efforts of police must be directed. The protection of life and property, the preservation of public tranquillity, and the absence of crime, will alone prove whether those efforts have been successful and whether the objects for which the police were appointed have been attained.[1]

'The prevention of crime', the 'detection and punishment of offenders', 'protection of life and property', 'the preservation of public tranquillity' (keeping the peace), 'and the absence of crime' are all things that are as resonant now as when Mayne wrote them more than 180 years ago. We might omit the *'punishment of offenders'* as this is more to do with the courts than with the police, and substitute *'bringing to justice'* to capture a more modern role and meaning. The essential point is that Mayne's list of police objectives preoccupies the Special Constable on duty today every bit as much as it occupied the first 'blue locusts' to patrol in London in 1830.

What is a Special Constable?

We shall start by asking you, the reader, to do this task:

Task
Make a list of the characteristics of a Special Constable.

Ours is not meant to be a model answer, but we shall assume that your list was something like this:

Characteristics of a Special Constable
- Volunteer
- Unpaid
- Part-time
- Is a warrant-holder under the Crown
- Has the same powers as a regular police officer
- Undergoes a comprehensive training programme
- Does many of the things that a regular police officer would do
- May have held other full- or part-time employment, or another full- or part-time occupation (such as student)
- Agrees to minimum of 4 hours a week or 16 hours a month of unpaid duty
- Is drawn from the community
- Understands local issues
- Can identify the local leaders
- Knows what concerns local people
- **Is enthusiastic, willing, committed, and possessed of a strong sense of public duty and obligation**.

You might not have included that last bullet point. We have highlighted this because, throughout our work for this *Handbook*, we have been continually impressed by how much Special Constables actually *do* in service across England and Wales, and how their enthusiasm for duty, their pleasure in serving as police officers, and their sense of social obligation, of 'putting something back', is immense.

It is impressive to note that Special Constables volunteer for roads traffic policing in Devon and Cornwall, for example, or that they are engaged closely in changing the attitudes of bored youths in Cheshire, or that they have created a 'Task Force' that intervenes in local instances of anti-social behaviour in Kent (all examples which we explore in the pages which follow).

The government has invested £2.25 million in funding a package to increase the numbers of Special Constables to 20,000 by 2012; both it and the police service can clearly see a percentage in having more police officers available, whose costs are minimal (see 1.1 and 1.2 below). They clearly think that a Special Constable is worth it. So do we.

We want to take you through an important national document—the fruit of many months of discussion, and born, too, of many years of 'Special' experience by most of those who took part: it is the National Strategy for the Special Constabulary.

National Strategy for the Special Constabulary

The need for a proper and coherent *national* strategy for the recruitment, training, and deployment of Special Constables was first debated in the months leading up to the annual Specials' National Conference in March 2006. A key element in this was partnership with the Association of Chief Police Officers (ACPO) so that there was 'buy-in' to the Special Constabulary on behalf of the whole police service. Another key relationship was with the National Policing Improvement Agency (NPIA) which now 'owns' policy on behalf of the Special Constabulary and the police service. Prior to this, obtaining national agreement to matters affecting the Special Constabulary was difficult, with many police forces pursuing individual recruitment and deployment agenda which might (and often did) run counter to that of a neighbouring force.

The situation is by no means fully coherent and consistent across England and Wales yet, but there has been steady progress towards consensus on what is required. It may be some time before a fully national standard is achieved on uniform, training, equipment, deployment, ranks, and advancement, but a solid start has been made. It is worth noting that individual police forces are quite often at minor variance from the norm in the police service (for example, in the matter of what vehicles or computer equipment a force uses), so it is not a surprise that the Special Constabulary should also show variation or individuality from force to force. The police will tell you, in relaxed moments, that getting police forces and their Chief Constables to do things together is like herding cats. (Writing a handbook which reflects the many variations in practice between Special Constabularies across England and Wales is sometimes like that too . . .)

The point is that, on all key *strategic* issues, there is national agreement following the drafting of the National Strategy in 2007 and its acceptance at the Specials' Annual Conference in March 2008. Significantly, there was full agreement that national standards should apply to the use of a two-part application form, the establishment of an assessment centre model, and the creation of a core national curriculum for initial and ongoing training (see the National Strategy).[2] This will enable consistency between forces and will signal to the regular police that the Special Constabulary is modernizing in step with them.[3]

Key Areas of Policing

The National Strategy identifies seven key areas of policing 'in which Specials can make a substantial contribution' (*National Strategy* document):[4]

Key Areas for Special Constabulary
- Public reassurance
- Crime reduction
- Anti-social behaviour and public order
- Investigation of minor crimes
- Drink/drugs driving
- ANPR vehicle checks
- Major incidents

These themes dominate this *Handbook*, and in the chapters that follow, we go into each of these key areas, and many more too, to give you a comprehensive description of the police work involved. NPIA has published *National Strategy Implementation Advice* (see Further Reading at the end of the Introduction) which builds on the National Strategy itself, by offering advice on good practice, case studies, and discussions of marketing, recruitment, training and development, deployment and tasking, human resources' management, performance management, and leadership. The philosophy of the *Implementation Advice* underpins the work we have done in this *Handbook*, but we also go into more detail and offer an independent (and we hope objective) view of the practicalities involved, based on the experience of the many Special Constables across England and Wales who have spoken to us. Many of the elements which appear here just as headline words, are explored in depth in the chapters that follow.

The Numbers Game

What size is the Special Constabulary? Bearing in mind that the government has set a target of 20,000 Special Constables by 2012, it is helpful to know the base figure. According to the latest Home Office figures available as we went to press at the end of 2009, there are 14,251 Special Constables in England and Wales.[5] This compares with 143,770 'full-time equivalent' police officers in the 43 police forces of England and Wales recorded on 31 March 2009.

However, whilst Special Constables seem on this basis to represent about 10 per cent of the full-time strength of regular police officers, the comparison is not exact, since Special Constables are not available for duty for hours comparable with those worked by salaried police officers. The Home Office has merely used a 'head count' rather than a full-time-equivalent (FTE) calculation. Given that the minimum hours which Special Constables agree to provide (4 per week) represent about 10 per cent of the hours worked by FTE regular police officers (approximately 40 per week), it would be a fairer comparison altogether if we noted that the Special Constabulary FTE strength therefore represents (at a minimum) 1 per cent of the strength of all police officers in England and Wales. Of course, many Special Constables work far more than the minimum number of hours.

This is not the whole picture. The overall Special Constabulary strength has dipped by 296 officers (representing 2 per cent fewer than last year). This drop in numbers follows a 3.8 per cent increase in March 2008, a 6.4 per cent increase in March 2007, and a 10.6 per cent increase in March 2006.[6] Some fluctuation in numbers is to be expected. People often say that they join the Special Constabulary intending to apply to be a regular police officer in time. Not many actually go on to do so, if the data are to be believed. In the year to 31 March 2009, only 3.2 per cent of new regular police officers had previously been Special Constables.

When we examine how Special Constables can be analysed in terms of gender and ethnic minority status, we find that the often-quoted adage that *Special Constables are drawn directly from the communities they serve*, is true:

Gender and minority ethnic proportions

Women accounted for 33 per cent of Special Constables, a much higher proportion than for regular police officers (about 25 per cent in 2008–2009).

Nearly 10 per cent of Special Constables were from minority ethnic communities (9.6 per cent). This was also higher than the proportion among the regulars. The Metropolitan Police had the highest proportion of minority-ethnic Special Constables (32.6 per cent), followed by West Midlands (20.6 per cent), and Leicestershire (18.9 per cent).

One other point to make is that the turnover (also known as 'wastage') of Special Constables was 21.5 per cent in the year to 31 March 2009, up from 18.5 per cent in the year to 31 March 2008. In figures, 3,358 special constables joined the Special Constabulary and 3,071 left.

The upshot of the numbers game is that there must be a determined campaign to attract new people to join the Special Constabulary if the government target of 20,000 is to be reached by 2012. Regional Leads for the Special Constabulary (see 1.8) have been appointed to help coordinate recruitment drives. We support any attempt to increase Special Constabulary numbers (provided there is no dilution of skills or enthusiasm for the role), but it is also probably true that, as many Special Constables have told us, the preferable 'paid' route into the regular police is through the PCSO role, and increasing numbers of Special Constables seem to be considering taking a PCSO post—for which they would be well qualified—because of the salary that comes with it. We freely admit that our evidence for this is anecdotal, though extensive; PCSO numbers are well up, there is no apparent shortage of applicants, and the turnover is relatively small. Losing one-fifth (or so) of Special Constables every year (see the shaded box above) would be worrying unless it could be shown that PCSOs were the gainers. We are confident, though, that numbers of Special Constables will rise again, provided always that police forces are prepared to offer challenge, variety, and a 'real' policing job to them. Special Constables have told us that they volunteer in order to be stretched and tested, not to be bored and resentful in 'nothing jobs'.

How to use this *Handbook*

We don't expect you to read this *Handbook* as you would a novel, starting at the beginning and reading in sequence through to the end. Riveting though our prose style is, we think you are more likely to dip into sections as you need them or as you want to remind yourself about the components of a law, or a power, or a procedure. To help you to do this, we have created within each chapter a series of stand-alone sections distinguished by numbered headings. Each of the major headings is glossed in the Index, so you can look up 'Neighbourhood Policing', for example, in a number of ways: in a discussion of the Special Constabulary's regional command structure (1.9), as related to a neighbourhood or community (7.1), as part of a Special Constable's deployment (6.4) or a Neighbourhood Policing Team (7.7). Additionally, other references to neighbourhood policing are located under this generic heading in the Index.

Each of the chapters is complete in itself and covers part of the Special Constable experience:

- What is involved in volunteering?
- The context of policing
- Recruitment
- Standards of professional behaviour
- Training, development, and learning
- Police powers (including stop, search and entry, investigation, arrest, detention and disposal, managing people and incidents, and roads and traffic)
- Criminal law (law and procedure, criminal investigation)
- Deployment partnerships
- Neighbourhood policing
- Crime scene management (crime scenes, forensic and other evidence, victims, witnesses, suspects, and offenders)
- Going to court
- The criminal justice system
- The future of policing.

The highlighted topics above are the largest in the *Handbook*, which is comprehensive and thorough. We test you from time to time, we highlight important things in shaded boxes, and we ask you to think for yourself at certain key points, mindful that our readers could equally be 1) someone thinking about joining the Special Constabulary, 2) someone who has just joined, or 3) a seasoned and experienced Special Constable who none-theless wants to brush up his or her knowledge or recall of some aspect of policing. We cater for all. For those who want to read more, we have Further Reading sections at the end of each chapter as well as a comprehensive Bibliography at the end of the book, where we have listed all the main thinkers, writers, commentators, and practitioners whose views have helped us in creating this *Handbook*.

However, *it is worth noting that this is not just a reference book, nor a compendium of Special Constables' duties; it is much more than that.* The *Handbook* gives **a context to policing** as a concept as well as to what is involved in being a police officer at the beginning of this century. It introduces discussions, research, controversies, and disagreements which may not always be evident to those outside policing, as well as looking at matters which dominate (and divide) criminal justice thinking.

We look at new ideas and evaluate the more tried and trusted methodologies, but we never forget that **this is first and foremost a Handbook for the Special Constable**—*not* for the regular police officer, *nor* the PCSO, and *not* for the general reader. They are welcome to use it, but it is intended for you, Special Constable, designed for you, written with you in mind. and, as often as possible, with clear understanding of both the constraints and freedoms which being a volunteer police officer may entail.

Further Reading

Although this *Handbook* is comprehensive and provides a full briefing for Special Constables, we understand, of course, that it cannot do absolutely everything. There are more detailed handbooks and specialist publications about particular aspects of policing or the law. What we want to do here is suggest some of them which might be useful to you and which you could consult with profit.

During March 2010 the NPIA launched version 6 of its new draft National Curriculum for Special Constables, entitled *The Initial Learning Programme for the Special Constabulary* or '*IL4SC*'. As we go to press, NPIA has asked five forces to trial *IL4SC* with a view to recommending it as best practice. IL4SC would achieve the establishment of a national standard in the Special Constabulary training curriculum, and would create a nationally-recognised training qualification for Special Constables. This in turn would make the Special Constabulary more flexible for individual officers who may need to move counties or force areas owing to work or family commitments and who wish to continue serving as Specials without having to undergo a full initial Special Constable learner programme again. It is too early to say if the programme will be widely adopted by forces (it is not mandatory), indeed, there has been no independent evaluation of its effectiveness yet.

Bryant, R and Bryant, S, (eds.), with Caless, B, Lawton-Barratt, K, Murphy, R, Underwood, R, and Wood, D, *Blackstone's Student Police Officer Handbook*, 4th edn. (2010, Oxford: Oxford University Press).

Now in its fourth edition, this is edited by Robin and Sarah Bryant, and has a posse of contributing authors, including some of those involved in this *Handbook*. The *SPOH* is a comprehensive introduction to policing in all its variety. However, it is designed primarily for the regular student police officer in the first two or so years of his or her career, and is aimed, obviously, at the generalist officer who has yet to specialize. It does not cater for the Special Constable, but we make extensive reference to it throughout this *Handbook*, and, along with many others, are indebted to its huge spread and detail.

A companion volume is:

Bryant, R and Bryant, S, (eds.) *et al*, *Blackstone's Student Police Officer Workbook* (2010, Oxford: Oxford University Press).

Other useful reference and 'context' books include:

ACPO/NPIA, *Practice Advice on Professionalising the Business of Neighbourhood Policing*, NPIA, (2006, Wyboston, Lincolnshire: National Centre for Policing Excellence, part of NPIA), available from: <http://www.neighbourhoodpolicing.co.uk/doclib/doclib_view.asp?ID=528>.

This covers most of the aspects of neighbourhood policing in which most Special Constables (but not all) will find themselves working at some point in their careers. It is well worth dipping into to refresh your recall of the aims and components of neighbourhood policing.

Police National Legal Database, *Blackstone's Police Operational Handbook: Law*, Bridges, I and Sampson, F (eds.), (2010, Oxford: Oxford University Press).

This detailed reference book is intended for those in the criminal justice system (but particularly police officers, Special Constables, and PCSOs) who have *to 'interpret and apply'* the criminal law. The Police National Legal Database (PNLD) is an ACPO-managed (not-for-profit) organization which is subscribed to by all police forces, the Public Prosecution Service (previously the Crown Prosecution Service, or CPS), and others in the criminal justice system. We strongly recommend that Special Constables refer to this excellent book for detail on the criminal law.

Caless, B (ed.), Bryant, R, Spruce, B, and Underwood, R, *Blackstone's PCSO Handbook*, 2nd edn. (2010, Oxford: Oxford University Press).

Designed primarily for PCSOs and members of neighbourhood policing teams, this *Handbook* deals comprehensively with communities, neighbourhoods, engagement with citizens and dealing with minor crimes, nuisance, infringement of by-laws, anti-social behaviour, vandalism, and criminal damage as well as giving a valuable context to policing for the newest member of the extended policing family.

Fitzpatrick, B, Menzies, C, and Hunter, R, *Going to Court*, Blackstone's Practical Policing, (2006, Oxford: Oxford University Press).

This is a very good review or introduction—depending on whether you are experienced or a new joiner—for Special Constables who are to attend court. It gives considerable detail on how courts are organized and how evidence is given.

Harfield, C (ed.), *Blackstone's Police Operational Handbook: Practice and Procedure*, (2009, Oxford: Oxford University Press).

This has a complete eight-chapter section—Part 3, *Neighbourhood Policing*—which was written by Bryn Caless and Barry Spruce to give a context for neighbourhood policing, and additionally 'considers its principles, parts and practices'. It is the most comprehensive treatment of neighbourhood policing available at the moment.

NPIA, *A National Strategy for the Special Constabulary* (2008, Strong Worldwide: on behalf of the National Policing Improvement Agency) also available from the NPIA website at <http://www.npia.police.uk/en/11813.htm>.

As we note throughout the *Handbook*, this is a seminal document for the Special Constabulary, since it sets out directions and deployments which can support regular policing activities. It is very much the Special Constabulary's own document, but it is of general interest too.

Tilley, N (ed.), *Handbook of Crime Prevention and Community Safety*, (2005, Devon: Willan Publishing).

Nick Tilley is a prominent academic commentator on the police and here he edits a range of contributions from different writers, on the theme of crime prevention, crime reduction, and a community's sense of safety. It has some excellent ideas for initiatives in local crime prevention, not least in 'designing-out crime' as long-term solutions to blighted urban areas.

The Bibliography at the end of this *Handbook* gives a wide selection of other contemporary specialist writings which reflect or impinge on the work of the Special Constabulary.

Notes

1 As reported on the Metropolitan Police history website, see <http://www.met.police.uk/history/definition.htm>, accessed 13 November 2009.

2 The full text of the *National Strategy for the Special Constabulary*, and much more besides in terms of its implementation, is available from <http://www.npia.police.uk/en/docs/Imp_Strategy_updated.pdf>, accessed 13 November 2009.

3 It is worth noting who the major stakeholders in the Special Constabulary are:

   The Home Office
   The Justice Ministry
   The Association of Chief Police Officers (ACPO)
   The National Policing Improvement Agency (NPIA, which includes national police training and publishes the *Specials* magazine)
   The Association of Police Authorities (APA)
   HM Inspectorate of Constabulary (HMIC)
   The Police Federation

   There are others, as well as interested parties from volunteering organizations and individual police forces, many of whom we shall refer to or cite in the rest of the *Handbook*. What may be concluded from the list shown here is that *the leading police organizations and the principal Departments of State support and endorse the work done for and through the Special Constabulary.*

4 See also Almandras, S, *Special Constables* (2008, Standard Note for the Library of the House of Commons SNHA/1154) Home Affairs Department, House of Commons, 31 October 2008, pp 8–9.

5 See Mulchandani, R and Sigurdsson, J, *Police Service Strength: England and Wales* (2009, Home Office Statistical Bulletin 13/09, 23 July, Crown Copyright). The statistics in this section are derived from the Mulchandani and Sigurdsson findings.

6 *Ibid.*

Chapter 1
Being Special

1.1 Introduction: 'A Manifest Sign'

> The Special Constabulary is a volunteer body designed to assist the regular police, drawn mainly from the communities served by each force. Special Constables perform Constabulary duties and exercise constabulary powers under the supervision of, and supported by, regular officers. They are expected to achieve and maintain a level of proficiency which will enable them to assist regular officers in solving local policing problems, and thereby to enhance the overall contribution and effectiveness of their local police force. *They are a manifest sign of partnership between the police and the public.* [our italics]
>
> (*Report of the Working Group on the Special Constabulary in England and Wales 1995–1996,* see Further Reading)

Some of the descriptions of the Special Constabulary in the extract quoted above no longer apply or are slightly misleading. For example, the idea of Special Constables being always 'under the supervision of [. . .] regular officers' is only true some of the time in some forces. It does not hold in all circumstances; and we are aware of many forces whose response/patrol function at weekends is made credible only by Special Constables working alone or in teams.[1] What is demonstrably still true however is that the 'volunteer body' supports the regular police and is 'drawn [. . .] from the communities'. Above all that is the primary characteristic of Special Constables expressed in the sentence we have highlighted:

They are a manifest sign of partnership between the police and the public

and this has never been more important than it is now. It has almost become something of a cliché to say that, pre-eminently, the Special Constable is a **citizen police officer**. Of course, so is the regular officer, but payment to a police officer for policing and security is relatively new (from 1830 or thereabouts), whilst *citizen police service from the community for the community, freely offered*, is ages old.

The salient characteristic of the Special Constabulary is precisely that it does its policing from a sense of community; it is policing by *volunteers* who want to perform a duty as citizens for the greater good. No one coerced them into deciding that this was what they wanted to do for society. We summarize the process this way:

Discussion points

Someone becomes a Special Constable as a result of:

a personal decision, voluntarily arrived at, in full recognition of the obligations that such office carries and the restriction which will be placed upon individual freedom, [which] has, as its outcome, service to the people.

This is a selfless and sociable act, but all such acts need a context if we are to understand them properly. The uniqueness of the Special Constabulary, and its place in the context of criminal justice, is what this chapter (and, indeed, this *Handbook*) is about.

1.2 **On Volunteers and Volunteering**

In February 2008, the Special Constabulary took part in the first ever national Police Support Volunteers (PSV) Conference, under the auspices of the NPIA. One of the guest speakers was Baroness Julia Neuberger, Adviser to the Government on Volunteering, who has overseen a 2008 review of volunteering in the criminal justice system.[2] She said this at the Conference, when referring to police volunteering:

Community ownership of policing services is absolutely critical and I don't think you can do it without volunteers.

(reported in *Specials*, March 2008, p 3)

It is necessary of course to note that Police Service Volunteers include more groups than solely the Special Constabulary (see 1.4.1, below), but the principle addressed by Baroness Neuberger applies precisely to the processes that we have been examining above. In a real sense the 'citizen police force' envisaged by Sir Robert Peel, in which *the public are the police and the police are the public*,[3] is exemplified in the Special Constabulary. Or, as the

Chief Constable of Greater Manchester Police, Peter Fahy (ACPO Lead for the Special Constabulary), remarked:

> You are [in the Special Constabulary] because of the personal right of every local citizen to exercise powers as a constable.
>
> (*Specials* magazine, May 2008, p 9)

1.3 **The Employer**

The other side of the volunteering equation for the Special Constable is the role of the employer. The use of the term 'equation' suggests a bipolar dimension, but actually, the relationship is more like a triangle than something linear:

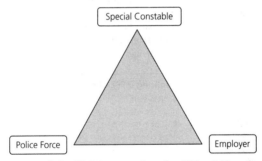

Figure 1.1: Relationship between employer, Special Constable, and police force

The Special Constable volunteer is usually employed at something else, and his or her commitment to the police impinges in some ways on that normal, full-time, paid employment, and upon the employer. It is therefore preferable always to engage the Special Constable's employer in the process of volunteering: at the very least the employer should be aware of activities which might affect the employee's activities at work. Normally, though, both the police force and the Special Constable would seek ways in which the employer can be more actively involved.

1.3.1 Employer-Supported Volunteering (ESV)

A template for engaging employers is found in **Employer-Supported Volunteering** (ESV). This encourages employers of all kinds to have a stake in employee volunteering in many different ways, from allowing periods of paid time off, to creating a positive public relations image for the individual company or organization. That said, a report in 2009 by Cathy McBain of Volunteering England and Joanna Machin of the Institute for Volunteering Research notes that 'business benefits are still not of sufficient weight to encourage employers to get involved'.[4]

1.3.2 Employer-Supported Policing (ESP)

A specific development from ESV, called Employer-Supported Policing (ESP), originally concerned Special Constabulary duties in and around the retail, public service, or commercial sector in which there is a direct and identifiable business benefit obtained from close linkage between a person's daily work and his or her work as a Special Constable. The general idea was that staff who are also Special Constables patrolled local areas or commercial or public premises relevant to their employers' occupations. There were six industry-specific schemes:

Employer-Supported Policing (ESP) schemes	
ShopWatch	for retail staff
BoroughBeat	for council staff
HospitalWatch	for staff in the NHS
BusWatch	for bus drivers and depot staff
CampusWatch	for students and teaching staff
ArtBeat	for those engaged in arts and crafts

(Source: adapted from *Specials*, March 2008, pp 9–10)

These schemes have been used in several police forces; however, more recently, the ESP scheme has extended to police staff.[5] This allows police service employees to have paid time for SC volunteering—the number of hours varies from force to force but tends to be between four and eight (these staff are then expected to make up the minimum requirement of sixteen hours per month from their own time). The NPIA has reinvigorated the ESP scheme to get other employers involved (although at the time of writing, developments are still in the preparatory stage).

Essentially, the ESP concept will be branded with a new identity and will be supported with new advertising to get more employers on board. Their staff will then be given paid time to volunteer as a SC. Some larger companies such as HSBC and Sainsbury's have already declared their support, but during

2010–11 each police force is expected to embark on new schemes to get local employers involved. It is too early to predict the success or otherwise of this rebranding of ESP, but it does show that the Special Constabulary is looking carefully at its strategic marketing.

The Metropolitan Police has recruited nearly a quarter of its serving Special Constables through the ESP scheme and the benefit to employers is obvious: there are knowledgeable staff serving as Specials who know the industry and its major players, and who are familiar with operations and procedures particular to the employment. Employers gain security and enhanced crime prevention (as well as crime detection) in exchange for investment in the scheme and allowing staff paid time off. In contemporary parlance, this is seen as a 'win/win' situation in which all parties to the triangular agreement gain benefit.

Some disadvantages to ESP schemes: a case study

West Midlands Police launched its own ShopWatch scheme in Birmingham in 2006. This was initially very successful and 15 Special Constables were recruited who made an impact on the levels of crime and anti-social behaviour in the shopping areas in the centre of the city, though it is important to note that most of the Specials recruited were support staff and cleaners (from the 'concierge business') rather than shop staff.

Some of those recruited in 2006 went on to join the regular police and others drifted away or left both the Special Constabulary and their employer. Only 4 Special Constables remained in 2008 from the original 15 recruited. The downside for the employers was that staff left specific employment to join the regular police, whilst others left the industry altogether.

The loss of 11 people over 2 years is high, even in volunteer schemes, and employer enthusiasm has demonstrably waned as a consequence. It proved difficult to recruit new volunteers and replacements after the first flush of enthusiasm. It has been equally difficult to persuade new employers of the benefits of allowing staff paid time off to do Special Constabulary duties.

Forces should be proactively engaging with employers in the triangular dynamic with which we began. If a force is not, it clearly

(Sources: *Specials* January 2008, pp 9–10, ESP and Institute for Volunteering Research websites, and SC blogs)

takes the role of the volunteer police officer more lightly than it should. As we move closer to 2012 and the Government target of 20,000 Special Constables becomes ever more pressing, new and innovative ways to engage employers must be sought. The impetus to join the Special Constabulary from an employee needing the support of his or her employer, may actually be pushing at an already open door, something which the 'new' ESP should encourage. But forces will not know if an employer is sympathetic unless they commit time and effort to explaining their needs, and take pains to spell out the business and social benefits—as the revamped ESP scheme suggests. Once the employer is enthusiastic, and says so publicly, employees are unlikely to be reticent or reluctant to come forward to volunteer. This is not a chicken-or-egg choice—some people will become Special Constables whether their employers support them or not—but it is clearly better to have an understanding and supportive employer, fully in tune with the aims of the Special Constabulary, than to have one who is not.

1.4 **The Extended Police Family**

Consider this diagram:

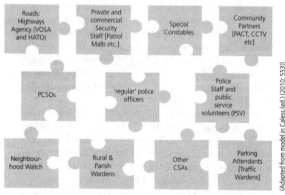

(Adapted from model in Caless (ed.) (2010: 553))

Figure 1.2: The 'Mixed Economy' model of the extended police family

This jigsaw diagram represents the relationship between the various organizations that make up the '**Extended Policing Family**'.

However, the diagram is not definitive because each police force will have other organizations that they bring into this 'family' to deal with specific and localized problems. Furthermore, the flexibility of these relationships will mean that some agencies move in and out of this arrangement in an informal and fluid way. Do not confuse this concept with 'partnership'. Although many of the Extended Policing Family operate within partnerships, the term as used by the police tends to indicate a more formalized arrangement, usually with organizations outside the law-enforcement family such as the Fire and Rescue Service or local authority departments (in Crime and Disorder Reduction Partnerships—CDRPs—for example). We're sorry if all this sounds convoluted: practice varies widely between police forces and we are merely trying to describe a relationship that may have infinite tiny variables.[6]

1.4.1 Extended Policing Family—three elements

We will look at three members of the Extended Policing Family to demonstrate the relationship they have with the Special Constabulary, and suggest to you that Neighbourhood Watch, which we examine in Chapter 7, is another example of the growing EP Family.

1.4.1.1 *Police Community Support Officer (PCSO)*

One significant development within the Extended Policing Family was the introduction of the Police Community Support Officer (PCSO) by the Police Reform Act 2002. In much the same way that auxiliary nurses and teaching assistants were seen as somehow subversive of the natural order in the NHS and schools, so the PCSO proved to be a contentious political issue at first. Opposition to the PCSO came principally from the Police Federation who described them and their role in the pejorative phrase 'numties in yellow jackets' [see Caless, 2007 and Caless (ed.) *et al*, 2010]. However in many communities, particularly those in rural locations, or those where the police presence had previously been sporadic, *the PCSO was welcomed as the visible personification of reassurance patrolling*. Most of the 16,000 PCSOs currently employed have become a very public representation of the police's commitment to Neighbourhood Policing (see Chapter 7 for a fuller explanation) and in many cases, PCSOs have been the first police to respond to low-level incidents and anti-social behaviour.

1.4.1.2 *PCSO Role Definition*

It was not until 2008, six years after their introduction, that the NPIA tried to define what PCSOs do. Because there are many regional and force 'variants' in both deployment and function, the PCSO role is not easy to pin down. NPIA's definition, which expresses some of this elasticity, depicts a PCSO who is

> integrated into a Neighbourhood Policing team (normally geographic but could be for a defined community of interest, for example. Safer Transport teams)
> Or
> deployed to directly support Neighbourhood Policing team(s) in their neighbourhoods (in both the above the PCSOs should spend the majority of their time within neighbourhoods and not be office/police station based and/or undertaking administrative roles).
> With *all* the below principles applying:
> - Undertake public facing non-confrontational duties in uniform
> - Visible in the communities on foot or cycle patrol (vehicle if rural community)
> - Deal with anti-social behaviour (ASB), low level crime and incidents, local problems/priorities and quality of life issues
> - Support and improve service to victims and vulnerable people
> - Conduct engagement and problem solving activity
>
> (NPIA, 2008)

> **Discussion point**
> Where a Special Constable works with a PCSO, in what ways can you see that this will ensure adherence to the above role specification?

1.4.1.3 *PCSO Powers*

To further complicate the PCSOs' position, their powers are divided between standard and non-standard (or 'discretionary'). The first are powers that all PCSOs across England and Wales have, although some will seldom be used, whilst the second are those that can be 'designated' (applied or granted) at the behest of each Chief Constable.[7] This has created a contradictory and inconsistent system under which a PCSO in Manchester may function in a very different way from, and even make use of different sets of powers to, a PCSO in Norwich. There has been some recent movement within the Home Office to standardize PCSO powers but this will require legislative change and therefore may take some time, and will entail the novel prospect of all Chief Constables agreeing to lose their discretionary input to the powers a PCSO has and therefore what a PCSO does or does not do.

1.4.1.4 *Police Service Volunteers (PSVs)*

More recent additions to the Extended Policing Family are Police Service Volunteers (PSVs), which we must note are *distinct in kind and degree from the more specialist and professional volunteering that the Special Constabulary does*. PSVs provide a 'gift' of time and commitment to the police in their community. A 2008 survey by the NPIA revealed that 32 of the 43 'home' police forces have volunteer programmes with over 6,000 people actively volunteering (NPIA website). Most volunteers, particularly those working in police stations, are vetted and undergo an interview and/or training process. Often the force has a Volunteer Coordinator to oversee the programme and, in particular, to work closely with the unions and staff associations to ensure that the volunteers are not taking the place of paid employees.

1.4.1.5 *PSV Roles*

These are some of the roles that PSVs perform across police forces in England and Wales:

- Administrative help in Neighbourhood Policing Teams
- Mystery shoppers
- Puppy walkers
- Maintaining memorial gardens
- Opening 'satellite' front counters in small towns and villages
- Organizing public meetings such as PACT (Partners and Communities Together)
- Data input, eg survey responses
- Washing police cars
- Emergency exercise role-players
- Search and rescue teams
- Role-players for training purposes
- Assisting at events.

It is anticipated that the scope for volunteers within policing will continue to grow. The NPIA report in 2008 also showed that the demographic profile of the PSV is different from those of both the regular police and the Special Constabulary, and brings considerable diversity to the policing family: 57 per cent are female, 25 per cent are over the age of 65, and nearly 8 per cent are from minority ethnic communities, whilst 1.5 per cent describe themselves as having a disability.[8]

> **Discussion point**
>
> Where a Special Constable works with a PSV, in what ways can you see that this will enhance both your role and the work of volunteers?

1.4.1.6 *Community Safety Accreditation Scheme (CSAS)*

The Community Safety Accreditation Scheme (CSAS) derives from the Police Reform Act 2002 and allows Chief Constables to 'accredit' employees of many organizations, both public and private, who work in the field of community safety. Such employees are known, rather stodgily, as 'Accredited Persons' and must display a standard 'accreditation badge' as part of any uniform. In practice, a Chief Constable will accredit employees only with those powers that help community safety; it is not a 'pick and mix' menu.[9] A Home Office audit in 2008 showed that 23 forces had accreditation schemes in place, involving 95 approved organizations and 1,406 accredited persons (Home Office website).

1.4.1.7 *CSAS Case Studies*

In 33 police forces in England and Wales the **Vehicle & Operator Services Agency (VOSA)** has been accredited with the power to stop vehicles for the purpose of conducting on-the-spot checks, such as those to ascertain vehicle roadworthiness. Previously the police had to actually stop vehicles with VOSA personnel doing the subsequent checks, so by accrediting and training VOSA to do the stopping as well as the checks, the police have freed up resources to concentrate on other targets.

Brunel University in partnership with the Metropolitan Police started a 12-month CSAS trial in which members of the university security team were accredited with some powers in respect of community safety, such as the power to require those acting in an anti-social manner to supply their name and address, or the power to confiscate alcohol from those drinking in a prohibited area (in this case, non-licensed parts of the university campus). A similar scheme operates at the **University of Surrey**'s campus in Guildford, where 'university security police' deal with students and public alike within the campus grounds and buildings.

1.4.1.8 *Advantages of CSAS*

For the police, the CSAS allows an innovative extension of community safety through partnerships with the public and private sectors. All 'accredited persons' are vetted and trained in their new powers by the police themselves, so some control is maintained, and when 'accredited persons' are on the streets, there is enhanced coverage at a time of scant resources. It is not surprising that the police find advantage in deploying others in non-confrontational, but visible (and therefore reassuring) roles. One prominent commentator noted that:

> Accreditation represents a form of arm's length governance through which the police aim to govern at a distance... It potentially allows a response to public demand for high-visibility reassurance policing without the cost.

> (Crawford, 2006, p 159)

1.4.1.9 *Disadvantages of CSAS*

Whilst the benefits to the police of extending their community safety remit through partnership with well-placed organizations are evident, there is a concomitant risk in managing those involved in policing who are not the police, do not have police powers, and have not had the benefit of extensive police training. Furthermore, some sections in the national press have highlighted what they see as an increase in 'irregulars', whom they caricature as nosy vigilantes, extending state control into all areas of life. Typical would be this headline: 'State recruits an army of snoopers with police-style powers' (*Daily Mail*, 26 May 2009).

Discussion points

Check what accredited persons are working with your force and what roles they occupy.

Where a Special Constable works with 'accredited persons', in what ways can you see that this will enhance the SC job role?

1.4.2 The Special Constabulary and the Extended Policing Family

In many publications, the Special Constabulary is cited separately in a diagram or description of the Extended Policing Family (as indeed we have done at the beginning of this section, though for different reasons). However, the Special Constabulary (which itself predates the paid regular force—see 1.5 below) could argue that it is part of the 'inner family circle' by virtue of length of service. Such arguments, whilst semantically correct, fail to understand the concept of the Extended Policing Family, which is not about past history but about present-day pluralization of policing. 'Policing' is no longer the sole preserve of paid, regular, warranted officers.

The systematic development of auxiliary civilian officers with limited powers (PCSOs) and volunteers (SC and PSV) has altered the internal composition of many forces, at a time when many traditional policing roles are being 'civilianized' (such as 'crime scene investigators' (CSIs), nearly all of whom are now police staff rather than police officers). The fiscal constraints on the police mean that many desk functions previously the sole preserve of police officers can be covered more prudently, even expertly, by police staff. The development of CSAS for example, has seen powers, previously jealously guarded as the prerogative of the police, being accredited to 'unwarranted persons' who are involved in community safety. Whatever resistance is offered by the Police Federation, it is behind the curve (and not for the first time), because the Extended Policing Family is likely to remain. It is popular with public and police managers alike, and offers flexibilities and partnerships of a sophisticated kind which did not previously exist.

Does this come at a price? Does the Extended Policing Family suggest that some tasks traditionally assigned to the police can be done just as well (or better) at a lower price by others? Is the EPF the thin end of a wedge that is subversive of the 'public' police? The jury is perhaps still out on these questions, which nonetheless need answers. More research needs to be undertaken to ascertain the true value and effectiveness of this 'pluralization' of policing.

1.5 A Short but Exciting History of the Special Constabulary

Where does the Special Constabulary come from? How has it developed? What milestones are there on the long road of history which explains why we are where we are now?

You might want to begin this journey with us by noting that the **Special Constabulary**, in function if not in name, is much, much older than the paid, regular, uniformed and detective police. The notion of a volunteer 'peace officer' being drawn from the community to help to regulate that community goes back at least as far as Alfred the Great in the ninth century. (So much for the 175th anniversary of the Special Constabulary in 2006; see Endnote 11 . . . .)

1.5.1 Policing in the 'Dark Ages'

The Anglo-Saxons, who ruled England from about the fifth century until the invasion by William the Conqueror in 1066, administered the country in small units of ten households called 'tythings' ('tenths'), and were themselves grouped under a 'hundredman' who controlled ten tythings. In turn, the hundredman was responsible for peace and order to the 'shire reeve' (from which we get the modern word 'sheriff'), who was the King's Officer in the county or shire and very broadly equivalent to today's Chief Constable. If someone committed a crime, his or her family members, or members of the tything to which he or she belonged, had to produce the offender to stand trial. If no person was produced, the shire reeve could raise a 'hue and cry' and call on those in the shire to join a 'posse' or group to hunt the fugitive down. It was an offence not to assist when asked to do so by a law officer in the King's name (still common law today).

1.5.2 1066 and all that

The arrival of the Normans in the eleventh century changed the Anglo-Saxon system of laws and responsibilities into something altogether more hierarchical and bureaucratic, known as 'frank-pledge'. What stayed the same, largely, was that law enforcement was locally based and communities were still heavily involved in the maintenance of their own peace and order. The Norman system of '**constables**' was applied across the country with, at the top, the Constable of a castle (the ceremonial role still exists, for example at Dover Castle in Kent), and beneath, in order, the constable of a county or shire, the 'high constable' of a hundred and the 'petty constable' of a tything or manor.[10]

1.5.3 Enter the Parish Constable

The next milestone was the **Statute of Winchester** in 1285, which obliged communities to keep their own peace and introduced the role of the **Parish** or **Town Constable**, who was responsible for local law and order, and who answered to the new 'Guardians of the Peace', forerunners of our more familiar Justices of the Peace (magistrates). The Statute also provided for towns to be guarded, strangers to be questioned, and curfews to be imposed. It bound every man to serve the King in case of invasion or revolt, and made it obligatory on all citizens to pursue felons when the hue and cry was raised against them. Local security was formalized in towns and cities through a system known as **Watch and Ward**. The 'Watch' was the name given to a mobile patrol which guarded the town gates and walls at night. Any wrongdoers caught during the night were then handed over to the Parish or Town Constable next day, as the latter exercised his daytime duty of patrol and peace-keeping called the 'Ward'.

1.5.3.1 *Producing the accused to answer charges*

The constable was then responsible for producing the offender at court under '**habeas corpus**' (Latin: *you must have the body*), a protection for the accused which dates back at least to Magna Carta in 1215, and which ensures that people arrested were not incarcerated and forgotten, but were brought before the 'justices' (magistrates or judges) to answer charges raised against them. This, like the obligation on citizens to assist a constable, is a legacy of ancient ('common') law-making which is alive and well today.

1.5.3.2 *From 'the community' to the 'agent of justice'*

Gill and Mawby (1990) describe the importance of the 1285 Statute to the Special Constable as follows:

> The Statute of Winchester, representing a fusion of Saxon and Norman influences, thus prioritised the role of 'the part-time constable, a local man with a touch of regal authority about him, enshrining the ancient Saxon principle of personal service to the community and exercising power of arrest under common law'.
>
> (Gill and Mawby, 1990, pp 13–14, quoting Critchley, 1978, p 7—see Further Reading)

A further development, almost 100 years later, formally brought constables under the authority of the law. This was the **Justices of the Peace Act** of 1361 under which JPs were recognized as superior in law to constables. What this meant was that the annually-elected constable became the person who implemented the JPs' policies; in other words, constables became **agents of the law** [Gill and Mawby, 1990, p 14].

1.5.3.3 *Decline of the constable to a functionary*

In fact, over the next 300 years, the JPs gradually took on much of the status and power which had formerly been exercised by the constable. The role of the constable was consequently downgraded and he became responsible for dealing merely with vagrants and those who were 'a burden on the parish', as well as inspecting walls and bridges, and enforcing lighting regulations (including the *curfew*, when all fires had to be extinguished and traders had to shut up shop, from the French *couvre feu*, 'cover [put out] the fire' or light). As this change took place, the declining status of the constable meant that prosperous citizens were reluctant to take on the annual role and so deputed it to others on their behalf, usually for payment (Critchley, 1978, p 6–11). The quality of those who undertook constable duties promptly declined too.

1.5.4 In times of crisis

Gill and Mawby describe the period from about 1650 to 1900 as a 'mixed economy of policing' (1990, p 16) when 'publicly paid police gained ascendancy but never achieved monopoly'. What this means is that the erosion of the status and effectiveness of the Parish and Town constable, allied to inefficiency in the discharge of office and the office's inherent unpopularity, eventually led to recognition that an 'integrated police service' was required. Until that recognition gained currency and led to the formation of 'a public police' in 1829, England particularly was beset by lawlessness and riot. The existing parish constable system was not adequate to deal with such events, and whilst the authorities did not hesitate to call in the military to deal summarily with the mob, magistrates had the power under section 15 of *An Act for the Better Relief* in 1662 to 'summon any man to the role of temporary peace officer in times of unrest' (Gill and Mawby, 1990, p 31, fn 2). This is a role which is recognizably that of the Special Constabulary, a body which, until the mid-twentieth century, was mobilized in support of the police whenever there was a crisis, but which had no standing membership.

1.5.4.1 *Industrial and political unrest*

In the eighteenth and nineteenth centuries, the requirement for male citizens to be sworn as constables was often invoked to deal with industrial unrest (such as the machine-breaking activities of the Luddites), and in Manchester in 1819, a Special Constable was killed during prolonged rioting. An Act of 1820 clarified the law allowing magistrates to summon 'special constables' but it was not until 1831, two years after the first establishment in law of the 'new police' of Metropolitan London, that *The Special Constables Act* was passed.

1.5.5 1831: The Special Constables' Act[11]

This Act is important, not only in that it placed on a statutory footing the appointment of Special Constables to supplement the regular police if order cannot be maintained, but also in that it accorded the Special Constabulary **equivalence to the police in terms of powers**. The Act declared that a Special Constable should be granted '*all powers, authorities, advantages and immunities*' such that a serving Constable enjoyed. The role was not yet voluntary, however, and the Act provided for fining those who refused to take the oath and turn out when instructed to do so. The voluntary element was introduced in a further Act three years later, giving us the essential characteristics of the Special Constabulary today: *part-time, voluntary, unpaid support to the police*. The major modification in the intervening years (from 1834 to the present) is that the Special Constabulary is not mobilized solely in crises and disasters, but routinely.

1.5.6 'The Year of Revolutions'

There were other milestones on this road, controversially in policing political demonstrations. The period from 1830–50 was characterized in Europe by great unrest. England and Wales were more peaceable but the middle classes still feared that mob rule needed only the slightest incitement to develop into anarchy and revolution. The 'Chartist movement' which emerged during this period was largely working-class in origin, and expressed resentment at the political status quo: those who owned substantial property could vote but those without could not. Chartists made a number of demands in their 'Charter', including the abolition of the property qualification to vote, the right to vote for all ('universal manhood suffrage'— meaning enfranchising men, of course), and annual parliaments.

The Chartists began as peaceable idealists, though a faction came to advocate violence, and their leaders could be fiery orators. Prominent amongst them was Feargus O'Connor, elected as an independent MP in 1847. The movement grew in popularity among working people and, in March 1848, the Chartist leadership announced that they would collect a massive petition and parade it to Parliament after a mass meeting. The authorities panicked. The Queen was evacuated to the Isle of Wight, military detachments were stationed in and around London, the threatened procession was banned, and the Duke of Wellington (the victor at Waterloo in 1815) was asked to take charge of the capital's security. Ever fearful of riot and disorder, the Duke increased the number of soldiers and swore in *170,000* Special Constables to patrol the streets, protect Parliament, and surround Kennington Common in south London, where the Chartists planned to assemble.

In the event the demonstration (though huge) was peaceful, the parade did not take place, and the petition (alleged to contain 6 million signatures but actually far fewer), was duly delivered to Parliament. When it was discovered that some names on the petition had been forged, or were patently untrue ('Victoria Rex', 'Mr Punch'), the Chartist movement attracted ridicule and disillusion in about equal measure, and slowly declined. Aspirations for political power among working men increasingly turned to the trades unions which grew in numbers throughout the century and led to the formation of the Labour Party in 1900.

1.5.7 Arrival of the 'blue-coated locusts'

Occurrences of affray, riot, and disorder continued to require the Special Constabulary to be called to service, though from 1830 onwards there was also a corps of paid, regular police officers, the 'Peelers' or 'Bobbies' (named for Sir Robert Peel, the Home Secretary who introduced the Metropolitan Police Act 1829 to Parliament). The 'Metropolitan Police', hated by the people at first, soon became a template for police forces raised in other cities and shires. By the 1860s, most towns and communities in England and Wales had their own paid, regular police forces; and Specials became an adjunct to be called up in times of crisis.

Thereafter, Special Constables were always invoked in support of the police, rather than in overt support for the ruling elite as they had been during the ill-fated Chartist 'uprising', though the effects were mostly the same. One unforeseen consequence of using middle-class men as Special Constables in time of unrest was that, in times of peace and order, it was extremely difficult to sustain numbers and the Special Constabulary spectacularly declined throughout the later nineteenth century. Indeed, it took a major war to bring the membership up again.

1.5.8 The First World War

In August 1914, Britain declared war on Germany and Austria and, by 1915, such was the enthusiasm to volunteer for military service that the Special Constabulary had to be called in to replace departing police regulars in England and Wales. The Specials were set to guarding key installations such as reservoirs (a task undertaken in the Second World War by the Home Guard), enforcing blackout regulations, and patrolling the darkened streets of cities and towns. Twenty thousand Specials were recruited to protect London alone, and similar numbers volunteered across England and Wales. An Order in Council in 1914 allowed for Specials to be maintained on a more permanent basis than before, but it was not until the police strike of 1919, when Specials were used to cover the work of striking regular police officers, that the Special Constabulary became a **permanent reserve**, enshrined legally in an Act of 1923.

1.5.9 Between the wars

A General Strike, called by the Trades Union movement in 1926, was countered with a rapid increase in volunteers for the Special Constabulary, largely from students and middle-class merchants, and by 1930, the number of Special Constables in England and Wales had reached a peace-time peak of 136,793 (Gill and Mawby, 1990, p 22). While this total seems very high, Seth (1961, pp 129–39) notes that there was a disparity between those who put their names down to become Specials and the much smaller number actually reporting for training and duty.

1.5.10 From reserve to air force

The recorded 130,000 Special Constables formed the basis of a wartime police reserve in 1939–40, augmented by retired police officers recalled to duty and a reserve recruited specifically for the duration. It was noted that many became full-time, salaried officers, whilst some contributed up to eight hours a week, and others still worked as Specials whenever they could. Leon (1989) notes that, in Surrey during the Second World War, the Specials contributed pilots and aircraft, and the Constabulary had its own air force of eleven planes.

1.5.11 Decline and (almost) fall

After the Second World War, numbers declined again, despite moves by the Home Office to allow Special Constables to deploy routinely with regular police officers 'more often than would be required for the purpose of training' (Home Office, 1949, cited in Gill and Mawby, 1990, p 23). Women became eligible to join the

Special Constabulary from 1949 (a year after female regular officers were allowed to join the Police Federation) but overall numbers continued to go down. The transition from an emergency police reserve used only in times of genuine crisis, to a peacetime permanent corps of volunteers who supported the regular police routinely, had happened, but such service evidently failed to find favour among the postwar generation. This may have had more to do with the largely 'non-policing' tasks which the Special Constables were often given, rather than the policing jobs they had volunteered to do.

Even though the Royal Commission on the Police of 1962 commended the existence of the Special Constabulary as 'bridging the gap between the police and the community', morale was low and stagnation in the role was rife. It was even suggested in 1976 that the Special Constabulary should be disbanded (Gill and Mawby, 1990, p 24). It should be noted, however, that recruitment to the regulars was not spectacularly better, and up to the end of the 1970s, full-time police officers regularly took supplemental jobs to eke out their painfully low salaries. 'Wastage' (officers leaving the service) was high. The new Conservative Government of 1979 under Margaret Thatcher restored police pay levels and, as a direct consequence, recruitment into the regulars began to pick up. The Special Constabulary, by contrast, continued to recruit in only small numbers and overall totals went down with ominous regularity.

What has happened in subsequent years is that there has been a slow realization by politicians (and indeed by senior regular police officers) that the Special Constabulary is a genuine asset. The realization has been slow to dawn that Specials are as skilled and as capable in many respects as their regular counterparts, and are uniquely qualified to perform effective roles in Neighbourhood Policing. In parallel with this waking-up to the Specials' potential, has been an understanding that, in times of economic stringency, Special Constables are a very cost-effective asset indeed. Cash-strapped Chief Constables, as well as a central government seeking reductions in its public services budget, view the Special Constabulary with favour and perhaps the true value of the volunteer police officer is now achieving widespread recognition. To be fair, of course, many Chief Officers and regulars, as well as Police Authorities, have long acknowledged the value of the Special Constabulary, but (perhaps paradoxically) at the very moment of recognizing the merits of volunteering in an economic recession, it is possible that recruitment may prove more difficult, and employers be more reluctant to offer support.[12]

1.5.12 Up to the present

Various attempts have been made since the early 1970s to put the Specials on a firm footing, and to arrest the steady decline in numbers, including Home Office studies in 1996–7 (see Further Reading); but it was not actually until 2007 that sustained efforts, involving a very public commitment from ACPO and the NPIA, as well as considerable commitment of time and expertise from the Special Constabulary itself, created a National Strategic Plan.[13] Concurrently, there was an announcement by the Government that it would seek to reverse the decline in numbers in the Special Constabulary, aiming to rise from the current base of 14,500 to 20,000 by 2012. The more sceptical among commentators noted that an augmented presence of Special Constables at the time of the London Olympics would look good for policing and also save the taxpayer lots of money, but the recruitment drive to increase Special Constabulary numbers is only part of a general picture of change for this volunteer police body. We have already looked at the National Strategy in the Introduction, and noted how it has provided the structural basis for this *Handbook*. However, if you wish to read the full text of the Strategy, you should go to the website <http://www.npia.police.uk/en/docs/National_Strategy_March_08.pdf>.

1.5.13 On history and context references

There are only a handful of histories of the Special Constabulary, all of them rare or out of print. If you can get hold of a copy, there is an excellent historical account in Martin Gill and Rob Mawby, *A Special Constable: A Study of the Police Reserve* (1990, published by Avebury, part of Gower Publishing, from Aldershot in Hampshire), particularly Chapter 2 'The Emergence of the Special Constabulary', pp 12–31. Another, even rarer, source is Ronald Seth's *The Specials*, published in 1961 by Victor Gollancz, but the most likely text still to be available is C Leon's 'The mythical history of the "specials" ', (1989) *Liverpool Law Journal* 11 (2): 187–97, available at <http://www.springerlink.com/content/104947/>.

There are good general histories of the police, notably by Clive Emsley, *The English Police: A Political and Social History*, 2nd edition (1996, Longman) and P Rawlings, *Policing: A Short History* (2000, Devon: Willan Publishing), but reference to the Special Constabulary in these tends to the incidental. A succinct but excellent historical outline of the regular police is provided in Robin and Sarah Bryant (eds.), *Blackstone's Student Police Officer Handbook*, 4th edition (2010, Oxford: Oxford University Press), and there is a short and rather cursory historical summary (unsourced) on the Special Constabulary website: <http://www.policespecials.com>. It is possible that, like some of the authors, you will be able to trace rare reference sources through Amazon.com, but a surer source is the Library at the Police Staff College at Bramshill in Hampshire. Your force will certainly have a link to Bramshill, and you may be able to borrow texts for short periods.

1.6 **Private Policing**

A prolonged debate in policing (at the close of the twentieth century and the early years of the current one) concerned overlaps between 'public' and 'private' policing, along with the proliferation of organizations and agencies which exercise a 'policing' function. In this section, we will look very briefly at the two themes and relate the debate and the considerable ethical concerns about 'private policing' to the work of the Special Constabulary, as well as providing an important context for public police work when boundaries are being moved and distinctions blurred. This is one of the 'contexts' of contemporary policing which has greater prominence amongst academic commentators than among the media, ACPO, or police officers themselves, perhaps because the former have more leisure to gaze reflectively at what is going on.

Many organizations, both public and private, now have a policing function which used to be the preserve of the 'public police'; for example, investigating benefit fraud, escorting prisoners, or attending road traffic collisions. The private security industry, which covers an enormous range of security duties from patrolling commercial premises at night, staffing 'gated communities', and keeping order in shopping malls, through to transporting or storing large amounts of money or running a prison, now employs more people than the public police. There are between 180,000 and 250,000 employees in various capacities in private security, compared with about 136,000 regular, and 14,500 Special Constabulary police officers (Jones, 2008).

Members of the public now find it hard to know which police function is exercised by what body. Do you? Try our test:

Discussion points

Who is responsible for these policing activities?

1 Identifying and investigating benefit cheats
2 Investigating poor food hygiene in shops and restaurants

---

3 Checking if children are 'bunking off' school
4 Evading duty on imports
5 Failure to pay for car insurance
6 Evasion of income tax
7 Diesel scams (stealing and selling agricultural or 'red' diesel)
8 Fraud in the supply of medicines and drugs
9 Recovering the cost of debts by seizure of goods
10 Dealing with rowdy or drunken behaviour in shops
11 Fraud in agricultural payments/subsidies
12 Crime on trains
13 Unauthorized (including terrorist) entry to a military site
14 Unauthorized (including terrorist) entry to a nuclear power station
15 Failure to pay a television licence

The public police, whether Special Constabulary or the regular police, may investigate all or any of these activities if on the site at the time they take place, and if not dealing with something else, and if the offence is serious enough (though the police tend not to deal with mere trespass, which in most instances is a civil offence). However, there are specialist government departments and other organizations that may well respond to a complaint, initiate an investigation, and proceed to a prosecution without any intervention by the public police.

How did you get on with our indicative test?

Here are the current answers ('current' because legislation, groupings, names, and alliances change rapidly in these fields: this is correct as we go to press):

1 Department of Work and Pensions (benefits agency security investigation service)
2 Environmental health officers (usually employed by a local authority)
3 Truancy Officers (employed by the local authority education department)
4 HM Revenue and Customs
5 Driver and Vehicle Licensing Authority (DVLA)
6 HM Revenue and Customs (import duty and income tax are now handled largely by the amalgamated organization, where until 2002 Customs and Excise dealt with imports and the Inland Revenue dealt with taxes)
7 Department of the Environment, Food and Rural Affairs (DEFRA)

> 8 Department of Health (Prescription Pricing Authority, Fraud Investigation Division)
> 9 Bailiffs (private or subcontracted to local authority)
> 10 Private security organizations, such as Group4 or Securitas
> 11 DEFRA (see 7)
> 12 British Transport Police
> 13 Ministry of Defence Police or the MOD Guard Force (civilian non-police) or, more rarely, bodies such as RAF Police or Royal Military Police
> 14 British Civil Nuclear Constabulary (CNC)
> 15 TV Licensing

(Johnston, 1992, which we have amended and added to)

What this demonstrates, quite graphically, is that there are many government departments and 'official' agencies which will investigate and prosecute offences, and some local authorities as well as some private organizations, together with some 'niche' or specialist police forces which have a jurisdiction over specific sites, areas, or facilities. Make no mistake though, the MOD Police, the Civil Nuclear Constabulary, and British Transport Police have full police powers within their jurisdictions.

What sort of things does the private sector do which the police largely have stopped doing?

> - A visible presence and reassurance
> - Paying for services gives the buyer some control: things are done *for* the buyer, not *to* him or her
> - Visible patrol has a tangible deterrent effect
> - Private companies have instant access to equipment, such as CCTV, electronic gates, razor wire, and other barriers
> - Private security can always summon the 'real' police if an incident gets out of hand
> - Visibility, frequent patrol, barriers, and restricted access all help to minimize petty crime—reduce shoplifting, theft, muggings, and graffiti—but 'private police' have **no capacity to investigate anything serious**, such as crimes of violence, fraud, and deception, or public order offences.

Where 'private policing' is carried out by commercial agencies, there is a profit motive which may have nothing to do with the 'public good'. A recurrent worry is that not all private investigations of crime and criminality will result in a prosecution since, in the case of a bank, retrieving money may be more important than punishment of an offender, whilst some companies (such as

IT firms) might not want any publicity about how they caught a 'hacker' lest they give away trade secrets or vulnerabilities. 'Public police' interest in crime investigation and the interests of a victim of that crime are probably identical in most cases. In 'private policing', the interest of the victim may be to choose an option other than prosecution; so public authorities might never know that a crime has been committed. In some well-documented instances, crime has been *connived* at by commercial companies (consider the paying of a ransom to kidnappers or institutional contract bribes).

1.6.1 How is 'private policing' accountable? And to whom?

The short answer is that it isn't: there is very little regulation, control, or licensing either of the organizations themselves or of the people whom they employ. Research by Button (2002) and Edwards (2005) suggests that the security checks on prospective employees are often token clearances and there have been instances of employees with serious criminal records joining reputable companies. Further, in private policing, training is likely to be rudimentary or inadequate, compared with between ten months' and two years' training in first years alone after enrolling in the public police, with continuous training periods and specialized learning thereafter. At the same time, low rates of pay make the use of private policing more attractive than using the public police (for example, in providing security at sports venues: from Wimbledon to Wembley, from the Oval to the Open). Like it or not, 'private policing' is now a tangible competitor with the Special Constabulary.

1.7 Ranks and Command

In 2005 an ACPO report on the Special Constabulary by Chief Constable Peter Fahy recommended that forces adopt a national Special Constabulary rank structure using the same designations as regulars but without the regular insignia. It was felt that this structure would ensure greater consistency and would create an incentive for those Specials who would welcome greater responsibility.

The Special Constabulary National Strategy Implementation Advice (2008) reiterated this suggestion, indicating that a national rank structure offers a standard. The Implementation Advice Document issued by ACPO and NPIA includes the following:

9.7.4: it is suggested that forces implement a rank structure for the Special Constabulary in accordance with the ACPO Guidance of 2005.

There is no compulsion on forces to do this, but it makes sense that a rank structure and command chain should parallel that of the regular force:

Table 1.1: Possible rank structure and command chain

Existing	Proposed	Regular equivalent
Special Constable	Special Constable	Police Constable
Section Officer	Special Sergeant	Police Sergeant
Area Officer	Special Inspector	Police Inspector
No existing rank	Special Chief Inspector	Chief inspector
Commandant	Special Superintendent	Superintendent
From Commandant	Assistant Chief Officer	Chief Superintendent
From Commandant	Deputy Chief Officer	Assistant Chief Constable
Chief Commandant	Chief Officer	Deputy Chief Constable

Police forces across England and Wales differ in number (that is the actual headcount) and in relative percentages of Special Constables measured against the regular police establishment. This means that, organizationally, command structures can vary from force to force. Depending on their local requirements, forces have either adopted this structure more or less as given or have made a slight variation to it; for example, Kent Police has no Specials Chief Inspectors because their structure has no requirement for the rank. At the other end of the scale, Sussex Police has one rank only: Special Constable. Essex Police has the full range of equivalent ranks. Typically, the Special Constabulary ranks broadly correspond with regular ranks. A **Special Sergeant** has supervisory responsibility for seven or so Special Constables. A **Special Inspector** has responsibility for a district. A **Special Chief Inspector** or **Special Superintendent** has responsibility for a basic SC command unit. A **Special Constabulary Chief Officer team** has responsibility for strategic matters through liaison with the ACPO senior management team in the regular police. Special Chief Officers also represent their respective Special Constabulary force contingent at regional and national level.

Here is an indication of what the Special Constabulary rank designation may look like in a typical police force:

Figure 1.3: Rank Insignia of the Special Constabulary for England and Wales

(Hats and epaulettes constructed and adapted from a variety of sources (including *The International Encyclopaedia of Uniform Insignia*) by Special Sergeant Mark Simpson)

Special Constable · Special Sergeant · Special Inspector · Special Chief Inspector · Special Superintendent · Assistant Chief Officer · Deputy Chief Officer · Chief Officer

1.8 **Special Constabulary Structures: The Regional Coordinators**

In 2008, NPIA established nine Regional Coordinators for the Special Constabulary, each based in a region formed from clustering counties or police force areas. The Coordinators have a remit to help Special Constabularies and ACPO to deliver the National Strategy for the Special Constabulary and also to develop mechanisms to achieve the recruitment of 20,000 Special Constables across England and Wales by 2012.

At the time of writing, it is impossible to establish through any objective correlative whether the appointment of the Regional Coordinators has been 'effective and efficient' or not. Certainly, there is a need to focus attention on Special Constabulary recruitment and training, and the coordination of the National Strategy across the regions may lead to greater consistency and fewer idiosyncratic variations between Special Constabularies. It remains to be seen whether the structure favoured by NPIA/ACPO is the best one to achieve these tasks. Regionalism, adherence to national guidelines, and suppression of parochialism have all failed spectacularly with **regular** police forces (corrupt or inefficient Regional Crime Squads, lack of consistency in, for example, information systems, and the ill-fated Amalgamation of Forces project in 2006, are all clear evidence of this). However, such regionalism *may* work for the less formalized and more flexible Special Constabulary; we must wait and see.

1.9 **The Structures and Remits of a Typical Police Force**

There are 43 'home' police forces and a number of other specialist police forces such as British Transport Police and the Civil Nuclear Constabulary in England and Wales. Scotland has eight separate forces (which nonetheless liaise closely with their counterparts in England and Wales),[14] and Northern Ireland has its own unified force, the Police Service of Northern Ireland (PSNI), which replaced the Royal Ulster Constabulary, GC, in November 2001. Forces in England and Wales vary in size from about 1,500 police officers and staff to 56,000 or so in the Metropolitan Police.

Correspondingly, the ways in which these police forces are structured vary a good deal, even among similarly sized forces, and there is no template which all forces fit exactly. What we suggest below may well vary in some details from your own force; this is not a concern. The principles of the 'hub and spokes' arrangement are common to most police forces, as is the distinction between crime investigation on one hand and territorial, or area, or neighbourhood policing on the other. One deals with criminality, the other with community; but the distinctions blur constantly. Terminology varies too; we have used the most common terms and descriptors, but your force may have its own.

1.9.1 'Hub and Spokes'

It is common to think of the relationship between a police headquarters and its outstations as being like the structure of a wheel, with the HQ at the hub or centre, and the outstations controlled and radiating out from the HQ. At its simplest, it would look like this:

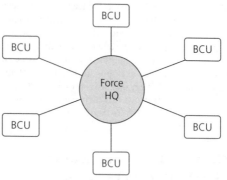

(BCU is Basic Command Unit)

Figure 1.4: Simplified 'Hub and Spokes' structure

This diagram if anything is *over*-simplified, because in terms of autonomy of operation, some finance, and budgeting, as well as in many aspects of organization, Basic Command Units (led by a Superintendent or Chief Superintendent) are often virtually independent of Police Headquarters (led by the Chief Constable and a 'top team' of chief officers), other than for performance and allied matters. The same 'hub and spokes' arrangement often characterizes the relationship at a local level between the BCU and the satellite Neighbourhood Policing Teams (NPTs):

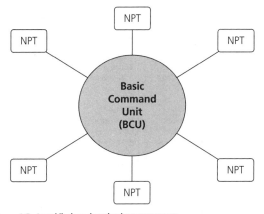

Figure 1.5: Local 'hub and spokes' arrangements

To get an idea of the complex structure of a police force we may need a more linear depiction:

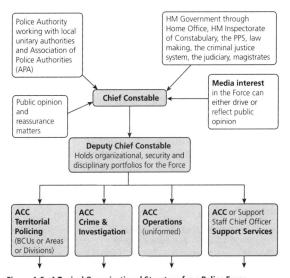

Figure 1.6: A Typical Organizational Structure for a Police Force

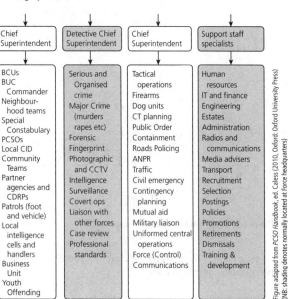

Chief Superintendent	Detective Chief Superintendent	Chief Superintendent	Support staff specialists
BCUs BUC Commander Neighbourhood teams Special Constabulary PCSOs Local CID Community Teams Partner agencies and CDRPs Patrols (foot and vehicle) Local intelligence cells and handlers Business Unit Youth Offending	Serious and Organised crime Major Crime (murders rapes etc) Forensic Fingerprint Photographic and CCTV Intelligence Surveillance Covert ops Liaison with other forces Case review Professional standards	Tactical operations Firearms Dog units CT planning Public Order Containment Roads Policing ANPR Traffic Civil emergency Contingency planning Mutual aid Military liaison Uniformed central operations Force (Control) Communications	Human resources IT and finance Engineering Estates Administration Radios and communications Media advisers Transport Recruitment Selection Postings Policies Promotions Retirements Dismissals Training & development

Figure adapted from *PCSO Handbook*, ed. Caless (2010, Oxford: Oxford University Press)
(NB: shading denotes normally located at Force headquarters)

Figure 1.6: *(Continued)*

The point of showing you all this is not just to examine the context within which you function as a police officer, although that is very important and underlines your role within the teams which comprise a police force. It is also directly relevant to you because your individual duties, such as your work in a neighbourhood policing team, may have a direct impact upon the force itself, in areas such as performance, reassurance, community engagement, detection, prevention and reduction of crime, clear-up rates, 'sanction detection' rates, 'brought-to-justice' data, and many other less measurable and tangible areas such as reduction in anti-social behaviour and arrests for criminal damage.

Further Reading

Anon., *Metropolitan Special Constabulary: an illustrated history from 1831 to today* (1989, London: Metropolitan Police)

Button, M, *Private Policing* (2002, Devon: Willan Publishing)

Caless, B, 'Numties in yellow jackets', *Policing, A Journal of Policy and Practice*, Vol.1, No.2, (August 2007, Oxford: Oxford University Press)

Critchley, T, *The History of Police in England and Wales* (1978, London: Constable)

Davis-Smith, J and Rankin, M, *Attracting Employer Support for the Special Constabulary*, Policing and Reducing Crime Unit (1999, Home Office, Crown copyright)

Emsley, C, *Crime and Society in England 1750–1900*, 3rd edn. (2004, London: Longman)

Epstein, J and Thompson, D (eds.), *The Chartist Experience: Studies in Working-Class Radicalism and Culture, 1830–1860* (1982, Basingstoke: Macmillan)

Flett, K, *Chartism after 1848: The Working Class and the Politics of Radical Education* (2006, London: Merlin Press)

Geary, R, *Policing Industrial Disputes 1893–1985* (1985, Cambridge: Cambridge University Press)

Home Office, *Report of the Working Group on the Special Constabulary in England and Wales, 1995–1996* (1997, London: Home Office Communications Directorate)

——, *The Government's Proposals for the Regulation of the Private Security Industry in England and Wales*, Cm 4254 (1999, London: HMSO (now TSO))

——, *The Volunteering Code of Good Practice* (2005, London: Home Office, Crown copyright)

Home Office White Paper: *Protecting The Public: supporting the police to succeed,* December 2009 (London: The Stationery Office, Crown copyright)

Hostettler, J, *A History of Criminal Justice in England and Wales* (2009, London: Waterside Press)

Johnston, L, 'Privatisation and the police function: from "new police" to "new policing" ', in Johnston, L, *The Rebirth of Private Policing* (1992, London: Routledge)

Jones, T and Newburn, T, *Private Security and Public Policing* (1998, Oxford: Clarendon Press)

Jones, T and Newburn, T, (eds.), *Plural Policing: a comparative perspective* (2006, London: Routledge)

Jones, T, 'Private Policing' in Newburn T and Neyroud, P (eds.), *Dictionary of Policing*, (2008, Devon: Willan Publishing)

Loveday, B, *Size isn't everything: Restructuring Policing in England and Wales* (2006, London: Policy Exchange Publication)

Mason, M, *Findings from the second year of the national Neighbourhood Policing Programme evaluation* (2009, London: Home Office RDS, available from: <http://www.homeoffice.gov.uk/rds/pfds09/horr14a.pdf>, accessed 11 June 2009)

Mather, F, *Public Order in the Age of the Chartists*, (1959, Manchester: Manchester University Press)

Morgan J, Conflict and Order: The Police and Labour Disputes in England and Wales, 1900–1939, (1987, Oxford: Clarendon Press)

Neuberger, J (Chair), *Report of the Commission on the Future of Volunteering and Manifesto for Change* (2008, available from <www.volunteering.org.uk/NR/rdonlyres/BAD29019–79A5–4F73–A401–051D38598DB6/0/Manifestofinal.pdf>, accessed 7 July 2009)

Neuberger, J, *Volunteering across the criminal justice system*, (2009. London: Cabinet Office/Third Sector Report, March, Crown Copyright, available from <http://www.cabinetoffice.gov.uk/third_sector/news/news_stories/090303_neuberger.aspx>, accessed 11 July 2009)

Police and Constabulary Almanac (2009, Dartford, Kent: Official Register, published annually by R Hazell and Co. (a trading name of Shaw & Sons Ltd.))

Rawlings, P, 'The Idea of Policing: A History', *Policing and Society*, (1995, Vol 5, No 2, pp 129–49)

Reiner, R and Cross, M (eds.), *Beyond Law and Order: Criminal Justice Policy and Politics in the 1990s* (1991, Basingstoke: Macmillan)

Roberts, S, *The Chartist Movement 1838–1848* (2002, BBC, available from <http://www.bbc.co.uk/history/british/victorians/chartist_01.shtml>)

Steedman, C, *Policing the Victorian Community: The Formation of English Provincial Police Forces, 1856–1880* (1984, London: Routledge)

Tuffin, R, Morris, J, and Poole, A, *An Evaluation of the Impact of the National Reassurance Policing Programme* (2006, Home Office Research Study 296. available from <http://www.homeoffice.gov.uk/rds/pdfs06/hors296.pdf>, accessed 12 June 2009)

Weinberger, B, *Keeping the Peace? Policing Strikes in Britain 1906–1926* (1991, New York and Oxford: Berg Publishing)

Wright, A, *Policing: An introduction to concepts and practice* (2002, Devon: Willan Publishing)

Notes

1 Indeed, one measure suggested by the Government to save money on policing (in its White Paper, ineptly titled *Protecting The Public: supporting the police to succeed*, published in December 2009) was that weekend police duties should be performed by the Special Constabulary. The implication is that this would be *all* the policing on Saturday and Sunday, not just some of it. The White Paper is available from: <http://police.homeoffice.gov.uk/publications/police-reform/protecting-the-public.html> accessed 3 December 2009.

2 *Ibid*. Disappointingly, the Baroness hardly refers to the Special Constabulary in her 2009 overview of volunteering in the criminal justice system, and her report is couched in often endearingly naïve terms, such as not understanding why the police are reluctant to use as volunteers those who have been imprisoned for offending.

3 Quoting Peel's 'Nine Principles' for the police. It is unclear whether the author of the Nine Principles was Sir Robert Peel in 1829, then the Home Secretary, or whether Charles Rowan and Richard Mayne, the first Commissioners of the Metropolitan Police, wrote it for him. Attributions vary and much is obscured by amateur historians claiming partisan ground. The point is that the Principle in question reads thus:

> Police, at all times, should maintain a relationship with the public that gives reality to the historic tradition that the police are the public and the public are the police; the police being only members of the public who are paid to give full-time attention

to duties which are incumbent on every citizen in the interests of community welfare and existence.

In fact, of course, the Special Constabulary exemplifies this principle more than the regular force, by virtue of its members being unpaid and volunteers.

4 In McBain, C and Machon, J, *Caring Companies: Engagement in employer-supported volunteering* (2009, London: Institute for Volunteering Research).

5 Not usually those engaged in front-line duty, such as PCSOs and Crime Scene Investigators (CSIs), but 'back office' staff who are employed by the force but are volunteer police officers as well.

6 In Caless's original diagram (2010), the distinction was between 'warrant holders' and other members of the 'extended policing family'. We have adapted the depiction to reflect minor differences between regular and volunteer police officers, and more extraneous (even temporary) additions to the policing family. This is a model which will flux and change constantly.

7 Full details of PCSO Powers can be found at <http://police.homeoffice. gov.uk/community-policing/community-support-officers> and in Caless (ed.) *et al*, *PCSO Handbook* (2010, Oxford: Oxford University Press).

8 Quoted in Neuberger, J, *Volunteering across the criminal justice system*, Cabinet Office/Third Sector Report, March 2009, Crown Copyright, available from: <http://www.cabinetoffice.gov.uk/third_sector/news/ news_stories/090303_neuberger.aspx> accessed 11 July 2009, pp 8–9, which refers to the NPIA Report of 2008, available from: <http://www. npia.police.uk/en/docs/2008_Final_Questionnaire_analysis.pdf> accessed 5 July 2009.

9 If the case is strong enough, Chief Constables could accredit people with powers very akin to those of a PCSO, by a process of 'designation'. However, since the employees concerned have had only limited police training, it would be foolish to give them any more powers than simple accreditation. The whole concept is subordinate to the notion of community safety, and in the view of a number of commentators the scheme panders to those who want to feel part of the police, and wear badges, but not share any of the dangers or discomforts that go with the job. This may or may not be the case, but the take-up has not been high across England or Wales.

10 The word 'constable' comes from the French *conestable* (derived from Latin *comes stabuli* meaning 'master of the horse', or 'count of the stable'). It was originally a high-ranking position in a royal household, but by 1252, a statute equated constables with mayors and bailiffs— still having some status and delegated power, but local rather than regional or royal.

11 Those who celebrated 175 years of the Special Constabulary in 2006 had their history a little astray, being led by name rather than function. The Statute of Winchester in 1285 created the local volunteer constable, which suggests that the 175th anniversary celebrants are out by some 500 years and the 1831 Act is *arriviste*.

12 An original draft of this chapter contained a comparative table of the relative costs of Special Constables, compared with their regular

police and PCSO colleagues. The Special is cheaper by an average factor of ten. There are about 330 Special Constables in each police force in England and Wales. Multiply by 43 forces, and 14,500 Special Constables save the police service the equivalent of 1,450 FTE regular police officers a year; at a minimum, the police service would have to expend £37.7–46.4 million in order to sustain such numbers for police duties. This is calculated using the 2008 numbers of Special Constables. If this overall total increases to the Government's target of 20,000 Special Constables by 2012, the 'unexpended costs' of SC policing (equating to 2,000 police officers) will benefit the government by something like £52–64 million annually. No wonder they think you're worth it.

13 NPIA, *A National Strategy for the Special Constabulary*, (2008, Strong Worldwide on behalf of the National Policing Improvement Agency), available from <http://www.npia.police.uk/en/docs/National_Strategy_March_08.pdf>, accessed 10 March 2009.

14 For information, the eight Scottish forces are **Dumfries and Galloway Constabulary**, **Strathclyde Police** (including Glasgow), **Lothian and Borders Police** (including Edinburgh), **Fife Constabulary**, **Central Scotland Police**, **Tayside Police** (which includes Dundee), **Grampian Police** (which includes Aberdeen), and **Northern Constabulary** (which is the largest geographically).

Chapter 2

Recruitment, Retention, and Resilience: The Process of Becoming a Special Constable

2.1 **The Recruitment Process**

This opening part of the chapter will have little interest for you if you are already a serving Special Constable, as you will have been through the procedures which we identify in the paragraphs below and you will have come out the other side. However, if you are now intending to become a Special Constable, the areas outlined below will be of real importance and will help you with your application process. One caution though: we cannot provide local and precise details of how each of 43 police forces in England and Wales conducts its Special Constabulary recruitment (nor other forces such as British Transport Police) so we have provided a generic explanation. Please make sure that you look at the website for the police force you want to join so that you have the most pertinent information available.

2.1.1 Recruiting a Special Constable

We need to note at the outset *how important the fact of continuous recruitment is* to the Special Constabulary and to the police force of which it is a part. Not only does this aid the retention of existing Special Constables (particularly apposite at this time of increased financial uncertainty in the public sector), but also 'gearing' recruitment can link individual expertise to specialist deployment roles.

2.1.1.1 *Avenues for recruitment*

There are many ways in which SC are recruited and the following text box, whilst not definitive, provides many examples of ways that police forces are reaching out to potential Special Constables:

- Newspaper advertisements
- Radio advertisements
- TV
- Police Force's own website
- Generic police websites
- Volunteer websites
- Community events, fetes, and fairs
- Posters
- Newspaper articles
- Local advertising
- Attendance at career fairs
- Talks at schools, colleges, universities
- Police station open days
- Community safety events
- Open evenings for potential recruits
- Blogs, Twitter, BEBO, MySpace, MSN, etc

These are all legitimate avenues for recruitment and many can be initiated and populated by current Special Constables themselves; after all, who is better to extol the virtues and pleasures (or frustrations) of the role than those already doing it? Furthermore, some of the examples listed above require very little or no expenditure and that has real resonance in a time of financial constraints. When a police force provides local media with a 'good news' story, there is also a real opportunity to include a sentence about how local people can apply to become Special Constables.

2.1.1.2 *Example of a Special Constabulary recruitment campaign*

The Metropolitan Police has been running a recruitment campaign with the strap line, 'Extraordinary People: Special Constables' since 2007. This provides a series of case studies from a 'first-person' perspective, using serving Special Constables. The campaign focuses on six motivational strands:

- To escape the 'rat race'
- To acquire new skills

- To gain job satisfaction
- To wear the uniform
- To be part of the team
- To make a difference.

The campaign features high-profile posters across the London Transport network, including buses and the Underground, as well as advertisements in free newspapers, and is cleverly targeted at the commuter population at its most passive (and receptive), travelling into and out of the capital.

2.1.1.3 *Basic eligibility criteria*

For *all* police forces, no matter which avenue of recruitment, there are basic eligibility criteria for joining the Special Constabulary:

Basic eligibility requirements are the same for the specials [*sic*] as for joining the regular police force; you must be over the age of 18, and there is no upper age limit, although you will need to be reasonably fit and in good health. In addition:

- there are no minimum or maximum height requirements
- there is no formal educational requirement, but applicants will have to pass written tests
- only applications from member states of the European [Union], or other nationals who have leave to enter or remain in the UK for an indefinite period, will be accepted
- convictions or cautions will probably make applicants ineligible, but this will depend on the nature and circumstances of the offence
- applicants must be judged physically and mentally able to undertake police duties.

(Source: <http://www.policecouldyou.co.uk/specials/eligible.html>, accessed 17 September 2009)

It is important that you satisfy these criteria before making an application; otherwise you will be wasting your own time. If you are uncertain whether you will meet all the criteria, then discuss this with the recruitment department (usually in HR or 'Personnel') of the force you wish to join. In particular, you must be aware that certain occupations can preclude you from becoming a Special Constable because of the potential for problematic cross-over in responsibility. One example is if your full-time job is being a Police Community Support Officer (PCSO). It would be confusing for any community to have the same person in two different uniforms, with two differing responsibilities and two differing sets of powers, patrolling the neighbourhood at different times. Other 'police' jobs may not preclude you.

2.2 Selection, Interview, Vetting

2.2.1 Selection

The forms used in Special Constable recruitment vary from force to force and so we are not able to provide anything other than a generic view of the process. Indeed, one of the recommendations contained within the NPIA's *Special Constabulary National Strategy Implementation Advice* (2008) is for a national application form that can be used by all forces, but a 'template' form is not yet in general use. The normal set of forms may come as an application pack with 16 or more pages to complete, along with medical and financial questionnaires and separate vetting forms. It is worth setting aside some time to complete all these documents as thoroughly as you can, since they will be used to sift the applications at an initial stage. It may be trite to say so, but these forms provide you with an opportunity to sell yourself.

2.2.2 Interview

If your application successfully negotiates the sifting phase then you will be invited to an interview/assessment centre. Again this will vary in time and place in the overall recruitment process, depending on which force you are seeking to join. There tend to be two approaches to Special Constable interview:

- the Police Initial Recruitment (PIR) approach, or
- an assessment centre approach.

More forces are beginning to use the latter as it encompasses a more holistic approach to recruitment and provides the force with a greater opportunity to assess candidates against a wide range of competences. These can include:

  verbal and written communication
  problem solving
  respect for race and diversity
  team working
  effective communication

Generally, the following will make up the various components of a Special Constable interview/assessment process, although (of course) the actual structure of the day will vary:

- Verbal-logical reasoning test
- Observation test
- Numeracy test
- Interactive role-playing scenarios
- Written problem-solving test
- Interview.

It is crucial that you check with the force to which you wish to apply what procedures they will use, so that you can plan and revise accordingly. Forces will often have more candidates than available spaces, so use your opportunity wisely.

2.2.3 **Vetting**

It is clearly appropriate for all members of the police service (warranted officers, PCSOs, police staff) to be vetted, given the nature of the work they undertake. The generic police role entails working with vulnerable persons and children, involves access to sensitive material, sometimes includes work with 'restricted' personal data from partnership agencies or police operations, and could involve working with intelligence material and accessing databases ranging from local force systems to the Police National Computer (PNC). It is therefore imperative that the police scrutinize applicants so as to exclude those who are unsuitable for the role. The risk otherwise is that criminals may seek to gain secret access by planting a mole within the police.

The vetting forms will ask questions about you and your family members and will also include a financial questionnaire. You should complete these honestly because any non-declared offences or irregularities which later come to light may damage your application, or require you to resign if you have concealed anything. None of this is a good start in a job built on honesty and integrity. If you are uncertain as to whether events in your past may exclude you from applying, then *ask*.

2.3 **Fitness and Medicals**

Applicant Special Constables are subject to a fitness and medical assessment. Given the nature of police work, applicants need to be fit and healthy so that they can cope with the wide variety of tasks involved in being a police officer. Dealing with confrontation or chasing a fleeing suspect requires levels of fitness and stamina that an office worker does not need (at least in a work capacity). Check with your intended force what its fitness requirements are and, because the recruitment time can be lengthy, you have a chance to get yourself up to standard if you are not already there.

2.3.1 Fitness test

All forces require their Special Constable applicants to take a fitness test, but the timing of this within the recruitment process can vary. Most forces will use the same test as that used for regular applicants and it will involve two distinct aspects:

1. **Endurance** (the 'bleep test')—this involves running between two fixed points on a measured track with a set time limit indicated by bleeps, which become faster as the test progresses.
2. **Dynamic strength** (the 'push/pull test')—this requires you to do five seated chest-pushes and five seated back-pulls on a machine designed to measure your strength.

2.3.2 Medical

Similarly, all forces will require Special Constable applicants to undergo a medical examination. This will probably be the same test that regular officers take, involving a medical assessment by a practice nurse or medical adviser, and is likely to include sight/vision/hearing tests. If you are uncertain what the requirements are for your chosen force, then check, as there can be subtle differences in application processes. If you have a medical condition that you think might preclude you from becoming a Special Constable, then check before applying. All queries will be treated confidentially and certain conditions, if managed correctly, do not prevent someone from having a long and fulfilling career within the police. Forces are used to applicants asking such questions. For example, some eyesight problems will exclude applicants, others will not. Some physical conditions may not disbar you if they are not severe, such as allergies. Others will.

One point worth making is that forces are looking for fit and healthy people who take their physical conditioning seriously and maintain sensible fitness levels.

2.4 **Considering Employment and Employers**

In 2008, Martin Stuart, Deputy Chief Constable of Bedfordshire Police and 'Project Executive' of the team which produced the *National Strategy for the Special Constabulary*, wrote this:

> As a business proposition the Special Constabulary is difficult to beat. Not only is it extraordinarily cost-effective, but it is more representative of the community (socio-economic groups and businesses) than any other body delivering policing services. It therefore brings greater involvement and improved communication with members of the public and the business community.
>
> (Executive Summary, *National Strategy*, 2008)

It is remarkable, given the brevity of the link here between employer, business, and Special Constable, that not more is made in the *National Strategy* of the importance to police forces of engaging with a supportive and flexible employer. A detailed reading of the *Strategy* produces very little in the way of guidance or commentary on the Special Constable's relationship with his or her employer. Such relationships are also grossly under-researched, despite the existence of organizations such as Volunteering England and the Volunteering Institute. We need to understand the complexity of the employer/employee relationship, the strains that work as a Special Constable may or may not place on employer and work colleagues, and the quantification of business benefits which can be quoted by prospective applicants to the Special Constabulary to win over their employers. Currently, these are either some years out of date or merely anecdotal.

It is worth turning our attention back to the employer for a moment and looking more specifically at the relationship between the employer and the Special Constable (whether putative—about to join—or already Special: the same considerations apply). In doing so, we should also re-emphasize the supportive and 'missionary' role which the police force itself must develop and nurture.

There will be times when the needs of the employer and the needs of the police are in collision, and often the expectation is that the higher sense of duty engendered by membership of the Special Constabulary will take precedence over any purely commercial concerns. Further, it is assumed that employers actually *like* the idea that members of their workforce have a calling to serve the community. And of course, most of the time for most employers that is perfectly true. What is also true is that the employer gets back, into the workplace, someone whose skills are being developed extensively at someone else's expense, which is a hefty bonus for Special Constable and employer alike.

Yet it is entirely reasonable for an employer, faced with the effects of having a Special Constable in his or her workforce (described dolefully by some as 'structured absenteeism'), to ask: **what is in this for me?** The question may very well be asked of you, quite literally, if you approach your employer with a request for time off for additional police duties, or with a request that s/he support you to join the Special Constabulary. Even if the question is not asked by your employer, it may be asked by colleagues at work, and so it is sensible for you to have responses well considered and prepared. The remainder of this section suggests *precisely* what is 'in it' for the employer, when you become a Special Constable.

2.4.1 The return-on-investment of a Special Constable

The society in which we live depends upon peaceable circumstances to be able to function. The 'work' undertaken by any organization, whether in public service or in private enterprise, flourishes under conditions of good order and withers under conditions of lawlessness or lack of social control. This is true whether the product or service being delivered is education or furniture, animal welfare or scientific research, trading standards or computer software. The Special Constabulary plays a significant part in sustaining or creating those conditions in which private and public businesses can thrive and develop. It follows that all of us, as citizens, have a **vested interest** in seeing the Special Constabulary (and the rest of the policing family) succeed in reassuring the public, carrying out visible patrol, dealing with nuisance, disorder, and anti-social behaviour, and being instrumental in crime prevention, crime detection, and the arrest and prosecution of criminal offenders. It follows equally that employers should have the same investment in those of their employees who become Special Constables.

The important thing is that no organization and no employer exists outside society: we are all citizens, we all belong to communities (sometimes to many of them), and we all have an obligation to support each other. Indeed, research by Tuffrey (1999) suggests that employers can have three principal motivations in contributing to the societies in which they are located:

Employers' social motivations:

1. *Moral and social responsibility*; response to society's expectations (such as ethical trading principles, or avoiding child labour).
2. Believing that companies have a *long-term interest in fostering a healthy community* (this is often called 'enlightened self-interest').
3. Knowing that interventions in communities by employees, customers, and suppliers can result in *increased profitability*, stronger morale among staff, and improved customer loyalty.

(source: Tuffrey, M: 1999)

If what Tuffrey says is true (and the research is now a little dated), then many employers will easily be persuaded that 'investing' in a member of staff becoming a Special Constable will have long-term beneficial impacts. But there is more to it than this, as noted in research by Davis Smith and Rankin (also in 1999):

Employer support for the Special Constabulary

- 70 per cent of respondents said that employers took a 'favourable' or 'very favourable' view of their work as Specials
- 40 per cent said employers could help with flexibility over time off
- 27 per cent said employers would take being a Special Constable into consideration in staff appraisals
- 20 per cent said employers would give favourable publicity to the Special Constabulary.

(source: Davis Smith, J and Rankin, M, 1999)

These are laudable elements in employers' responses to Special Constabulary staff in the workforce, but the percentages are hardly overwhelming. They serve to emphasize, again, that the relationship between employers and the Special Constabulary is under-researched, a little piecemeal, and seldom definitive. However, from the employer's perspective the 'return on investment' becomes clearer:

What's in it for the employer:

- Having a Special Constable on the staff is actually beneficial to staff morale

---

- Staff enjoy flexibility: it works both ways, so a flexible employee is an added benefit to employer
- Having additional positive things to note at appraisal is helpful to the employer's assessment of the staff member
- Favourable publicity for the Special Constabulary is also favourable publicity for the employer: sponsorship of the SC with a company logo, for example, is very cost-effective advertising
- Staff want *work–life balance*: encouraging membership of the Special Constabulary is a direct contribution to that balance
- Employer gets a person with continuously enhanced skills, for which s/he did not have to pay.

Most employers will agree that a motivated employee, with a high sense of social responsibility, treated like an adult and equal partner, and given flexibility and trust, is more likely to work productively than one who has none of these things. At least with Special Constables on their staff, employers may be assured that positive treatment will result in positive outcomes.

2.4.2 Don't forget the Force

The force for which you work can also influence your employer for good. Mention of the sponsoring organization when publicity is generated about the work of a Special Constable is one way in which the force can 'pay back' the employer's support, as can mentions on the Special Constabulary section of the force website. There are many ways to 'spin' the force's involvement with the Special Constabulary/employer and most will reinforce the strength of the 'triangular relationship' between force, employer, and Special Constable. Further sponsorship of police activity may also be a force benefit, once positive links with employers are made. And there's nothing to stop your employer making it clear to shareholders, stakeholders, customers, communities, neighbourhoods, boards, trusts, and oversight committees that s/he strongly supports Special Constables. Altruism is sometimes very good business.

2.4.3 Summary

It is worth summarizing here the very positive outcomes of the relationship between an employer and the Special Constable (and you can use this freely to persuade and influence):

Positive Outcomes: Special Constables and their employers

- It is mutually beneficial: both sides gain
- The employee's skills levels are enhanced in many ways and new skills learned, all of which can positively affect an employer's bottom-line profitability or efficiency
- It generates positive images (and good publicity if well handled) for the employer, which directly assists in the 'marketing' of his or her organization
- Flexibility and understanding are needed on both sides, the outcomes of which are very positive in terms of productivity and employment relations
- Employers appreciate being informed of likely impacts of police work, whilst Special Constables appreciate reciprocity in planning their duties
- A Special Constable demonstrates qualities which employers value, not least of which are loyalty and commitment; whilst a Special Constable relishes working for a flexible and compassionate organization aware of its community obligations
- Each needs to sustain an open dialogue
- The police force can support both sides and can play an important part in 'oiling the wheels' by showing sensitivity and understanding. After all, the Force is an employer too.

2.5 Special Constable—The Main Role

The following is an extract from a Home Office recruitment site for Special Constables—you will probably already be familiar with it—which seeks to provide a broad 'job description'. What is immediately noticeable is its breadth and depth—this is not a role that can be handily condensed to one side of A4. Furthermore, the activities described will vary from day to day, from force to force, from operation to operation. Despite being generic, the description shows how important the role of the Special Constable is and how central that role is to the business of visible and 'reassurance' policing. After all, if somebody wishes to volunteer his/her time, to make a gift of it, and can cover all of these areas, how much of a boon is that to the police force?

Generally speaking, a [Special Constable's] main role is to conduct local, intelligence-based patrols and to take part in crime prevention initiatives, often targeted at specific problem areas.

In many forces, Special Constables are also involved in policing major incidents, and in providing operational support to regular officers.

Depending upon their individual force, Special Constables can:

conduct foot patrols

assist at the scene of accidents, fights or fires

enforce road safety initiatives

conduct house-to-house enquiries

provide security at major events

present evidence in court

tackle anti-social behaviour

tackle alcohol related incidents

spend time at local schools educating youths about crime-reduction and community safety.

(Extract from Home Office website <http://www.policecouldyou.co.uk/specials/whats_it_like.html>, accessed 17 August 2009)

Let's look at a couple of these elements in case studies.

2.5.1 Tackle anti-social behaviour

Anti-social behaviour is a problem that blights the lives of many people and the fear that such behaviour generates can have a huge impact on the quality of life for many neighbourhoods. It is therefore important that, once identified, this problem is tackled firmly, tactics for which are explored in greater detail in Chapter 7 when we look more closely at Neighbourhood Policing. It is not surprising, then, that the Special Constabulary is involved in such high-profile activity, as the following example demonstrates:

Sending a strong message in Gloucestershire

Operation Ballymore was undertaken by the Stroud Police 'Safer Community' Team. This operation was mounted in response to residents' complaints about speeding, anti-social behaviour, and criminal damage, principally by young people within their area. Having identified these local priorities, an integral component of neighbourhood policing, the Safer Community team provided high-visibility policing with strong enforcement capability. Twelve Special Constables were drafted in to assist their regular colleagues with reassurance patrolling and speed checks, and thus helped to play a key part in the successes, where arrests were made, cautions given, and fines imposed, bringing a sharp decrease in the behaviours complained of. The successes were noted not just by the police but by the residents themselves.

(adapted from: <http://www.gloucestershire.police.uk/Latest News/Press Releases/2009/July/item12440.html>, accessed 24 August 2009)

2.5.2 Spend time [. . .] educating youths

Another key strand of government policy has been the **inclusion** of young people in a series of projects designed to help them avoid becoming victims of crime, to engage them in crime prevention, or to deter them from embarking on a career in crime. Such projects include going into schools or youth projects to deliver talks on road safety and 'stranger danger', or even helping with National Curriculum citizenship projects on community safety. All forces employ specialist officers to deal with youth offending, but local PCSOs, Neighbourhood Policing Officers, and Special Constables can make a significant impact, as the following example demonstrates:

After-School Café

In South Yorkshire, a team of Special Constables and community volunteers is running an after-school programme, the Dinnington ROC (Redeeming Our Communities) Café which provides facilities and activities for pupils from the local school.

These pupils gain extra achievement points at school for their attendance at the 'Café' and gain additional awards for working in the local community. The team has recently set up a new project to get the young participants looking at the issue of 'distraction burglaries' in the area.

(adapted from: *Specials, the Voice of the Special Constabulary*, NPIA, April 2009)

2.5.3 Fitting this into the minimum of four hours' duty

The issue of hours is not set in stone, because volunteering requires flexibility both in the hosting organization and in the individual. The police increasingly recognize that Special Constables have other commitments—work, family, studies, social lives (maybe all four)—so most forces will adapt to your needs. It is not unknown for police supervisors to order Special Constables to go home, because the latter have volunteered for too many shifts and need a break. You, working alongside your family, your employer, and the police, must determine how many hours you can commit to and when. What you offer, of course, is an 'added value' to each force; so it may make more sense for you to think not simply about the number of hours you put in, so much as the qualitative difference you can make when volunteering.

2.6 The Standards of Professional Behaviour

Police Regulations which gave guidance for ethical behaviour were revised in 2008 and a Schedule (No 3) was added in a Statutory Instrument (SI 2864) which reflected a new emphasis. The following are the revised **standards of professional behaviour**, full details of which may be found at <http://www.opsi.gov.uk/si/si2008/plain/uksi_20082864_en_8>, accessed 30 July 2009. In each case we have used the SI 'headline' wording, and followed it with our brief commentary.

2.6.1 Honesty and integrity

Police officers are honest, act with integrity and do not compromise or abuse their position.

This is about probity (ethical or 'right' action), and is part of the Nolan Principles which govern proper behaviour in public office.[1] Without honesty, a Special Constable cannot be trusted; without integrity, the job s/he does is partial or biased in some way; and the position of sworn officer is one where considerable powers are granted in the expectation that those powers are applied 'without fear or favour'; in other words, the Special Constable should never do something because of unethical pressures or expectations of favours.

2.6.2 Authority, respect, and courtesy

Police officers act with self-control and tolerance, treating members of the public with respect and courtesy.

Police officers do not abuse their powers or authority and respect the rights of all individuals.

Abuse of powers is among the major public complaints about police officers' actions, manifested often as high-handedness, incivility, and arrogance. Nick Hardwick, Chair of the Independent Police Complaints Commission (IPCC) said this in 2008:

> It is unacceptable that nearly half of all complaints [against the police] involve neglect or rudeness. There is absolutely no excuse for being rude to the public.[2]

and, of course, Mr. Hardwick includes the Special Constabulary, PCSOs, and other members of the extended policing family in his reference to 'complaints against the police'. It is sometimes difficult, in the face of deliberate provocation or abuse from the public, for a Special Constable to remain cool and calm, but the abiding characteristic of the 'good copper' is imperturbable fairness and impartiality, not loss of temper or abuse of power. 'Respecting the rights of all individuals' is much easier to write about than to do; and it does not simply refer to people who are different in terms of skin colour, or gender, or sexual orientation. Discriminatory behaviour of any kind has no place in the Special Constabulary, and no place anywhere else in policing. However, treating a paedophile or child murderer with tolerance and respect *can be very difficult*, and some crimes which Special Constables have to investigate are abhorrent by any civilized standard. For all one's individual feelings of repugnance and disgust at what people might have done, the external treatment of and attitude towards such offenders must still be exemplary.

2.6.3 Equality and diversity

Police officers act with fairness and impartiality. They do not discriminate unlawfully or unfairly.

We noted above that discrimination is not tolerated in the Special Constabulary, and this extends to age, disability, and belief, as well as to skin colour or race, gender or sexual orientation. Indeed, most of these forms of discrimination are unlawful. But **diversity is about difference**, and the positive way to approach difference is to accept it and learn from it, not to oppose it or seek to act prejudicially against it.

2.6.4 Use of force

Police officers only use force to the extent that it is necessary, proportionate and reasonable in all the circumstances.

Most forces have a mnemonic or handy reminder of the principle of proportionality guiding the use of force or compulsion. The most common is **PLAN**:

P	Proportionate
L	Legal
A	Authorized
N	Necessary

but there are other examples which say more or less the same things. This professional behaviour Standard is about what is right and appropriate to do in the circumstances, and the majority of Special Constables have plenty of common sense to guide them. Occasionally, the use of force is authorized, for example, to compel protesters to move away from obstructing a highway, in order to allow access to emergency vehicles; but in almost every instance except aggressive resistance, it is better to persuade someone to do something than to make that person do something. Much criticism was directed at the Metropolitan Police, for example, for using anti-terrorist powers to deal with protesters at the G20 economic summit in London in April 2009.[3]

There is a spectrum of responses which usefully illustrates the point:

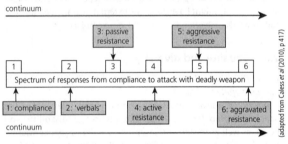

(adapted from Caless *et al* (2010), p 417)

Figure 2.1: Aggression response spectrum

or we might remember the point behind this deceptively simple model:

Figure 2.2: Betari's Box

where sometimes (but importantly, not always) your aggression *can* provoke aggression; your incivility *can* produce an equally dismissive response. There are other times when you will have to cut across this pattern, impose your will, and make an arrest.

With care, common sense, and some luck, such occasions ought to be uncommon.

2.6.5 **Orders and instructions**

Police officers only give and carry out lawful orders and instructions. Police officers abide by police regulations, force policies and lawful orders.

Special Constables should only ever give **lawful orders** and instructions, and only ever receive them. You cannot hazard the safety of members of the public, for example, by telling them to cross a busy road, or to drive faster than the speed limit, except under highly unusual conditions such as the urgent and overriding need to save lives. Common sense plays a large part in the orders and instructions which a Special Constables gives and receives; but always, at the back of any action or order, is the spectre that, if things go badly wrong, it might be in the dispassionate and clinical atmosphere of a court that such actions and orders are scrutinized. Remember the police shooting of Jean-Charles de Menezes in London in July 2005, and how the media coverage, consequent Inquiry, accusations, and strong emotions surrounding that unfortunate event, completely overshadowed the excellent work which the Metropolitan Police and the other emergency services had performed in dealing with the aftermath of the terrorist attacks on public transport on 7 July 2005.[4]

2.6.6 **Duties and responsibilities**

Police officers are diligent in the exercise of their duties and responsibilities.

The technical legal term for not doing what you should do in public office is '**non-feasance**': this applies to diligence, or 'careful and persistent industriousness'.[5] A Special Constable should never ignore situations where someone is breaking the law, creating a nuisance, or upsetting other people. That said, whilst there is always an absolute duty to save life, a Special Constable can exercise discretion whether or not to apply the law in some circumstances. That is *not* the same as turning a blind eye. In addition, diligence entails enthusiasm for the job of policing, a readiness to take responsibility, and a willingness to go into places and to do things which ordinary members of the public might reasonably refuse to do (such as stopping a fight, defusing an angry quarrel, going into a rowdy pub, entering a house where death is suspected, and so on).

2.6.7 Confidentiality

Police officers treat information with respect and access or disclose it only in the proper course of police duties.

Relationships between Special Constables and the media (particularly a friendly local journalist who often casts the police in a favourable light), have to be carefully managed, to avoid crossing the line between protecting information and improperly disclosing it. In general terms, **confidentiality** means that Special Constables should not discuss any police activity with anyone from the media, always referring enquiries to the force media spokesperson or media centre. The principle of **'need to know'** should be paramount: as a police officer, you only tell someone something confidential about policing if s/he *needs* to know it in order to do his or her job.

2.6.8 Fitness for duty

Police officers when on duty or presenting themselves for duty are fit to carry out their responsibilities.

This is a straightforward principle about being able, physically or mentally, to do the job, and not doing something (or refraining from doing something) which would compromise that ability. The classic example is being unfit through drink to drive a car, and in some forces police officers face dismissal if convicted of drink-driving. Other forces are more tolerant, but there can be no reasonable excuse for turning up for rostered duty impaired by drink.[6] The same principles apply to drugs, with the additional observation that the taking of illegal drugs is a criminal offence.

2.6.9 Discreditable conduct

Police officers behave in a manner which does not discredit the police service or undermine public confidence in it, whether on or off duty.

Police officers report any action taken against them for a criminal offence, any conditions imposed on them by a court or the receipt of any penalty notice.

A Special Constable who has a court order for bankruptcy proceedings must declare it, as must one who has been ordered by a court not to approach an ex-partner, for example. A Special Constable convicted of a crime may be dismissed if the offence is grave enough: normally crimes of deception, theft, sexual predation, or violence fall into the dismissal category, depending upon severity and any court ruling or comment.

2.6.10 **Challenging and reporting improper conduct**

Police officers report, challenge or take action against the conduct of colleagues which has fallen below the Standards of Professional Behaviour.

This is an internal measure, designed to ensure that Special Constables treat their colleagues in the rest of the Constabulary, and in the extended policing family, with respect. It is important that the kinds of attitude which characterized Mark Daly's exposé of racist police trainees in the BBC's *The Secret Policeman* in 2003,[7] are challenged internally by colleagues and fellow officers, so that discrimination and intolerance are eliminated from the police service. This applies as much to any other form of discriminatory behaviour as it does to racism, and will cover bullying, intolerance, and offensive language as well as behaviour. This is not intended to create a breed of police 'informants' but to ensure that the police become and remain non-prejudiced non-discriminators.[8]

2.6.11 **Police Regulations apply in their entirety to Special Constables**

The Explanatory Note in the Police (Conduct) Regulations 2008 makes it clear that

> [t]he Regulations establish procedures for the taking of disciplinary proceedings in respect of the conduct of members of police forces and special constables ('police officers') and [. . .] special constables are treated as if they are non-senior officers regardless of their actual level of seniority.
>
> (Police (Conduct) Regulations 2008 SI No 2864)[9]

In other words, whatever applies to the regular police officer in terms of required behaviour and professional standards applies equally *in law* to the Special Constable, which is, of course, how it should be.

2.7 **Uniform**

The British police uniform, particularly the traditional pointed police helmet, is one of the most recognizable uniforms in the world (so much so that it is used for souvenir purposes, as any visitor to the tacky souvenir shops in central London can testify). This distinctive image is perhaps diminishing, as patrol uniforms across the country are adapted to deal with the requirements of twenty-first century policing.[10] All officers on patrol or working outside police stations now routinely wear stab vests/body armour for example, as the threat of 'sharps' has become more pronounced (see below). Some forces have adopted a black polo shirt instead of the traditional white shirt and black tie, and some forces have moved wholesale from the time-honoured tunic with silver buttons to the 'blouson' jacket (known irreverently in Special Constabulary circles as the 'bum-freezer'). Many officers wear high-visibility vests when on duty, as we note below.

The development of police uniform and equipment is one that has been going on since police officers were first introduced and changes have been brought about to reflect the environment within which policing occurs. The whistle has given way to the Airwaves radio, the truncheon to the ASP baton, and so on. North Wales Police has issued its officers with polo shirts (with special anti-sweat protection) instead of shirts and ties, together with cargo trousers and even baseball caps (*The Sharp End*, 28 July 2007). These changes may not prove universally popular, especially with those people more used to the appearance of the traditional 'bobby'; but for the advocates of the newer, less formal, uniform, polo shirts and baseball caps are reflective of the need to adapt to changing circumstances. Whilst undue American influence might be regrettable, it is worth noting that firearms officers have been wearing baseball-type caps for some years now, without provoking much adverse comment.

These changes have also been incorporated within the Special Constabulary uniform, which is virtually identical to that of regular officers (except, perhaps, for 'SC', and sometimes a crown, on the collar badge or epaulette). It is clear that there is more to the Special Constabulary uniform than merely being items of occupational or protective clothing. Actually, in our experience, nothing in policing is more likely to produce a long and sometimes heated discussion than the topic of uniform and equipment. We do not take sides in any debate, but we have devoted some of this chapter to uniform and equipment, largely because it looms so large in many officers' experience. No doubt you too will be drawn into discussion of preferences and whether 'hi-sole tab-backed boots' are preferable with or without 'splash tread'. It is a topic which can become very arcane.

2.7.1 **Uniform issue**

The following is a list of uniform elements that can be issued to a
Special Constable. This can vary from force to force and should be
seen as generic. It does not include all the forms/books of forms
that the average officer takes with him or her on patrol.

Police Uniform
- Shirts (black polo-necks in some forces)
- Trousers (skirts for female officers is an option)
- Waterproof Trousers
- Cap + cap badge
- Helmet + helmet badge
- Epaulettes + sliders with force insignia
- Clip-on tie
- Fleece
- Blouson jacket or formal tunic
- Motorway 'hi-viz' jacket (traffic officers can have a fluorescent cap
  cover too: see 2.8.2)
- Gloves
- Belt (see 2.8.3.1 for descriptions of load vests and equipment belts)
- Boots (some forces provide a boot allowance to help with the cost,
  others leave it to you to shoe yourself).

2.7.2 **Uniform standards**

All forces will have a force policy on uniform standards, and these
apply equally to members of the Special Constabulary, and will
include details of what uniform should be worn for what occasion, as well as details about hair colouring, body jewellery, tat-
toos, and even the number of tiepins or badges an officer may
display.

2.7.3 **Female uniform**

Another important development within police uniform has
been the long-overdue move towards properly fitting uniforms
for female officers, including customized stab vests (see 2.8.3).
Some police forces continue to issue uniforms only in male sizes,
which is archaic and scandalous. There is a need for properly fitted uniform that conforms to the different physiological needs
of female officers, which in turn helps with issues of confidence
and self-esteem.

2.8 'Going Equipped'— Police Equipment

Whilst the make, model, and style of police equipment may differ from force to force, all provide the following equipment to Special Constables as a minimum. It is obligatory to carry with you the following:

2.8.1 Airwave radio

Every operational police officer is required to carry a personal radio (PR), when on duty: these may be personal issue or from an equipment pool. PRs are essential and invaluable pieces of equipment. Not only do they allow you to pass and receive timely information about the events you are attending, or intelligence or warning markers on persons or vehicles stopped, but they allow you to call for emergency assistance should a situation deteriorate and urgent back-up be required. Earpieces (on 'curly-wurly' wires) are now becoming standard issue with the handsets to safeguard the integrity and security of information passed over the radio network.

'Airwave' is the operational name for the police service's encrypted digital trunked radio system that replaced the old analogue radio. Distribution of Airwave was completed in May 2005 and currently every territorial police force in the United Kingdom, including the British Transport Police, the Serious Organized Crime Agency, and other policing organizations make use of the technology (NPIA, 2009).[11] Both the fire and rescue, and the ambulance services received Airwave radios at the end of 2009, so that in the event of a national emergency, or major incident (such as the flooding in Cheshire in November 2009), all three emergency services are able to coordinate resources and responses, using a communication system common to all (NPIA, 2009).[12]

2.8.2 Hi-visibility jackets/tabards

The Health & Safety at Work Act 1974 places a statutory responsibility on both the employer and each individual employee to ensure his/her health, safety, and welfare, so the police service provides its staff with the necessary protective equipment for them to be able to carry out their work safely and to minimize any risks they might face on duty.

'High-visibility' ('Hi-Viz') jackets and tabards are provided because they enhance officers' visibility to others. This has the dual advantage of increasing public awareness of a police presence (whilst patrolling a neighbourhood foot beat, for example), and also enhances officers' safety on roads and motorways (at the scene of a road traffic collision, say). Hi-visibility jackets are waterproof, and ordinarily come with a detachable, quilted inner lining for additional warmth. These versatile jackets are quickly replacing the black 'town beat' coats used in the past by officers when patrolling on foot.

Figure 2.3 (below) illustrates both the fluorescent and reflective properties of the hi-visibility clothing worn by police officers in darkened conditions. Note how the officer becomes more conspicuous when an oncoming light source is directed towards the officer whilst wearing the jacket, this is particularly useful when operating on roads in hours of darkness.

Figure 2.3: A police officer wearing a hi-visibility jacket

Figure 2.4 details and explains the classification system found on the garment labels for hi-visibility jackets and tabards ordinarily issued to Special Constables, and describes in which operational circumstances they may be used.

X – Class for the conspicuity (maximum surface area exposure) of the fluorescent and reflective surfaces – 3 levels of conspicuity.
(1) Minimum level visibility;
(2) Intermediate level visibility;
(3) Highest level visibility.

NB. This is what we refer to when detailing a jacket's Class and determining what road types a garment should be used on.

Y – Class for the performance of the reflective tape (furthest distance visible from) – 2 levels of performance.
(1) Minimum level performance;
(2) Highest level performance.

Figure 2.4: Hi-visibility clothing classification system

You should never wear a black load vest or duty belt over a hi-visibility jacket, unless it is of hi-visibility specification. A useful tip is to fasten your jacket up only by its poppers so that, should you need to grab any of your Personal Protection Equipment (PPE), such as your baton, you can do so quickly and easily by pulling open the coat.

2.8.3 Body armour—'stab vests'

In most forces the wearing of body armour when on duty away from the police station is mandated by force policy to meet the legislative provisions of the Health and Safety at Work Act. Failing to wear issued body armour not only risks injury, but it also endangers your colleagues because, if you are wounded, you cannot help them. The standard body armour has been designed to provide a level of protection against knife, glass, blade, slash, spike, and other sharp-instrument attacks.[13] Body armour also substantially safeguards an officer from sustaining an injury from the effects of 'blunt force trauma' during a physical attack from punches, kicks, dog bites, pinching, or weapons that might be used against them such as bats, sticks, or stones. Standard body armour offers *some* protection against the ballistic impact from light firearms (Home Office, 2007d).[14]

2.8.3.1 *Load vest/duty belt*

Load vests and duty belts are a means of carrying police equipment whilst on patrol. A **load vest** is simply an adjustable webbing mesh worn over body armour which has sewn-on 'docks' and 'holsters' for storing the Airwave radio, ASP baton, rigid handcuffs, incapacitant spray, mobile telephone, torch, disposable gloves, and first aid pouch, whereas the **duty belt** carries holsters for this equipment on a webbing belt worn around the waist.

In some forces new officers may have the choice of either a load vest or a duty belt and it is very much personal preference which is selected. Both have advantages and disadvantages. Increasingly, though, load vests are being favoured by police forces because of the perceived future long-term risks which duty belts might pose to an officer's lower spine (Home Office, 2007d).[15] Load vests can feel very heavy and may obstruct officers because they restrict movement, or get in the way if you have to climb obstacles. A duty belt is less of a problem. Moreover, it allows the ASP baton to be drawn from the hip, which is often the preferred and natural way to pull out a defensive weapon (rather than from the chest which is how you draw it from a load vest). Duty-belt holsters also allow for extendable batons to be carried either in their 'open' or 'closed' modes.

2.8.3.2 Baton

The symbolic yet impractical wooden truncheon has been replaced with a variety of different police batons modelled mostly on American law enforcement designs such as the PR–24 telescopic baton, the side-handled tactical baton, or the ASP extendable baton. Each baton has a set of strikes and techniques for safe and effective use. These will have been taught to you by specialist staff safety trainers during your officer safety training phase.

Batons are provided to all operational Special Constables as defensive weapons and form part of an officer's PPE and must be carried when booked on duty and in the public domain. They are usually uniquely identifiable to an individual officer because of an etched serial- or collar-number marking on the base. Lawful authority to be in possession of such an article ceases when the officer books off duty. Whilst police officers are authorized by law to use force on other people in certain circumstances, the decision to deploy or utilize a baton is the officer's own, and s/he alone is accountable for justifying its use in court and to supervisory officers.

2.8.3.3 Rigid cuffs

Rigid 'speed' or 'quick' cuffs have replaced the 'bracelet'-style handcuffs. The major advantage with modern rigid cuffs is that they restrain a non-compliant subject effectively and can also be used to force a person to the ground if necessary to allow officers to gain better control.

The application of handcuffs to another person amounts to use of force and must be justified and recorded in your pocket note-book (ACPO, 2009).[16] Handcuffs should always be checked for tightness on a person's wrist and then double-locked to prevent the cuff from closing and tightening further.

2.8.3.4 *Incapacitant spray*

Incapacitant sprays, whether of the CS or PAVA (synthetic pepper spray) varieties, form part of a Special Constable's PPE. Both sprays are classified under s 5 of the Firearms Act 1968 as **prohibited weapons** and accordingly very few people have lawful authority to possess such items. Special Constables *are* authorized to do so, but only when booked on duty.

The aim of incapacitant sprays is to enable Special Constables to gain control over a violent or non-compliant subject so that an arrest or other procedure can be executed swiftly and as safely as possible for everyone involved. Incapacitant sprays are useful tools for enforcing compliance, or as a distraction, allowing an officer time to disengage from a violent subject and employ a different tactic, or call for back-up. Sprays are generally thought of as the safest and lowest levels of force an officer can utilize because there are no lasting physical effects on a person after use.

2.8.3.5 *Personal equipment or property*

Finally, you should never supplement force-approved equipment with your own. Should any incidents occur whilst you are on duty at which you are found to have used equipment not approved or issued by your force, you might be liable in any possible future litigation, and might have made void any claims to compensation. Similarly, you should think twice about wearing expensive rings or watches in case of loss or damage. It is unlikely that police forces will offer you compensation for the loss of such items. Cheap substitutes worn for duty purposes are much easier to replace and have much less sentimental value.

Further Reading

Association of Chief Police Officers, *Guidance on the Use of Incapacitant Spray* (2006, ACPO)
ACPO, *Guidance on the Use of Handcuffs* (2009, ACPO)

Caless, B (ed.), with Bryant, R, Spruce, B, and Underwood, R, *Blackstone's PCSO Handbook*, 2nd edn. (2010, Oxford: Oxford University Press)

Croft, J and Longhurst, D, *HOSDB Body Armour Standards for UK Police (2007): Part 1: General Requirements*, Publication No. 39/07/A (2007, London: Home Office Scientific Development Board)

Davis Smith, J and Rankin, M, *Attracting employer support for the Special Constabulary* (1999, Home Office Policing and Reducing Crime Unit, Occasional Paper)

Davis Smith, J and Locke, M (eds.), *Volunteering and the Test of Time; Essays for policy, organisation and research*, (2008, Volunteering England, available to order from: <http://www.volunteering.org.uk/Resources/Publications/Volunteering+and+the+test+of+time>, accessed 7 July 2009)

Douse, K, *Carriage of Police Equipment* (2006, Home Office Scientific Development Board)

Health & Safety Executive 2008, 'High visibility clothing', available at <http://www.hse.gov.uk/workplacetransport/factsheets/clothing.htm>

Holton, V, Grayson, D, and Wilson, A, *Small firms and employer-supported volunteering: developing a strategy to take forward the work of Volunteering England* (2006, available on <www.volunteering.org.uk/smes>, accessed 24 August 2009)

Home Office, *Report of the Working Group on the Special Constabulary in England and Wales, 1995–1996* (1996, Home Office Communications Directorate)

Neuberger, J (Chair), *Report of the Commission on the Future of Volunteering and Manifesto for Change* (2008, available from <www.volunteering.org.uk/NR/rdonlyres/0B8EC40C-C9C5-454B-B212-C8918EF543F0/0/Manifesto_final.pdf>, accessed 7 July 2009)

Neuberger, J, *Volunteering across the criminal justice system* (2009, Cabinet Office/Third Sector Report, March, Crown copyright, available from: <http://www.cabinetoffice.gov.uk/third_sector/news/news_stories/090303_neuberger.aspx>, accessed 11 July 2009)

NPIA, *A National Strategy for the Special Constabulary* (2008, Strong Worldwide on behalf of the National Policing Improvement Agency, available from <http://www.npia.police.uk/en/11813.htm>, accessed 10 March 2009)

NPIA, 'Airwave Radio', (2009, available at <http://www.npia.police.uk/en/10506.htm>)

O'Connor, D, *Adapting to Protest*, HMIC's Report on policing the G20 protests, (2009, Home Office, Crown copyright)

Tuffrey, M, 'Getting the measure of community involvement', available from the *Corporate Citizenship Company* website <http://www.corporate-citizenship.co.uk>, originally published in *The Guide to UK Company Giving* (1999, Directory of Social Change) and quoted in Millie, A and Jacobson, J, *Employee Volunteering and the Special Constabulary: a review of employer policies* (2002, Police Foundation))

Notes

1 Lord Nolan, a prominent Law Lord, was appointed by the Conservative Government under John Major in 1994 to look into the standards of behaviour in public office, following a 'cash for questions' scandal amongst Members of Parliament. Lord Nolan issued his first report in 1995 and the seven Principles for Public Office which he enunciated then have since become a yardstick for probity in public office (however compromised by the scandal over MPs' expenses in 2009). See Nolan (1995).

2 See *Daily Telegraph* 'Police "rudeness" attacked by watchdog', available from <http://www.telegraph.co.uk/news/uknews/3074592/Police-rudeness-attacked-by-watchdog.html>, accessed 2 December 2008.

3 See an account at <http://news.bbc.co.uk/2/hi/uk /7975597.stm>, accessed 30 July 2009, and also <http://www.politics.co.uk/news/policing-and-crime/-heavy-handed-police-misuse-terror-laws-$1281978.htm>, accessed 30 July 2009.

4 See particularly the Independent Police Complaints Commission's report, *Fatal shooting of Jean Charles de Menezes*, 8 November 2007, available from <http://www.ipcc.gov.uk/index/pr081107_stockwell1_statement.htm>, accessed 28 February 2010. A considerable literature has built up on the subject of police shootings, but it is important to bear in mind always that post-fact enquiries always have the luxury of hindsight and time to mull over split-second decisions. Most firearms officers know this risk, and persist in their calling despite possibly harmful consequences for themselves. Consider this in the case of de Menezes: what criticism would have been levelled at MPS firearms officers if the unarmed Brazilian electrician had indeed been a terrorist with a bomb, which he had triggered on a crowded train? In the police service, 'pure' and meritorious actions are sometimes only a hair's breadth away from culpable homicide or awful accident.

5 As defined by the *Oxford English Dictionary* (1996, Oxford: Oxford University Press).

6 Being called in, in an emergency, after being at a party (for example) is different and attracts no penalty. All the same, the drink-drive laws apply and Special Constables cannot use emergency call-outs as an excuse for 'driving while unfit . . .'.

7 See <http://news.bbc.co.uk/1/hi/programmes/panorama/7650207.stm>, broadcast 3 October 2003, accessed 30 July 2009.

8 See Allport, G, *Nature of Prejudice* (1988, New York: Perseus Books).

9 Available from <http://www.opsi.gov.uk/si/si2008/plain/uksi_20082864_en_1>, accessed 26 June 2009.

10 Indeed, the Government's White Paper on the police, *Protecting The Public: supporting the police to succeed*, December 2009 ((London: The Stationery Office, Crown copyright), available from: <http://police.homeoffice.gov.uk/publications/police-reform/protecting-the-public.html>, accessed 3 December 2009), stated that one of its objectives was to standardize the police uniform across England and Wales.

Relations with your community
Dealing with the vulnerable
Communications
Negotiating and persuading
Developing partnerships
Working as part of a team

If you think that some of these learning topics entail overlaps between various parts of KUSAB, you would be right. This is our suggested answer:

Learning Topic	KUSAB elements
Your powers in law	K, U
Discretion	K, U, A
Structure and organization of your police force	K, U, A
The criminal justice system	K, U, A
Anti-social behaviour	K, U, A, B
House-to-house enquiries	K, U, S, A, B
Missing persons enquiries	K, U, S, A, B
Human rights	K, A, B
Standards of Professional Behaviour	K, U, S, A, B
Relations with your community	U, A, B
Dealing with the vulnerable	U, A, B (maybe K too)
Communications	K, U, S
Negotiating and persuading	K, U, A, B (some S too)
Developing partnerships	K, U, S, A, B
Working as part of a team	K, U, A, B

We can think of many instances across the entire range of learning topics for Special Constables in which all the elements of KUSAB apply at some point, for the simple reason that *knowing and understanding something modifies your behaviour and attitude towards it*. Often, a skill of some mechanical or intellectual kind is needed to ensure that the **K** and **U** are able to modify the **A** and **B**. None of what we learn takes place in isolation, and in policing that is especially so, since knowledge is **applied** to situations and circumstances, unlike, say, some kinds of academic knowledge, where the knowledge sought is the thing itself (some abstruse 'large-number' theoretical mathematics, say, or the function of colour symbolism in late medieval English Literature): better known as 'knowledge for its own sake'.

We can summarize the nature of **applied learning** through this case example:

> **Case Example (applied learning)**
>
> *Offence*: *Domestic violence*
>
> **K** Knowledge—the law, the circumstances, police powers
>
> **U** Understanding—common causes for domestic violence, common inhibitors, awareness that injured party often subsequently declines to prosecute, (knowing that 27 is average number of assaults before first reporting)
>
> **S** Skills—calming a situation, rendering first aid, encouraging assailant and victim (separately) to talk to you, taking notes, collecting evidence (including prompt photographing of alleged injuries)
>
> **A** Attitudes—no assumptions, not demonizing any of those involved, but alert to evidence, ready to caution
>
> **B** Behaviours—calm, authoritative, non-judgemental, protecting children or the elderly

There are many other examples of how KUSAB applies 'across' your actions as a Special Constable, and it is rare that one single aspect of KUSAB applies in isolation.

We are going to look quickly at two more aspects to learning: **learning domains** and the **experiential learning cycle** (ELC). The reason for doing so is that the greater your awareness of how you learn, the more likely it is that you can choose the best method of learning for you. This means that you are likely to learn more thoroughly, and retain more of what you have learned, once you know what is involved (and which best suits you).

3.1.1 Learning domains

Areas in which you commonly learn most easily and effectively are called **learning domains** (Bloom and Krathwohl, 1956).

The first domain is linked with your ability to **reason**, to work things out logically in your head, and your ability to remember how to reason and think about problems. An example is learning the 'rule of law' and how individual laws (such as those concerned with begging or with theft) apply in certain circumstances. This is often called the **cognitive domain**. Another area, or domain, is to do with **feelings** and emotional responses to situations, such as how you respond when someone swears at you, or when you are dealing with a baby or very young child. Your emotional response to a child's vulnerability is very deep-seated in your psyche as an adult human being, and you are likely to respond protectively and positively to vulnerable people (after all, caring about people was one of the reasons which led you to become a Special Constable). It may help to think of this as to do with your heart: it is normally termed the **affective domain**. The third domain is associated with how you can do things physically, such as using a screwdriver or catching a ball, and involves things like hand/eye coordination and **physical dexterity**. A primary professional example for the Special Constable is in first-aid skills, where stopping bleeding or bandaging a wound requires such coordinated and dextrous (skilful) abilities. This area of learning is usually referred to as the **psychomotor domain**.

One complication is that the three domains do not function on a single plane, but they progress, systematically, from a simple to a very complex level indeed. We might express it programmatically in a table like this:

Table 3.1: A dynamic for 'simple to complex' learning

Domain	*move from simple* ⟶ *to very complex*
Cognitive	*facts about law*: apply, invoke law to control a riot, use law to bring criminal charges, case files
Affective	*missing person*: search, time passes, media campaign, partnerships in search, find alive and unharmed
Psychomotor	*resuscitate accident victim*: airways, breathing, circulation, heartbeat, sustain breathing, recovery position, paramedical aid, hospitalization of victim

In practice, it is difficult to try to separate which domain is doing what as you are learning, but you are more likely to recall experience (**affective**) when the emotion is re-created; more likely to be able to apply **psychomotor** skills if you practise them regularly; and more likely to remember **cognitive**ly if you use a mnemonic or memory aid to 'bring up' key words.

3.1.2 The Experiential Learning Cycle (ELC)

This sounds complicated and difficult, but isn't. What it refers to is **learning through experience**. You can probably remember some examples from your past in which a decision or judgement you made turned out to be faulty. Let's use a really silly example to illustrate what we mean: it is February in the North Midlands, it is snowing lightly, but there is a strong wind which reduces the temperature even further. It is growing dark, even though it is only 1400 hours, and you, in T-shirt and shorts, are having trouble lighting the barbecue. The remainder of your family and friends are watching, with some anxiety, from the safety and warmth of the house as you stubbornly try to coax a blaze, ignoring the icicle forming on the tip of your nose. To spread the flame and increase the heat, you reach for a petrol can . . .

Well, if you survived the resultant conflagration, you are unlikely to do it again (we hope), and this is how you learn from experience. Try as you might, you will find it hard to recreate the conditions of late July in early February, even with global warming. Not in the North Midlands anyway.

We can express the process of learning by experience graphically as a cycle:

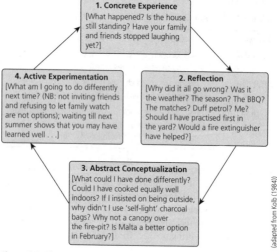

Figure 3.1: The Experiential Learning Cycle

The diagram shows how you can pass from the experience itself through a period of hard thinking and remembering (review and reflect), then through a process of working out what had been involved, ending with a decision to adapt to circumstances or to change actions in the light of what originally happened. The original cycle, presented by David Kolb (1984) is more abstract and theoretical than we have made it here, but the principle is a very simple, age-old, human one: how often do you have to plunge your hand into a fire to learn that fire burns and is painful? Most of us can even reason that, given sets of circumstances which entail danger, the best action is withdrawal or approaching differently (abstract conceptualization), but at the same time, most of us learn best through making mistakes.

You use this experiential cycle not just in your formal classroom and on-the-job training, but also in your normal span of duty, because only by being alert to what we do less well, can we improve what we do next time. This should offer us a **learning strategy**.

3.2 Special Constables' Training

Significantly, when it sees a police uniform the public does not distinguish between experienced and novice, any more than it distinguishes between a regular police officer and a Special Constable. Whether it is your first tour of duty after your initial foundation training, or you are a seasoned veteran, in any given crisis, or emergency, the public will assume that the person wearing the uniform can and should cope, ensuring everybody's safety and well-being. The sole exception is probably a firearms incident, but even there the public would expect uniformed police officers, Special or not, experienced or not, to contain the situation, get the public into safety, and call for support.[1]

3.2.1 Initial foundation-level training—a synopsis

Before you are let loose to perform operational police duties, you will receive *initial foundation-level training* from your chosen force. This usually this takes place at police headquarters, or in another designated police training establishment operated by them. The average initial foundation training course lasts between 12 and 16 weeks, with at least one and probably two evenings and a weekend day each week. There is an expectation that you will be able to commit to, and attend all of these training sessions. There is usually a limited 'run' of training courses at various points throughout the year, often following a recruitment drive. It is important that you choose a course at dates that you are able to commit to fully, without diversion, previous arrangements, or leave. You also need to ensure that your employer is aware of your commitment, so that you are not subject to in-work pressures at the same time.

Because you are to perform identical duties, hold exactly the same powers, and share the same responsibilities as a regular police officer, your foundation training is likely to be very intensive, bearing in mind your volunteer status, and the fact that a probationary police constable's initial taught training is approximately 36 weeks in duration (Bryants *et al*, 2010). A typical training timescale outlining key milestones in your development as a special constable might look like this:

Table 3.2: Typical training timescales

Time scale (months)	Training phase
0–3	Foundation training: induction and skills
3	**Attestation**
3–5	Foundation training: criminal law BCU or local station induction
3–6	Mentored patrol and evidencing of policing skills Ongoing local or BCU-based training
6–12	Supervised Patrol and evidencing of policing skills Ongoing BCU-based training
12	**Independent Patrol status**
12+	Advanced training Ongoing local or specialist occupational training

Timescales to achieve independence will of course vary depending on the number of hours you are able to work as a special constable, your availability to perform duties, the activities and training modules that you complete satisfactorily, and reflection on the experiences you gain when on duty, allied to your levels of confidence, skill, and knowledge. It is not a race to force you into independence, though it is anticipated that most Special Constables, under average conditions, will be able to achieve Independent Patrol status in 12 months (NPIA, 2008b).

The content of your foundation training, and when you are likely to receive each topic input, varies from force to force, of course. However, as a minimum it has been suggested by the NPIA in the *Special Constabulary National Strategy* (NPIA, 2008a) that Special

- **Small-group work**—in small groups you will be asked to research a set topic, analyse and discuss it amongst the group, and present your findings to the rest of the class. The trainers will usually act as facilitators to ensure that the key learning points are drawn out to aid the students' understanding of the topic

- **Individual work**—you may be set individual tasks to ensure that you can work unsupervised. These might include reading your 'pre-read' notes, revising for a knowledge check, giving a presentation to the rest of your group about your findings on a set topic, or (less formally) asking questions to clarify any learning points and consolidate your understanding during lessons

- **Lectures**—usually kept to a minimum, though sometimes they are an important way of getting across key learning points quickly, effectively, and without confusion

- **Electronic learning**—using computer-based learning (CBL) packages designed by your force or by the NPIA through their National Centre for Applied Learning Technologies (NCALT) system. E-learning aims to present topics in an interactive audio-visual manner that asks questions of the user to check his or her understanding of the material. The advantage is that the user can progress with the training at his or her own pace

- **Presentations**—used for certain topics such as aspects of the criminal law. A speaker will present and discuss the key points, whilst the presentation itself acts as a reference point for those who prefer to learn by reading than by listening. Presentations also aid those who wish to take concise training notes. Copies of the presentations may be given out as paper notes or as disks after the session

- **Role-play**—often used to simulate a set scenario, for example performing a stop and search or making an arrest. Student Special Constables play one of the roles in the scenario—for example the lead police officer, the support police officer, or the suspect—and will follow the scenario through to its conclusion. Role-plays are normally used when students have sufficient knowledge and understanding of police procedure and the law to make scenarios meaningful. They are useful in consolidating this knowledge and understanding by allowing you to practise your skills actively in a safe learning environment. A trainer or assessor will oversee the role play and will conduct a debrief at the end explaining how well you performed and any learning points that need to be highlighted for your awareness, to learn from or bear in mind, when you perform the procedure, possibly in a real situation, next time

- **Practical sessions**—usually first aid, radio, and OST are the key practical or physical elements of training based on the 'learning by doing' philosophy. Student Special Constables will be shown a technique and then practise it in pairs until proficient. There will be many 'reinforcement' sessions to consolidate the knowledge and skills involved, such as CPR (cardiopulmonary resuscitation) or using rigid handcuffs

- **Facilitated/led discussions**—very useful when exploring attitudes, values, and behaviours. Often a facilitated/led discussion will be stimulated initially by a film or DVD clip, or by reflecting on a written passage, or by a guest speaker's presentation. The trainer will encourage student Special Constables to discuss, share views, feelings, and thoughts in the safe learning environment of the classroom. It is important that confidentiality is maintained since participants might disclose personal, private, or sensitive matters that they may not wish others outside the training environment to know about. That said, remember that students will constantly be assessed, monitored, and observed by trainers and directing (or 'Di') staff. The safe learning environment of the classroom does not protect or insulate anyone from any disciplinary proceedings for inappropriate language, attitudes, or behaviour.

(adapted and augmented from Bryant *et al* (2009))

In most cases, foundation training courses are delivered to a maximum of 20 student Special Constables with a class ratio of approximately one trainer to ten student officers at most, though other assessors and trainers are brought in to monitor smaller groups, for example when performing role-plays, as appropriate. You will have plenty of quality contact time with your trainers and they will normally show interest in your progress.

3.2.3 Assessment

Assessment is an ongoing process throughout your training period. You will be visually assessed, monitored, and observed by your trainers from the outset of your training. It is therefore essential that you take a professional and mature approach to your training. Whilst you are not attested as a Special Constable immediately on commencing to train, the force will almost certainly view you as a voluntary employee of the police authority and also as a trainee police officer. You are therefore subject to the same professional and organizational standards as the regular police, police staff, and police authority employees, and other volunteers. Most importantly, this includes the Standards of Professional Behaviour for police officers (see 2.6). Any inappropriate language, attitudes, or behaviours are likely to incur disciplinary proceedings against you. Role-plays are often used to assess your performance during your foundation training because they are a useful means of assessing your practical skills, such as your abilities to stop and search a person safely whilst complying with your legal obligations, or demonstrating that you can issue a form HORT/1. This will usually take the form of a visual assessment by a training officer, or an experienced Special Constable assessor. Your PNB entries, and any practice statements, tickets, and forms that you fill in during your role-play sessions, are also likely to be collected and assessed to ensure your compliance with the PNB and statement rules, and force policy in relation to your forms and tickets.

Furthermore, the first aid, radio, and OST elements of your training are visually assessed by your trainers and are pass/fail aspects of training because of their importance to your personal safety and that of the public. Should you not reach the required standard in any of these training elements, your trainers will conduct a debrief with you to identify why you have difficulties and discuss what you can do to develop for next time. You would probably be 'recoursed' (that is, put through the training for that particular element again) so that you can attempt this practical aspect of your training with a greater understanding of what is expected of you. Your trainers may also provide additional training notes and perform one-to-one training with you to iron out any shortfalls and improve your performance next time. Having to start again at the beginning (a complete 'recourse') is unusual but not unknown—but failure to reach the required standard a second time might mean that you are asked to leave. Every effort will be made to help you succeed—no one wants to see you fail after all the effort that has been put into your learning, not least by you.

More common and regular forms of assessment are '**knowledge checks**'. These written or verbal tests are designed to assess whether you have attained the required levels of knowledge and understanding about your role, responsibilities, powers, procedures, and other material covered by your foundation training. These knowledge checks take place periodically throughout your foundation training period, culminating in a final written knowledge check covering all aspects of the course before you will be deemed suitable for attestation. Whilst these assessments should not be viewed as exams to get stressed about, they *are* important for your trainers to gauge whether you have the levels of knowledge to be able to carry out your role as a Special Constable and support your police colleagues safely and effectively when you are attested and deployed on your police area. Written knowledge checks are also used throughout Phase 2 of your foundation-level training to gauge your understanding of the criminal law.

3.2.4 Attestation

Your attestation is the formal ceremony in which you take the oath of office in front of a magistrate, your family, a command officer in the force you have chosen to serve, your Special Constabulary chief officer, and other invited guest representatives from the community, the police service, or other community safety partnership agencies. Your making the oath of attestation in front of the magistrate marks your formal swearing-in as a 'warranted' police officer. You will receive your warrant card and from this moment you hold full police powers. You will be viewed as a police officer by the public, your friends and family, and the police service. The ceremony is a prestigious event and is the culmination of your foundation-level training, and recognizes all your commitment, work, and learning to date. Ordinarily, it will take place after you have completed your foundation training on about week 12 or 13, where you demonstrate sufficient fundamental policing knowledge, understanding, and vocational skills to merit being granted your executive police powers.

3.2.5 Supervised Patrol, tutoring, mentoring, and performance reviews

Once you are attested, you are able to perform operational police duties, but you will not yet be capable of **Independent Patrol**. As a Special Constable, you may be allocated to a section of special constables, usually between five and ten strong, and each with different lengths of service and experience levels. The section may be supervised and led by a Special Sergeant or by a regular police sergeant, or very occasionally by a senior regular constable. It is the supervisor's job to look after your welfare, to monitor your performance, and to help your professional development. The Special Sergeant will usually assign you to an experienced Special Constable, or one who has undergone additional mentor training, to take you on a tour of the police station, get you fully equipped with the forms that you will need, and take you on a tour of the district you will now police, highlighting problem areas or crime hot spots. The 'mentor Special' or 'tutor constable' (terms vary) may arrange to perform duties with you for a set

proficient and confident. The variety of skills to evidence under the PAC headings includes:

- **Safety**—including dynamic risk assessments and use of radio
- **Information management**—including intelligence reporting in accordance with the NIM
- **Patrol**—including crime reporting, knowledge of offences, and abilities to deal with them
- **Search**—safe and competent skills at searching persons, vehicles, and property
- **Investigation**—including evidence gathering, writing and taking statements, accurate note taking in your PNB, use of caution, and arrest procedure
- **Disposal**—including reporting for summons, PND, and street cautions
- **Custody procedures**—including booking in a prisoner
- **Finalize investigations**—including charging suspects, giving evidence at court, and submitting case files
- **Roads policing**—including issuing FPNs, HORT/1s and VDRS, and dealing with drink-drive offences
- **Property**—including dealing with found and special property, handling, preserving, and managing physical evidence.

(adapted and augmented from Bryant et al (2009))

The evidence of attaining each skill will come in various forms. It could be evidence from your PNB, from any forms or 'tickets' you have competed or issued during your tour of duty, written witness testimony from colleagues who have observed you performing one of your PAC skills, or from any forms or reports generated from your actions, such as arrest summary reports. Collecting the evidence is far from difficult, because it is simply the collation and grouping of the actions and activities you perform on every duty. Part of the skill is organizing the mass of evidence you will quickly accumulate into the appropriate PAC heading or sub-heading. Most officers find the taxing part is recording the evidence in their PDP; however, this is usually because they do not keep on top of their PDP and do not record the evidence as they achieve it. This makes it a fairly hefty job later on, so best practice is to record your PDP/PAC evidence as you go, and write it up at the end of each tour of duty you perform.

3.2.7 Ongoing professional development

In addition to your operational policing hours, most forces run weekly or bi-weekly, uniformed Special Constabulary training or 'parade' nights at your police station, or the main district station in larger BCUs. Your attendance is expected, and should take precedence over performing operational police duties. Not only are these meeting nights an invaluable chance to catch up on any admin or process that you might have outstanding, but they are also an opportunity for your supervisory special officers or Area Special Constabulary Coordinator (ASCC) to share important information with you, such as impending operations, or events that extra officers are required at and that you might wish to take part in, or to advise you about important area news, changes to force policy, or indeed the law. They might also conduct an intelligence briefing so that you are aware of the BCU priorities, crime hot spots, and prolific offenders relevant to your patrol during the forthcoming duty.

Sometimes, training inputs are arranged to enhance officer skills on a specific offence or aspect of policing, such as the completion of crime reports, or common problems in dealing with a road traffic collision. On other occasions other specialist departments (such as Fraud, or Professional Standards) might come along to inform you about their work and how your work as a Special Constable can support them. Essentially, this ongoing training is about keeping you as up-to-date as possible, bearing in mind that crime and policing can change very quickly. It is also valuable, as you have more limited exposure to these experiences since you are not a regular officer and can only commit a limited number of hours each week or month to performing policing duties.

3.2.8 Independent Patrol status and advanced training

At about 12 months' service, you should be ready for Independent Patrol status, if you have not already achieved this. Independence allows you to patrol unsupervised—that is, without the direct supervision of another independent Special Constable or regular officer—and allows you to patrol solo, or take out up to two other non-independent Special Constables to help them achieve their independence, and act as lead officer when dealing with incidents or emergency situations.

Whilst achievement of Independent Patrol status would seem to make the Special Constabulary more flexible for you, it does carry increased responsibilities. By patrolling as an independent officer, you will take ownership of everything you deal with, and you will be responsible for supervising any non-independent officers you take out on patrol with you. You should not rush to achieve independence, therefore: rather, you should wait until you feel able enough to deal with any given incident by yourself, confident that, as a result of your training and learning, and the consolidation of your experience, you will get it right.

3.3 **The National Occupational Standards (NOS)**

The NOS show what a Special Constable can do, what s/he cannot do quite so well, and where the learning gaps are. The problem with the NOS is that evidencing each of the skills, to the competency required, involves lots of cross-checked paperwork, evidencing of examples, assessment and attestation ('testimony'), and the investment of considerable amounts of time. Since the Special Constable's time is limited, this seems to many to get in the way of operational policing rather than complementing it. It is in this context that we wish briefly to explore the subject of NOS—which, to be fair, do exactly what it says on the tin:

> National occupational standards describe the **standards of performance** that people are expected to achieve in their work and **the knowledge and skills** they need to **perform effectively**. National occupational standards have been developed to cover most occupational areas in the UK

(Skills for Justice, 2006, p 3; our italics)

There can be no doubt that the key terminology here is that which we have highlighted in the box—*standards of performance, knowledge and skills, perform effectively*. Therefore it is not surprising that police forces, the Home Office, and Skills for Justice (the organization that administers and develops NOS) have placed great emphasis on individual Special Constables achieving such competence.

3.3.1 **Developments within NOS**

At the time of writing, there are quite profound developments taking place in the world of NOS and no one knows precisely where it will end. It is quite possible that, by the time you read this, the details which we outline below may have changed. The onus, we are afraid, is on you to check out any changes, amalgamations, joinings-together, or omissions with either your in-force training or local personal development units. **At present there are 22 NOS units** that a Special Constable must achieve and *it is proposed that this be reduced to 10*. What is entirely unclear is which NOS will go and which will stay.

3.3.1.1 *Present Special Constable NOS*

Current (22) regular police officer and Special Constable NOS

The first 11 are at Level 3:

1A1 Use police actions in a fair and justified way
1A4 Foster people's equality, diversity, and rights
2C1 Provide an initial police response to incidents
2C3 Arrest, detain, or report individuals
2C4 Minimize and deal with aggressive and abusive behaviour
2H1 Interview victims and witnesses
2I1 Search individuals
2K2 Present detained persons to custody
4C1 Develop one's knowledge and practice
4G2 Ensure your own actions reduce risks to health and safety
4G4 Administer first aid

The second 11 are at Level 4:

1A2 Communicate effectively with all members of the public and its communities
1B9 Provide initial support to individuals affected by offending or anti-social behaviour and assess their needs for further support
2A1 Gather and submit information that has the potential to support policing objectives
2C2 Prepare for, and participate in, planned policing operations
2G2 Conduct investigations
2G4 Finalize investigations
2H2 Interview suspects
2I2 Search vehicles, premises, and land
2J1 Prepare and submit case files
2J2 Present evidence in court and at other hearings
2K1 Escort detained persons

The NOS as currently structured above provide a detailed list of those things in which the public would expect a Special Constable to be competent. However, things will not stay like this.

3.3.1.2 *The proposed new Special Constable NOS*

We noted above that there are to be new Special Constable NOS by late 2010 or early 2011 but, at the time of writing, we simply don't know when the publication/start date will be. We have provided a list below of what we *believe* the new NOS will be, but we must emphasize again that you must check at the time of publication—in policing, things change regularly and quite quickly.

Proposed New Special Constable (consolidated) NOS

BE2   Provide initial support to victims, survivors, and witnesses

CD1   Provide an initial response to incidents

CD5   Arrest and detain or report individuals

CK1   Search individuals

CK2   Search vehicles, premises, and open spaces

GC10   Manage conflict

CB1   Gather and submit information

CI101   Conduct priority and volume investigations

CJ101   Interview victims and witnesses

CJ201   Interview suspects

If adopted in this format, the new NOS will provide a more streamlined, although still rigorous, examination of the Special Constable role. The NOS as proposed are still areas in which the public would wish their police officers to be competent, but this tightened format, reducing the NOS from 22 to 10, may ensure that attaining competence in the NOS is much more about *workplace-based assessment* and much less about tedious and interminable form filling for portfolios of evidence.

3.3.2 'An appropriate core set of NOS for the Special Constabulary'

It is worth our noting here that the use of the NOS within the Special Constabulary is dependent on which force you are in or are joining. Each police force has tended to interpret the NOS for Special Constables in slightly different ways and, in particular, many forces have been keen to avoid some of the more excessive bureaucracy that comes with the NOS—a point which NPIA has been quick to acknowledge:

> The Special Constabulary, owing to the limited time and availability of students to complete a full course, would be unlikely to achieve the full 22 NOS and work is needed to identify *an appropriate core set of NOS for the Special Constabulary*.
>
> (NPIA, 2008, 5.2.4; our italics)

How do you ensure that volunteer police officers are assessed as being competent for their role, as they should be, whilst not making their limited volunteering hours all about assessment? It could be quite dispiriting for a Special Constable to spend his or her designated 16 hours per month of volunteering in a continual round of NOS completion and form filling. A balance is required; and it is fair to acknowledge that one is being sought through a dialogue between NPIA, the Special Constabulary Strategic Command, and Skills for Justice. What balance will be struck is not yet clear.

3.3.2.1 *How could NOS be used in the Special Constabulary?*

By themselves, NOS do not improve individual performance; they need to be put into a *performance management* context. This requires the NOS to become part of the annual appraisal process and, in particular, they are crucial in the first year to eighteen months, during which a new Special Constable works towards independence. Furthermore, the NOS need to be utilized in all forms of training for the Special Constabulary, so that competence can be assessed and gaps in knowledge or skills identified, and then addressed. It is only in this way that the NOS can begin to be used correctly for the benefit of both the individual and the organization, in what is a cyclical process as outlined in the figure below:

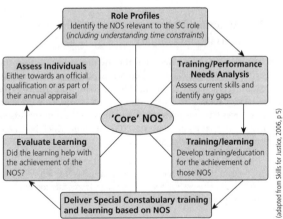

Figure 3.2: NOS as cyclic skill determinants

(adapted from Skills for Justice, 2006, p 5)

3.3.2.2 *Delivering on the NOS*

It is evident that, as a species of work-based assessment, the NOS can be used to the benefit of individual performance and therefore can contribute to the achievement of overall organizational aims. Furthermore, used within a training context, the NOS can help with retention and 'job satisfaction' by providing Special Constables with access to training and assessment that truly matters—individual Special Constables will feel valued by their forces as a consequence of a substantial investment in their skills and development. However, this can tend to the utopian. Bureaucracy still dominates the NOS and there are many difficulties in properly utilizing them within the Special Constabulary as we summarize here:

Some difficulties in utilizing the NOS within the SC

- *Time constraints*—Special Constables volunteer to help with policing, and might be frustrated by continuous and bureaucratic assessment. They might see the NOS as getting between them and the job, rather than being an effective way of evaluating how well they do the job
- *Use of regular officer NOS*—they are not bespoke for the Special Constabulary and therefore do not take into account the unique volunteering perspective.
- *Achievement of NOS*—if a Special Constable volunteers for 16 hours per month, s/he may find it difficult to achieve all the NOS in a specified period, particularly if s/he does not encounter some given or routine situations upon which the NOS are predicated
- *Assessing the NOS*—as Special Constables predominantly work in the evenings/weekends, some assessors might not be available to observe the Special Constable in action and to assess completion of a NOS indicator.
- *Training the NOS*—as above, it can be difficult for training to be given to Special Constables in a standard 'Mon–Fri, 9–5' training context; weekend training tends to be crammed anyway
- *Utilizing the NOS*—many Special Constables do not receive annual appraisals that take the NOS into account. This lack reduces the effectiveness, relevance and utility of the NOS.

3.3.3 Conclusion

Competence is, of course, the *minimum* level of attainment of NOS by the Special Constabulary that the public should expect.

We anticipate that the 'new'—or at least revised and consolidated—NOS destined for launch in 2010 or 2011 will seek to ensure that competences are focused more on achieving credible ends than on bureaucratic means. However, it remains to be seen how Special Constables can be 'assessed for competence' under the NOS (full or 'core') without making individuals dissipate their available time in pursuit of a paper exercise. The NOS must be made brisker, more practical, and more meaningful to the Special Constabulary role without compromising operational effectiveness and without devaluing the Special Constables' gift of time.

3.4 Appraisal and Assessment

> Appraisal of employee performance is among the most controversial of management practices. Although many organizations have implemented formal procedures for evaluating their employees, the level of dissatisfaction with this process among both managers and employees has remained high.
>
> (Lilley and Hinduja, 2007, p 137)

This paints a bleak picture of appraisals but, if you think about either your own career as a Special Constable or your main employment history, we suspect that there are very few of us who have not, at some point, had an annual review that we have disagreed with or found irritatingly inadequate. At one end of the spectrum, the annual appraisal can be a quick corridor chat that established nothing and appraised even less, and at the other, it can be a bureaucratic nightmare of page filling and box ticking. For many managers, the objective lies in simply completing the assessment, not in using the opportunity to develop the individual employee's career.

This has produced a widespread scepticism about the appraisal process and what it is supposed to do. We can itemize some of the problems associated with appraisal like this:

Criticisms of annual assessment
- Can be too subjective
- Focuses on mistakes/part of blame culture
- Not necessarily reflective of the real job

- Can be a bureaucratic process
- Linked to performance pay, therefore no one gets top marks
- Problems might not be mentioned until end of year
- There may be no review period
- There may be a lack of appeal rights
- Too often based on one person's opinion
- Often there is no evidence to back up claims
- Fairness and consistency can suffer, or not appear.

3.4.1 Why have appraisals at all?

Given these identified problems, would it make any difference if performance was not appraised or assessed? After all, it is what the organization achieves that is the most important outcome, isn't it? Yes, but the organization's achievements are the sum total of lots of individual efforts. Therefore improving on each of these small parts *will* make a difference cumulatively. This produces, often, a collective effort which is far greater in impact than all the individual parts considered separately. It is called *synergy*, and you will hear this word used a lot in the higher reaches of the Special Constabulary, where it is often a strategic aim. Equally persuasive is the need, in any organization (but especially in policing), to identify those individuals who are not performing well or competently, so that shortfalls can be addressed. Imperfect as the system is, and sceptical of the outcomes as we may be, nonetheless, the appraisal of employees is crucial in order to reward strengths on the one hand and to address and change weaknesses on the other:

3.4.1.1 *Appraisal and assessment within the Special Constabulary*

Within the Special Constabulary appraisal and assessment will always be an area where different forces adopt different strategies, depending on the role that Special Constables perform and upon the management/supervision structure and the internal administrative systems employed. However, common to all forces will be the logistical difficulty of assessing volunteers who work at different times and whose attendance is not mandatory. Furthermore, by employing a highly structured and comprehensive system of assessment, police forces could end up with the time gifted to the force by the volunteer mainly taken up by systems of appraisal and assessment. This point has been recognized by the NPIA:

> Individual performance management for volunteers is an area that requires a balance between the positive motivation and development aspects that individual appraisal can provide and the potentially demotivating impact. With Special Constabulary officers generally giving 16 hours per month, *any individual appraisal system needs to be proportionate* in terms of the time taken and the benefits to be obtained.
>
> (NPIA, 2008b, Section 8; our italics)

3.4.2 Developments in police assessment

A move to work-based assessment, where performance of **policing** tasks is assessed, has been highlighted by many forces exploring options for the development of regular officers. A report into the concept of 'assessing at work through work' undertaken by West Midlands Police identified a need to move away from a traditional NVQ approach in favour of one that put the student officer at the heart of the process:

> The strategy [for work-based assessment] aims to have trained and competent police officers and a seamless process which is not driven by the qualification. This can only be progressed and developed if the right organisational culture is in place.
>
> (*Police Professional*, 11 September 2008, p 24)

However, discussions during 2009 appear to suggest that the issue of qualifications is back on the agenda as police forces seek to improve leadership potential. Whatever approach is utilized for regular officers, there is clear crossover potential for the Special Constable. The focus on organizational culture is crucial:

> The context of officer development is inherently less confrontational and encourages employees to continually improve on performance, rather than dwelling on past deficiencies. Further, the developmental context may be even more important in police agencies, where the professional model has been used to highlight officer mistakes and has resulted in a risk-averse culture.
>
> (Lilley and Hinduja, 2007, p 147)

Lilley and Hinduja make a vital point here and, although their research is based on US police experience, the idea of focusing on continuous improvement rather than dwelling on mistakes has real resonance for policing in the UK, particularly in a time of inclusivity and citizen focus fostered by neighbourhood policing. It may be time to say goodbye to a culture predominantly based on *blame* which has dominated policing for decades and which, more than anything, has contributed to a current climate of risk-aversion.

3.4.3 The future of assessment

As we noted above, there is much that can go wrong with the assessment process for anyone in any organization, but there is little doubt that some sort of appraisal or formal assessment needs to be completed on a regular basis by those who manage others, so that developmental issues for the individual can be addressed. Within policing at large there is much discussion of how assessment should be done, what the process should include, and what the content and regularity of the appraisal of performance should be. Such a process of evaluation applies to police forces as much as it does to individuals working or volunteering for those forces. Recent national developments are about giving the public more say in how police forces are rated—what has been termed *Rounded Assessment*. This entails Her Majesty's Inspectorate of Constabulary's (HMIC) taking into account what local people feel about local policing—a real departure from a centralized and centrist past. The proposal is that 'Rounded Assessment' will concentrate on five areas:

The Five Domains of Rounded Assessment
- Confidence and Satisfaction
- Local Crime and Policing
- Protection from Serious Harm
- Value for Money
- Managing the Organization

(HMIC (2009), *Assessing Police Performance: Giving the Public a Voice. Proposals for Consultation on Rounded Assessment*)

Whilst there are no plans yet for these five areas of police force performance to be incorporated into individual assessments, it would seem logical to suppose that this might happen, because the individual should be working towards the completion of organizational objectives. As a Special Constable it would be worth assessing your own performance against these key areas because if you are achieving against these objectives, then your appraisal should be a positive one. At the same time, we cannot divorce Rounded Assessment from fulfilment of the **Policing Pledge** (see 10.2), which seeks to evaluate the service which policing gives to the public. It might even be that some kind of synergy between Rounded Assessment and the Policing Pledge emerges over the next few years to take appraisal of a Special Constable's performance into a new and perhaps effective dimension.

Further Reading

ACPO/NPIA, *Practice Advice on Professionalising the Business of Neighbourhood Policing*, (2006, Wyboston, Lincolnshire: National Centre for Policing Excellence, part of NPIA), available from: <http://www.neighbourhoodpolicing.co.uk/doclib/doclib_view.asp?ID=528>, accessed 19 December 2008

Bloom, B and Krathwohl, D, *Taxonomy of Educational Objectives: The Classification of Educational Goals, by a committee of college and university examiners. Handbook I: Cognitive Domain* (1956, New York: Longmans, Green), and others in the series to 1964

Bryant, R and Bryant, S (eds.), *Blackstone's Student Police Officer Handbook*, 4th edn. (2010, Oxford: Oxford University Press)

Caless, B (ed.), with Bryant, R, (Morgan, D), Spruce, B, and Underwood, R, *Blackstone's Police Community Support Officer's Handbook*, 2nd edn. (2010, Oxford: Oxford University Press)

Fahy, P *et al* (Strategy working group members), *National Strategy for the Special Constabulary*, (2007, Working Group on Strategy, NPIA Conference, 3 December), also available from <http://www.npia.police.uk/en/9353.htm>, accessed 2 July 2008

HMIC, *Assessing Police Performance: Giving the Public a Voice. Proposals for Consultation on Rounded Assessment* (2009, London: Home Office, Crown copyright)

Kolb, D, *Experiential Learning, experience as a source of learning and development*, (1984: New Jersey: Prentice Hall)

Lilley, D and Hinduja, S, 'Police Officer Perfomance Appraisal & Overall Satisfaction', *(2007) Journal of Criminal Justice*, 35, 137–50

Moon, J, *Reflection in Learning and Professional Development Theory and Practice* (1999, London: Kogan Page)

Mullins, L, *Management & Organisational Behaviour*, 7th edn. (2005, Harlow: FT Prentice Hall)

NPIA (2008a), *A National Strategy for the Special Constabulary* (2008, Strong Worldwide on behalf of the National Policing Improvement Agency), available from <http://www.npia.police.uk/en/11813.htm>, accessed 10 March 2009

NPIA (2008b) *Special Constabulary National Strategy Implementation Advice*

NPIA, *Special Constabulary*, (2009) Police Recruitment and *Specials* Magazine, available from <www.npia.police.uk/en/10040.htm>, accessed 9 June 2009

Pohl, M, *Learning to Think, Thinking to Learn: Models and Strategies to Develop a Classroom Culture of Thinking* (2000, Cheltenham, Victoria, Australia: Hawker Brownlow)

Police Professional, 'Breaking the Mould', (2008) 11 September

witness is able to remember something about what the suspect(s) looked like, but the identity of the suspect is probably not known to any of those involved. The Police and Criminal Evidence Act (PACE Act) 1984 Codes of Practice outline a process to safeguard the rights of a possible suspect. The Codes specify that a record must be made of the **first description** of the suspect that is given by a witness, and describe the procedures for taking a witness to a particular neighbourhood or place to identify the suspect. If the witness can point out the suspect to you, the circumstances under which the identification was made must be recorded in line with the precedent set in the case of *R v Turnbull* [1976] 63 Cr App R 132. The following subsections provide more detail of the procedures involved.

4.3.1 Circumstances for identifying a suspect

The only circumstance under which you can carry out such an identification is when the identity of the suspect is **not known**; that is, you do not have reasonable grounds to suspect a particular person or group of people of committing that offence (Code D 3.2)).

Do not take a witness to identify a suspect who has already been arrested. In such circumstances, the suspect's identity is regarded as being **known** (Code D 3.4). Other identification procedures are used once a suspect has been arrested—for example, identification parades, video identification, or group identification.

4.3.2 The first description

Where it is practicable, a record should be made of the witness's description before asking him/her to make any kind of identification (Code D 3.2a). This first description must be clearly recorded in a visible and legible form which can be given to the suspect or the suspect's solicitor. Ideally, it should be recorded in your PNB, and a copy made for the suspect or the solicitor.

4.3.3 Support for the witness during the identification

Care must be taken not to direct the witness's attention to any individual, unless, taking into account all the circumstances, it cannot be avoided (Code D 3.2b). However, this does not prevent a witness being asked to look carefully at the people around, or towards a group, or in a particular direction. This might be necessary to ensure that the witness does not overlook a possible suspect, or to enable the witness to make comparisons between any suspect and others who are in the area.

The identification may be compromised if you specifically draw the witness's attention to the suspect (see Code D, Note 3F), or the suspect's identity becomes known before the procedure. Therefore do not point at the suspect or ask the witness to verify your choice.

4.3.4 More than one witness

Witnesses should be taken **separately** to see whether they can identify the particular person independently. This may mean that you will have to call for other patrols to help you with the identification process (Code D 3.2c).

4.3.5 Recording an identification

The student police officer or police support employee accompanying the witness must record as soon as possible in his/her PNB full details of the action taken (Code D 3.2e).

The record should include:

1. the **date, time, and place** of the occasion when the witness claims to have previously seen the suspect
2. **where** any identification was made
3. **how** it was made
4. the **conditions** at the time (for example, the distance the witness was from the suspect, the weather, and lighting conditions)
5. whether the witness's attention was drawn to the suspect
6. the reason for his/her attention being so drawn
7. **anything said** by the witness or the suspect about the identification or the conduct of the procedure.

4.3.6 Evidence to be gathered from the witness

The witness has had two opportunities to see the suspect. First, at or around the time the offence was committed, and second, when taken to the location of the incident. Always note that the visual evidence from the first sighting may be disputed in court. You should try to minimize that possibility by applying the guidelines set by case law in *R v Turnbull* [1976] 63 Cr App R 132. A helpful way to remember the component parts of *Turnbull* (as it is commonly referred to in police circles) is to use the mnemonic ADVOKATE, an approach common within police training (though we think that the mnemonic is rather weak and inaccurate in places—see below):

A Amount of time the suspect was under observation

D Distance between the witness and the suspect

V Visibility (for example what was the lighting like, what were the weather conditions?)

O Obstructions to his/her view of the suspect

K Known or seen before (does s/he know the suspect and, if so, how?)

A Any reason for remembering the suspect (this would apply if the witness has seen the suspect before and such reasons could include a distinguishing feature or peculiarity of the person, or the nature of the incident itself, which made the person memorable; this can relate to previous or present sightings)

T Time lapse between the first and any subsequent identification to the police (this is not the time between first seeing the suspect and the writing of the statement)

E Errors: differences between the first recorded description of the suspect and his/her actual appearance.

4.4 **Stop, Search, and Entry**

4.4.1 **Stop and search under s 1 of PACE 1984**

Sections 1 and 2 of the PACE Act 1984 give you the power to stop, search, and detain individuals and vehicles. The PACE Act 1984 Codes of Practice safeguard the rights of an individual while you carry out such a search.

4.4.1.1 *Grounds for 'stop, search, and detain'*

Section 1(3) of the PACE Act 1984 states that you do not have the power to search unless you have **reasonable grounds** for suspecting that you will find stolen or prohibited articles. Reasonable grounds for suspicion depend on the circumstances in each case (see Code A, para 2.2), but the following factors can all be considered:

• a suspect's behaviour, for example trying to hide something
• accurate and current intelligence or information, and/or
• reliable information that members of a particular group habitually carry prohibited articles.

Reasonable grounds do *not* include personal factors, such as ethnicity, age, appearance, or previous convictions (either alone, or in combination with each other, or with any other factor). You must never generalize or stereotype groups of people as being more likely to take part in criminal activity, nor should a person's religion contribute to forming grounds for reasonable suspicion.

If you discover an article which you have reasonable grounds to suspect to be stolen or prohibited, you can seize it (s 1(6), PACE Act 1984).

4.4.1.2 *Appropriate locations for 'stop, search, and detain'*

Section 1(1) of the PACE Act 1984 states that you may search:

(a) in any place to which [. . .] the public or any section of the public has access, on payment or otherwise, as of right, or by virtue of express or implied permission;

(b) in any other place to which people have ready access at the time when [you propose] to exercise the power, but which is not a dwelling.

The public have a **right** to use roads and footpaths and other public areas during opening hours. They have **express permission** to enter cinemas, theatres, or football grounds having paid an entrance fee and they can remain there until that particular entertainment is over, when permission to be there ends. There is an **implied permission** for persons to enter buildings to carry out business transactions with the owners, and even to use a footpath to a dwelling-house for the purposes of paying a lawful call upon the householder. That implied permission remains until withdrawn by the householder or the owner of the business premises. Places to which the public has **ready access** include places such as a private field if that field is regularly used by trespassers, or a garden if it is accessible by jumping over a low wall.

This power can never be used to search inside a place of residence (a dwelling). If the search is to be carried out on land attached to a dwelling (including a garden or yard), you cannot search any person who lives in the dwelling, nor any other person who has the resident's permission to be on the attached land. The same principles apply to searching vehicles; you cannot search a vehicle located on land attached to a dwelling if the person who lives in the dwelling has permitted the vehicle to be on that land.

You must carry out the search at or 'nearby' the place where the person or vehicle was first detained. Code A, para 3.4, note 6 defines 'nearby' as 'within a reasonable travelling distance', but gives no indication of actual distance. Without any further guidance from case law, the term should be interpreted relatively cautiously.

4.4.1.3 *Who or what can be 'stopped, searched, and detained'?*

Having made sure that you first of all satisfy the above requirements concerning the location, under s 1(2)(a) of the PACE Act 1984 you can search:

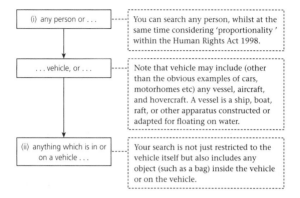

4.4.1.4 *Items you may search for under 'stop, search, and detain'*

Section 1 of the PACE Act 1984 can *only* be used for searching for stolen or prohibited articles. Stolen articles include any article which you have reasonable grounds for suspecting to be stolen. The table below provides further details about prohibited articles.

4.4.1.5 *Requirements regarding the search of persons and vehicles*

You must take reasonable steps to provide information to the person to be searched (or to the person in charge of the vehicle to be searched), and this can be best remembered by the use of the mnemonic **GO WISELY**:

G	Grounds of the suspicion justifying the search
O	Object/purpose of search
W	Warrant card (if you are not in uniform or if requested by the person)
I	Identity of the officer performing the search
S	Station to which the officer is attached
E	Entitlement to a copy of the search record
L	Legal power used
Y	You are detained for the purposes of a search.

Table 4.1: Articles for which you may *not* 'stop, search, and detain' under the PACE Act 1984

Prohibited article	Description
Offensive weapons	Includes any article made, intended, or adapted for causing injury to a person (see 4.6.5 below), for use either by the person having it with him/her or by someone else. A firearm, as defined by s 57 of the Firearms Act 1968 (for example an air weapon: see 4.6.6 below). See: • s 1(9), PACE Act 1984 • Note 22 Code A, Codes of Practice, PACE Act 1984.
Bladed or sharply pointed articles	Includes any article which is bladed or sharply pointed, but excludes a small folding pocket-knife (see 4.6.5 below).
Any articles used in the course of or in connection with certain criminal offences	Includes any article made, intended, or adapted for use (by either the person having it with him/her or by someone else) in the course of or in connection to any: • burglary (see 5.2.4 below) eg screwdriver, gloves • theft (see 5.2.2 below) eg pliers, large bag • taking a conveyance (see 5.2.5 below) eg master keys • fraud (see 5.2.8 below) eg false identity documents • criminal damage (see 5.2.7 below) eg spray cans.
Fireworks	Only includes fireworks possessed in contravention of a prohibition imposed by any of the firework regulations (see 4.6.8 below).

After searching an **unattended vehicle** or anything in or on it, you must leave a record of the search inside the vehicle. However, if the vehicle has not been opened (see Code A, para 4.8), or it is not reasonable or practical to leave the record inside without causing damage (see s 2(7), PACE Act), the record should be attached to the outside of the vehicle.

4.4.1.6 *Conducting the search*

When searching persons:

- You must seek the **cooperation** of the person to be searched. Reasonable force may be used as a last resort (under s 117 PACE Act 1984), but only after your attempts to search have been met with resistance (see Code A, para 3.2)
- You must keep the search **relevant**: the extent of the search must relate to the object you are searching for, and if the

4.4.3.1 *Searching premises under s 18(1) of the PACE Act 1984*

Section 18(1) of the PACE Act 1984 states that:

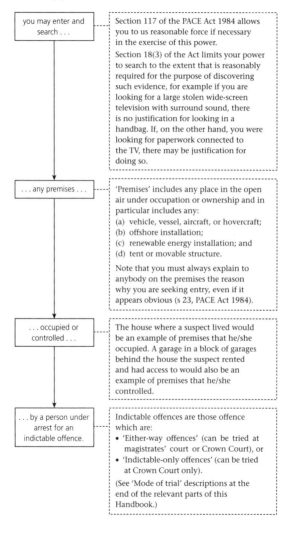

you may enter and search . . .

Section 117 of the PACE Act 1984 allows you to us reasonable force if necessary in the exercise of this power.

Section 18(3) of the Act limits your power to search to the extent that is reasonably required for the purpose of discovering such evidence, for example if you are looking for a large stolen wide-screen television with surround sound, there is no justification for looking in a handbag. If, on the other hand, you were looking for paperwork connected to the TV, there may be justification for doing so.

. . . any premises . . .

'Premises' includes any place in the open air under occupation or ownership and in particular includes any:
(a) vehicle, vessel, aircraft, or hovercraft;
(b) offshore installation;
(c) renewable energy installation; and
(d) tent or movable structure.

Note that you must always explain to anybody on the premises the reason why you are seeking entry, even if it appears obvious (s 23, PACE Act 1984).

. . . occupied or controlled . . .

The house where a suspect lived would be an example of premises that he/she occupied. A garage in a block of garages behind the house the suspect rented and had access to would also be an example of premises that he/she controlled.

. . . by a person under arrest for an indictable offence.

Indictable offences are those offence which are:
• 'Either-way offences' (can be tried at magistrates' court or Crown Court), or
• 'Indictable-only offences' (can be tried at Crown Court only).

(See 'Mode of trial' descriptions at the end of the relevant parts of this Handbook.)

4.4.3.2 *Evidence requirements*

Section 18(1) of the PACE Act 1984 states that you must have reasonable grounds to suspect that there is evidence on the premises that relates to that offence or to some other indictable offence connected with or similar to that offence. For example, if you arrest a suspect who was in the process of stealing an iPod from a store, you might want to search his/her car for other stolen property. S/he could well have received other items and be in the process of selling them on: this would constitute the offence of 'handling stolen goods', a similar offence to theft.

You may:

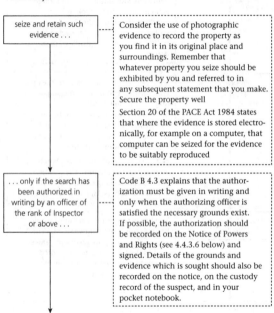

seize and retain such evidence . . .	Consider the use of photographic evidence to record the property as you find it in its original place and surroundings. Remember that whatever property you seize should be exhibited by you and referred to in any subsequent statement that you make. Secure the property well
	Section 20 of the PACE Act 1984 states that where the evidence is stored electronically, for example on a computer, that computer can be seized for the evidence to be suitably reproduced
. . . only if the search has been authorized in writing by an officer of the rank of Inspector or above . . .	Code B 4.3 explains that the authorization must be given in writing and only when the authorizing officer is satisfied the necessary grounds exist. If possible, the authorization should be recorded on the Notice of Powers and Rights (see 4.4.3.6 below) and signed. Details of the grounds and evidence which is sought should also be recorded on the notice, on the custody record of the suspect, and in your pocket notebook.

. . . or you can carry out the search before the arrested person is taken to the police station without obtaining the authorization (s 18(5)).

For example, you arrest a suspect for theft of CDs at a store and he/she tells you that he/she has some other stolen CDs at home amongst his/her lawfully obtained collection. You may therefore have justification to search his/her home before attending the police station in order that he/she can identify the stolen CDs amongst the others. If you do make such a search without authorization, then you must inform an Inspector or above that you have made a search as soon as practicable afterwards.

4.4.3.3 *The timing of searches*

Searches should be made at a reasonable hour. However, they may be carried out at any time if the results of the search might otherwise be prejudiced (Code B, para 6.2).

4.4.3.4 *Using force to enter*

Reasonable and proportionate force may be used if necessary (Code B, para 6.6):

- if the occupier has refused entry, or
- if it is impossible to communicate with the occupier.

4.4.3.5 *Communication with people on the premises during a search*

If you are in charge of the search, you should communicate with people on the premises (Code B, para 6.4), unless there are reasonable grounds for believing that alerting the occupier would frustrate the object of the search or put you in danger.

4.4.3.6 *Documentation to be left on the premises after a search*

A copy of the Notice of Powers and Rights should be given to the occupier or left on the premises if they are empty (Code B, para 6.7).

4.4.4 Entering premises to arrest and save life

The PACE Act 1984 provides you with a power to enter premises in which you believe a person you are seeking to arrest is located, or to save life.

4 Special Constables' Powers

4.4.4.1 *Entering premises to arrest*

There are a number of situations in which you have the power to enter premises in order to arrest a person, such as having a relevant warrant, or in order to arrest for certain offences.

As to the scope of such an entry and search, s 17 of the PACE Act 1984 states that:

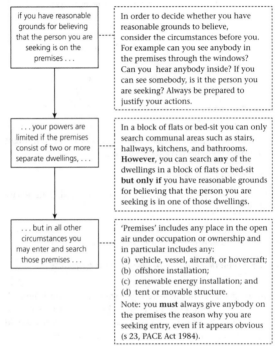

if you have reasonable grounds for believing that the person you are seeking is on the premises . . .	In order to decide whether you have reasonable grounds to believe, consider the circumstances before you. For example can you see anybody in the premises through the windows? Can you hear anybody inside? If you can see somebody, is it the person you are seeking? Always be prepared to justify your actions.
. . . your powers are limited if the premises consist of two or more separate dwellings, . . .	In a block of flats or bed-sit you can only search communal areas such as stairs, hallways, kitchens, and bathrooms. **However**, you can search **any** of the dwellings in a block of flats or bed-sit **but only if** you have reasonable grounds for believing that the person you are seeking is in one of those dwellings.
. . . but in all other circumstances you may enter and search those premises . . .	'Premises' includes any place in the open air under occupation or ownership and in particular includes any: (a) vehicle, vessel, aircraft, or hovercraft; (b) offshore installation; (c) renewable energy installation; and (d) tent or movable structure. Note: you **must** always give anybody on the premises the reason why you are seeking entry, even if it appears obvious (s 23, PACE Act 1984).

4.4.4.2 *Entering premises to arrest on warrant*

You may enter to arrest a person and search those premises under the execution of the following warrants:

- An **arrest warrant** issued in connection with or arising out of criminal proceedings: Home Office Circular 88/1985, para 8, states that this section 'is deliberately widely drawn and the words 'in connection with' enable a constable to enter and search premises for the purpose among other things of executing a warrant for the arrest of a person for non-payment of a fine'

- A **warrant of commitment** (that is: for commitment to prison): this goes further than a default warrant (which orders an offender to appear before a court to explain the reasons for non-payment of a fine). A warrant of commitment requires the offender to be taken straight to prison unless the money stated in it is paid, and is issued under s 76 of the Magistrates' Courts Act 1980 (for failure to pay fines).

4.4.4.3 *Entering premises to arrest for specified offences*

You may also search and enter premises in order to arrest a person for any indictable offence (this includes either-way and indictable-only offences, see 9.1 and 9.2), and also for certain non-indictable offences shown below:

Table 4.2: Circumstances in which you may search and enter premises to arrest a person under the PACE Act 1984

Non-indictable offence for which you can use the power of entry to arrest	Explanation
s 163 of the Road Traffic Act 1988	This legislation requires a person driving a mechanically propelled vehicle or riding a cycle on a road to stop if you require him/her to do so. Failing to stop is an offence. Note that you can only use this power when you are in uniform.
s 4 of the Road Traffic Act 1988	This is an offence of driving or being in charge of a mechanically propelled vehicle on a road or other public place when unfit through drink or drugs (see 4.7.3 below).
s 27 of the Transport and Works Act 1992	This offence may be committed by certain staff operating the railways and other guided transport systems when they are under the influence of drink or drugs.
ss 6, 7, 8, or 10 of the Criminal Law Act 1977	These offences include using violence to secure entry (s 6), trespassing with a weapon of offence (s 8), and entering and remaining on premises (s 7), also known as 'squatting'. Note that you can only use this power when you are in uniform.
s 4 of the Public Order Act 1986	The result of the suspect's conduct in this offence is to bring about a feeling of fear or provoke a reaction of violence in the victim or recipient (note that this power of entry does not extend to s 4A of the same Act).

(Continued)

Table 4.2: (*Continued*)

Non-indictable offence for which you can use the power of entry to arrest	Explanation
s 61 of the Animal Health Act 1981	This offence relates to the control of rabies and sets out a power for you to arrest any person you have reasonable cause to suspect to be committing (or to have committed) an offence in relation to bringing animals into the UK.
ss 4, 5, 6(1) and (2), 7, and 8(1) and (2) of the Animal Welfare Act 2006	These are offences relating to the prevention of harm to animals.

4.4.4.4 *Entering premises to arrest for other specified circumstances*

You also have a power of entry to arrest anyone whom you are immediately **pursuing**. This could include a person who had escaped from you having just been arrested, as well as a patient who has escaped from involuntary custody at a psychiatric unit. Note, however, that the chase must be under circumstances of 'hot pursuit', for example the person must have only just escaped from lawful custody or a hospital; it cannot be used after a period of days or weeks.

You also have the power of entry to arrest anyone who is liable to be **detained** in a prison, remand centre, young offenders' institution, or secure training centre. Section 32(1A) of the Children and Young Persons Act 1969 gives you a power to arrest a **child** who is absent from care, but only if the child is in care after having been remanded or committed to local authority accommodation (s 23(1) of the same act).

4.4.4.5 *Searching premises for a suspect*

The power of entry to arrest under s 17 of the PACE Act 1984 permits you to search premises in order to find the person to be arrested, but does not allow you to search for anything else unless you have other justifications for searching (s 17(4) PACE Act 1984).

4.4.4.6 *Entering premises to save life and property*

Subsection 17(1)(e) of the PACE Act 1984 gives you the power to enter premises 'to save human life and limb' and also to prevent serious damage to property. Under subsection (e) you can enter and search:

- even if you do not have reasonable grounds for believing any person is on the premises, and
- all the flats within a block of flats and not just one of them.

(Note that s 17(1)(e) does not give you power of entry in order to arrest a person.)

In the case of *Mandy Baker v Crown Prosecution Service* (2009) EWHC 299 (Admin), it was further decided that you can enter and search under part (e):

- without seeking the permission of the occupant (otherwise this might be self-defeating)
- to save someone from him/herself as well as from a third party
- without having to give an occupant a reason for using the power of entry if it is impossible, impracticable, or undesirable to do so, but
- only to the extent that was reasonably required to satisfy the objective for using the power of entry. For example, if the reason was the danger to life or limb posed by a knife, then the powers available would relate only to a search for that knife (s 17(4) PACE Act 1984).

4.4.4.7 *Power of entry and breach of the peace*

Nothing in s 17(6) of the PACE Act 1984 affects any power of entry to deal with or prevent a breach of the peace. You are entitled to enter either private or public premises in order to make an arrest for a breach of the peace or to prevent a breach of the peace. However, you should *always* make sure that the circumstance you are faced with really constitutes a breach of the peace (see 4.6.9 below).

4.4.4.8 *Searching suspects and premises upon arrest*

The powers of search under Section 32 of the PACE Act 1984 can only be used at the time of an arrest when you have reasonable grounds for believing that the suspect might have concealed anything for which a search is permitted (see 4.4.1). Similarly, you may not search premises unless you have reasonable grounds for believing that there is evidence for which a search is permitted (see 4.4.3) and the suspect has been arrested for an indictable offence.

Section 32(1) of the PACE Act 1984 states that you can search any person who has been arrested elsewhere than at a police station if you have reasonable grounds for believing that the arrested person may present a danger to him/herself or others. This is *not* a power to search everybody after arrest: you must have reasonable grounds for believing that the person to be searched might have concealed on his/her person anything that could be used to effect an escape or which might provide evidence of an offence:

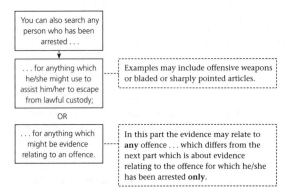

When using these powers to search a person, you only have a power to search to the extent required to find the item you are seeking. You cannot require the person being searched to remove any clothing in public other than an outer coat, jacket, or gloves, but you may search a person's mouth.

Under s 32(2)(b) of the PACE Act 1984 you may search premises, but only if the offence for which the person has been arrested is an **indictable offence**. Further details about your powers in this instance are in the *Police Operational Handbook* (POH) edited by Ian Bridges (2006), pages 659–61.

4.4.4.9 *Seizing items*

You can **seize** (take into police possession) anything you find on the person or premises as a result of searching (under s 32), apart from items protected by legal privilege—for example letters from the suspect's legal representative (ss 19, 32(8), and 32(9) of the PACE Act 1984).

4.5 **Investigation, Arrest, Detention, and Disposal**

4.5.1 **Cautions**

From the moment you start dealing with anybody you suspect of having committed an offence, you must remember that s/he has the right to **a formal warning** or **caution** at certain points during the investigative process (Code C, paragraph 10 of the PACE Act 1984 Codes of Practice).

The type of caution given depends on the stage of the investigation. The caution may be given:

- at the very beginning of an investigation, when s/he is first arrested and interviewed, or interviewed without having been arrested. In this case use the **when questioned** caution (see below), or
- at the end of the investigation, before s/he goes to court (whether arrested or not), as a result of charge or reporting the suspect. This is the **'now'** caution, and is his/her last chance to have what s/he says recorded before going to court.

4.5.1.1 *The three parts to a caution*

There are three parts to a caution (Code C, para 10.5):

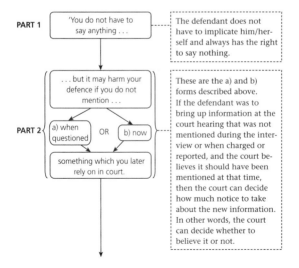

PART 1 — 'You do not have to say anything . . .

The defendant does not have to implicate him/herself and always has the right to say nothing.

PART 2 — . . . but it may harm your defence if you do not mention . . . a) when questioned OR b) now . . . something which you later rely on in court.

These are the a) and b) forms described above. If the defendant was to bring up information at the court hearing that was not mentioned during the interview or when charged or reported, and the court believes it should have been mentioned at that time, then the court can decide how much notice to take about the new information. In other words, the court can decide whether to believe it or not.

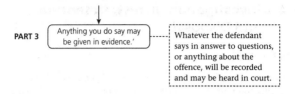

PART 3

Anything you do say may be given in evidence.'

Whatever the defendant says in answer to questions, or anything about the offence, will be recorded and may be heard in court.

4.5.1.2 *When to caution a suspect*

If you have arrested your suspect, you must caution him/her at the time of the arrest unless:

- it is impossible for you to do so because of his/her condition or behaviour: for example, where he/she is unconscious, drunk, or fighting (Code C, para 10.4 and Code G, para 3.4), or
- the suspect has already been cautioned before s/he was arrested, because s/he was suspected of committing an offence (Code C, para 10.4 and Code G, para 3.4).

The correct time to give a caution was explained succinctly in *R v Nelson and Rose* [1998] 2 Crim App R 399:

> The appropriate time to administer the caution [. . .] is when, on an objective test, there are grounds for suspicion, falling short of evidence which would support a *prima facie* case of guilt, not simply that an offence has been committed, but committed by the person who is being questioned.

4.5.1.3 *Is a caution required?*

If you have not arrested your suspect, and your questions are for other purposes (Code C, para 10.1), *you do not need to use a caution*. Examples of such situations are:

- when you ask for a driver's name and date of birth under the Road Traffic Act 1988 (see Code C, para 10.9)
- when you ask for a person's identity or the identity of the owner of a vehicle
- when you ask a suspect to read and sign records of interviews and other comments (see Code C, para 11 and note 11E)
- whilst you carry out a search using an appropriate power and at the same time following the PACE Codes of Practice.

4.5.1.4 *Other times when a caution is needed*

You need to use a caution when informing someone that s/he may be prosecuted for an offence: for example, when:

- you **charge** (a charge is a written accusation) a detained person with an offence or inform a person that s/he may be **prosecuted** (reported for an offence). At this stage, use the word *'now'* in part 2 of the caution in 4.5.1.1 above (see Code C 16.2)
- you inform a person not under arrest that s/he may be prosecuted for an offence. At this stage, use the word *'now'* (as above). This is not a requirement within the Codes of Practice, *but* if the 'now' caution is not given at this point, the court cannot draw its own conclusions if the defendant subsequently provides new information at the hearing. The court might be more likely to believe the new information (see Code C, Note 10 G). The advice is therefore to use the 'now' caution after informing a person that s/he may be prosecuted.

4.5.1.5 *Recording a caution*

Always write down in your PNB (or on a record of the interview) when you give a caution. You must also record whether it was the *'when questioned'* or the *'now'* version (see Code C, para 10.13). There is no need to write out the caution in full in your PNB. Something like 'the subject was cautioned, using the "when questioned" formula, at 1855', would do.

4.5.1.6 *Understanding the caution*

The caution is a necessary warning that must be given to a person to protect his/her rights and keep him/her informed of the consequences of what s/he says during an investigation. This can only be done if you yourself have a thorough understanding of the *'when questioned'*, *'now'*, and *'restricted'* variants of the caution, so that you can convey the shades of meaning to the suspect. The suspect can be made more aware of the importance of a caution if you are yourself aware of its significance.

4.5.2 **Making an arrest**

On making an arrest you are consequently responsible to protect the suspect's rights. This entails knowing:

- what information should be given to the suspect on arrest
- how much force you can use when making an arrest
- under what circumstances you can release the suspect before arriving at the police station
- what you can and cannot ask the suspect before arrival at the police station

- how long that journey should take
- under what circumstances you can search the arrested person
- when you should inform him/her that s/he is under arrest for a further offence.

4.5.2.1 *Information to be given on arrest*

Section 28 of the PACE Act 1984 states that:

. . . an arrest is not lawful unless at the time or as soon as practicable [you] inform the person they are under arrest (s 28(1)) . . .	Although it is recommended, it is not necessary to say words such as 'I arrest you' for an arrest to be lawful. Code C 10.3 states the suspect must be informed at the time or as soon as practicable that he/she is under arrest and Code C Note 10B states the suspect must be given sufficient information to enable him/her to understand that he/she has been deprived of his/her liberty.
. . . when [you] arrest a person, [you] must still inform him/her that he/she is under arrest even though that fact is obvious . . .	Do not think that making the most obvious actions alone will be enough, for example placing your hand on the shoulder of the suspect and preventing him/her from going anywhere after you have just seen him/her seriously injure a person. It will not be sufficient! You must still apply s 28(1) above.
. . . an arrest is not lawful unless at the time or as soon as practicable [you] inform the person of the grounds for the arrest.	There is no need for technical or precise language providing the suspect knows why he/she has been arrested. There is no need to refer to the power of arrest but the reason must be the correct reason, otherwise it is unlawful. Also, the information given must be sufficient for the suspect to respond.
	The suspect must be informed at the time or as soon as practicable of the grounds for the arrest, Code C 10.3. The suspect must be given sufficient information to enable him/her to understand the reason for the arrest (Code C Note 10B).
	However, you are not required to inform the suspect of the grounds for the arrest if it was not reasonably practicable to do so (s 28(5)), for example because he/she escaped from you before you could give the information.

According to Code G, paragraph 2 of the PACE Act 1984 Codes of Practice, you are required to inform the arrested person about the circumstances surrounding his/her involvement, suspected involvement, or attempted involvement in the commission of a criminal offence, and the reason(s) why the arrest is necessary (see 4.5.3.4 below).

4.5.2.2 *The use of force to arrest a person*

You may need to use force to arrest a person, but the amount of force you use must be **reasonable**. Two pieces of legislation will help you here: s 3 of the Criminal Law Act 1967 and s 117 of the PACE Act 1984.

Section 3(1) of the Criminal Law Act 1967 states that:

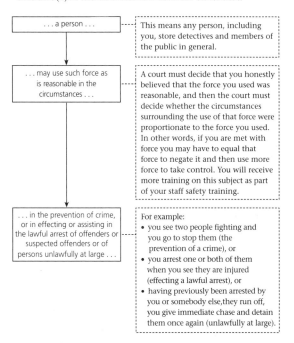

. . . a person . . .	This means any person, including you, store detectives and members of the public in general.
. . . may use such force as is reasonable in the circumstances . . .	A court must decide that you honestly believed that the force you used was reasonable, and then the court must decide whether the circumstances surrounding the use of that force were proportionate to the force you used. In other words, if you are met with force you may have to equal that force to negate it and then use more force to take control. You will receive more training on this subject as part of your staff safety training.
. . . in the prevention of crime, or in effecting or assisting in the lawful arrest of offenders or suspected offenders or of persons unlawfully at large . . .	For example: • you see two people fighting and you go to stop them (the prevention of a crime), or • you arrest one or both of them when you see they are injured (effecting a lawful arrest), or • having previously been arrested by you or somebody else, they run off, you give immediate chase and detain them once again (unlawfully at large).

Section 117 of the PACE Act 1984 states that where any part of the PACE Act 1984:

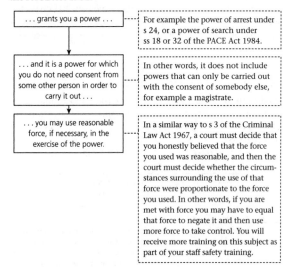

. . . grants you a power . . .	For example the power of arrest under s 24, or a power of search under ss 18 or 32 of the PACE Act 1984.
. . . and it is a power for which you do not need consent from some other person in order to carry it out . . .	In other words, it does not include powers that can only be carried out with the consent of somebody else, for example a magistrate.
. . . you may use reasonable force, if necessary, in the exercise of the power.	In a similar way to s 3 of the Criminal Law Act 1967, a court must decide that you honestly believed that the force you used was reasonable, and then the court must decide whether the circumstances surrounding the use of that force were proportionate to the force you used. In other words, if you are met with force you may have to equal that force to negate it and then use more force to take control. You will receive more training on this subject as part of your staff safety training.

4.5.2.3 *What to do immediately after an arrest*

Do not forget to caution the suspect (see 4.5.1 above and the PACE Act 1984, Code G, para 3.4). Then, unless it is impracticable to do so, record in your PNB:

- the nature and circumstances of the offence leading to the arrest
- the reason or reasons why the arrest was necessary
- the fact that you gave a caution, and
- anything said by the person at the time of arrest.

4.5.3 Statutory power of arrest

In the course of your duties whilst on Supervised or Independent Patrol, you may need to arrest without a warrant someone who you suspect of committing a criminal offence. Apart from the power to arrest for a breach of the peace (see 4.6.9 below), and specific powers of arrest from other legislation, you also have a statutory power of arrest without a warrant that stems from s 24 of the PACE Act 1984. Using this power, you may arrest a person whether you are in uniform or not, but only if certain criteria are met.

4.5.3.1 *The two conditions for an arrest to be lawful*

The two conditions for an arrest to be lawful are:

1. that a person is about to commit an offence, or is in the act of committing an offence, or that there are reasonable grounds to suspect that a person is involved, or has attempted to be involved in the commission of an offence, and
2. that there are reasonable grounds for believing that the person's arrest is necessary.

You must not arrest a person solely because of his/her involvement, or suspicion of involvement, in a criminal offence. You must make an arrest **only if it is necessary**. The reasons for which an arrest may be necessary are specified in s 24(5) of the PACE Act 1984 and its Code G, paragraph 2.9.

Before we look further at the power of arrest, it is important that you understand the term 'reasonable grounds to suspect', as it is a central component part of the power.

4.5.3.2 *Reasonable grounds to suspect*

Although words such as 'suspicion', 'grounds', and 'belief' are in common use, they have particular meanings within the law. Whether or not something is **reasonable** is a conclusion that one or more people reach in agreement as a result of personal experience or understanding. **Grounds** for something include a reason or argument for a thought to exist. To **suspect** something is to think that it is probably true, although you are not certain. To **believe** something is a stronger and more concrete conclusion.

Therefore, in order to decide whether you have 'reasonable grounds to suspect', consider the offence, the component parts of that offence, and whether or not a like-minded person would draw the same conclusion as you about the suspect and the offence. For example, did the person have the means, the opportunity, the motive, the presence of mind, and the incentive to commit the offence?

Note however, that **an arrest can never be justified simply on the basis of obeying the orders of one of your supervisors or managers** (*O' Hara (AP) v CC of the RUC* (1997) 1 CrAppR 447). Equally, it is insufficient for you to infer that your supervisors or managers had reasonable grounds for suspicion (see *Commissioner of Police of the Metropolis v Mohamed Raissi* (2008) EWCA Civ 1237). To justify an arrest, you must have been given sufficient information by a supervisor or manager to generate your own reasonable grounds to suspect that it was necessary to arrest that person: (see *(1) Sonia Raissi (2) Mohamed Raissi v Commissioner of Police of the Metropolis* (2007) EWHC 2842 (QB)).

4.5.3.3 *Involvement in the commission of a criminal offence*

The first condition for an arrest to be lawful is that you know, or have reasonable grounds to suspect, that a criminal offence is in the process of being committed (or is about to be committed). This is shown in the table below:

Table 4.3: Circumstances in which you can know, or have reasonable grounds to suspect, that a criminal offence is in the process of being committed (or is about to be committed) under the PACE Act 1984

Level of involvement	Example
A person is **about to commit** an offence	You are on duty, not in uniform, in an electrical store when you see a woman, not a member of the shop staff, walk up to a display of iPods, select one, and put it under her coat. You see her walk towards the entry/exit of the shop, making no attempt to pay for the item. You stop her as she is about to leave the shop, as she is about to commit an offence. If it is **necessary**, you may arrest her (see 4.5.3.4 below).
A person is **in the act of committing** an offence	You are on duty, not in uniform, in an electrical store when you see a man walk up to a display of DAB radios, cut a security link, pick up a radio, and walk towards the door of the shop past the pay-points, without paying for the radio. The store alarm is activated and the man continues to walk out of the shop. You decide the man is stealing the radio and stop him just outside the shop as he is in the act of committing the theft of the radio. If it is **necessary**, you may arrest him (see 4.5.3.4 below).
You have **reasonable grounds** for **suspecting** a person to be **about to commit** an offence	You are on duty, not in uniform, in an electrical store when you see a man walk up to a display of mobile phones. You see him take a metal cutter out of his pocket. He then reaches out towards the security chain of the mobile and appears to be about to cut the chain when he is disturbed. He puts the tool back in his pocket and walks away. A few seconds later he returns to the display of mobiles, takes out the same tool, places the cutter on the security chain, and sets off the alarm. You walk up to the man having decided you have reasonable grounds for suspecting he is about to commit an offence. If it is **necessary**, you may arrest him (see 4.5.3.4 below).

Level of involvement	Example
You have **reasonable grounds** for **suspecting** a person **to be** committing an offence	You are standing outside a store that sells electrical goods when you see a person just inside the store near the doorway, carrying an unpacked, new DVD player underneath his arm with the lead and plug dragging behind. He also has a rucksack on his back. You see him use a tool to cut away the security tag from the DVD player and put the player in his rucksack. The person then walks towards the door as if to leave the store.
	You possess 'reasonable grounds for suspecting' that he has been found to be in the process of committing an offence of theft of a DVD player. If it is **necessary**, you may arrest him or her (see 4.5.3.4 below).

You may also arrest someone on suspicion of committing an offence on an earlier occasion, but you must be certain that it is **necessary** to arrest the suspect, and have clear **reasons** in mind (see 4.5.3.4 below).

In these circumstances, you may arrest:

- **anyone who is guilty of the offence, and/or**
- **anyone who you have reasonable grounds for suspecting to be guilty.**

4.5.3.4 *Reasons that make an arrest necessary*

A Special Constable would decide on the basis of each particular situation:

- what action to take when first in contact with the suspect—for example, when to caution, search, or use personal safety equipment, and
- whether to arrest, report for summons, grant street bail, issue a fixed penalty notice, or take any other action.

In 4.5.3.1 above, we explained that there are two conditions which need to be satisfied before an arrest should be made. The first concerns the existence of an offence, and we discussed this in 4.5.3.3 above. The second condition is that one or more of a number of **reasons** make the arrest **necessary**. The possible reasons are set out in the PACE Act 1984, Code G, para 2.9 (Code G is available at <http:// police.homeoffice.gov.uk/publications/ operational-policing/ PACE_Chapter_Ge42d.html?version=1 >).

An arrest is deemed to be necessary if one or more of the following reasons apply.

4.5.3.4.1 To obtain someone's name or address

You must always explain, if the person refuses to provide his/her name or address, that it may lead to his/her arrest. Remember, this is not a power to arrest a person who simply refuses to give you his/her name or address. Instead, this is just one of several reasons that make a person's arrest necessary in particular circumstances. You may arrest someone in a situation where:

1. *You do not know and cannot readily ascertain the person's name or address*   Do not just ask him/her for his/her name and address once, or in a manner that lacks confidence. Make it clear to him/her that you need his/her name and address, and explain that you suspect that s/he has committed an offence and that you require his/her name and address in order that the process of investigation can be followed.
2. *You have reasonable grounds for doubting whether a name or address given by the person is real*   You must have a logical reason for not believing that the name or address s/he gave you is correct, for example:
   • S/he cannot give you anything which identifies him/her with the name or address (for example a driving licence with a photograph)
   • You suspect s/he is using the name or address of a close relative with the same details (which are therefore false)
   • There is no record of the name or address s/he provided in the voters' register or telephone directory
   • You suspect his/her name or address is fictitious because it is the name or address of a famous person or character.

Code D of the PACE Act 1984 Codes of Practice provides more detailed information about the definition of a satisfactory address.

4.5.3.4.2 To prevent injury, damage, indecency, or obstruction

A reason for arresting someone could be to prevent the person

• *causing physical injury to another person:* for example, if you were investigating an offence of throwing fireworks in a street or public place under s 80 of the Explosives Act 1875, you might reach the conclusion that the suspect could harm him/herself or somebody else
• *suffering physical injury:* for example, if you were investigating a person for an offence of being a pedestrian on the carriageway of a motorway under s 17(4) of the Road Traffic Regulation Act 1984, you might decide that the suspect could suffer physical injury him/herself from passing vehicles

- *causing loss of or damage to property:* for example, if you were investigating someone for the offence of 'interference with a motor vehicle or trailer' under s 9 of the Criminal Attempts Act 1981, you might conclude that the suspect caused damage to a vehicle during the interference
- *committing an offence against public decency:* for example, if you were investigating a person for an offence of using obscene language under the Town Police Clauses Act 1847, you might decide that the suspect was committing an offence against public decency (however, this legislation can only be used when the acts are committed in the presence of members of the public who cannot avoid the suspect)
- *causing unlawful obstruction of the highway:* for example, if you were investigating a person for an offence of wilful obstruction of the highway under s 137 of the Highways Act 1980 and the suspect was stopping or slowing vehicular traffic on the highway, you might conclude that the person should be removed.

4.5.3.4.3 To protect a child or other vulnerable person

If you were investigating a person for any offence and you suspected that the suspect was putting the health and safety of a vulnerable person or child at risk as a result of his/her conduct, you might arrest the person.

4.5.3.4.4 To allow the prompt and effective investigation of the offence or of the conduct

There may be many reasons why you could feel that an investigation might be jeopardized if you did not arrest the suspect, such as grounds to believe that the person:

- has made false statements (for example, dates of birth, denials of disqualification from driving)
- has made statements which cannot be readily verified (for example, ownership of property for which s/he has no records, such as vehicle registration documents)
- has presented false evidence (for example, forged driving licence)
- might steal or destroy evidence (for example, disposing of stolen property from a burglary)
- might make contact with fellow suspects or conspirators (for example, using a mobile phone to warn an associate)
- might intimidate, threaten, or make contact with witnesses (for example in cases where the identities of the suspect and victim are known to each other).

Other instances might include an arrest in connection with an **indictable** offence where there is an operational need to:

- enter and search any premises occupied or controlled by the person being considered for arrest: if you do not arrest him/her, you will not be able to use s 18 of the PACE Act 1984 (see 4.4.3 1 above)
- search the person: if you do not arrest him/her, you will not be able to use s 32 of the PACE Act 1984 (see section 4.4.4.8 above) to search and seize property
- prevent contact with others: if you do not arrest him/her, you will not be able to seek the authority to delay the right of the detained person to have someone informed of his/her detention
- take fingerprints, footwear impressions, samples, or photographs of the suspect: if you do not arrest him/her, you will not be able to obtain forensic evidence from the suspect
- test him/her for drugs, thereby ensuring compliance with statutory drug-testing requirements: if you do not arrest the person, you will not be able to use s 63B of the PACE Act 1984 to obtain samples from the suspect to ascertain whether s/he has taken a Class A drug.

4.5.3.4.5 To prevent the disappearance of the person in question

This may arise if there are reasonable grounds for believing that if the person is not arrested, s/he will fail to attend court: for example, there is currently a warrant for the arrest of the person for failing to appear at court and s/he has now committed another offence.

4.5.4 Power to retain property from a detained person

There will be occasions when it is necessary to **seize and retain** a suspect's property. This normally occurs when the property is potentially to be used as evidence. The main guidance for this is found in s 22 of the PACE Act 1984, which explains that the property 'may be retained so long as is necessary in all the circumstances' but does not elaborate further on the meanings of '*necessary*' and '*circumstances*'. However, common respect for the property rights of others (as described, for example, in the Human Rights Act 1998) would suggest that property which is no longer relevant to an investigation should be returned to its owner as soon as possible. Your force is likely to have a Property Management Policy that sets out the protocols for return.

The legislation describes two main reasons for seizing and retaining property:

    (a) anything seized for the purposes of a criminal investigation may be retained
        • for use as evidence at a trial for an offence, or
        • for forensic examination or for investigation in connection with an offence . . .
    (b) anything may be retained in order to establish its lawful owner [. . .] where there are reasonable grounds for believing that it has been obtained in consequence of the commission of an offence.

When seizing and retaining property, bear in mind the need to minimize contamination and to maintain a **continuity record**, and also the rules concerning 'Retaining, Recording, and Revealing' (see 5.3.2 below).

4.5.5 The Pocket Notebook

There are a number of fundamental aspects relating to the PNB that are common to virtually all Special Constabularies:

* The PNB notes the start and finish time of each period of duty
* It is used to keep a contemporaneous account (unless impossible) of information collected during an incident: for example, a statement made by a suspect or a description given by a witness
* It should note where you consulted another police officer (for example your assessor whilst on Supervised Patrol) over the writing of an entry
* It may be used to increase the extent and accuracy of recall in court
* There is a need to ensure that the language used is clear, factually based, and is not exclusionary.

4.5.5.1 *How to use the Pocket Notebook*

Your PNB is important. Your force places obligations upon you to record matters within it and, if you use it to give evidence, the courts will have the opportunity to examine it. As a consequence, rules have been established in relation to completion of the PNB: and, if these rules are not followed, then the correctness or even the authenticity of the entries will be questioned.

Top ten hints for using a PNB
1. Carry it at all times on duty
2. Use it to record evidence (*not* your opinion, except in cases of drunkenness)
3. Use it for drawing diagrams as well as for writing
4. Do not use additional pieces of paper, either to supplement your PNB, or as an alternative
5. You may refer to it when giving evidence
6. It is, and remains, police property
7. Don't lose it!
8. It is a supervisor's responsibility to issue you with a new one
9. It often contains other useful information
10. Always apply the general rules (see below)

4.5.5.2 *Summary of PNB rules*

PNB rules can be summarized using the mnemonic 'no ELBOWS(S)', commonly mentioned in Special Constable training:

No
E Erasures
L Leaves torn out/Lines missed
B Blank spaces
O Overwriting
W Writing between lines
S Spare pages
(S) Statements should be recorded in 'direct speech'

4.5.6 Presentation of detained persons to custody officers

The experience of being arrested can be highly charged, and the start of a long process for the suspect. You have a responsibility to protect his/her rights throughout the whole process.

4.5.6.1 *Arrival at the police station with an arrested person*

When an arrested person reaches a police station, s/he should be taken before a **custody officer** as soon as practicable after arrival (Code C, para 2.1A).

The time that the arrested person arrived at the police station is relevant because s/he can only be kept in custody for 24 hours after arrival. The arrival time is referred to as the **relevant time**. Therefore, make a note of this time in your PNB.

4.5.6.2 *The custody officer*

A custody officer is a police officer of at least the rank of sergeant, or a police support employee designated as a staff custody officer (such an arrangement is unusual). His/her main duty is to ensure that all persons in police detention are treated as required by the PACE Act 1984 and the Codes of Practice, and that such treatment is recorded on a custody record.

You are required to inform the custody officer of the relevant circumstances of the arrest in relation to both criteria of s 24 of the PACE Act 1984, including the suspect's **involvement in the commission of a criminal offence** and the **reason(s)** why the arrest was necessary (Code G, para 2.2, see 4.5.3.4 above). You remain with the arrested person during this initial custody process.

4.5.6.3 *The decision to charge a suspect*

The custody officer will decide if there is enough evidence to charge your arrested person at this point (s 37(2), PACE Act 1984). If the custody officer decides there is *not* enough evidence to charge the suspect, s/he can still detain the arrested person if there are reasonable grounds for believing that detention without being charged is necessary to:

- secure or preserve evidence relating to an offence for which s/he is under arrest: for example to carry out searches for evidence, or
- obtain such evidence by questioning the suspect.

The time at which the custody officer authorizes the detention of the arrested person is important, as it is from this time that the **review times** of the detention are calculated. The reviews are carried out by an Inspector not more than:

- six hours from the time of authorized detention, then
- nine hours after the first review, then
- at nine-hour intervals after that.

4.5.6.4 *The detainee's rights after the arrest*

If the custody officer decides to detain your arrested person s/he must inform the detainee of the following rights which continue throughout his/her detention (PACE Act 1984, Code C, para 3.1):

1. the right to have someone informed of his/her arrest
2. the right to consult privately with a solicitor and receive legal advice, and
3. the right to consult the PACE Act 1984 Codes of Practice.

The detainee must be given two written notices (Code C para 3.2). The **first notice** sets out:

- the three rights noted above
- the arrangements for obtaining legal advice
- the right to a copy of the custody record, and
- an explanation of the caution, for example what it means to him/her (see 4.5.1 above).

The **second notice** sets out the detainee's entitlements while in custody: for example, the provision of food and drink.

The detainee will be requested to sign the custody record to confirm his/her decision about legal advice and informing someone of his/her arrest (Code C, para 3.5). The custody officer will also determine whether the detainee requires:

- medical attention, for example as a result of an injury or lack of medication
- an '*appropriate adult*', for example the parent or guardian for a juvenile, or a relative or guardian for a mentally vulnerable person
- help to check documentation, for example clarification of any of the rights or procedures, or
- an interpreter, for example for detainees who do not speak English or those with speech or hearing impairments.

4.5.6.5 *Searching the detainee*

The custody officer has the power to search detainees, though s/he may ask you to carry out the search instead, perhaps so that s/he can observe (if appropriate). The custody officer will decide the extent to which the search will be made (s 54(6), PACE Act 1984) but the search must not be intimate (it must not involve the physical examination of orifices other than the mouth). The search must be carried out by a Special Constable or regular police officer of the same sex as the detainee (s 54(7)).

A **strip search** can be authorized, but only if it is necessary to remove an article which the detainee would not be allowed to keep (Code C, Annex A 10), and if it is reasonably considered that the detainee has concealed such an article. A strip search must be carried out:

- by an officer of the same sex
- in an area away from other people
- in a safe place with at least two other people present, and
- with regard to sensitivity.

4.6.2.2 *Anti-social Behaviour Orders*

Anti-social Behaviour Orders (or ASBOs) may be used for individuals over ten years of age who continually behave in such a way as to cause '**harassment, alarm, or distress**' to members of the local community. Section 1 of the Crime and Disorder Act 1998 enables a magistrates' court to make an ASBO against such an individual. An ASBO is intended to prevent problem behaviour in the future rather than punishing behaviour that has already occurred; if the individual breaches an ASBO, s/he commits a criminal offence. This is intended to act as a deterrent.

An ASBO is made following a complaint about a behaviour that occurred in the preceding six months and:

• lists the types of behaviour that are prohibited for that particular individual
• lasts at least two years
• can be discharged (discontinued) if both parties agree
• may be varied (changed) if new and different complaints are made.

A breach of such an order is an offence under s 1(1) of the Crime and Disorder Act 1998.

This offence is triable either way (depending on seriousness: at a magistrates' court or at a Crown Court);

• summarily: six months' imprisonment and/or a fine
• on indictment: five years' imprisonment and/or a fine.

4.6.2.3 *Local child curfews*

Local 'child curfews' ban children under 16 from being in a specified area of a public place between 2100 and 0600 hours unless they are under the effective control of a parent or a responsible person aged 18 or over. This legislation is covered in s 14 of the Crime and Disorder Act 1998. A local authority or a chief officer of police may introduce a local child curfew scheme for a specified period not exceeding 90 days.

Before making a local child curfew scheme, the applicant will consult with the chief officer of police in the area and with appropriate bodies such as the local authority. A local child curfew scheme will not come into effect until it is confirmed by the Secretary of State. The notice will be given by displaying it in the area or by any other suitable method.

Section 15 of the Crime and Disorder Act 1998 describes the action you should take if you find a child contravening a local child curfew. If you have reasonable cause to believe that a child is in contravention of a ban imposed by a curfew notice, you must inform the local authority (s 15(1)). You may take the child back to his or her home unless you have reasonable cause to believe that the child would be likely to suffer significant harm (s 15(3)).

4.6.2.4 *Dispersal and removal powers for anti-social behaviour*

Section 30 of the Anti-Social Behaviour Act 2003 describes police powers that may be used if a senior police officer of, or above the rank of, superintendent has reasonable grounds for believing:

a) that any members of the public have been intimidated, harassed, alarmed, or distressed as a result of the presence or behaviour of groups of two or more persons in public places within the relevant locality, and

b) that anti-social behaviour is a significant and persistent problem in the relevant locality.

The senior police officer can issue an authorization under s 30(2) that provides you with the power (should the need arise) in the relevant locality to:

• give directions to groups of people (any age), and
• remove a person under 16 years of age to his/her place of residence.

The authorization is for a period not exceeding six months. You must be in uniform to give such directions, and a direction may be given to either a group or an individual.

4.6.2.5 *Dispersal of groups*

The term 'group' is not defined in the legislation but has been held to include protesters (see *R (on the application of Singh and another) v CC of West Midlands Police* [2006] EWCA Civ 1118) and must be two or more persons. Once the authorization has been issued (see above) and if the circumstances recur (as detailed above) you have the power (s 30(4)) to give a direction requiring the people in a group to disperse (either immediately or within a certain time limit). You can also direct any person in the group whose place of residence is not within the relevant locality to leave (either immediately or within a certain time limit) and not to return within a specified period (not exceeding 24 hours).

Section 32 of the Anti-Social Behaviour Act 2003 provides more guidance on how to give a direction for the purposes of s 30(4) above. Under s 32(1) a direction may be:

a) given orally
b) given to any person individually or to two or more persons together, and
c) withdrawn or varied by the person who gave it.

Section 32(2) states that it is an offence to knowingly contravene a direction.

This offence is triable summarily and the penalty is three months' imprisonment and/or a fine.

4.6.2.6 *Removal of young people under 16*

The authorization will have been made in response to a group of people, but it empowers you to remove particular individuals too. This applies to a young person found:

• in any public place within the relevant locality, and
• only between 2100 and 0600 hours.

Therefore, under s 30(6), if you find such a young person and you have reasonable grounds for believing s/he is both:

• under the age of 16, and
• not under the effective control of a parent or a responsible person aged 18 or over,

you may remove that person to his/her place of residence (unless you have reasonable grounds for believing that s/he would be likely to suffer significant harm once there). If s/he is unwilling to go voluntarily, the word 'remove' has been held to mean 'take away using reasonable force if necessary': (*R (W) v Commissioner of Police for the Metropolis and another, Secretary of State for the Home Department, interested party* [2004] EWCA Civ 458.

4.6.3 **Protection from harassment**

Sections 1 to 5 of the Protection from Harassment Act 1997 can be applied in a wide range of situations, including the investigation of disputes between partners in a relationship and disputes between neighbours. More recently, the Government has made additions to the Act to protect people from extremist campaigns, and *it is now an offence to harass two or more people on separate occasions.*

The definition of harassment is in terms of **the effect it has on the victim** rather than the actual events that took place. The victim must be distressed and the perpetrator must know that his/ her actions were likely to cause distress. However, the behaviour must be consistent with the behaviour that a **reasonable person** would see as harassing (s 1(2), Protection from Harassment Act 1997). The final decision of whether or not particular behaviour led to a person being alarmed or distressed is taken by the court.

Only individuals can suffer harassment under the Act. Companies or corporate bodies cannot be harassed, but their employees can, and so references to 'a person' in the context of harassment refer to a person or persons as **individuals** (s 7(5), Protection from Harassment Act 1997).

The harassment must consist of a **course of conduct** (s 7(3) (a)(b), Protection from Harassment Act 1997). Harassment is not just a one-off event; it must occur on more than one occasion. A course of conduct exists when conduct is directed towards:

- an individual on at least two occasions (s 7(3)(a)), or
- two or more people, and on at least one occasion in relation to **each** of those persons (s 7(3)(b)).

Conduct includes speech, letters, and emails, so you will need to gather evidence from a wide range of sources. What might begin as a bona fide enquiry to a company for example, could become harassing if it is followed up in a manner that is unreasonable and persistent (see *DPP v Hardy* (2008) All ER (D) 315 (Oct)).

Two **offences** described in the Protection from Harassment Act 1997 are:

- harassment (without violence) (ss 1 and 2), and
- putting people in fear of violence (s 4).

4.6.3.1 *Harassment*

It is an offence under ss 1 and 2 of the Protection from Harassment Act 1997 for a person:

- to pursue a course of conduct (s 1(1)), or
- to aid, abet, counsel, or procure the pursuance of a course of conduct (s 7(3A)),

which involves harassment of one or more persons (s 1(1) and (1A)) which they know (or ought to know) amounts to harassment of the other(s) (s 1(1A)(b)).

It will be up to the court or jury to decide whether it believes a reasonable person would have considered that the conduct was alarming or distressing in the particular circumstances.

In addition to the harassment of two or more persons in s 1(1A) (a), an offence can also be committed when the course of conduct is intended to persuade any person to change his/her current routine (s 1(1A)(c)(i) and (ii)). Such attempts to persuade may form part of a wider campaign about political or social issues. The attempt to persuade any person must:

- be directed towards two or more person(s) in the first instance, and
- must occur on at least one occasion in relation to **each** of those persons.

The offender might try to persuade any person (not only the two or more persons to whom the contact is directed) **to do something** that s/he is **not** under any obligation to do (s 1(1A)(c)(ii)).

This offence can be also be committed when there is an intention to persuade any person (not just the two or more persons to whom it is directed) to **not** do something that s/he is **entitled or required to do** (s 1(1A)(c)(i)).

These offences are triable summarily and the penalty is six months' imprisonment and/or a fine. This offence can be racially or religiously aggravated (see 4.6.10 below).

4.6.3.2 *Isolated events causing distress*

If distress is only caused on one occasion then, under the Protection from Harassment Act 1997, this does not constitute a course of conduct. Instead an actual or apprehended harassment may be the subject of a claim in **civil proceedings** by the distressed or alarmed person under s 3(1) of the same Act.

The main points of this option are:

- A 'course of conduct' is not necessary
- The result of such a civil claim can be **damages** (a court order to pay money) and/or an **injunction** (a court order to impose sanctions on a person, to make the person cease an action) against the offender
- A company can apply for an injunction (as well as individuals).

If such an injunction is breached, the offence is triable either way:

- on indictment: five years' imprisonment and/or a fine
- summarily: six months' imprisonment and/or a fine.

4.6.3.3 *Putting people in fear of violence*

This offence is described under s 4 of the Protection of Harassment Act 1997 and involves more than sending threatening letters or emails. The victim must experience a real fear of violence, and s/he must believe that whatever s/he is frightened of will really happen (as opposed to the possibility that it *might* happen).

There are several key differences from the harassment (s 2) offence we described earlier. In s 4 offences:

- the victim must fear the violence personally, not on behalf of somebody else, such as a family member (*Mohammed Ali Caurti v DPP* [2002] Crime LR 131)
- the fear of violence cannot be achieved through a third party: in other words, an individual cannot be put in fear of violence via an intermediary.

This offence is triable either way:

- summarily: six months' imprisonment and/or a fine
- on indictment: five years' imprisonment and/or a fine.

This offence can be racially or religiously aggravated (see 4.6.10 below).

4.6.3.4 *Restraining orders*

A court may make **a restraining order** under s 5 of the Protection from Harassment Act 1997 against a person convicted of the offences described above. A restraining order will place restrictions on a defendant's future behaviour and, in particular, aim to inhibit any further harassment of the victim. The order may last indefinitely or for a period stated by the court. You can use the PNC to find out if a person is subject to a restraining order.

If such a restraining order is breached, an offence is committed, and is triable either way:

- summarily: six months' imprisonment and/or a fine
- on indictment: five years' imprisonment and/or a fine.

4.6.4 **Section 5 of the Public Order Act 1986**

The offence is also referred to as **non-intentional** harassment, alarm, or distress. Section 5 of the Public Order Act 1986 states that a person is guilty of this offence if s/he:

a) uses threatening, abusive, or insulting words or behaviour, or disorderly behaviour, or

b) displays any writing, sign, or other visible representation which is threatening, abusive, or insulting, within the hearing or sight of a person likely to be caused harassment, alarm, or distress thereby.

The key features of s 5 offences are that:

- The conduct does not have to be aimed towards a specific person
- The conduct must take place within the presence of a person who can see or hear the conduct, but that person does not need to be identifiable
- The type of conduct must be likely to cause harassment, alarm, or distress
- Any material used (such as a poster) is not distributed
- The suspect must intend or be aware that his or her conduct is threatening, abusive, or insulting in general terms.

However, there is no need to prove s/he actually intended to cause any person to be harassed, alarmed, or distressed, because a suspect might intend his/her conduct to be threatening, abusive, or insulting but still have no intention to harass, alarm, or distress any particular person.

4.6.5 Offensive weapons, bladed and sharply pointed articles

Serious wounding and possibly death can result from the use of these items, but you will hear plenty of excuses from people found in possession of them, almost always predicated on self-defence. In some cases, the individuals concerned may be genuinely vulnerable to attack by others; however, it is your responsibility to attempt to prevent crimes involving the use of these weapons, and, if at all possible, to detect their presence before they are used, especially as such weapons might serve to 'aggravate' (make worse) any fight, attempted resistance, or action to recover 'loss of respect' in front of peers.

The legislation covered here concerns offensive weapons, bladed, and sharply pointed articles in public places and on school premises, and is to be found in:

- s 1 of the Prevention of Crime Act 1953
- s 139A(2) of the Criminal Justice Act 1984
- s 139 of the Criminal Justice Act 1988.

You have the power to search for offensive weapons or bladed or sharply pointed articles under s 1 of the PACE Act 1984 (see 4.4.1 above).

4 Special Constables' Powers

4.6.5.1 *Offensive weapons in a public place*

Section 1 of the Prevention of Crime Act 1953 is an important piece of legislation relating to the discovery of an offensive weapon in the possession of a member of the public.

Section 1(1) of the Act states that it is an offence for:

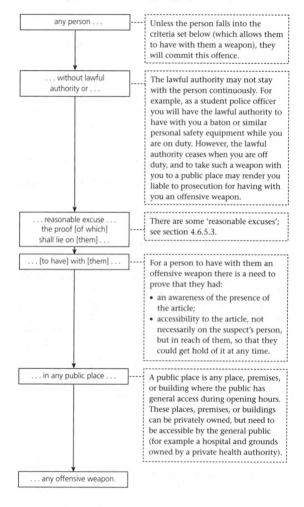

any person . . .

Unless the person falls into the criteria set below (which allows them to have with them a weapon), they will commit this offence.

. . . without lawful authority or . . .

The lawful authority may not stay with the person continuously. For example, as a student police officer you will have the lawful authority to have with you a baton or similar personal safety equipment while you are on duty. However, the lawful authority ceases when you are off duty, and to take such a weapon with you to a public place may render you liable to prosecution for having with you an offensive weapon.

. . . reasonable excuse . . . the proof [of which] shall lie on [them] . . .

There are some 'reasonable excuses'; see section 4.6.5.3.

. . . [to have] with [them] . . .

For a person to have with them an offensive weapon there is a need to prove that they had:

- an awareness of the presence of the article;
- accessibility to the article, not necessarily on the suspect's person, but in reach of them, so that they could get hold of it at any time.

. . . in any public place . . .

A public place is any place, premises, or building where the public has general access during opening hours. These places, premises, or buildings can be privately owned, but need to be accessible by the general public (for example a hospital and grounds owned by a private health authority).

. . . any offensive weapon.

4.6.5.2 *Definition of an offensive weapon*

An offensive weapon (s 1(4)) is any article made, adapted, or intended for causing injury:

1. A **made** article includes any article which has been made or manufactured with the intention of causing injury to people, for example a flick knife. These are offensive weapons *per se*; the courts need no proof of their intended use, but do require proof that the defendant had no reasonable excuse for possessing such an item.

2. An **adapted** article includes any article which has been modified in some way with the intention of causing injury, for example a broken bottle with sharp edges. A jury decides whether or not articles have been specifically **adapted** to be offensive weapons.

3. An **intended** article includes any article in the suspect's possession with which s/he intends to cause injury. The precise nature of the article is not important: it is what the suspect intends to do with it. A pillow could become an offensive weapon if it can be proved that the suspect intended to use it to cause injury to an elderly relative. Once again, gathering evidence through interview is important here.

Of course some items that may be classed as offensive weapons might have innocent uses, and the person would therefore have a reasonable excuse for carrying such an item. An example might be a Forestry Commission Ranger carrying an axe along a woodland path. If the Ranger were to walk down the High Street of a town carrying the axe, the possession is not so reasonable.

4.6.5.3 *Reasonable and unreasonable excuses*

A person **might** have a reasonable excuse if s/he fears for his/her safety: for example a security guard who fears attack while picking up or dropping off money at a bank. Other reasonable excuses include having an **innocent reason**, such as a chef carrying knives.

Unreasonable excuses include:

- **Forgetfulness**—a person might not have a reasonable excuse if s/he has forgotten s/he has an offensive weapon with him/her
- **Ignorance**—a person might not have a reasonable excuse just because s/he does not know the true identity of the item, for example not knowing that an antique but functioning swordstick is not a walking stick
- **General self-defence**—a person does *not* have reasonable excuse to have an offensive weapon with him/her generally

for self-defence, '*just in case*' s/he is attacked. This is an excuse that Special Constables hear all the time. Be sure you know the law on this, as it is possible that confiscation could prevent escalation of violence.

In any prosecution the burden of proving a reasonable excuse for possession of an offensive weapon lies with the defendant: if the defendant can persuade the court to consider the likelihood that s/he had a reasonable excuse, that could be enough for a Not Guilty verdict. This offence is triable either way:

- summarily: six months' imprisonment and/or a fine
- on indictment: four years' imprisonment and/or a fine.

4.6.5.4 *Bladed or sharply pointed articles in a public place*

The offence of having a bladed or sharply pointed article (s 139(1), Criminal Justice Act 1988) was created in an attempt to prevent serious crimes involving the use of everyday items. An offence is committed by any person who possesses a bladed or sharply pointed article **in a public place**.

4.6.5.5 *The definition of 'bladed' and 'sharply pointed' articles*

The definition of **'bladed'** includes any kind of article with a blade, for example a kitchen knife, scissors, a craft knife, a pocket knife, a dagger, a scalpel, or any other article which has been given a cutting edge or blade. Pocket-knives with a blade less than 7.62 cm long which cannot be locked in the open position are not classed as bladed under this legislation.

The definition of **'sharply pointed'** includes any kind of article with a point, for example a needle, geometry compasses, a bradawl, or any other article which has been given a sharp point.

A court must decide whether or not an article has a blade or is sharply pointed, so the prosecution must be able to prove that the article fits this description.

4.6.5.6 *Defences for having bladed or sharply pointed articles*

There may be a good reason for a person having a bladed or sharply pointed article in their possession, such as a carpet layer carrying a specialist knife for cutting carpet at work. But neither general self-defence, nor ignorance, nor forgetfulness are suitable defences; see the descriptions in 4.6.5.3 above.

Table 4.4: Other grounds for defence (s 139 of the Criminal Justice Act 1988)

Defence	Example
Lawful authority	The lawful authority may not stay with the person continuously. For example, as a Special Constable, you have the lawful authority to have with you a bladed or sharply pointed article after seizure and before placing it into a special property store. Members of the Armed Forces also have lawful authority to carry articles such as bayonets whilst on duty, but if such an article was carried off duty they might be liable for prosecution.
For use at work	A joiner uses wood chisels with very sharp cutting edges during the course of his/her work and might need to carry them in a bag while moving between jobs in the street. S/he would, however, not be able to use this claim if s/he had a chisel in a night club whilst socializing.
Religious reasons	Genuine followers of the Sikh religion carry *kirpans* (a small rigid knife) for religious reasons.
Part of any national costume	Whilst wearing national costume, some Scots carry a *skean dhu* (a small dagger, tucked in the top of a sock). However, this defence could not be used if the person was carrying the knife but was not wearing national costume.

This offence is triable either way:

- summarily: six months' imprisonment and/or a fine
- on indictment: four years' imprisonment and/or a fine.

4.6.6 Air weapons

An air weapon is usually less dangerous to other people than many other firearms, because the pellets are discharged from the barrel relatively slowly and have less mass than, for example, a handgun bullet. The velocity is relatively low because the pellets are propelled by air pressure only, rather than by an explosive charge. However, **air weapons are capable of producing serious injury** including causing blindness. Indeed, air-weapon offences make up more than half of all recorded firearms offences. Fatalities are also not unknown, particularly among children. Air weapons include air pistols, air guns, and air rifles which are different in shape and size.

4.6.6.1 *Definition of lawful air weapons*

The missiles from this category of weapon are pellets propelled by air. The **kinetic energy rate** (the energy used to fire the pellet) must not exceed 6 ft-lb (for air pistols), or 12 ft-lb (for air weapons other than air pistols).

A lawful air weapon does not require a certificate under s 1 of the Firearms Act 1968. However, if the air weapon **exceeds** the authorized kinetic energy, it becomes a s 1 firearm and must be certificated as such. A forensic laboratory will be able to measure the kinetic energy of the pellets expelled by an air weapon. A weapon with a self-contained gas cartridge system (containing both a charge of compressed air or other gas and the pellet) is not classified as a lawful air weapon, and is a prohibited weapon under s 5 of the Firearms Act.

4.6.6.2 *Age limits and firing restrictions for air weapons*

For a person under the age of 17, it is an offence to possess an air weapon or ammunition for an air weapon (s 22(4), Firearms Act 1968), unless (s 23) the child or young person:

- is accompanied by someone over 21 years of age, in which case s/he can be allowed to fire the air weapon on premises, but the missiles must not go beyond the premises (otherwise both the firer and the supervisor commit an offence), or
- is aged 14 years or over, in which case s/he may possess the weapon on premises with the permission of the occupier, and can fire the air weapon, but the missiles must not go beyond the premises, or
- is a member of an approved club for target shooting, or
- is at a shooting gallery with only air weapons or miniature rifles not exceeding 0.23 calibre.

Firing an air weapon (or allowing its missile to pass) beyond the premises within which it is lawful to fire it, is also an offence (s 21A of the Firearms Act 1968). However it will be a defence (for the firer or the supervisor) to show that the occupier of the premises into or across which the missile was fired, had consented to the firing of the missile (whether specifically or by way of a general consent).

'Premises' is not defined in this Act but examples will include houses, gardens, and other private places which are enclosed.

These offences are triable summarily and the penalty is a fine.

4.6.7 **Alcohol-related offences**

Many of the incidents you will investigate whilst on Supervised and Independent Patrol will be alcohol-related, particularly on late shifts. Remember, you must consider your own health and safety and the health and safety of everybody around you when dealing with incidents fuelled by alcohol; the potential for injury can be very high. Drunken people are sometimes subject to rapid mood swings, happy one minute, violent the next, whilst people who are normally quite reserved may lose some of their normal social inhibitions and behave unpredictably.

Alcohol-related offences are dealt with under the following legislation:

- s 12 of the Licensing Act 1872
- s 2 of the Licensing Act 1902
- s 91(1) of the Criminal Justice Act 1967.

4.6.7.1 *The definition of being 'drunk'*

The terms 'drunk' and 'drunkenness' are not defined in law, but the *Oxford Reference Dictionary* (1996) is blunt and to the point: **drunk** is defined as '*rendered incapable through alcohol*'. The general rule that the 'lay' opinion of a witness is inadmissible does not apply in this particular context: a competent witness may give evidence that, in his/her opinion, a person was drunk (*R v Davies* [1962] 1 WLR 1111). A competent witness is a person who understands questions put to them and gives answers that can be understood. As a Special Constable, you can therefore state as a competent witness your opinion whether a particular person was drunk. You should also be able to give the facts on which your opinion is based, such as:

- he was unsteady on his feet
- her eyes were glazed
- his speech was slurred, or
- you could smell intoxicating liquor on her breath.

The court itself must decide whether or not a suspect was drunk.

4.6.7.2 *Drunkenness as an offence*

Section 12 of the Licensing Act 1872 states that it is an offence for a person to be:

4 Special Constables' Powers

drunk in any highway, public place or licensed premises;	**Highway** shall be understood to mean all roads, bridges, carriageways, cart ways, horse ways, bridleways, footways, causeways, 'church ways', and pavements.
	Public places include any place where the public have or are permitted to have access, whether on payment or otherwise, whether it is a building or not.
	Licensed premises are premises with a Justices' licence authorizing the sale of intoxicating liquor (a pub or club) or an occasional licence (such as a village hall for the purposes of a wedding reception). However, such a venue only becomes licensed premises during the times specified on the occasional license, after which it reverts to its usual status.
drunk in charge of any carriage, horse or cattle in any highway or public place;	**Carriages** include vehicles such as trailers, bicycles (being pushed or not) and steam engines. It also includes motor vehicles, though the offence of driving or being in charge while over the prescribed limit (s 5 of the Road Traffic Act 1988) may be more appropriate. For aircraft, other offences may also be more appropriate.
	Cattle includes pigs and sheep as well as cows.
drunk in possession of a loaded firearm.	**Firearm**—a lethal barrelled weapon of any description from which any shot, bullet, or other missile can be discharged and may include an air weapon, but not an imitation.

- you are satisfied on inspecting the licence and its counterpart that the driver would not be liable to disqualification, and
- the driver accepts an EFPN.

The procedure for issuing an EFPN is the same as that for a NEFPN, except for the procedures described in 4.7.1.5 below.

4.7.1.5 *The significance of the driver's licence*

If the driving licence contains fewer than 12 points and the driver accepts an EFPN then:

- ask the driver to surrender the licence and provide a receipt to the driver
- issue a FPN and explain to the driver that s/he needs to pay within the specified time or face an increased fine (as for NEFPN; see 4.7.1.3 above).

If the licence contains more than 12 points an EFPN cannot be issued: **you must report the driver for prosecution**. If the driver does not have a driving licence available, you should issue a provisional EFPN and instruct him/her to produce the licence for inspection at a police station (of his/her choice) within seven days.

4.7.1.6 *Reporting for the purposes of issuing a written charge*

You may choose to report a person for the purposes of issuing a written charge as the method of disposal. Remember that you will still need to report a driver for the offence even if s/he has elected for the VDRS scheme or a FPN, as s/he might not comply subsequently with the VDRS or FPN requirements.

To report a person for the purposes of issuing a written charge, **you will always** need to go through the following process:

1. examine the vehicle or see the offence being committed
2. decide what offence was detected
3. point out the offence to the driver
4. caution the driver using the 'when questioned' form of caution and ensure you meet the PACE Act 1984, Code C10.2
5. write down questions and answers about the offences in your PNB
6. offer your PNB to the driver to read and sign that the notes were a true record of the interview
7. offer the driver (if appropriate) the opportunity to have his/her vehicle rectified or pay the penalty notice
8. tell the driver 'I am reporting you for the offence of [. . .]'
9. caution the driver (using the 'now' caution).

4.7.1.7 *Notice of Intended Prosecution (NIP)*

You must give notice to a suspect if s/he is to be prosecuted for certain categories of motoring offence. This is known as a **Notice of Intended Prosecution** (NIP). *If you do not issue such a notice, the prosecution cannot proceed.* An NIP specifies the nature of the offence, and the time and place where it is alleged to have been committed. It must be given to the offender (the driver or the registered keeper of the vehicle), at the time of the offence (or sent within 14 days of the offence). An NIP is not required when the vehicle concerned has been involved in an accident or if a FPN (see 4.7.1.2 above) has been issued.

The following offences require a NIP (s 1, Road Traffic Offenders Act 1988):

- dangerous driving
- careless and inconsiderate driving
- dangerous cycling
- careless and inconsiderate cycling
- failing to conform with the indication of a police officer when directing traffic
- failing to comply with a traffic sign
- speeding offences.

A person cannot be prosecuted for any of the offences listed above unless s/he has been:

- **warned** at the time of the offence of the possibility of prosecution (s 1(1)(a))
- **given a notice** setting out the possibility of prosecution, and
- **served with a written charge** within 14 days of commission of the offence (s 1(1)(b)).

It is advisable to provide a NIP as a document.

4.7.2 **Powers to stop a vehicle**

When you are on foot or mobile patrol, it may be necessary for you to investigate offences connected with a variety of vehicles being used on roads.

If a vehicle is in motion on a road, you will need to stop it safely in order to speak to the people inside. To do this **you must be on duty in full uniform**, and give a clear direction (whether from a police vehicle or while you are on foot patrol).

The power to stop a mechanically propelled vehicle on a road is to be found in s 163 of the Road Traffic Act 1988, which states that:

4.7.3.7 *Evidential tests*

The results of these tests (for drugs, alcohol, and impairment) can be used as evidence in a court. The tests are usually carried out at a police station (or hospital if the suspect is a hospital patient) but some may also be conducted at the roadside.

We don't have the space to go into the details of taking evidential tests (breath, blood, or urine). Look at the *Police Operational Handbook* (Bridges, 2006), sections 10.10 and 10.11, pp 527–40.

4.7.4 Driving licences

It is inevitable that you will investigate and detect a number of offences relating to driving licences in the course of your Special Constable's duties.

The table below shows the age requirements for driving particular categories of vehicle.

Table 4.9: Age requirements for driving particular categories of vehicle

	Vehicle category	Minimum age requirement
A	Motorcycles	17
B	Cars and light vans	17
C	Large goods vehicles	21
D	Passenger-carrying vehicles with nine to sixteen passenger seats	21
E	Trailers	18
F to K	Other vehicles	16
P	Mopeds	16

4.7.4.1 *Information shown on driving licences*

Driving licences have two parts: the photocard and the counterpart. Photocard full licences are pink, but provisional licences are green. The driver number contains information about the driver.

Table 4.10: How to interpret the driver number

The Driver Number is:	**GARDN 605109C99LY**
The first five characters are the first five of the surname:	**GARDN**
The first and last digits are derived from the year of birth:	605109 shows the year of birth is 19**69**
The second and third digits represent the month of birth and the gender of the licence holder:	6**05**109 shows that the person was born in May and is male. For females, 5 is added to the second digit so for a female born in May the number would be **655**109. For females born in the months of October, November and December, the second digit becomes 6.
The fourth and fifth digits show the day of birth:	605**10**9 shows that the date of birth was the 10th of the month.
The first two characters of the final cluster represent the initials:	**C** (if there is only one initial, **9** is used in place of a second initial)
The middle number of the final cluster is computer-generated, in order to avoid duplicate records:	**9** (can be any digit between 0 and 9)
The final two letters are also computer-generated:	**LY** in this case

Full details concerning the driving licence, including the meaning of the various symbols and codes, may be found at the DVLA website: <http://www.dvla.gov.uk>.

4.7.4.2 *The photocard*

Figure 4.3 describes the main features of the front of the photocard.

The reverse of the photocard contains the information shown in Figure 4.4.

4.7.4.3 *The counterpart*

The counterpart is a paper document (see Figure 4.5 below) showing additional information, such as the vehicle categories the holder is entitled to drive provisionally, the entitlement history (superseded categories), and any endorsements. It is green and pink for both full and provisional licences.

National sign

Date of issue

Date of expiry

Issue number

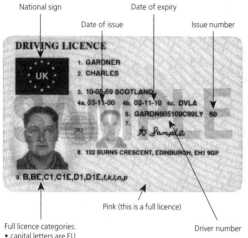

(Image reproduced with the permission of the DVLA)

Pink (this is a full licence)

Driver number

Full licence categories:
• capital letters are EU categories
• lower case letters are national categories

Figure 4.3: Driving licence photocard—front

Vehicle categories as listed on the front of the photocard, with pictograms for clarity.

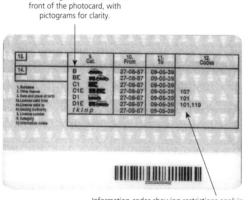

(Image reproduced with the permission of the DVLA)

Information codes showing restrictions applying to the adjoining category. For example, 101 means that the licence holder cannot drive that category of vehicle for hire or reward.

Figure 4.4: Driving licence photocard—reverse

List of categories for which the holder
is entitled to drive provisionally

The issue number on the counterpart
will be followed by a letter

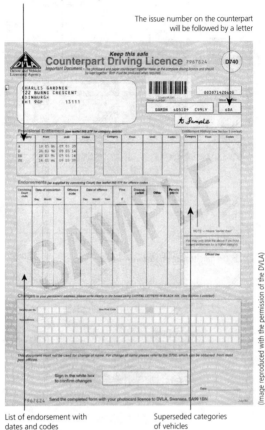

List of endorsement with
dates and codes

Superseded categories
of vehicles

(Image reproduced with the permission of the DVLA)

Figure 4.5: Driving licence counterpart

4.7.4.4 *Requiring to see a driver's licence*

Under s 164(1) of the Road Traffic Act 1988 you may require a person to produce his/her driving licence. This applies to any person:

a) **driving** a motor vehicle on a road
b) who you have reasonable cause to believe to have been
   driving a motor vehicle involved in an **accident** on a road

c) who you have reasonable cause to believe to have **committed an offence** in relation to the use of a motor vehicle on a road, or

d) supervising a provisional-licence holder in any of the above three circumstances.

A failure to produce the licence is an offence unless the driver produces it within specified time limits (see 4.7.4.6 below).

4.7.4.5 *Requiring a person to state his/her date of birth*

Under s 164(2) of the Road Traffic Act 1988 you may require a person to state his/her date of birth if s/he:

- has failed to produce his/her licence
- has produced a licence that is unsatisfactory (for example it seems to have been altered or if it contains information you suspect to be incorrect), or
- is the supervisor of a learner driver at the time of an accident or an offence, and you have reason to suspect that s/he (the supervisor) is under 21 years of age.

4.7.4.6 *Offences relating to failing to produce a licence*

Under s 164 of the Road Traffic Act 1988 it is an offence for a person to fail to:

- produce his/her licence and its counterpart, or
- produce his/her certificate of completion of a motorcyclist's training course (CBT; Compulsory Basic Training), or
- state his/her date of birth.

Under s 164(8) of the Road Traffic Act 1988 it will be a *defence* for that person to produce the relevant licence either:

- within **seven days** in person at a police station (specified by her/him at the time of the request)
- as soon as **reasonably practicable**, or
- at a **later time** if s/he can prove it was not reasonably practicable to do so before the day on which written charge proceedings were commenced.

It will be a question of fact for the court to decide when is 'as soon as is reasonably practicable', given the circumstances of the case.

4.7.4.7 *Seizing a vehicle*

Under s 165A of the Road Traffic Act 1988, there is a power to seize a vehicle if there are reasonable grounds for believing that the driver does not have a suitable licence or that the vehicle is not adequately insured. To seize a vehicle a Special Constable must be in uniform and must have:

- requested to see the driver's licence and counterpart or evidence of insurance, but the appropriate document has not been produced, or
- warned the driver that the vehicle will be seized unless s/he produces the required documentation immediately (it might not be practical to warn the driver; if so, this stage may be omitted) (s 165A(6)).

A vehicle can also be seized if a Special Constable has required that vehicle to stop (a police officer must be in uniform to require a vehicle to stop: see 4.7.2 above), but it has not stopped, or has not stopped long enough for appropriate enquiries, **and** a police officer has reasonable grounds for believing that the driver does not have a suitable licence, or that the vehicle is not adequately insured. If the vehicle cannot be seized immediately because the person driving it has failed to stop or has driven off, the vehicle can be seized at any time within 24 hours after the incident. In order to seize a vehicle a police officer can enter premises (other than a private dwelling-house) if there are reasonable grounds for believing the vehicle to be present, using reasonable force if necessary. Note that a private dwelling-house does not include any outbuildings or adjacent land, so vehicles can be seized from areas such as driveways and garages.

Note: Details of qualifications to drive and disqualifications from driving, including insurance, defective eyesight, driving a class of vehicle for which the driver is not licensed, driving without a test certificate, and so on, are all to be found in the Police Operational Handbook (Bridges, 2006), 10.14 to 10.16, pp 550–69. We shall not repeat them here.

4.7.4.8 *Provisional licence holders*

A person holding a provisional driving licence must not drive a vehicle unless s/he is accompanied and supervised by a qualified driver (see 4.7.4.9 below). Details are provided in reg 16(2)(a) of the Motor Vehicles (Driving Licences) Regulations 1999.

There are exceptions; supervision is not required when:

- driving a motor vehicle in certain categories: for example three-wheeled vehicles
- riding a moped or motor bicycle (with or without a sidecar)
- driving a motor vehicle on an exempted island (except large goods vehicles and passenger-carrying vehicles)
- driving a motor vehicle having just passed a test (having been given a certificate authorizing the person to drive the respective class of vehicle).

4.7.4.9 *Displaying learner driver plates correctly*

A person holding a provisional driving licence must not drive a vehicle unless 'L' plates are displayed on the vehicle in such manner as to be clearly visible to other road users from within a reasonable distance in front of and behind the vehicle. Details are provided in reg 16(2)(b) of the Motor Vehicles (Driving Licences) Regulations 1999.

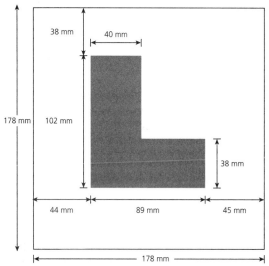

Figure 4.6: Specification for learner driver plate

'D' plates can be displayed in Wales, but if such a vehicle is driven in England these must be replaced with 'L' plates. The appropriate sizes and measurements of an 'L' Plate are shown in the diagram. The corners can be rounded, but the dimensions of the 'L' plate must be as shown.

4.7.4.10 *Provisional licence holders and towing*

A person holding a provisional driving licence must not drive a vehicle while it is being used to draw a trailer. Details are provided in reg 16(2)(c) of the Motor Vehicles (Driving Licences) Regulations 1999. There are exceptions, such as for those holding provisional licences in certain categories, such as articulated lorries.

4.7.4.11 *Provisional licences for mopeds or motorcycles*

A motorcycle rider with only a provisional licence is subject to certain restrictions. No passengers may be carried on a moped or a motor bicycle (with or without a sidecar) if the driver has a provisional driving licence. Details are provided in reg 16(2)(b) of the Motor Vehicles (Driving Licences) Regulations 1999.

A Certificate of **Compulsory Basic Training** (CBT) is required by all holders of provisional licences for motorcycles and mopeds before they ride on a road (except during the training itself). The CBT lasts for two years and then has to be renewed. This legislation is described in s 97(3)(e) of the Road Traffic Act 1988.

For a provisional licence holder, a breach of these conditions amounts to an offence of driving otherwise than in accordance with a licence under s 87(1) of the Road Traffic Act 1988.

These offences are triable summarily.

4.7.4.12 *Motorcycle training and licensing arrangements*

These arrangements are complicated and are summarized below. The power of the motorcycle engine is an important factor for the type of licence required.

4.7.4.13 *Category 'P' licence*

A category 'P' licence is for riding a moped only. The following conditions must be met:

- rider age: minimum 16 years, and
- engine size: maximum 50cc capacity/50kph speed.

New riders and drivers need a provisional licence and CBT before riding on the road (apart from riding on the road during training). The CBT certificate is valid for two years. Other conditions apply for moped riders who already have a licence that allows them to ride a moped:

- **Full Category P holders** who took the Category P test after 1 December 1990 need to complete CBT; the Certificate is valid for two years

- **Car drivers** with a full car Category B licence automatically have a full Category P licence, but if the Category B test was passed on or after 1 February 2001, CBT is still required; (the CBT Certificate does not have to be periodically renewed).

4.7.4.14 *Category 'A' motorcycle licence*

There are different types of Category A motorcycle, and the licence requirements also depend on the rider's age.

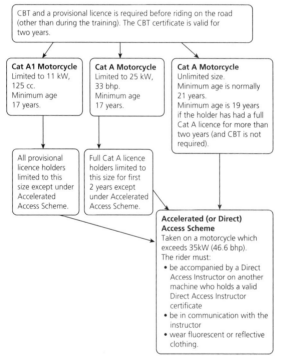

CBT and a provisional licence is required before riding on the road (other than during the training). The CBT certificate is valid for two years.

Cat A1 Motorcycle
Limited to 11 kW, 125 cc.
Minimum age 17 years.

Cat A Motorcycle
Limited to 25 kW, 33 bhp.
Minimum age 17 years.

Cat A Motorcycle
Unlimited size.
Minimum age is normally 21 years.
Minimum age is 19 years if the holder has had a full Cat A licence for more than two years (and CBT is not required).

All provisional licence holders limited to this size except under Accelerated Access Scheme.

Full Cat A licence holders limited to this size for first 2 years except under Accelerated Access Scheme.

Accelerated (or Direct) Access Scheme
Taken on a motorcycle which exceeds 35kW (46.6 bhp).
The rider must:
- be accompanied by a Direct Access Instructor on another machine who holds a valid Direct Access Instructor certificate
- be in communication with the instructor
- wear fluorescent or reflective clothing.

Figure 4.7: Category A motorcycle licence requirements

4.7.4.15 *'Mini-motos', 'go-peds', and electrically assisted pedal cycles*

The use of miniature motorbikes ('mini-motos') and petrol-driven scooters ('go-peds') may pose risks to the health and safety of other road and pavement users, and are considered by many members of the public as examples of anti-social behaviour. There have been a number of fatalities and serious injuries as the result of the use of mini-motos.

The Department of Transport has specified that mini-motos and go-peds are in fact 'lightweight powered motor vehicles' and must therefore comply with the usual road traffic and vehicle excise licence laws. *It is illegal to use a mini-moto or go-ped on the pavement under s 72 of the Highways Act 1835.*

Further information can be found in a government publication at the Department for Transport website <http://www.dft.gov.uk/transportforyou/roads/miniaturemotorbikesminiature6076>. For case law on go-peds, refer to *DPP v Saddington* [2000] The Times, November 1 QBD and *Burns v Currell* [1963] 2 QB 433, 440.

An electrically assisted pedal cycle is classified as a pedal cycle as long as:

- it is no heavier than 40kg
- it can be propelled by its pedals as well as by its electric motor
- the electric motor does not exceed 0.2kW and the maximum speed (due to the motor alone) is less than 15mph.

Similar exemptions are made for powered wheelchairs and powered scooters designed for people with disabilities.

4.7.5 Road traffic collisions (section 170 of the Road Traffic Act 1988)

We often refer to collisions between vehicles (of various degrees of seriousness) as 'accidents' and the older police term 'RTA' (for Road Traffic Accident) has entered the popular language. However, it is usual now in Special Constabulary and regular police circles to refer to road traffic **collisions** rather than accidents, partly to reflect that incidents of this kind are often due to driver error rather than simply a random occurrence or entirely unforeseen event.

The Road Traffic Act 1988 takes a common-sense approach to collisions (referred to as 'accidents' in this Act) and requires that **the driver of a vehicle involved in a collision must stop** and be prepared to provide details to anybody who reasonably requires information. This information might be needed for compensation claims for repairs, injuries, or deaths. As a Special Constable, likely to happen across road traffic collisions in the course of your duties, you should have an understanding about what information must be exchanged after a collision, and what offences may be committed by a person who fails to meet his/her obligations in this regard. We have little space to devote to this, and refer you to section 10.9 of the *Police Operational Handbook* (Bridges, 2006), pp 522–6 and also Bryants *et al* (2010).

4.7.6 **Lights on vehicles**

The following information relates in part to the Road Vehicles Lighting Regulations 1989.

There is a possibility of underestimating the importance of lights on vehicles when placed alongside other demands on your time, particularly when compared with incidents involving violent criminal activity. However, the position, style, maintenance, and colour of vehicle lights are all very important for road safety. Your many Special Constabulary responsibilities include identifying vehicles with lights that are not working properly, testing and inspecting lights, and bringing the faults to the attention of the owner and/or driver.

Drivers are also expected to employ their lights with consideration towards other road users; you can offer advice to drivers about how they use their vehicles' lights—for example lights should not be used in a way that causes undue dazzle or discomfort to other persons using the road.

4.7.6.1 *Obligatory lights*

On the **front of a car**, the following lights are obligatory:

- front position lights ('side lights')
- dipped-beam headlights
- main-beam headlights, and
- direction indicators.

On the **back of a car**, the following are obligatory:

- rear position lights
- direction indicators
- rear stop (brake) lights
- rear fog light
- rear registration-plate lamp
- rear reflector (not strictly a light, but obligatory).

A 'hazard warning-signal device' to operate the direction indicator lights on the front and back of the car is also obligatory.

These obligatory lights may be clustered as a group of lights underneath a plastic or glass cover.

4.7.6.2 *Sunrise, sunset, lighting-up times, and hours of darkness*

To establish when position lamps or sidelights must be illuminated, published sunrise and sunset times may be consulted. Times can be found in diaries, the internet, or local publications such as newspapers, and databases accessible by your Control Room.

> Remember: Sunset and Sunrise for Sidelights

For the purposes of finding out when dipped headlights must be used, hours of darkness can be calculated by adding 30 minutes to sunset time and taking away 30 minutes from sunrise time, in other words half an hour after sunset and half an hour before sunrise.

> Remember: Hours of Darkness for Dipped headlights

Further Reading

Bland, N and Read, T, *Policing Anti-Social Behaviour* (2003, Police Research Series Paper 123, Crown Copyright)

Home Office (2007c), *Police and Justice Act 2006*, Home Office, Police Reform Unit, HO Circular 21/2007 [this act extends the jurisdiction of Specials to whole of England and Wales]

Jefferson, M, *Criminal Law*, 8th edn. (2007, London: Pearson Longman)

Povey, D and Smith, K (eds.), with Hand, T and Dodd, L, *Police Powers and Procedures: England and Wales 2007/08*, 07/09 (2009: Home Office, Research and Development Studies Directorate (RDSD), 30 April, also available from the Research Development Statistics website: <http://www.homeoffice.gov.uk/rds/index.html>, accessed 1 May 2009)

Notes and Acknowledgements

We acknowledge, with grateful thanks, the kind permission of Robin and Sarah Bryant (editors of *Blackstone's Student Police Officer Handbook*, 2010) and the Delegacy of Oxford University Press for its agreement that we could amend and modify some material on powers and law, originally prepared for the *Handbook*. This is a huge quarry to which many will come to dig out the stones, and we were glad to have the chance to swing our picks.

We also acknowledge with some awe the quantity of legal detail in the excellent *Blackstone's Police Operational Handbook*, Police National Legal Database, edited by Ian Bridges (2006), also published by Oxford University Press. We strongly recommend that readers who want more detail than we can supply should go to Bryant and Bridges.

1 A throwdown is a firework containing impact-sensitive explosive and grains of inert material (wrapped in paper or foil) which produces a sound when thrown on to the ground to explode.

Chapter 5
Criminal Law

5.1 Introduction

This is another reference chapter, following on logically from considering your powers (Chapter 4), which we expect you to dip into as needs arise. It is in two parts. The first (5.2) is about **criminal law and procedure**; the second part (5.3) concerns **criminal investigation** and again concentrates on the most prevalent of a Special Constable's experiences on duty.[1]

5.2 Criminal Law and Procedure

5.2.1 Unlawful personal violence

Here we cover several different types of offence:

> - **Common assault** under s 39 of the Criminal Justice Act 1988
> - **Common assault by beating (battery)** under s 39 of the Criminal Justice Act 1988
> - **Assault occasioning actual bodily harm** under s 47 of the Offences Against the Person Act 1861
> - **Grievous bodily harm** under s 20 of the Offences Against the Person Act 1861
> - **Grievous bodily harm with intent** under s 18 of the Offences Against the Person Act 1861.

The law concerns two groups of offences, *assaults* and *batteries*: each has separate legal meanings. An **assault** does not actually mean physical attack; instead it is any act, such as a threat made by an assailant, which makes a victim believe that s/he is going to be subjected immediately to personal violence. An example would be someone shouting 'I'm going to kick your head in!'

A **battery** is the *actual use of force* by an assailant on a victim, such as a punch.

5.2.1.1 *Common assault*

Common assault is an offence under s 39 of the Criminal Justice Act 1988. It consists of *either* an assault *or* a battery. If there is a serious outcome, then the injuries may constitute **actual bodily harm** (ABH) and the offender will receive a greater penalty if found guilty at court. If the outcome is even more serious, then the injuries may constitute **grievous bodily harm** (GBH).

5.2.1.2 *Assault*

An assault (s 39, Criminal Justice Act 1988) is:

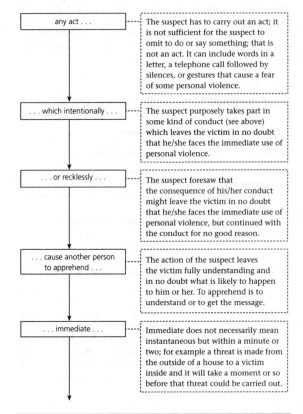

any act . . .	The suspect has to carry out an act; it is not sufficient for the suspect to omit to do or say something; that is not an act. It can include words in a letter, a telephone call followed by silences, or gestures that cause a fear of some personal violence.
. . . which intentionally . . .	The suspect purposely takes part in some kind of conduct (see above) which leaves the victim in no doubt that he/she faces the immediate use of personal violence.
. . . or recklessly . . .	The suspect foresaw that the consequence of his/her conduct might leave the victim in no doubt that he/she faces the immediate use of personal violence, but continued with the conduct for no good reason.
. . . cause another person to apprehend . . .	The action of the suspect leaves the victim fully understanding and in no doubt what is likely to happen to him or her. To apprehend is to understand or to get the message.
. . . immediate . . .	Immediate does not necessarily mean instantaneous but within a minute or two; for example a threat is made from the outside of a house to a victim inside and it will take a moment or so before that threat could be carried out.

5.2.1.9 *GBH with intent*

The full name for this offence is 'wounding or causing grievous bodily harm with intent to do grievous bodily harm or to resist or prevent arrest'.

Section 18 of the Offences Against the Person Act 1861 states it is an offence to:

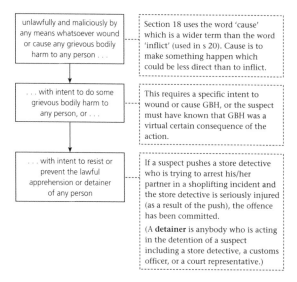

unlawfully and maliciously by any means whatsoever wound or cause any grievous bodily harm to any person . . .	Section 18 uses the word 'cause' which is a wider term than the word 'inflict' (used in s 20). Cause is to make something happen which could be less direct than to inflict.
. . . with intent to do some grievous bodily harm to any person, or . . .	This requires a specific intent to wound or cause GBH, or the suspect must have known that GBH was a virtual certain consequence of the action.
. . . with intent to resist or prevent the lawful apprehension or detainer of any person	If a suspect pushes a store detective who is trying to arrest his/her partner in a shoplifting incident and the store detective is seriously injured (as a result of the push), the offence has been committed. (A **detainer** is anybody who is acting in the detention of a suspect including a store detective, a customs officer, or a court representative.)

The main difference between s 18 and s 20 offences is that s *18 offences have the element of intent* whilst s 20 refers to the offence only as 'malicious'.

This offence is triable on indictment only and the penalty is life imprisonment.

There is no need to include a racially or religiously aggravated offence as the maximum sentence is in any case life imprisonment.

5.2.2 Theft

Theft is a 'volume crime' and likely to be the offence you deal with most commonly. The primary source of legislation relating to theft is to be found in ss 1–6 of the Theft Act 1968. Offences of theft include shoplifting and stealing from an employer, but there are legal complexities surrounding theft and we will examine here only the basic principles involved. It is worth clarifying at this point two particular examples of theft that occur commonly: *robbery* (theft from a person, accompanied by violence or the threat of violence: see 5.2.3 below), and *burglary* (theft or the intention of theft from a building: see 5.2.4).

5.2.2.1 *The definition of theft*

Section 1 of the Theft Act 1968 states that a person is guilty of theft if s/he 'dishonestly [appropriates] property'. We examine in turn each of *dishonesty*, *appropriation*, and *property*.

5.2.2.2 *Dishonesty*

Dishonesty is not defined by the Act, but s 2(1) of the Theft Act 1968 outlines when a person will *not* be treated as dishonest. The person is not acting dishonestly if s/he believes that:

- s/he had the lawful right to take the item (for example, a person mistakenly taking the wrong coat from a changing room, believing it was his or her own)
- s/he would have had the owner's consent if the owner had known of the circumstances, and
- the owner could not have been discovered by taking reasonable steps.

But s 2(2) of the Theft Act 1968 states that a person may be treated as dishonest even though s/he was willing to pay for the property (for instance, where a person wants to buy a particular garden ornament, but the shopkeeper cannot be found, so the person takes the ornament and leaves behind what s/he thinks it is worth in money). In the end, a court must decide whether a person acted dishonestly or not.

5.2.2.3 *Appropriation*

With reference to theft, the term **to appropriate** is given the following meaning in the Theft Act 1968, s 3(1):

- assuming the rights of an owner of property by stealing it (for example, by shoplifting), or
- obtaining property innocently and later keeping it and using it as one's own (for example, hiring a piece of machinery and not returning it).

However, when an innocent purchaser pays the right price to a person who is selling some kind of property which later turns out to be stolen, the innocent purchaser will not have committed theft. For example, if a person buys a second-hand bicycle in good faith and then discovers it is stolen, the innocent purchaser will not have committed theft (s 3(2), Theft Act 1968).

5.2.2.4 *Property*

The definition of **property** (s 4, Theft Act 1968) is not straight-forward. Property includes:

- *money*
- *personal property*, for example personal effects or pets
- *real property*, for example land and things forming part of the land, such as plants and buildings. However, land can only be stolen:
  a) by a *trustee* (someone who has the legal control over the land), for example during its transfer in some kind of a legal process
  b) by *persons who do not own the land*, for example by removing turf, topsoil, or digging up cultivated trees and shrubs
  c) by *tenants*, for example by removing fixtures and fittings
- *things in [an] action*, for example patents, copyrights, and trademarks
- *plants or fungi growing wild*, but only if they are picked for sale, reward, or a commercial purpose (and always consider other legislation that might prohibit such activities, such as the Wildlife and Countryside Act 1981)
- *wild creatures*, but only if they are tamed and have not been lost or abandoned since they were kept in captivity, and
- *tangible property*, for example gas.

    (Note that electricity is not legally property, so it cannot be stolen.)

The offence of theft is triable either way:

- summary: six months' imprisonment and/or a fine
- on indictment: seven years' imprisonment.

5.2.3 **Robbery**

Robbery is *the act of stealing from a person whilst using (or threatening the use of) force or violence*. It is an **aggravated form of the primary offence of theft** and therefore, for robbery to be proved, theft has to be proved first. Robbery is covered in s 8 of the Theft Act 1968.

First, note that a robbery must involve at least one of the following elements:

- force or a threat of force is used on any person, immediately before, or at the time of the theft, or in order to carry out the theft, or

- any person is *'put in fear'* that force will be used to carry out a theft.

There are two main ways of establishing the 'put in fear' element of the offence:

- the victim's statement: the fear of being subjected to force must be genuine: the fear could be evidenced by what s/he saw the suspect do and felt as a result, or
- to seek to put in fear: the state of mind of the offender is what is important, and this could be evidenced from the suspect's statement.

The offence of robbery is defined by s 8(1) of the Theft Act 1968 which states that a person is guilty of robbery if:

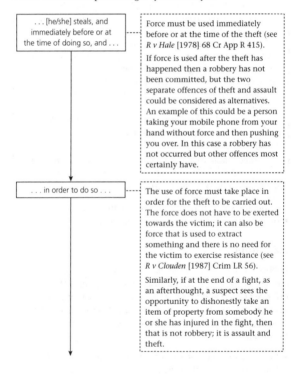

... [he/she] steals, and immediately before or at the time of doing so, and ...

Force must be used immediately before or at the time of the theft (see *R v Hale* [1978] 68 Cr App R 415).

If force is used after the theft has happened then a robbery has not been committed, but the two separate offences of theft and assault could be considered as alternatives. An example of this could be a person taking your mobile phone from your hand without force and then pushing you over. In this case a robbery has not occurred but other offences most certainly have.

... in order to do so ...

The use of force must take place in order for the theft to be carried out. The force does not have to be exerted towards the victim; it can also be force that is used to extract something and there is no need for the victim to exercise resistance (see *R v Clouden* [1987] Crim LR 56).

Similarly, if at the end of a fight, as an afterthought, a suspect sees the opportunity to dishonestly take an item of property from somebody he or she has injured in the fight, then that is not robbery; it is assault and theft.

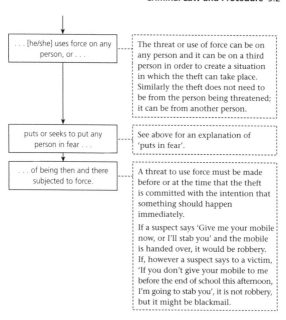

. . . [he/she] uses force on any person, or . . .	The threat or use of force can be on any person and it can be on a third person in order to create a situation in which the theft can take place. Similarly the theft does not need to be from the person being threatened; it can be from another person.
puts or seeks to put any person in fear . . .	See above for an explanation of 'puts in fear'.
. . . of being then and there subjected to force.	A threat to use force must be made before or at the time that the theft is committed with the intention that something should happen immediately. If a suspect says 'Give me your mobile now, or I'll stab you' and the mobile is handed over, it would be robbery. If, however a suspect says to a victim, 'If you don't give your mobile to me before the end of school this afternoon, I'm going to stab you', it is not robbery, but it might be blackmail.

The offence of robbery is triable by indictment only and the maximum penalty is life imprisonment.

5.2.4 Burglary

Despite being a 'volume crime', burglary is a serious offence: aggravated burglary for example, carries a maximum sentence of life imprisonment. There is also the phenomenon of *distraction burglary* (in some forces called 'burglary by artifice'), where entry is gained to the home of a person (usually an elderly person) by an offender pretending to be an official such as the gasman. The criminals usually work in pairs, with one stealing from the household whilst the other 'distracts' the householder.

5.2.4.1 *The basic offence*

The basic offence of burglary is set out in s 9 of the Theft Act 1968 which states that a person is guilty of burglary if:

(a) [s/he] enters any building or part of a building as a trespasser and with intent to commit any such offence as is mentioned in subsection 2 below; or

(b) having entered into any building or part of a building as a trespasser [s/he] steals or attempts to steal anything in the building or that part of it or inflicts or attempts to inflict on any person therein any grievous bodily harm.

The sub-section 2 offences (referred to in the law quoted above) are listed in s 9(2) of the Theft Act 1968. They are:

- 'stealing anything in the building or part of a building in question', or
- 'inflicting on any person therein any grievous bodily harm' (the entry has to be with intent to inflict GBH and thus enough evidence is required to satisfy a charge under s 18 of the Offences Against the Person Act 1861 (see 5.2.1.7 and 5.2.1.9 above), or
- 'doing unlawful damage to the building or anything therein' (see 5.2.7 below and s 9(2) of the Theft Act 1968).

Note that part (a) offences involve a person entering a building with the **intent** to steal or cause injury or damage (but these actions do not actually need to be carried out). For part (b) offences, the theft or injury must be **carried out** or at least attempted.

5.2.4.2 *Part (a) burglary*

Certain terms, such as 'entry', 'building', and 'intent' need to be carefully defined in order to fully appreciate the range of activities that might count as burglary under s 9(1)(a) of the Theft Act 1968.

5.2.4.2.1 Entry as a trespasser

Trespass means entering without the consent of the owner (but see below for further detail). **Entry** can be gained in a number of clearly defined ways:

- *In person*, by walking or climbing into a building, either completely or by inserting a body part (such as an arm or a leg) through a window or letter box. However, there must be more than minimal insertion: sliding a hand between a window and frame from the outside of a building in order to release the catch would be insufficient
- *Using a tool or article* as an extension of the human body to carry out one of the relevant offences. In these circumstances no part of the body needs to be inserted, only the article that

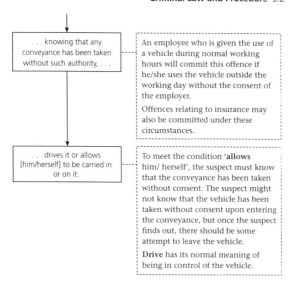

... knowing that any conveyance has been taken without such authority, ...	An employee who is given the use of a vehicle during normal working hours will commit this offence if he/she uses the vehicle outside the working day without the consent of the employer.
	Offences relating to insurance may also be committed under these circumstances.
... drives it or allows [him/herself] to be carried in or on it.	To meet the condition '**allows him/ herself**', the suspect must know that the conveyance has been taken without consent. The suspect might not know that the vehicle has been taken without consent upon entering the conveyance, but once the suspect finds out, there should be some attempt to leave the vehicle.
	Drive has its normal meaning of being in control of the vehicle.

As a possible defence, s 12(6) of the Theft Act 1968 states that a person does not commit this offence if s/he:

1. believes that s/he has the consent of:
   • the owner, or
   • other lawful authority to do it, or
2. mistakenly holds such belief.

This offence is triable summarily and the penalty is six months' imprisonment and/or a fine.

The basic offence of *taking a conveyance* cannot be attempted as the offence is not indictable; more appropriate offences might include vehicle interference or tampering with a motor vehicle. Note that theft is an indictable offence, so the offence of theft could also be considered if some form of attempt has taken place.

5.2.5.1 *Aggravated vehicle-taking*

A further offence may have been committed under s 12A(1) of the Theft Act 1968 if damage or injury is caused when a vehicle is taken without consent. Injuries may also include shock to the person who is attacked. Damage includes any damage caused during the whole incident and does not have to have been deliberately inflicted: it could have been accidental. Note that the damage can be caused to any property including the vehicle itself.

Section 12(A)(1) of the Theft Act 1968 states that a person commits the offence of aggravated vehicle-taking if s/he first of all commits:

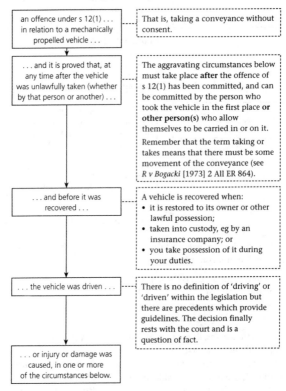

an offence under s 12(1) . . . in relation to a mechanically propelled vehicle . . .	That is, taking a conveyance without consent.
. . . and it is proved that, at any time after the vehicle was unlawfully taken (whether by that person or another) . . .	The aggravating circumstances below must take place **after** the offence of s 12(1) has been committed, and can be committed by the person who took the vehicle in the first place **or other person(s)** who allow themselves to be carried in or on it. Remember that the term taking or takes means that there must be some movement of the conveyance (see *R v Bogacki* [1973] 2 All ER 864).
. . . and before it was recovered . . .	A vehicle is recovered when: • it is restored to its owner or other lawful possession; • taken into custody, eg by an insurance company; or • you take possession of it during your duties.
. . . the vehicle was driven . . .	There is no definition of 'driving' or 'driven' within the legislation but there are precedents which provide guidelines. The decision finally rests with the court and is a question of fact.
. . . or injury or damage was caused, in one or more of the circumstances below.	

The aggravating circumstances for this offence are that:

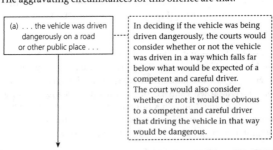

(a) . . . the vehicle was driven dangerously on a road or other public place . . .	In deciding if the vehicle was being driven dangerously, the courts would consider whether or not the vehicle was driven in a way which falls far below what would be expected of a competent and careful driver. The court would also consider whether or not it would be obvious to a competent and careful driver that driving the vehicle in that way would be dangerous.

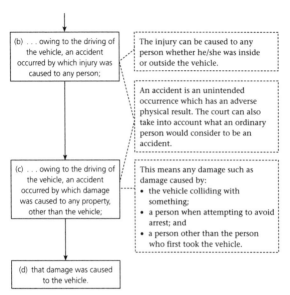

(b) . . . owing to the driving of the vehicle, an accident occurred by which injury was caused to any person;

The injury can be caused to any person whether he/she was inside or outside the vehicle.

An accident is an unintended occurrence which has an adverse physical result. The court can also take into account what an ordinary person would consider to be an accident.

(c) . . . owing to the driving of the vehicle, an accident occurred by which damage was caused to any property, other than the vehicle;

This means any damage such as damage caused by:
• the vehicle colliding with something;
• a person when attempting to avoid arrest; and
• a person other than the person who first took the vehicle.

(d) that damage was caused to the vehicle.

This offence is triable either way:

• summary: six months' imprisonment and/or a fine
• on indictment: two years' imprisonment and/or a fine.

If the accident (under s 12A(2)(b)) caused death, the penalty is 14 years' imprisonment.

5.2.6 Unlawful possession of a controlled drug

The most important piece of legislation available to the police in countering the street-level use and distribution of illegal drugs is s 5(2) of the Misuse of Drugs Act 1971. Drugs that are subject to legal control are referred to as **controlled drugs**. Some controlled drugs are addictive and/or dangerous. Unless you have a great deal of experience in relation to controlled drugs, recognizing them is very difficult as they may appear in many different forms, shapes, colours, and sizes including pills, tablets, liquids, powders, and resins. Therefore, your first thoughts when finding substances without pharmaceutical company packaging, should be to *suspect that the person might be in possession of controlled drugs*.

Many crimes are linked to drug-related activities, so you will frequently be faced with such situations. Remember, you must assess risk and hazard levels carefully when dealing with people who have been taking drugs as they may behave unpredictably. Always be prepared to use your personal protection equipment (PPE); remember too the possible consequences of contamination from bodily fluids or equipment used by a drug addict. *The merest micro-cut from a sharp article contaminated by a transferable virus could infect you and cause a serious illness.*

5.2.6.1 *What is a controlled drug?*

Drugs are controlled because of their effect on the human body, and are divided into classes A, B, and C (Misuse of Drugs Act 1971) according to the potential for harm they are thought to present to individuals and to society at large:

Table 5.1: Some of the more common controlled drugs

Class A	eg Ecstasy, Heroin, Cocaine, Crack Cocaine, 'Magic Mushrooms' (containing Psilocin), and LSD
Class B	eg cannabis leaves, cannabis resin, 'skunk,'[2] amphetamines, and barbiturates
Class C	eg tranquilizers (such as Temazepan), some painkillers, and gamma hydroxybutyrate (GHB)

You will find a full list of controlled drugs by accessing the website <http://www.drugs.gov.uk>.

5.2.6.2 *Unlawful possession*

As a Special Constable, the most common offence that you will deal with in relation to the misuse of drugs is that of **unlawful possession**.

It is an offence under s 5(2) Misuse of Drugs Act for a person unlawfully to:

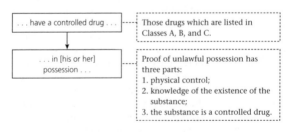

. . . have a controlled drug . . .	Those drugs which are listed in Classes A, B, and C.
. . . in [his or her] possession . . .	Proof of unlawful possession has three parts: 1. physical control; 2. knowledge of the existence of the substance; 3. the substance is a controlled drug.

5.2.6.3 *The three parts of the proof for unlawful possession*

The following are the three parts required for proof of unlawful possession of a controlled drug ('part' is our own term, not that of the law):

Table 5.2: The three parts of the proof for unlawful possession

Part 1—Physical control	The drug must be in the physical control of the suspect and the suspect must know where the drug is, though it does not have to be on his or her person. For example, if a suspect keeps drugs in a lock-up garage and gives the keys to an innocent person, the drugs remain in the suspect's control and possession, but in the custody of the innocent person. However, if two people use a car and they both store drugs that they use in the glove compartment, they both *possess* the drugs.
Part 2—Knowledge of the existence of the substance	What is important is that the suspect knows of, or suspects the existence of, the substance in question. If the substance was in a small tin, for example, you must show that the suspect knew that the tin contained a substance. It does not matter whether or not the suspect knows if the substance is a controlled drug.
Part 3—The substance is a controlled drug	The drug must be a controlled drug in Class A, B, or C (see above, 5.2.6.1).

5.2.6.4 *Defences to unlawful possession of a controlled drug*

Section 28 of the Misuse of Drugs Act 1971 provides a suspect with a potential defence in terms of satisfying Part 1 together with either Part 2 or Part 3 as described earlier. The flow charts below provide more explanation of the ways each part could be used in defence.

Part 1, remember, is about the suspect having *physical control* of the drug. His/her defence could be that s/he did not have possession of it.

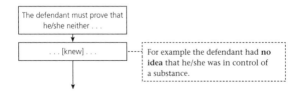

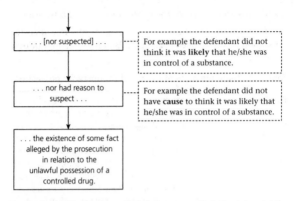

For example, if a package containing controlled drugs is mistakenly delivered to a person's home, so long as the package has not been requested by the homeowner, s/he can claim s/he does not possess the drugs.

In addition to Part 1, *either* Part 2 *or* Part 3 must be satisfied as part of the defence.

Part 2 is about the defendant's *knowledge about the substance*. A defence could be that s/he did not *believe, suspect* or have *reason to suspect* that the substance was a controlled drug.

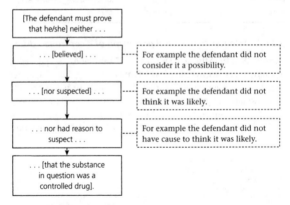

Part 3 is about the substance being a *controlled drug*. A defence could be that the defendant believed it was a drug s/he was lawfully entitled to possess:

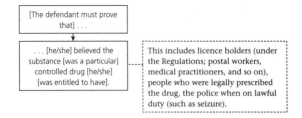

[The defendant must prove that] . . .

. . . [he/she] believed the substance [was a particular] controlled drug [he/she] [was entitled to have].

This includes licence holders (under the Regulations; postal workers, medical practitioners, and so on), people who were legally prescribed the drug, the police when on lawful duty (such as seizure).

5.2.6.5 *Mode of trial and penalty for unlawful possession of drugs offences*

Offences involving *class A drugs* are triable either way and the penalty is:

- summary: six months' imprisonment and/or prescribed fine
- on indictment: seven years' imprisonment and/or fine.

Offences involving *class B drugs* are triable either way and the penalty is:

- summary: three months' imprisonment and/or fine
- on indictment: five years' imprisonment and/or fine.

Under the Criminal Justice and Police Act 2001, unlawful possession of cannabis can also be dealt with by way of a PND for £80 (see 5.3.4 below).

Offences involving *class C drugs* are triable either way and the penalty is:

- summary: three months' imprisonment and/or fine
- on indictment: two years' imprisonment and/or fine.

5.2.6.6 *Unlawful possession of cannabis*

During the last decade, cannabis was initially reclassified to class C but more recently (2009) has been returned to class B.[3] With the aim of providing a consistent national approach during these periods of change, ACPO has produced guidance including various models of intervention for unlawful possession of cannabis. ACPO recommends that the term 'Cannabis Warning' is used (rather than 'Street Warning') and a typical format for the warning is given below.

5.2.6.7 *Intervention model for the unlawful possession of cannabis*

The ACPO guidance provides you with an opportunity to give a justifiable and proportionate response, and aims to send out a message that cannabis remains harmful and illegal. Three levels of escalating intervention are provided for, but the guidance emphasizes that, although your discretion can be used at all times, arrest remains your first presumption:

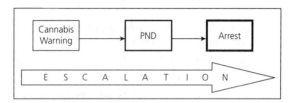

Figure 5.1: Intervention model for the unlawful possession of cannabis

The model only applies to a person who is:

- aged 18 years or over
- not vulnerable
- competent enough to grasp the meaning of your questions and his/her replies
- not under the influence of alcohol or drugs at the time a warning or PND is issued
- in possession of an amount of cannabis suitable for personal use only, and
- verifiable in relation to his or her personal details, such as name, date of birth and address.

For a 'Cannabis Warning' s/he must also be willing to admit the offence.

Suspects aged 17 years and under cannot be issued with a Cannabis Warning or a PND for unlawful possession of cannabis. They will have to be dealt with by way of reprimand, final warning, or prosecution.

5.2.6.8 *Aggravating factors*

These must be taken into consideration when deciding which option to take in the intervention model. If, for example, there are no aggravating factors, then a Cannabis Warning is the likely outcome; however if one or more aggravating factors are present, a Special Constable should use his or her discretion to decide whether to issue a PND or make an arrest.

Aggravating factors include a suspect who:

- was smoking cannabis in a public place or in the view of the public, eg at a sports ground, on a bus, near a pub, or on educational premises
- is a repeat offender (other criminal offences) or someone who continually engages in anti-social behaviour, or
- appears not to recognize the seriousness of possessing cannabis.

The location where the person is found to be in possession of cannabis may also be an aggravating factor, for example:

- previously identified 'hot spots' for anti-social behaviour due to cannabis use, eg shopping centres, street corners, parks, and shops, or
- schools, playgrounds, or youth clubs—places where young people might come into contact with cannabis users.

Cannabis warnings can only be issued when there are no aggravating factors (see above), and only to a person who is compliant with the procedure and:

- has no previous records of Cannabis Warnings, PNDs, or convictions, and
- is not listed on police intelligence records as a persistent offender.

There is no formal wording for a Cannabis Warning: you might say that it will:

- be recorded by you and will be added to local police databases for future reference
- produce a record of a detected crime for the purposes of statistics as a recordable crime
- not amount to a criminal record or conviction against him or her, and
- lead to the issuing of a PND or arrest if s/he is found in unlawful possession of cannabis in the future.

A PND (see 5.3.4 below) must be issued or the suspect arrested if s/he has previously received either:

- a Cannabis Warning after 26 January 2009 (you can either issue a PND or arrest the suspect), or
- a PND—your only option is to arrest (even if s/he has not received a Cannabis Warning previously).

5.2.6.9 *Unlawful possession of small amounts of cannabis: practical aspects*

For suspects unlawfully in possession of small amounts of cannabis you should:

1. Investigate the suspected unlawful possession, remembering your obligations under the PACE Codes of Practice to protect the rights of the individual (see 4.5.1 above), and determine if there is:
   • any lawful excuse (see 5.2.6.2–5.2.6.4 above), or
   • evidence of a further offence such as intent to supply.
2. Seize the cannabis (see 4.5.4 above) and secure it according to your local policy.
3. Record the incident contemporaneously in your PNB (see 4.5.5 above).
4. Manage the recorded information effectively, remembering to complete stop and search forms (see 4.4.1 above), intelligence, and crime reports.
5. Any arrest you make must be necessary (see 4.5.3 above).

5.2.7 Damage to property

The kind of criminal damage that you will meet as a Special Constable is commonly graffiti and minor damage to fences, cars, and bus shelters. Occasionally, the damage can be more serious, when, for example, the damage has been caused by fire (arson).

Section 1(1) of the Criminal Damage Act 1971 states that an offence is committed by:

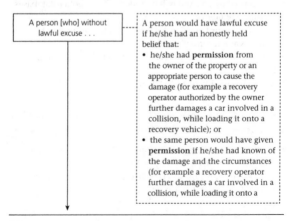

A person [who] without lawful excuse . . .

A person would have lawful excuse if he/she had an honestly held belief that:
• he/she had **permission** from the owner of the property or an appropriate person to cause the damage (for example a recovery operator authorized by the owner further damages a car involved in a collision, while loading it onto a recovery vehicle); or
• the same person would have given **permission** if he/she had known of the damage and the circumstances (for example a recovery operator further damages a car involved in a collision, while loading it onto a

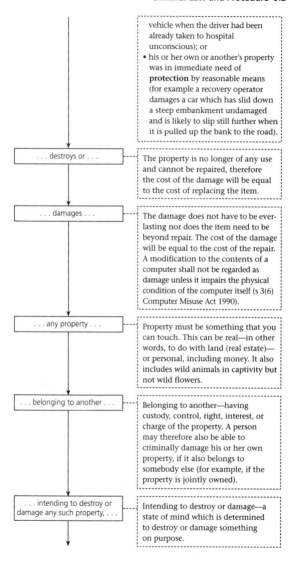

vehicle when the driver had been already taken to hospital unconscious); or
• his or her own or another's property was in immediate need of **protection** by reasonable means (for example a recovery operator damages a car which has slid down a steep embankment undamaged and is likely to slip still further when it is pulled up the bank to the road).

. . . destroys or . . .

The property is no longer of any use and cannot be repaired, therefore the cost of the damage will be equal to the cost of replacing the item.

. . . damages . . .

The damage does not have to be ever-lasting nor does the item need to be beyond repair. The cost of the damage will be equal to the cost of the repair. A modification to the contents of a computer shall not be regarded as damage unless it impairs the physical condition of the computer itself (s 3(6) Computer Misuse Act 1990).

. . . any property . . .

Property must be something that you can touch. This can be real—in other words, to do with land (real estate)—or personal, including money. It also includes wild animals in captivity but not wild flowers.

. . . belonging to another . . .

Belonging to another—having custody, control, right, interest, or charge of the property. A person may therefore also be able to criminally damage his or her own property, if it also belongs to somebody else (for example, if the property is jointly owned).

. . . intending to destroy or damage any such property, . . .

Intending to destroy or damage—a state of mind which is determined to destroy or damage something on purpose.

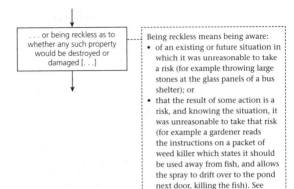

. . . or being reckless as to whether any such property would be destroyed or damaged [. . .]

Being reckless means being aware:
- of an existing or future situation in which it was unreasonable to take a risk (for example throwing large stones at the glass panels of a bus shelter); or
- that the result of some action is a risk, and knowing the situation, it was unreasonable to take that risk (for example a gardener reads the instructions on a packet of weed killer which states it should be used away from fish, and allows the spray to drift over to the pond next door, killing the fish). See *R v G and G* [2003] UKHL 50.

This offence is triable either way and the penalty is:

- summary: six months' imprisonment and/or a fine
- on indictment: ten years' imprisonment.

Note that if the value of the property damaged or destroyed is less than £5,000, the offence is tried summarily only (s 22, Magistrates' Courts Act 1980) but it still remains an 'either-way' offence.

5.2.8 Fraud offences

Much of the modern law surrounding the crime of fraud is in the Fraud Act 2006, which came into effect in January 2007. Given how recent the law is, there are as yet few precedents to help with a deeper understanding of some parts of the new fraud legislation. For example, it might well be that an intention to carry out a 'phishing' crime could be prosecuted as a s 2 offence but this has not yet been tested.

Section 1 of the Fraud Act 2006 states that the offence of fraud can be committed in one or more of three distinctive ways:

1. by **false representation**, eg returning stolen goods to a shop to try to obtain a refund (s 2, Fraud Act 2006)
2. by **failing to disclose information** such as omitting important information when applying for a job or health insurance (s 3, Fraud Act 2006)
3. through **abuse of position**, for example where the driver of a local authority mini-bus demands fares from local residents when the service is actually free (s 4, Fraud Act 2006).

5.2.8.1 *False representation*

Section 2 Fraud Act 2006 states that a person commits an offence if s/he:

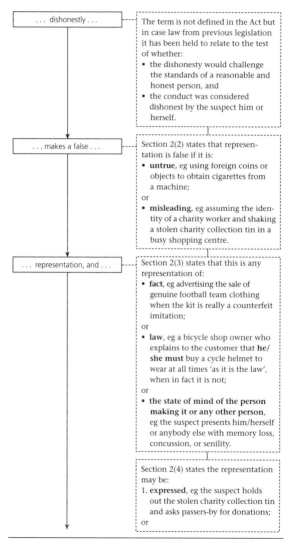

. . . dishonestly . . .

The term is not defined in the Act but in case law from previous legislation it has been held to relate to the test of whether:
- the dishonesty would challenge the standards of a reasonable and honest person, and
- the conduct was considered dishonest by the suspect him or herself.

. . . makes a false . . .

Section 2(2) states that representation is false if it is:
- **untrue**, eg using foreign coins or objects to obtain cigarettes from a machine;

or
- **misleading**, eg assuming the identity of a charity worker and shaking a stolen charity collection tin in a busy shopping centre.

. . . representation, and . . .

Section 2(3) states that this is any representation of:
- **fact**, eg advertising the sale of genuine football team clothing when the kit is really a counterfeit imitation;

or
- **law**, eg a bicycle shop owner who explains to the customer that **he/she must** buy a cycle helmet to wear at all times 'as it is the law', when in fact it is not;

or
- **the state of mind of the person making it or any other person**, eg the suspect presents him/herself or anybody else with memory loss, concussion, or senility.

Section 2(4) states the representation may be:
1. **expressed**, eg the suspect holds out the stolen charity collection tin and asks passers-by for donations;

or

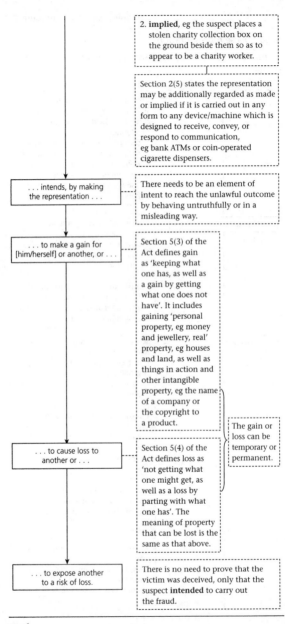

2. **implied**, eg the suspect places a stolen charity collection box on the ground beside them so as to appear to be a charity worker.

Section 2(5) states the representation may be additionally regarded as made or implied if it is carried out in any form to any device/machine which is designed to receive, convey, or respond to communication, eg bank ATMs or coin-operated cigarette dispensers.

... intends, by making the representation ...

There needs to be an element of intent to reach the unlawful outcome by behaving untruthfully or in a misleading way.

... to make a gain for [him/herself] or another, or ...

Section 5(3) of the Act defines gain as 'keeping what one has, as well as a gain by getting what one does not have'. It includes gaining 'personal property, eg money and jewellery, real' property, eg houses and land, as well as things in action and other intangible property, eg the name of a company or the copyright to a product.

The gain or loss can be temporary or permanent.

... to cause loss to another or ...

Section 5(4) of the Act defines loss as 'not getting what one might get, as well as a loss by parting with what one has'. The meaning of property that can be lost is the same as that above.

... to expose another to a risk of loss.

There is no need to prove that the victim was deceived, only that the suspect **intended** to carry out the fraud.

5.2.8.2 *Failure to disclose information*

Section 3 of the Fraud Act 2006 states that a person commits an offence if s/he:

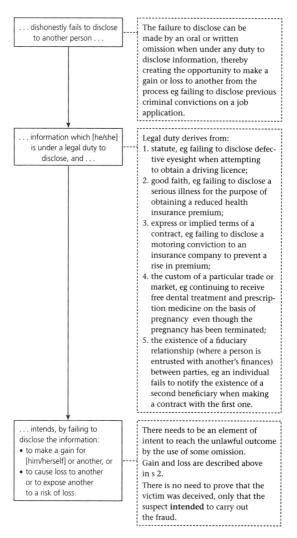

... dishonestly fails to disclose to another person ...

The failure to disclose can be made by an oral or written omission when under any duty to disclose information, thereby creating the opportunity to make a gain or loss to another from the process eg failing to disclose previous criminal convictions on a job application.

... information which [he/she] is under a legal duty to disclose, and ...

Legal duty derives from:
1. statute, eg failing to disclose defective eyesight when attempting to obtain a driving licence;
2. good faith, eg failing to disclose a serious illness for the purpose of obtaining a reduced health insurance premium;
3. express or implied terms of a contract, eg failing to disclose a motoring conviction to an insurance company to prevent a rise in premium;
4. the custom of a particular trade or market, eg continuing to receive free dental treatment and prescription medicine on the basis of pregnancy even though the pregnancy has been terminated;
5. the existence of a fiduciary relationship (where a person is entrusted with another's finances) between parties, eg an individual fails to notify the existence of a second beneficiary when making a contract with the first one.

... intends, by failing to disclose the information:
• to make a gain for [him/herself] or another, or
• to cause loss to another or to expose another to a risk of loss.

There needs to be an element of intent to reach the unlawful outcome by the use of some omission.
Gain and loss are described above in s 2.
There is no need to prove that the victim was deceived, only that the suspect **intended** to carry out the fraud.

5.2.8.3 *Abuse of position*

Section 4 of the Fraud Act 2006 states that a person commits an offence if s/he occupies a position in which s/he:

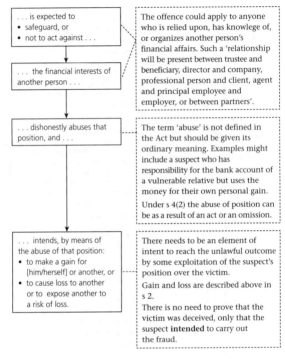

. . . is expected to
• safeguard, or
• not to act against . . .

. . . the financial interests of another person . . .

The offence could apply to anyone who is relied upon, has knowlege of, or organizes another person's financial affairs. Such a 'relationship will be present between trustee and beneficiary, director and company, professional person and client, agent and principal employee and employer, or between partners'.

. . . dishonestly abuses that position, and . . .

The term 'abuse' is not defined in the Act but should be given its ordinary meaning. Examples might include a suspect who has responsibility for the bank account of a vulnerable relative but uses the money for their own personal gain.
Under s 4(2) the abuse of position can be as a result of an act or an omission.

. . . intends, by means of the abuse of that position:
• to make a gain for [him/herself] or another, or
• to cause loss to another or to expose another to a risk of loss.

There needs to be an element of intent to reach the unlawful outcome by some exploitation of the suspect's position over the victim.
Gain and loss are described above in s 2.
There is no need to prove that the victim was deceived, only that the suspect **intended** to carry out the fraud.

This offence is triable either way and the penalty is:

• summary: 12 months imprisonment and/or a fine
• on indictment: ten years imprisonment and/or a fine.

Section 7 of the Fraud Act 2006 states that a person commits an offence if s/he:

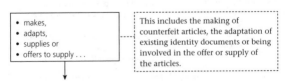

• makes,
• adapts,
• supplies or
• offers to supply . . .

This includes the making of counterfeit articles, the adaptation of existing identity documents or being involved in the offer or supply of the articles.

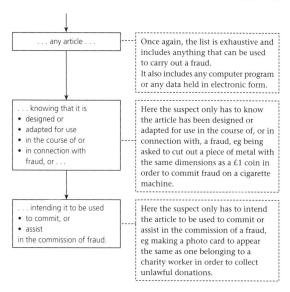

Under s 1 of the PACE Act 1984, you have the power to search for articles made or adapted for use in fraud (see 4.4.1 above).

This offence is triable either way and the penalty is:

- summary: 12 months' imprisonment and/or a fine
- on indictment: ten years' imprisonment and/or a fine.

5.2.8.4 *Fraudulent obtaining of services*

Where a service has been provided, such as a taxi ride or a stay in a hotel room, there is no gain or loss of property, only the provision of a facility or service. For this reason, an additional offence is provided for by the Fraud Act 2006 when *a service is obtained by dishonest means*.

Section 11 of the Fraud Act 2006 states that a person commits an offence if s/he:

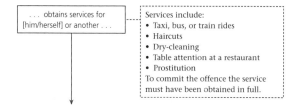

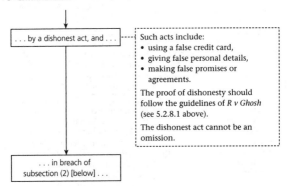

... by a dishonest act, and ...

Such acts include:
- using a false credit card,
- giving false personal details,
- making false promises or agreements.

The proof of dishonesty should follow the guidelines of *R v Ghosh* (see 5.2.8.1 above).

The dishonest act cannot be an omission.

... in breach of subsection (2) [below] ...

Section 11(2) of the Fraud Act 2006 states that a person obtains services in breach of this subsection if:

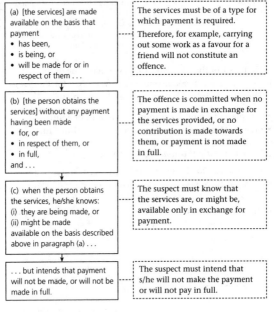

(a) [the services] are made available on the basis that payment
- has been,
- is being, or
- will be made for or in respect of them ...

The services must be of a type for which payment is required.

Therefore, for example, carrying out some work as a favour for a friend will not constitute an offence.

(b) [the person obtains the services] without any payment having been made
- for, or
- in respect of them, or
- in full,
and ...

The offence is committed when no payment is made in exchange for the services provided, or no contribution is made towards them, or payment is not made in full.

(c) when the person obtains the services, he/she knows:
(i) they are being made, or
(ii) might be made
available on the basis described above in paragraph (a) ...

The suspect must know that the services are, or might be, available only in exchange for payment.

... but intends that payment will not be made, or will not be made in full.

The suspect must intend that s/he will not make the payment or will not pay in full.

This offence is triable either way and the penalty is:

- summary: 12 months' imprisonment and/or a fine
- on indictment: five years' imprisonment and/or a fine.

5.2.8.5 *Making off without payment ('bilking')*

If no fraud is practised but goods are still obtained dishonestly and without payment, it is an offence under s 3 of the Theft Act 1978 rather than fraud under s 1 of the Fraud Act 2006. This particular offence is often referred to as **'bilking'**. For example, a person might fill up with petrol on the forecourt of a filling station, but on seeing the staff otherwise engaged and no other customers around, decide to drive off without paying.

Note that this offence only applies if 'payment on the spot' is the norm in that particular situation, such as collecting goods on which work has been done (for example, shoe repairs) or paying for a service which has been provided (for example, a haircut). This offence does not cover circumstances in which a customer has a credit arrangement or a 'tab' with the service provider.

This offence is triable either way and the penalty is:

- summary: six months' imprisonment and/or a fine
- on indictment: two years' imprisonment and/or a fine.

5.3 **Criminal Investigation**

5.3.1 **Interviewing**

Interviewing witnesses, victims, and suspects may be a core part of your role as a Special Constable in investigations, or something which you do periodically. Whether a frequent part of your duties or a rare episode, it is an important police investigative activity because *interviewing is the way to obtain evidence or information in relation to something that has happened* (which might or might not be a crime). Interviews are the best ways to obtain accurate information from suspects, victims, or witnesses in order to discover the truth about matters which you are investigating as a police officer. We have space to visit the principles of interviewing only briefly.

5.3.1.1 *Obtaining initial accounts*

You need to ask a few preliminary questions to determine whether anyone present could reasonably be suspected to have been involved in a criminal offence, based upon your initial appraisal of the situation. If this initial assessment provides you with 'reasonable grounds for suspicion' that a person has been involved in a criminal offence, you should caution him/her at this stage (see 4.5.1 above for further details) before asking any further questions.

Any conversation that takes place before a caution is given should be summarized in your PNB, as the court may take this into consideration. The PACE Act Codes of Practice do not affect your ability to speak to or question a person in the ordinary course of your duties (PACE Act Code of Practice A, Note 1). This Note explains that, when trying to discover whether, or by whom, an offence has been committed, *you may question any person from whom useful information might be obtained*. Once a decision has been made to arrest a suspect, s/he cannot be interviewed about the offence except at a police station (Code C 11.1), unless the delay would irretrievably hinder the investigation.

Another priority is to identify possible witnesses. You need to exercise judgement in establishing who was a **material witness** to the event (who actually saw it) and who was not; and eliminate from your enquiries anyone not directly involved, or who did not see what happened. This is not as easy as it sounds: people can become over-excited when they think they have witnessed a crime and will be keen to give you their (possibly derivative) account.

The most beneficial way of using witness evidence is to ask him/her to explain to you what s/he saw, in the presence and hearing of the suspect(s), and record in your PNB exactly what the witness says. You will then be able to use your record as evidence in court, because it contains what was originally said by a witness in the presence and hearing of the accused.

Remember, too, that you need to think about compliance with the Criminal Procedures and Investigation Act 1996 (CPIA) because there have been occasions when Special Constables have not recorded 'relevant material', to the detriment of the prosecution or defence of the suspects. You must make sure that you have recorded in your PNB information about *all* the witnesses, and any actions, statements, comments, or other relevant material. It might not be used by the defence, *but it could be*. We look at the need to 'record, retain and reveal' in 5.3.2 below.

Legislation such as the PACE Act 1984 has helped to reassure the public, the courts, and the police themselves that interviewing is now more tightly controlled, more ethical, and often more effective. However, the crucial question remains *whether the evidence obtained from interviewing will stand up to scrutiny in court*, and that question should perhaps be at the forefront of your mind during an interview.

It might help you to have copies of the PACE Act 1984 and the Criminal Justice and Public Order Act (CJPOA) 1994; available from <http://www.opsi.gov.uk/legislation/about_legislation> by following the relevant links.

5.3.1.2 *The 'PEACE' approach to Interviewing*

To assist Special Constables and regular officers with structuring interviews, police forces have adopted the '**PEACE**' approach. PEACE is an acronym which stands for:

P	Planning and **P** Preparation
E	Engage and **E** Explain
A	Account, Clarify, and Challenge
C	Closure
E	Evaluation

You will often hear the process referred to in your force as the 'PEACE interview'.

The key points to consider are:

• *your objectives* (focus on what you hope to achieve and how you intend to achieve it—remember, the aim is to establish the truth)
• *the relevant law* (research the law and recent stated cases)
• *possible defences* (consider coercion, duress, self-defence)
• *possible mitigating and aggravating factors*, and
• *pre-interview disclosure.* (consider what you should tell legal representatives)

5.3.1.3 *PEACE—planning and preparation*

One of the first things you need to decide is what potential offence(s) you are investigating. You should consult the relevant legislation and work out what you need to know. Once you have information such as witness statements and any other available evidence, you will be able to decide what contribution the interview is going to make to your investigation. Remember that, if an offence has actually occurred, you have to prove the existence of:

1. **Criminal intent** (*mens rea*): What was in the suspect's mind at the time? Why did s/he commit the offence?
2. **Criminal action** (*actus reus*): What did he/she actually do? How did s/he do it?

An interview should plan and explore these aspects carefully. The suspect might be guilty or, if the course of the interview suggests otherwise, a 'refused charge' might be the outcome.

5.3.1.4 *PEACE—account, clarify, and challenge*

This is the main part of the interview. In the following order you should:

- *Seek a 'free' account*, without any interruption from you if possible
- *Develop the account* by moving systematically from one phase to another, clarifying or seeking greater detail. You may need to bear in mind *Turnbull* and the ADVOKATE checklist (see 4.3.6 above)
- *Summarize the account* and then select topics that are checkable for examination in greater detail. Does the account make chronological sense? Are there gaps?
- *Seek new/additional information* and summarize each topic with commitment and agreement if possible
- *Clarify and challenge* but restrict your challenges to inconsistencies and checkable, admissible facts. When challenging, do not criticize or accuse—instead ask for explanation, especially where discrepancies emerge.

5.3.1.5 *Interviews with suspects*

A suspect interview is defined as '*the questioning of a person regarding* [his or her] *involvement or suspected involvement in a criminal offence or offences which must be carried out under caution*' (PACE Code of Practice C 11.1A). This definition covers any conversation (no matter how short, and wherever it takes place) once a caution has been given, and whether the suspect has been arrested or not is irrelevant.

For further detail on the conducting of interviews see Bryants *et al* (2010).

5.3.1.6 *The role of the defence solicitor*

The PACE Act 1984 Codes of Practice Code C, Note 6D states that:

> The solicitor's only role in the police station is to protect and advance the legal rights of his client. On occasions this may require the solicitor to give advice which has the effect of his client avoiding giving evidence which strengthens the prosecution case.

A 'duty solicitor' comes from a retained panel of solicitors available to advise arrested people who do not have a solicitor of their own (or, if they do, that person is not available for the interview). Duty solicitors provide 'free and independent legal advice' (FILA) and advise their clients independently of the police and the PPS. The defence solicitor is obliged to prevent his/her client from further assisting the police by way of self-incrimination, if that is not in the client's interest. It is sometimes difficult for a new Special Constable to accept that a solicitor's advice can stop a suspect giving details about a crime, or admitting to committing a crime. Indeed, more experienced police officers may also argue that there is not a 'level playing field' with the accused. However, a jury may form an adverse interpretation from a suspect's silence in the face of reasonable questioning, where that suspect relies on evidence in court which s/he could have provided earlier (NB the caution).

5.3.2 Record, Retain, Reveal, and Disclose

Here we look at the need to 'record, retain, and reveal' information that you gather in the course of your duties as a Special Constable. The 'revealed' material is considered by the PPS, who then decide which parts of it should be *disclosed* to the defence. You should be aware that, although this process involves ' "revealing" to the PPS and "disclosing" to the defence' (*two completely separate processes*), *both* are often referred to as 'disclosure'. The legislation around disclosure is complex.

In general terms, all police officers have a responsibility to record and retain *relevant material* obtained or generated, either through their own efforts or through those of others, during the course of the investigation, even if it is not subsequently used by the prosecution ('unused evidence'). If this is not recorded, recorded wrongly, or not retained, then it is 'lost' to the defence, and hence has not been properly shared with them through the PPS. This could be a serious loophole that the defence may exploit.

You will need to identify and record all 'relevant material'. These last two words have a precise meaning in law and it is important to note that **relevant material** has a much wider meaning than, for example, the term 'evidential material':

• **material** refers to information and objects obtained in the course of a criminal investigation, and includes written materials, videotapes, audiotapes, and information given in speech

- these materials are **relevant** when they have a bearing on any offence under investigation, or any person being investigated, or on the surrounding circumstances of the case
- **unused material** is 'material that may be relevant to the investigation that has been retained but does not form part of the case for the prosecution against the accused'.

It may be difficult to recognize whether materials are relevant. However, you will often need to make such a decision very quickly. You should also note that the responsibility to record and retain relevant material does not relate just to prosecution material, but also to any material which might assist the defence (see above).

What follows is more detailed guidance for you in terms of the relevance, recording, and retaining of material in the course of your initial investigation of a crime, or arising from being an officer involved in a response to an incident. We call this the '3 Rs': **Record, Retain, and Reveal** (this is an approach common in national police training). The information presented here is drawn largely (but not exclusively) from the CPIA 1996 and its associated Code of Practice.

5.3.2.1 *The importance of 'record' and 'retain': 'record'*

It is the responsibility of the officer in charge of the investigation to ensure that the material is **recorded** in a durable or retrievable form, for instance in writing, on video- or audiotape, or on computer disc.

The following is a list of materials which you and colleagues are routinely required to record and retain, as described in paragraph 5.4 of the CPIA Code of Practice:

1. *Crime reports* (including crime report forms, relevant parts of incident report books, and your PNB)
2. *Custody records*
3. Records which are derived from *tapes of telephone messages* (for example, 999 calls) containing descriptions of an alleged offence or offender
4. *Final versions of witnesses' statements* (and draft versions where their content differs from the final version), including any exhibits mentioned (unless these have been returned to their owner on the understanding that they will be produced in court if required)
5. *Interview records* (written records, or audio- or videotapes, of interviews with actual or potential witnesses or suspects)

5.3.3 **Penalty Notices**

These provide offenders with an opportunity to pay a fine for an offence without going to court. Fixed Penalty Notices (FPNs) were introduced for motoring and road traffic offences. Following their success, the Penalty Notice for Disorder (PND) scheme was introduced (ss 1 to 11 of the Criminal Justice and Police Act 2001).[5]

The key aims and objectives of penalty notice schemes are to reduce the amount of time that police officers spend completing paperwork and attending court, to reduce the burden on the courts, to increase the amount of time officers spend on the street dealing with more serious crime, and to deliver swift, simple, and effective justice that carries a deterrent effect. Under the Criminal Justice and Police Act 2001 the following procedures are adopted:

1. If you have reason to believe that a person has committed a penalty offence, you may give that person a penalty notice for that offence (see your local policy for the minimum age of the recipient).
2. The notice may be issued either:
   • on the spot by an officer in uniform, or
   • at a police station by an authorized officer (in the majority of cases, this takes place in the custody area of a police station, by the custody officer, after the person has been investigated).
3. The issue of a penalty notice gives the recipient the opportunity to pay the penalty, in order to discharge liability to conviction for the offence.
4. Once the notice has been issued, the recipient may elect to either:
   • pay the penalty, or
   • request a court hearing.
   • S/he must do one or the other within 21 days of the date of issue.
5. Failure to undertake either option may result in:
   • the registration of a fine of one-and-a-half times the penalty amount as a fine against the recipient, or
   • court proceedings against him/her.

Note to avoid confusion

The PND scheme involves fixed penalties. The term 'Fixed Penalty Notice'(FPN) is normally reserved for use in motoring offences, but the Anti-Social Behaviour Act 2003 also provides for local authority personnel and PCSOs to issue penalty notices (also known as FPNs) for graffiti, littering, and other minor disorder offences.

5.3.3.1 Offences included in the PND scheme for which the penalty is £80

The table below summarizes which offences may be dealt with under the PND scheme by an £80 fine for those aged 16 years and over. For the same offence committed by 10–15 year-olds, the fine is £40.

Table 5.4: Offences included in the PND scheme for which the penalty is £80

Offence	Legislation
Wasting police time/giving false report	Criminal Law Act 1967, s 5(2)
Using public electronic communications network in order to cause annoyance, inconvenience, or needless anxiety	Communications Act 2003, s 127(2)
Knowingly giving a false alarm to a person acting on behalf of a fire and rescue authority	Fire and Rescue Services Act 2004, s 49 (England only) Fire Services Act 1947, s 31 (Wales only)
Causing harassment, alarm, or distress	Public Order Act 1986, s 5
Throwing fireworks	Explosives Act 1875, s 80
Drunk and disorderly	Criminal Justice Act 1967, s 91
Selling alcohol to person under 18 (anywhere)	Licensing Act 2003, s 146(1)
Supply of alcohol by or on behalf of a club to a person aged under 18	Licensing Act 2003, s 146(3)
Selling alcohol to a drunken person	Licensing Act 2003, s 141
Purchasing or attempting to purchase alcohol on behalf of a person under 18 (includes licensed premises and off-licences)	Licensing Act 2003, s 149(3)
Purchase of alcohol for consumption in licensed premises by person under 18	Licensing Act 2003, s 149(4)
Delivery of alcohol to under 18 or allowing such delivery	Licensing Act 2003, s 151
Destroying or damaging property valued at less than £500	Criminal Damage Act 1971, s 1(1)
Unlawful possession of cannabis and its derivatives	Misuse of Drugs Act 1971, s 5(2)
Theft (retail) valued at less than £200	Theft Act 1968, s 1

Offence	Legislation
Breach of fireworks curfew (2300–0700 hours)	Reg 7 of the Firework Regulations 2004 (Fireworks Act 2003, s 11)
Possession of a category 4 firework	Reg 5 of the Firework Regulations 2004 (Fireworks Act 2003, s 11)
Possession by a person under 18 of an adult firework in public	Reg 4 of the Firework Regulations 2004 (Fireworks Act 2003, s 11)

5.3.3.2 *Offences included in the PND scheme for which the penalty is £50*

The table below summarizes the offences which may be dealt with under the PND scheme by a £50 fine for those aged 16 years and over. For the same offence committed by 10–15 year-olds, the fine is £30.

Table 5.5: Offences included in the PND scheme for which the penalty is £50

Offence	Legislation
Trespassing on a railway	British Transport Commission Act 1949, s 55
Throwing stones at a train	British Transport Commission Act 1949, s 56
Drunk in the highway	Licensing Act 1872, s 12
Consumption of alcohol in designated public place, contrary to a requirement by a constable not to do so	Criminal Justice and Police Act 2001, s 12
Depositing and leaving litter	Environmental Protection Act 1990, ss 87(1) and 87(5)
Consumption of alcohol by a person under 18 in a bar	Licensing Act 2003, s 150(1)
Allowing consumption of alcohol by a young person (aged under 18) in a bar	Licensing Act 2003, s 150(2)
Buying or attempting to buy alcohol for a young person (aged under 18)	Licensing Act 2003, s 149(1)

5.3.4 **Policing Domestic Violence**

You should note that *there is no legal definition of domestic violence*, nor is it a legally separate and distinct category of crime (although it involves criminal activity, such as unlawful violence). The term domestic violence relates to the **context** within which various crimes and acts of violence occur.

The boundaries of what constitutes domestic violence are continually refined in terms of the meanings we attribute to both 'domestic' and 'violence'. These boundaries have varied historically as well as from force to force. Some police forces have adopted narrow definitions, deciding that offences are limited to married heterosexual couples where there is evidence of physical violence. Others forces have broadened the definition to include same-sex and couples cohabitating outside marriage. Others more recently have included violence against the old, disabled, or terminally ill by their carers (often members of the family). 'Violence' can also include emotional and psychological abuse. A description provided by the Home Office Violent Crime Unit in 2004 demonstrates the broad understanding of the term 'domestic violence':

> Any incident of threatening behaviour, violence or abuse (psychological, physical, sexual, financial or emotional) between adults who are or have been intimate partners or family members, regardless of gender or sexuality.
>
> (Home Office, 2004b: p 12)

It has been noted by a number of commentators that in the past domestic violence had been seen by police officers as 'messy, unproductive, and not "real" police work' (Reiner, 1997). This attitude is not officially accepted today and the Crime and Disorder Act 1998 established in legislation the need for the police and local authorities to work through partnerships with appropriate local bodies to address the problem of domestic violence locally.

5.3.4.1 *The Police response to domestic violence*

Despite this, domestic violence remains a difficult area in practical terms for the police. This is partly because of the relationship of the offender to the victim. By definition, the offender and victim within a domestic context are part of a more complex relationship than is the case in most non-domestic crimes. There will be, or at least will have been, a loving and caring aspect of the relationship, and there will be many shared memories, friends, family, and possibly children involved.

In the past the police were guilty of under-recording because their experience suggested that victims of domestic abuse would later withdraw complaints. You will often hear this rendered as '*IP declines*' (that is, the 'Injured Party' declines to give evidence or charge against the alleged injurer). Data about domestic violence are imprecise, in terms of incidence, prosecution, *and* proportion (estimates suggest that domestic violence comprises 16–25 per cent of all violent offences). However, we do know that an average of *two women die every week* in domestic violence incidents (Home Office, 2003b: p 6). Because it is not always an easy crime to identify, and because the consequences can be fatal, domestic violence is one of the most serious aspects of police work as well as one of the most fraught.

In cases where the violence is persistent, domestic violence is often seen as part of a cycle of abuse: children who witness domestic violence may become domestic violence victims, and/or some victims of domestic violence may become offenders, at a later date. Knowledge of this cycle of abuse links domestic violence to child protection, and this is not simply historical, because there is also evidence to suggest that, where a man is beating his partner, he may also be beating his children. Alternatively, where a man is beating his wife, his wife may in turn be beating the children.

5.3.4.2 *The Government response*

The Home Office Circular 60/1990 (revised 19/2000) is an important influence upon the development of a proactive policing policy towards domestic violence. There were three main recommendations:

1. *The police should take a more interventionist approach to domestic violence cases, with a presumption in favour of arrest*

   All forces have adopted 'positive action' policies to ensure that officers attending the scene of a domestic incident treat it seriously. Positive action, not necessarily arrest, is required. Indeed making an arrest could be counterproductive. There is research which suggests that many women want nothing more than an immediate break from the violence and a warning given to their partners.

2. *Domestic violence crimes are recorded in the same way as other violent crimes*

   The problem of under-recording has already been mentioned but this recommendation suggests that, not only should all incidents of domestic violence be recorded, but also such reports should indicate the seriousness of the alleged offence.

3. *The police adopt a more sympathetic and understanding attitude towards victims of domestic violence*

As far as victims of domestic abuse are concerned, the Home Office circular emphasized *the need for the police to adopt a duty of care*. In this respect the policing of domestic violence should be less concerned with instrumental goals and more concerned with doing the right thing.

However, this presents the police with important questions: should they give greater priority to tackling domestic violence (and treat it as a core mandate of police work) or should other agencies become more involved? What happens when there is a clash between, on one hand, supporting the wishes of a victim who decides not to press charges and, on the other, responding to a perceived social need to punish domestic offenders?

Note: there are many documents dealing with different aspects of policing domestic violence available online at the Home Office. See the 'Violence against Women' section at <http://www.homeoffice.gov.uk/rds/violencewomen.html>. Other offences, such as forced marriages, come into the general area of domestic violence, and your force may have specialists in these areas, whom you should consult if you have concerns.

5.3.5 Police Protection

The police can act to prevent further harm to a child. Whether a child would otherwise be likely to suffer significant *harm* will be a matter for you (as a Special Constable) to decide. The Children Act 1989 provides you with the powers to take into police protection children (under 18 years of age) who are at risk of significant harm. However, paragraph 15 of Home Office Circular 17/2008 states that:

Police protection is an emergency power and should only be used when necessary, the principle being that wherever possible the decision to remove a child/children from a parent or carer should be made by a court.

Apart from in exceptional circumstances (for example, an imminent threat to a child's welfare), no child is to be taken into police protection until an **initiating officer** (trained to respond to such incidents) has seen the child and assessed his or her circumstances.

5.3.6 Incidents involving deaths

In addition to encountering death and injury as the result of major and critical incidents, you are likely as a Special Constable to experience occasions where someone is found dead because of illness and/or old age. The local police station may be called by the neighbours of an elderly person to report that they have not seen their neighbour for some time or that there are other circumstances which give cause for concern. Of course, these situations are not restricted to the elderly; you may have the particularly distressing task of attending the scene of the death of a child or young person.

Any death which occurs other than in a hospital, and is in some way unexpected, is referred to in police circles as a '*sudden death*'. All sudden deaths will be subject to some form of investigation, but of course this does not mean that the death is necessarily associated with criminal activity. However, at any event involving a dead body it is essential that Special Constables are never afraid to ask questions and, above all, if you believe an incident is suspicious, it is *your responsibility* to say so. If you do not understand something, you should ask: if you are puzzled, or you see something that doesn't add up, you *must* ask questions. In particular, if you are the Special Constable in early attendance at the scene of a fatality, ask yourself:

- Is the event which probably caused death at this scene accidental or deliberate?
- If it is a suicide, were the means available to the victim?
- Was the victim physically capable of the act?
- Is there any sign of a struggle?
- Is anything missing?
- Is there evidence of a forced entry?
- Is there anything at the scene which is strange or doesn't seem in keeping?
- Does the position or state of the body logically fit with the information received?

5.3.6.1 *Attending incidents with deaths*

The general procedure to follow for sudden deaths will vary from force to force although all subscribe to certain basic principles (and relate to the procedures for attendance at a crime scene: see 8.1 below). You should:

1. Ensure your own safety before approaching, as the scene of a death can be dangerous.
2. Establish and use a Common Approach Path (CAP) (see 8.2 below) to preserve the scene.
3. Beware of bodies in contact with live electrical systems, as well as the existence in the vicinity of toxic fumes, poisons, firearms, needles, and body fluids.
4. Touch nothing until you have made a visual inspection.
5. Is there a chance the person is still alive? Can you administer first aid and is an ambulance/paramedic required?
6. Consider that any death might be the result of crime if it is in any way suspicious.

Next, begin a PNB entry (see 4.5.5 above) which records the following information:

- the location and position of the body
- any physical evidence in the immediate area
- a general description of the body, including any visible injuries
- the evidence of any witnesses, and
- the identity of the deceased, if known.

As can be seen from the above, the circumstances in which you might encounter a deceased person vary widely, and your response must be appropriate. Whatever the cause of death, there are common processes that occur in all bodies after death, that you need to be familiar with, and some of these changes are described in 5.3.6.3 below. All deaths also need to be *certified* for legal and administrative purposes.

5.3.6.2 *Certifying death*

If there is the slightest chance that a victim is alive, seek medical assistance. If a victim has been beheaded, you may presume death has occurred; in all other cases a 'certified medical practitioner' is required to attend the scene. You will need to call a doctor (or arrange for one to be called) either to provide medical advice or to certify that life is extinct. The procedure to be followed depends on whether the death was expected or unexpected (see below).

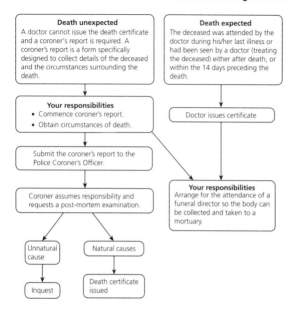

Certainly, in the case of 'unnatural cause' a police investigation would ensue, although in most cases of this kind it would already be under way.

5.3.6.3 *Changes to the body after death*

There are several changes that take place in a body after death, and some of these are externally evident and might contribute to an investigation:

5.3.6.3.1 Hypostasis

When people die, the blood settles to the lowest parts and enters the skin where it creates a port-wine-coloured stain. This is also known as 'post-mortem lividity' or *livor mortis*. Where a body is upright, blood drains to the lower parts of the limbs, cheeks and ears.

In addition to this discoloration, wherever pressure is exerted on the skin, blood and tissue fluid cannot enter and is displaced into adjacent areas of tissue. As a result, the deceased's skin may take on an impression of the surface beneath it (for example from a tiled floor). The pattern of the fabric or seams from the victim's clothing may also be very clearly imprinted on the skin. After some time (around three to four hours), the blood clots (solidifies) and can no longer flow, so if the body is subsequently moved, the signs of hypostasis will no longer be on the lower or underside parts of the body.

5.3.6.3.2 Rigor mortis (stiffness after death)

After death, chemical changes in the muscles gradually cause them to stiffen. The process normally begins in the head and works down the body. In very general terms it might start after 4 hours and disappear after 24 hours (when the body begins to break down biologically). However the process is dependent upon a number of factors, not least of which is the ambient temperature (the process is quicker at higher temperatures). Immediately after death the body becomes limp and will flop to rest on adjacent structures, and if left for a number of hours, *rigor mortis* will stiffen it in that position. If subsequently moved, the body will be rigid and will not flop against the surrounding structures.

5.3.6.3.3 Body temperature

The core temperature of the deceased will equalize with the ambient temperature after death (so it will usually cool down) and then, owing to decay and insect activity, the body temperature may increase. The relationship between the lowering of the core temperature and the ambient temperature is well documented but not so precise that a pathologist can give an estimate of the time of death to within a few minutes. The ambient temperature, amount of clothing, and general health of the victim may all affect the temperature drop.

5.3.6.3.4 Suicide by cutting

Where a suicide victim has stabbed him/herself or severed an artery, often in the throat, wrist, or groin, one would normally expect to see *tentative cuts*—minor cuts carried out prior to the lethal wound.

This concludes our outline survey of the commonly-used criminal law in situations that Special Constables routinely encounter.

Notes

1 We have not tried to cover every eventuality and, indeed, discuss only the commoner offences and legislation. We refer you to *Blackstone's*

- Where is the *most appropriate place* to take the statement from the witness? The police station is usually the best choice for the Special Constable, but it may be done at the witness's home address.
- What is the *current physical state* of the witness? If s/he received any injuries from the crime or is traumatized, emotional, heavily intoxicated, or suffering from the effects of any medication or controlled drugs, it may be better to obtain a statement later, when things are calmer.

6.1.2 Format

Statements should always include the time, day, month, and year when they are taken, and refer immediately to the event witnessed. The opening paragraph should record the witness's occupation and address. It is also important to record what the witness or victim was doing at the time of the incident and how s/he became involved. The body of the statement should consist of the events witnessed. *A separate paragraph should be used for each event or aspect witnessed* (Calligan, 2007). The ending of the statement will depend very much on the offence being dealt with, as it is often here that 'points to prove' will go. If the witness is content with what has been written, s/he should sign at the bottom of each page, and you must witness the signatures in the appropriate box at the bottom of the page(s). You should close the statement by writing:

> This statement consisting of X pages, was taken by me, [rank, force number, first name, SURNAME] at [location], commencing at [24-hour time] hours. Upon conclusion at [24-hour time] hours, I read it over to [name of witness] and invited [him/her] to read and sign it in my presence.

You should sign next to this certification and add your force identification number. This not only distinguishes your signature from that of the witness but means that you are easily identified by others in the case as the statement taker.

6.1.3 Errors, amendments, and additions

If a witness does not fully agree with what is written, or wishes to make an amendment, possibly to a single word, a sentence, or indeed a whole passage, then the error in the original statement must only be crossed through by a single line. This also applies to any mistakes you might have made whilst taking the statement. It is important that the original words and content are still visible, and readable, behind this line to ensure that, for the accused, the trial is as fair and transparent as possible. Never use correction pens or fluid. Next to each crossed-through error, the witness should sign.

6.1.4 Vulnerable or intimidated witnesses

The Youth Justice and Criminal Evidence Act 1999 Part II provides that vulnerable or intimidated witnesses may use 'an intermediary' when making a statement to the police. An intermediary is a neutral person who is present when a statement is being taken from a witness and who aims to assist with the free flow of information between the witness and the police officer taking the statement, explaining processes to the witness in ways s/he will understand (Calligan, 2007).

Definitions
Vulnerable witnesses:
- under 17 years of age at the time of a relevant court hearing, or
- a witness whose evidence would, in the opinion of a court, be weakened by reason of a mental disorder, or significant impairment of intelligence and social functioning (learning disability), or a physical disability or physical disorder.

Intimidated witnesses are defined as:
- All complainants in sexual offence cases—unless they say that they do not want to be treated as an intimidated witness.
- A witness whose evidence would, in the opinion of a court, be weakened because of their fear and distress in connection with testifying. The factors which should be taken into account include:
  a) the nature and alleged circumstances of the offence to which the proceedings relate
  b) the age of the witness
  c) the social and cultural background and ethnic origins of the witness
  d) the domestic and employment circumstances of the witness, and
  e) any intimidating or threatening behaviour towards the witness on the part of the defendant, members of the defendant's family or associates, or from any other person who is likely to be a defendant or a witness in the proceedings.

(HMCS, 2006)

6.1.5 Negative statements

Negative statements are often taken from witnesses who state that they did not hear or see anything and are thus unable to support the police investigation. This is done to prevent them from coming forward at a later date, perhaps after having made up a story to help a guilty associate.

6.1.6 Where a witness becomes a suspect

When you are taking a statement from a witness, it may emerge that s/he has had some involvement with the criminal offence under investigation. You should immediately stop taking the statement, noting in your PNB the time and record, and why you stopped. The individual is no longer to be treated as a witness, but as a suspect. You should administer the caution and advise that s/he is not under arrest and is free to leave at any time. You must also record any unsolicited comments made by the person before or after the caution that led you to suspect his or her criminal involvement in or with the offence, offering your PNB or the statement to the 'now suspect' to sign. You should speak to a supervisor immediately and agree a course of action to be taken. The statement must be retained as evidence.

6.1.7 Voluntary statements made under caution

Occasionally, a suspect may elect to make a statement. This is covered by Annex D to Code C of the PACE Act 1984: all voluntary statements must contain a declaration signed by the offender before any content of the statement is recorded. Where a suspect wishes to write his or her own statement, s/he must be directed to write out the following declaration:

> I make this statement of my own free will. I understand that I do not have to say anything but it may harm my defence if I do not mention when questioned something which I may later rely on in court. This statement may be given in evidence.

S/he must then add his or her signature. Voluntary statements should be written without any prompting by police officers, except that a police officer may question any ambiguity or indicate any matters that are material to the statement, such as the time(s) of the offence.

6.2 **Personal Safety**

It is evident that the duties of a Special Constable carry an implicit risk of danger from threat, physical assault, or other injury. Table 6.1 illustrates the total number of recorded assaults on police officers, Special Constables, and other members of police staff (for example PCSOs) between 1 April 2005 and 31 March 2009:

Table 6.1: Recorded assaults on the police in England and Wales 2005–9

Year	Fatal	Serious injury*	Minor/no injury**
2005/06	3	423	11,592
2006/07	0	506	10,993
2007/08	1	502	10,890
2008/09	1	433	9,882

* Serious injury—assaults on police where officer sustained serious wounds and where offenders were charged under ss 18 or 20 of the Offences Against the Person Act 1861.

** Minor injury/no injury—assaults on police where officer sustained no physical injury or minor wounds and where the offender was charged with an offence under ss 47 or 38 of the Offences Against the Person Act 1861, s 89(1) and 89(2) of the Police Act 1996, or s 39 of the Criminal Justice Act 1998.

(adapted from Home Office (2008a)[1] and (2009a)[2])

We hope that you thought about these risks when you joined the Special Constabulary, since you attend the same incidents as regular officers, including crimes involving firearms or bladed weapons, drink- or drug-fuelled public order incidents, violent assaults, and volatile domestic incidents. Sometimes you will be alone, or with other Special Constables who might have lower levels of experience than you.

6.2.1 Officer safety training

Special Constables are authorized to use reasonable force on another person to ensure compliance. These legal rights are established both under common law (self-defence and breach of the peace) and by various statutes including section 3 of the Criminal Law Act 1967 and section 117 of the PACE Act 1984. However, in all cases where 'authorized force' is used on another, it helps to remember proportionality and the rights of the individual.

In many forces, practical training in protecting both yourself and others from assault or attack is called *Officer Safety Training* (OST), though others prefer *Personal Safety Training* (inevitably

At the time of writing (late 2009), there is some uncertainty as to which of the **National Occupational Standards** (NOS) will be retained as evidence of competence for Special Constables. However, there is currently one very specific NOS relating to health and safety, and it is **Unit 4G2:** *Ensure that your own actions reduce risks to health and safety.* 4G2 is in two parts; the first is 4G2.1, *identify the hazards and evaluate the risks in your workplace.*

Task

Make a quick list of Health and Safety aspects of policing which are quite specific to the role.

We have some thoughts about this but we cannot cover all circumstances in all police forces, so the following should not be taken as in any way definitive:

Some suggested answers
- Intervening in fights and disputes
- Searching land, buildings, and other places for evidence, missing children, bodies
- Dealing with angry, frightened, stressed, bewildered, or injured people
- Taking charge of drugs paraphernalia, including hypodermic needles
- Searching people who may be armed with weapons or have sharp objects (needles, knives) concealed
- Taking charge at a road traffic collision
- Informing someone of the death of a relative, dealing with the subsequent grief, incomprehension, or anger
- Dealing with scenes of crime, often as first officer attending (FOA)
- Rendering first aid to injured people
- Resuscitation, including CPR* or mouth-to-mouth
- Calming situations where emotions are high
- Controlling crowds
- Getting quickly to a reported incident on foot or by vehicle
- Dealing with a terrorist threat
- Dealing with the aftermath of a terrorist attack
- Responding to reported domestic violence
- Responding to any civil emergency, from fire to plane crash, flooding to derailment, building collapse to gas explosion

(* cardio-pulmonary resuscitation)

It's quite a list, isn't it? And it's not complete or comprehensive. The chances are that over the course of a year's duty or so as a Special Constable, you will find yourself dealing with most of the incidents and situations we have outlined. They are all inherent in policing which, shorn of its complex specialisms, is still really about dealing with people's problems in an infinite permutation of circumstances.

This leads us to one last point. The motivation for many who choose to become Special Constables is helping people. In emergencies, officers may disregard their own safety in order to rescue others from dangerous situations. This is public-spirited and brave, but it might sometimes be a bit daft. Trying to rescue someone from a burning building might place your own life in danger if you have not been trained or properly equipped (such as with flame-retardant overalls and breathing apparatus). Ineffective bravery is not really enough for a professional, is it? There is no point in throwing away your life (and not saving others either) when there are risk-assessed alternatives, such as throwing lifebelts to people in water. This may mean acting **counterintuitively**—against what your instinct tells you to do—but it may nonetheless be the *right thing to do*. Foolish bravery may be brave, but it *is* foolish: a moment's thought and dynamic risk assessment might mean that the people in difficulties can be rescued without hazarding your life as well.

6.4 **Deployment and Varieties of Tasking**

Let's start with an important observation: Special Constables are by no means limited to working in Neighbourhood Policing Teams, nor should they be. We show below that Special Constables can perform fast-roads policing, can operate Automatic Number Plate Recognition (ANPR), can assist in investigations, can be utilized in 'Misper' (missing persons) enquiries, can patrol, can control crowds and can play a part in keeping public order, and, of course, can provide reassurance to communities through high-visibility foot and anti-social behaviour patrols. Whilst we are fully persuaded of the importance of neighbourhood policing (indeed, the next chapter is devoted to it), and we are signed up to the proactive role of Special Constables within Neighbourhood Policing Teams, nonetheless we do not think that this is all that they can do or that it is in the force's best interests to circumscribe them in such a way.

Special Constables bring into the police service an extensive range of skills, talents, knowledge, competencies, and experience from their full-time work or private lives (NPIA, 2008a). Thus, the National Strategy holds that there is 'no single area of policing that cannot benefit from Special Constabulary support', and enjoins regular command officers to utilize the Special Constabulary where there is the greatest need for their support that fits with the Special Constabulary's strengths (*ibid*). Indeed, the National Strategy outlines, though not exhaustively, many tasks and functions that Special Constables can capably and competently be used to perform in support of the regular police:

Crime reduction: eg bail checks, anti-social behaviour deterrent patrols

Crime detection: drink-driving checks, use of ANPR to support intelligence-led policing approaches to detecting offences and stopping vehicles

Crime investigation: investigating minor traffic offending, or volume crimes

Public reassurance/safety: conducting multi-agency road-traffic-vehicle checks, uniformed foot patrols

Incident response: responding to emergency calls or other incidents requiring police attendance

Neighbourhood policing and anti-social behaviour: supporting the work of NPTs in responding to, solving problems of, and combating specific issues identified by local communities in partnership with other community safety agencies through the PACT process

Critical incidents: supporting major incident teams in their work by carrying out low-tier investigation or evidence gathering, eg assisting with house-to-house enquires, taking statements from witnesses

(adapted and augmented from NPIA, 2008a)

We examine some of these in more detail below. Today, the Special Constabulary is increasingly viewed by regular command officers as a tactical resource. This is solidly based on the extraordinary cost-efficiency of volunteer police officers, the fact that they have the full complement of warranted powers, and that Special Constables can augment regular officer strength at times of peak demand when their volunteering hours are mostly performed (weekends and public holiday periods). As a result, some police leaders are steadily becoming more imaginative when it comes to tasking and deploying Special Constables.

Special Constables can play a significant part in supporting police responses to major or critical incidents, and in carrying out incident response duties. Moreover, there is also a growing trend by individual forces (in recognition of the cost-efficiency of the Special Constabulary) to use Specials who have been given advanced training within previously exclusive regular officer units such as the Roads Policing Units (RPUs, see below), ANPR intercept teams (6.5), and public order support units.

Some police forces have sought to exploit the skills, talents, and experiences that individual Special Constables bring with them into the police service from their external 'civilian' jobs, or that they have gained from study or learning. Such skills and specialist knowledge can enhance the efficiency of certain specialist policing or investigatory fields such as hi-tech and computer crime, financial and economic crime, and fraud; as well as 'test purchasing' (NPIA, 2008a). Experienced independent Special Constables may take advantage of some of the following specialist opportunities made available to them by their chosen forces:

Examples of deployment and Special Constables' utilization in England and Wales

The **Metropolitan Police** uses dedicated Special Constables in their *fine art and antiquities squad*. Duties include gathering evidence to help combat art and antique thefts, offering crime prevention advice to art and antiques buyers and sellers, and attending high-profile art and antiques fairs.

Bedfordshire Police has recently established a *Cannabis Factories Team* including Special Constables with enhanced levels of training. The team is tasked with carrying out arrest warrants, raiding and searching cannabis factories, and gathering and preparing evidence for trial. The force also has a dedicated *Specials Trading Standards team* that deals with reports of rogue traders, and often patrols local boot sales or fairs to detect traders in counterfeit goods such as CDs, DVDs, and clothing.

Suffolk Special Constabulary has created a *Specials Support Team* which assists their regular colleagues with high-profile policing operations such as executing drugs warrants. The officers often work in plain clothes as spotters and relay information about possible suspects to their uniformed colleagues to action.

In **Leicestershire**, Special Constables serve as *Force Wildlife Officers* and work in partnership with charitable agencies such as the RSPB and the World Wildlife Fund. Duties include seizing illegally imported exotic animals (such as tortoises) and prosecuting wildlife vandals, poachers, and unauthorized hunters.

Special Constables in **Surrey** and **Cumbria Constabulary** work alongside regular officers in *Roads Policing Units* and on *ANPR intercept teams,* and help tackle all forms of offending through vehicles, vehicle documentation, and roads traffic offending.

The **City of London** Police use Specials to help *investigate fraud, economic, and financial crime.* In addition there are several officers authorized to use marked police motorcycles to perform operational duties. The force has a squad of Special Constables who patrol on cycles and another team that combats taxi-touting.

In **Hertfordshire**, Specials with additional computer skills support the investigation *of hi-tech and computer crime.* They are also used to police demonstrations, football and rugby matches, and those with enhanced training are deployed to support public order operations.

Kent and **Devon and Cornwall** Specials are deployed in areas identified as crime, disorder, or anti-social behaviour hot spots and work in Special *Neighbourhood Task Teams* (SNTTs) or Special Constabulary *Tactical Policing Teams.* Working with regular officers and PCSOs in the Neighbourhood Policing Teams, the Specials target, combat, and address specific issues that adversely affect the community's quality of life, for example littering, vandalism and criminal damage, under-age drinking, anti-social or unruly behaviour, or nuisance use of motor vehicles.

Independent Specials in **West Yorkshire** work on the force's *Operational Support Unit* (OSU) and have the opportunity to undergo *advanced public order, method of entry, and response driver* training. The OSU works to support neighbourhood policing, but is often deployed in support of specific public order operations, or to make arrests, or execute search warrants.

Special Constabulary officers in **Dorset** are deployed on numerous operations specifically aimed at targeting *anti-social behaviour and under-age drinking,* working alongside Neighbourhood Policing Teams.

Merseyside and **Cleveland** Specials are involved in supporting the regular force in the wake of *critical or major incidents*.
The Special Constabulary has played a fundamental part in
supporting police interventions and responses to the immediate incidents, and in helping to reassure local
communities affected by them. Moreover, Specials have
assisted with any subsequent criminal investigations by
helping with house-to-house enquiries and by helping to
gather information and evidence.

(Collated and abridged from: NPIA, 2008a, and, *Specials Magazine*
editions; January 2008–Summer 2009)

Now, a specific case study:

**Devon and Cornwall Police: Specials in Fast-Roads Policing,
a case in point**
This description of how Special Constables get into
fast-roads policing is adapted from the words of their duty
Inspector, Andrew Turner:

Context
Involving Special Constables in Fast-Roads Policing is new to
Devon and Cornwall and only really took shape just
over a year ago; although I know that other forces like
Warwickshire and Gwent are further along than we are.
We now have 12 Special Constables fully enrolled in Roads
Policing and hope for 35 across the force within two years.

Getting in
Existing Special Constables apply and are 'paper-sifted' and
then we hold a selection interview with a matrix scoring
system. From this the successful Special Constable applicants
get a working Personal Development Plan (PDP) which may
take the individual officer as much as 200 hours to complete.
Once this has been completed and is signed off by the traffic
training unit and line management, the Special Constable is
welcomed as a full member of the roads policing team.

Getting on
Once the Special Constables have passed a test, they
can drive the traffic car and police Range Rover under
supervision and later on their own, and when they are fully
on board, Special Constables can start doing other courses,

such as the standard three-week police driving course, can learn to deploy the Stinger equipment for safe stopping of suspect vehicles, or they can learn and use the 'Vascar' on-board computer (a device which registers the speed of other vehicles).

Getting the rewards
Motivation is a big key and we all work as a team and enjoy a good laugh and have some fun and support each other. I think we do it because it is always different every shift and you never know what is going to happen.

The Special Constables always put in a lot more than their 'conditioned' 16 hours each month, one put in nearly 100 hours last month. We all love it.

(based on correspondence with the Editor, and reproduced with kind permission of Inspector Turner and the Chief Constable, Devon and Cornwall Police, Stephen Otter)

It's your turn to do some research:

TASK

Using the force intranet, or by speaking to other Special Constables, find out what specialist deployments and taskings are available, or offered, to the Special Constabulary in your force. List them and compare what you find with the sorts of duties your regular colleagues undertake.

Is there anything you could do that is not yet on offer to Special Constables?

Do you know of any Special Constables with particular talents or specialist areas of knowledge who could add to or help the regular units?

Whilst there appears to be a range of possible deployments it must be noted that the hard reality of serving as a Special Constable with your chosen force is that, although you are an unpaid volunteer, fundamentally you are an additional resource for the police service to utilize as *it deems most suitable or appropriate*. As such, your exact duties are likely to be at the discretion of the chief constable of the police force you choose to serve with, and those duties may not always be what you would prefer to do.

If you expect that, because of your volunteer status, you will always get your preferred duties or taskings, you may well be disappointed. Remember, you are part of a bigger policing picture and the Special Constabulary has an established place within all police forces. You need to understand, willingly accept, and be prepared for the utterly unglamorous aspects of police work, for example patrolling on foot on a cold, dark, wet, winter's evening; or standing with cold feet protecting a crime scene from any unauthorized access. You may even find yourself conducting constant supervision duties in custody on a suicidal detainee. These tasks are of equal importance to and need completing as much as the duties in your preferred field of policing.

Pragmatism and the good of the service are the important things. So, whilst you might not always get a say in what you do and how you do it, you should take positive steps to ensure that your force knows all about your skills and abilities, against the time when they may be needed. Keep pushing at the orthodoxy of the regular force 'envelope': if they don't realize that you can do something, perhaps that's your fault for not telling them that you want to do it, or not volunteering to be considered for it in the first place.

6.5 Automatic Number Plate Recognition (ANPR)

6.5.1 What is ANPR?

ANPR is a complex network of specially-adapted CCTV cameras that have the capability to read the 'characters' (numbers and letters) on vehicle registration plates, and then cross-reference and compare this information against database records held on file by law enforcement agencies and other government departments.[6] The cameras may be **static** (fixed site, or temporarily fixed site, such as ANPR Spectrum vans), **CCTV-integrated** (infrastructure-based, including cameras mounted on motorway gantries), or **mobile** (fitted in cars) sets. Each ANPR camera is linked, usually by remote feed, to the central **Nexus database**, an integrated criminal intelligence system, situated alongside the Police National Computer in the National ANPR Data Centre (NADC), London.[7]

6.5.2 How does ANPR work?

Sorry about the number of abbreviations in what follows. ANPR cameras capture still digital images of vehicle registration marks (VRM) that pass in front of them at speeds of up to 100 mph.[8]

Each camera is linked to a number-plate reading device (NRD), and each captured image is sent via the connection to this device for conversion to read data.[9] The NRD works by first locating the VRM within the image, as on each vehicle it may be at a slightly different height or position. It then crops the VRM so that only this part of the image is now visible, and thereafter, using Optical Character Recognition (OCR) software, it identifies the dark groups of pixels, comprising each character and digit of the registration plate, as the pre-set numbers and letters that make up the actual VRM.

Once the OCR software has read the VRM, this data is cross-referenced with the Nexus database.[10] Any VRM that returns, classified as a 'hit' or 'ping', indicates that a match has been found between a cross-checked number-plate and a record held on the database being searched.[11] It is 'hit data' that is most important for Special Constables engaged on roads policing duties, for hits mean that a vehicle should be stopped, if safe and possible to do so, and the driver questioned under caution if applicable.

The continued roll-out of ANPR has led to many older cameras being replaced with newer versions equipped with infrared (IR) technology. IR has a greater capacity to 'read' vehicle registration plates, even where visibility is poor,[12] or registration plates are partially obscured by dirt, or even where they have been deliberately altered by drivers wanting to escape detection, using black insulation tape to change (for example) an F to an E, a P to an R, or a 0 into an 8.[13]

The following figure summarizes the typical set-up and operation of ANPR and the actions that may be taken after a positive hit or 'ping':

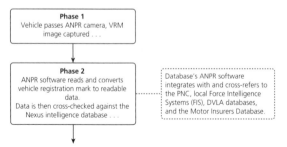

Figure 6.2: ANPR operation

Phase 3	
If a successful hit, or 'ping', is returned, ANPR Intercept Team notified. Decision is then taken whether to stop the subject vehicle (some Health and Safety considerations)	'Pings' can include action markers or alerts such as 'no MOT', 'no vehicle excise licence', 'no insurance held', or 'stolen vehicle', among others.
Phase 4	
Subject vehicle stopped if safe to do so and 'appropriate action' taken.	'Appropriate action' can take many forms including giving words of advice to inform the driver of his or her vehicle's defect, or missing documentation, issuing a Non Endorsable or Endorsable FPN, CLE2/6, or HORT/1, seizing the vehicle, issuing a PG9 notice or VDRS requirement, searching the driver/passengers or vehicle, arrest, or summonsing an individual to court.

Adapted and augmented from PA Consulting Group (2004a; 2004b)

Figure 6.2: (*Continued*)

6.5.3 The increasing use of ANPR by Specials

The number of police officers specializing in road-traffic policing is in decline, with only 6 per cent of the total police officer numbers nationally dedicated to this policing field.[14] This has been beneficial for the Special Constabulary since Specials Roads Policing Units or Special ANPR intercept teams are becoming established in forces across England and Wales (as we saw in Devon and Cornwall, or Gwent) and this allows you to challenge and deny criminals use of the roads.

6.6 Investigating Minor Crime

Averagely 20 per cent of police officer duty time is spent attending, dealing with, and investigating instances of volume crime (ACPO, 2001). Volume crime includes offences such as:

- Street robbery
- Burglary (dwelling and non-dwelling)
- Theft (including shoplifting)
- Vehicle crime (theft of and theft from)
- Petty drugs offences (small-time dealing and possession)
- Criminal damage
- Common assault.

(ACPO, 2001)

6.6.1 **Roles and responsibilities of the First Officer Attending (FOA)**

The first officer attending (FOA) the scene of a reported volume crime should be mindful that s/he is attending as a proactive criminal investigator, and not simply reactively as going to take a crime report from the victim, or the person reporting the incident. On arrival at the crime scene, the FOA assumes the role of *investigator*. It is the investigator's responsibility to *identify* and *pursue all reasonable lines of enquiry* that will help to establish the truth about what happened at the crime scene, and establish who has committed the offence. It is also the FOA's duty to ensure that *any material that may be relevant to the investigation*, or indeed physical evidence, *is recorded and retained* (see 5.3.2).

6.6.2 **Initial actions for investigating 'minor crime'**

On arriving at a volume crime scene, the FOA should:

- *Obtain initial information from control room/victim/witnesses:*
    a) record personal and contact details of victim/witness, and
    b) establish what has happened/is happening, where the incident is, and when it occurred. Ask open ended questions to elicit better responses from witnesses, such as what, why, where, when, who, and how (5WH + 1).
- *Ensure own personal health and safety, and that of any other person present at, or attending the scene, is safeguarded and maintained at all times:*
    a) perform a dynamic risk assessment
    b) stabilize the scene
    c) cordon and secure the scene
    d) identify what support the victim requires immediately, and
    e) advise the victim to remain where they are and not to touch anything in the crime scene to avoid contamination of any forensic evidence that might have been left there by the perpetrator(s).
- *Survey and assess the crime scene and identify sources of potential evidence:*
    a) preserve evidence
    b) look for discarded items in the immediate vicinity, or places where evidence might have been concealed by offenders fleeing the scene, eg in refuse bins, under hedges, and
    c) identify and establish entry and escape routes of offenders.

- *Identify what response is needed*:
  a) is anyone injured, or is life threatened?
  b) is anybody in the act of committing an offence?
  c) is immediate action required to:
    - preserve evidence, or
    - prevent further offending, or offences being committed?
  d) what support does the victim/witness require at the present time?
  e) are further officers required?
  f) is an ambulance required?
  g) does the incident require the attendance of a supervisor?
  h) does CSI need to attend to record or capture forensic evidence?
  i) if the offence is recent, or offenders have recently made off from the crime scene, is a dog unit available to provide assistance locating them?
  j) does the duty detective sergeant/constable need to be made aware of the offence, or attend the scene?
  k) if applicable, is air support available to help search for and locate the offenders?
- *Obtain supplementary information and disseminate to control room*:
  a) full descriptions of offender(s) and their direction of travel
  b) establish ownership of any property in question
  c) full details and descriptions of any damaged or stolen property
  d) provide a brief situation report (sit-rep) to the control room and describe what has happened/is happening
  e) inform control room if further resources are required to attend the scene, and if so, what type of resource, and
  f) any other relevant information dependent on the offence and type of incident you are dealing with.
- *Provide advice and guidance to the victim or witness*:
  a) provide basic crime prevention advice to avoid repeat victimization
  b) inform victim(s) of their entitlements to services of Victim Support, and their rights under the Victim's Code (2006, replacing the old Victim's Charter);[15]
  c) inform the victim of the appropriate point of contact within the police organization that will be dealing with their case, and
  d) provide the victim with their crime or incident reference number.
- *Maintain an accurate PNB entry and complete documentation*:
  a) record all information or material obtained during your initial investigation
  b) record details of any actions you have undertaken since arriving at the scene
  c) complete a crime report for the incident
  d) if necessary, commence a crime scene log, and
  e) take a description of the suspect using ADVOKATE if applicable.

- *Commence and complete initial investigative enquiries:*
  a) gather CCTV footage (if available)
  b) complete house-to-house enquiries after having made contact with the victim to identify any witnesses—all premises within line of sight and in hearing distance should be contacted
  c) in the case of stolen vehicles, inform control to cross-refer VRM with ANPR cameras to establish its heading or rough location
  d) record information from any witnesses present
  e) pursue any other reasonable line of enquiry to establish what has happened at the scene, who is responsible for the crime, and, if stolen property is involved, where this may be recovered
  f) conduct an intelligence check and identify whether any similar crimes have happened in the local area recently, and whether any known or suspected offenders are indicated to have been potentially responsible for their commission, and
  g) maintain contact with the victim. Provide regular updates on progress or actions taken.

(adapted and augmented from ACPO, 2001)

6.6.3 Crime reports

As FOA it is your responsibility to complete a crime report for the incident you are attending, on your return to the police station, or at the latest before booking off-duty. To do this properly, it is essential that you get information from the victim, witnesses, and the crime scene itself, so that your crime report can be as full and detailed as possible. The information and detail the report contains may help other investigators allocated to deal with the offence at a later stage, and ease the identification of lines of enquiry that remain uncompleted. Generally, crime reports comprise:

- *Type of offence*: often subdivided, eg burglary (dwelling), or theft (shoplifting)
- *Day, date, month, year, time,* and exact *location* of offence
- *Day, date, month, year, time when,* and *location where* offence was first reported to police
- *Name, address,* and *contact details* of person reporting the offence to police
- *Name, address, contact details, date of birth, sex, occupation of victim*
- *Details of the offence*: eg what exactly happened (if known), how the offence was carried out, or the *modus operandi* (method of operating—how they work) of the offender(s). *This is essential*

because it can help identify any links or patterns in a series of similar offences and crime scenes, and better help to identify the perpetrators

- *Property* stolen/damaged and full descriptions, including value of items to replace or repair
- *Special property* recovered from scene, vicinity, or from suspects
- *Full and comprehensive description of the suspect*: this is also important because it may link offenders to other crimes, or help identify offenders based on previously recorded offender descriptions
- *Person(s) suspected/wanted* for the offence
- *Person(s) cautioned*/reported/arrested
- *Names and force identification numbers of officers* attending the scene, including police staff such as crime scene examiners or investigators
- *Details of the OIC* (officer in charge)
- *Enquiry log* (investigative actions completed so far, and by whom, eg if CCTV has been obtained, and from where, and which houses/premises you have attended. Also any witnesses you have spoken to, whether or not they have provided you with a statement, what they have said, or their witness account, and their full contact details). It is also important to note down any steps you have taken to locate offenders/stolen property so far
- *Further enquiries* to be completed, by whom, and by when.

(Adapted from Barron, 1994)

When detailing and describing the *modus operandi* (MO) for an offence in a crime report, it is important to consider the following points, which can be summarized by the mnemonic STOPCRIMES:

S Style – the actual method by which the offender committed the offence.

T Time – time, day, and date of offence, and the occasion, eg market days, Sunday nights, during school hours, late-night shop openings.

O Object – what was the motive or objective for committing the crime, eg revenge, lust, hate, personal or financial gain, etc.

P Pal – did the offender have any accomplices, and if so, how many people were involved in the crime?

C Classification – the type of person (age, occupation, wealth, beliefs, etc) or property falling victim to the crime, eg religious buildings, schools, fast-food outlets. Relevant occupations might include such persons as police officers, teachers, doctors, scientists, etc, that may be expressly targeted because of their job.

R Reason – given by a suspect for being at the crime scene, in the vicinity of it, or for possessing any articles or property.

> **I** Implement – was an implement used to effect entry: for example, brick thrown through window, ladder used, confidence trick/deception, smash and grab, or tool used such as a crowbar, screwdriver, or a jemmy.
>
> **M** Mode – of transport used by the offender to arrive at the crime scene, and depart it.
>
> **E** Entry – the exact point of entry to the premises: for example, through the roof, a skylight, window, etc.
>
> **S** Signature – was there anything peculiar or unusual done at the crime scene: for example, consumption of any food, use of the toilet, urination, defecation, or any attempt by the offender to leave a trademark or tag.

(adapted and augmented from Barron, 1994)

Crime reports are disclosable documents, so care should be taken to protect the privacy of witnesses and the victim, whilst providing enough relevant information accurately to record the offence and identify further lines of enquiry to be completed.

6.7 Problems with the Job and 'Duty of Care'; Trauma, Stress, and Counselling

Many jobs have stresses, strains, pressures, and difficulties. Examples range from social workers coping with caseloads of 'problem' families, through coroner's officers dealing constantly with the bereaved, to maxillofacial surgeons painstakingly reconstructing a person's jaw and face after an accident. The contrary state, too little stress and strain, such as in a purely mechanical and repetitive task, also has adverse effects. It seems that, to enjoy their work fully, humans need some stress and challenge, but not too much and certainly not all at once.

There are particular occupations where continual stress and *trauma*, cumulatively or repeatedly experienced, can wreak havoc. These are the Armed Forces and the Emergency Services, where the sudden awfulness of an event can affect any who are involved in it. You might think of things like bomb attacks, train and plane crashes, a motorway 'pile-up', or a civil emergency such as a building collapsing or flooding, all of which are largely unpredictable events and may incur widespread injury and loss of life. Those actually involved in the event can suffer searing consequences, months or even years afterwards. It can be much worse for those who are continually exposed to abnormal experiences of this kind, through what they have to do as a routine: think of staff in hospital Accident and Emergency Departments, aid workers, fire-fighters, paramedics, and, of course, police officers. One of the writers of this *Handbook*, working in Northern Ireland in the mid-1980s, still recalls clearly the effects and aftermath of a bomb exploding near him in Belfast. However, such things are not within 'normal' experience and few Special Constables will have dealt with the result of a terrorist attack.

Doctors and other health professionals used to call this 'syndrome' or set of symptoms 'shell shock' (for other ranks) and 'neurasthenia' (for officers) when describing the Army's experiences in the First World War. Later it became more democratically known as 'battle fatigue', 'extreme exposure to stress', 'war weariness', and many other names, until the word *trauma* began to describe, neatly enough, the nightmare-like quality of post-event distress.[16]

A particularly intense form of the recollection of stressful horror has been labelled **post-traumatic stress disorder** or **PTSD**, which we will look at shortly. But there are many instances of how the job can bring very powerful stresses in tow. Let's examine what they might be:

> **Task**
> Make a brief list of stress factors and traumas commonly encountered in policing.

Our own response to this, shown in the box below, is by no means definitive and we are conscious that there can be many other examples of stress inherent within the task of policing, but we have concentrated in our list of traumas on the commoner examples affecting Special Constables, rather than those affecting regular and specialist police officers (such as those in Firearms or in police search units such as POLSA). It is worth noting that stress counselling and knowledge of PTSD is more widespread in specialist units like Firearms than it is in the general run of policing. Compare your list with ours:

> **Discussion points: Some stresses and traumas in policing**
> • Attending a crime scene where there has been extreme violence
> • Injured children and elderly people in great distress

- Finding an adult who has been dead for some time
- FOA a murder scene
- Dealing with a would-be suicide
- Finding a dead child
- Missing-person enquiry (*misper*) resulting in finding the person injured or dead
- Dealing with continual hostility and abuse from aggressive members of the public
- Being isolated and fearful of attack
- Dealing with casualties after a fire or building collapse
- Dealing with the aftermath of a serious road traffic collision in which there are injuries and deaths
- Attending a 'domestic' where children or vulnerable people have been systematically abused
- Interviewing a paedophile
- Searching a suspect for drugs and being pricked by a used hypodermic needle
- Being spat on or attacked by suspects who claim to be HIV-positive or even have AIDS
- Dealing with casualties as the result of a crowd panicking and stampeding
- Intervening in a fight and being badly beaten oneself
- Assisting at a train or plane crash
- Dealing with a body on a railway line
- Searching the site of a gang rape for forensic evidence
- Being attacked with a deadly weapon
- Having a gun pointed at you from very close range
- Being taken prisoner or hostage.

We are not saying, of course, that all of what we list in the box is commonplace and therefore *likely* to happen to any Special Constable (though at least some of these examples will be familiar to experienced officers); what we *do* say is that each of these sometimes extreme examples has been the experience of one or more Special Constables and regular officers at some time during their careers.

6.7.1 **Post-Traumatic Stress Disorder**

How PTSD may show itself is described by a psychotherapist, Dr Walter Busuttil (2009):

[Those experiencing PTSD] suffer from night sweats and suddenly wake up, terrified or anxious, having had nightmares. Some have invasive memories where things keep popping into their minds, a bomb going off, a friend's death or being shot at. Worse still, they can get flashbacks where they actually see a snapshot or replay a film. Sometimes they are looking at the film and sometimes they are actually in it, it is happening to them again.

Reliving the episodes which caused such horror in the first place is very distressing indeed to the individual, who might think that the nightmares and flashbacks are symptoms of insanity or impending mental breakdown, and who often has recourse to alcohol to block the images out. That in turn, if taken to extremes, intensifies the individual's distress and vulnerability. Keith and Nicola Guy note that, averagely, 'five in 100 men and 10 in 100 women will experience PTSD',[17] though we may expect the incidence to be higher in those occupations which are regularly exposed to traumatic events, such as policing, paramedical/ medical staff, or service in the Armed Forces.

Of course, it might be that, in all your time as a Special Constable, you will never yourself experience PTSD and not encounter its symptoms in any of your colleagues. But it is now a recognized clinical condition and help exists to get people better, even if this does take time. *The worst thing anyone can do is to try to cope alone.* Having read this brief description of the extremities of stress, you might now be able to assist and advise those who need help, and know how to seek help yourself, if need be.

Most Special Constables most of the time experience less intense trauma and stress than we have discussed above, but those lesser anxieties and worries are still real enough and can gnaw away at you just as destructively. Most police forces have small teams of people who provide a confidential Counselling and Welfare Service to deal with problems such as these. No one can force you to go to Counselling Services unless you want to, just as no one can force you to adopt a healthy lifestyle unless you want to do so. Counselling and Welfare Services respond to approaches and are available to be consulted, but they are not prescribed like medicines. But what they offer does work: research by Professor John Mcleod of Tayside Institute for Health Studies found that:

> counselling interventions are generally effective in alleviating symptoms of anxiety, stress and depression in the majority of workplace clients, and have been found, in the majority of studies that have examined this factor, to reduce sickness absence rates in clients by up to 60 per cent.[18]

and up to 6.5 per cent of a workforce made use of counselling services. There have been specific studies and programmes to help stressed Special Constables and regular police officers (notably work by Gersons *et al*, 2000), in which a higher percentage has been supported, but only if police officers wanted such support and sought it out.

6.7.2 Trauma Risk Management (TRiM)

A more recent development in the treatment of 'lesser stress' (lesser in the sense of being more moderate in its effect than full-blown PTSD, but real enough to those suffering from it) is a stress management methodology called TRiM. Fewer than 8 per cent of people suffer PTSD as a result of their jobs, but everyone will react to abnormal events in some way. It is usually impossible to avoid people getting ill as the result of traumatic stress, but it is possible to manage this if it is identified early enough (within three days is the norm). TRiM was first developed in the Armed Forces to cope with just such an eventuality, and it has begun to make a relatively straightforward transference to policing and the Special Constabulary. Put simply, it uses regular in-house debriefing sessions with colleagues which are usually supported by, and sometimes facilitated through, in-force Occupational Health departments. This entails going over the details of any recent operational deployment, which might include things like witnessing 'armed conflicts or other aggression, extreme suffering or incidents such as kidnappings, road traffic accidents (*sic*) and fatalities' [TRiM, Centurion Risk Assessment, 2009].[19]

6.7.3 Conclusions

Special Constables are subject to stress in their normal 'day' jobs which their voluntary work may intensify. Such stresses are born of the often unpleasant and occasionally abnormally stressful work which policing entails. At its most extreme, stress can lead to the serious condition of post-traumatic stress disorder, which requires considerable investment in long-term counselling and psychotherapy to resolve. Other, lesser, stresses and tensions nonetheless take their toll, and police forces routinely provide, and encourage staff to use, in-house counselling and welfare services. Such use is voluntary, even though strongly advised and it may be down to the individual force culture whether or not the services are used.

Further Reading

Association of Chief Police Officers, *ACPO Investigation of Volume Crime Manual* (2001, London: ACPO)

Association of Chief Police Officers, *National Automatic Number Plate Recognition User Group: ECHR, Data Protection & RIPA Guidance Relation to the Police use of ANPR* (2004, London: ACPO)

ACPO (2005a), *ANPR Steering Group: ANPR Strategy for the Police Service— 2005/2008* (2005, London: ACPO)

ACPO (2005b), *Roads Policing Strategy* (2005, London: ACPO)

ACPO, *Police Health and Safety: a Management Benchmarking Standard* (2007, London: ACPO)

ACPO, *Strategy for a healthy police service* (2007b, London, ACPO)

Barron, T, *The Special Constable's Manual* (1994, London: Police Review Publishing)

Bryant, R and Bryant, S (eds.) with Caless, B, Lawton-Barrett, K, Underwood, R and Wood, D *Blackstone's Student Police Officer Handbook*, 4th edn. (2010, Oxford: Oxford University Press)

Busuttil, W, 'Some veterans have trauma from four conflicts', *The Independent*, 28 February 2009

Caless, B (ed.) and Bryant, R, Morgan, D, Spruce, B, and Underwood, R, *Blackstone's PCSO Handbook*, 2nd edn. (2010, Oxford: Oxford University Press)

Calligan, S, *Taking Statements*, 6th edn. (2007, Goole, East Yorkshire: The New Police Bookshop)

Clark, D, 'Life and Limb: the enforcement of health and safety law on the police service', *Police Professional*, No 61, 21 September 2006, pp 50–52

Emmott, J, 'Managing a Police Welfare Function', *Executive Development* (1994) Vol 7, No 3, MCB UP Ltd, pp 13–15

Gersons, B, Carlier, I, Lamberts, R, and van der Kolk, B, 'Randomised clinic trial of brief eclectic psychotherapy for police officers with post-traumatic stress disorder', *Journal of Traumatic Stress*, 2000; Vol 13, pp 333–47

Greenbery, N, Langston, V, and Jones, N, 'Trauma Risk Management (TRiM) in the UK Armed Forces', *Journal of the Royal Army Medical Corps* (2008) Vol 154, No 2, pp 123–6; available from: <http://www.kcl.ac.uk/kcmhr/information/publications/articles/screening/123TraumaRisk.pdf>, accessed 15 September 2009

Guy, K and Guy, N, 'Psychological Trauma', *Counselling at Work* (2009) Spring, pp 19–22

Hall, J, 'Trauma and Stress in high-demand conflict and emergency settings', *Counselling at Work* (2006) Autumn, pp 2–4

Health and Safety Executive (2005), 'A short guide to the Personal Protective Equipment at Work Regulations 1992', available at <http://www.hse.gov.uk/pubns/indg174.pdf>, accessed 5 October 2009

Health and Safety Executive (2009), 'RIDDOR—Report an Accident', available at <http://www.hse.gov.uk/riddor/>, accessed 5 October 2009

HM Courts' Service, *Definitions of vulnerable and intimidated witnesses*, 2006, available from <http://www.hmcourtsservice.gov.uk/infoabout/attend/witness/special-measures.htm>, accessed 1 March 2010

HMIC (1997), 'Officer Safety: Minimising the Risk of Violence', available at <http://inspectorates.homeoffice.gov.uk/hmic/inspections/thematic/os/>, accessed 5 October 2009

Home Office (2008), 'Statistics on the number of police officers assaulted on duty from 2005/06 to 2007/08 in England and Wales', available at <http://www.homeoffice.gov.uk/rds/pdfs08/hosb0808supptab1.pdf>, accessed 5 October 2009

Home Office (2009a), 'Statistics on the number of police officers assaulted on duty for 2008/09 in England and Wales', available at <http://www.homeoffice.gov.uk/rds/pdfs09/hosb1309supp.pdf>, accessed 5 October 2009

Home Office (2009b), 'Police Numbers', available at <http://police.homeoffice.gov.uk/human-resources/efficiency-and-productivity/Police-numbers/>, accessed 5 October 2009

Larcombe, M, 'Counselling isn't for the completely bonkers!' *Counselling at Work* (2007) February, pp 16–7

Mcleod, J, 'Research into the effectiveness of workplace counselling: new directions', *Counselling at Work* (2008) Winter, pp 7–8

National Institute for Clinical Excellence, *Post-traumatic stress disorder (PTSD): the management of PTSD in adults and children in primary and secondary care* (2005, London: NICE)

National Policing Improvement Agency, *Practical Advice on the Policing of Roads* (2007, London: NPIA)

NPIA, *Practice Advice on the Management and Use of Automatic Number Plate Recognition* (2009, London: NPIA)

PA Consulting Group (2004a), *Home Office/Association of Chief Police Officers—Denying criminals use of the road* (London: PA Consulting Group)

PA Consulting Group (2004b), *Driving Crime Down: Denying criminals the use of the road* (London: The Stationery Office)

Police Professional (2009a), 'A case for clarity', 4 June 2009

Police Professional (2009b) 'The Information Debate', 2 July 2009

Readhead, I, 'Question Time', *Police Review*, 24 August 2007

Rivers, K, 'Traumatic Stress: An Occupational Hazard', *Journal of Workplace Learning* (1993) Vol 5, No 1, MCB UP Ltd, pp 4–6

Specials Magazine, January 2008 (London: Story Worldwide, published on behalf of the NPIA)

Specials Magazine, March 2008, *ibid*

Specials Magazine, May 2008, *ibid*

Specials Magazine, August 2008, *ibid*

Specials Magazine, December 2008, *ibid*

Specials Magazine, April 2009, *ibid*

Specials Magazine, Summer 2009, *ibid*

Webster, B, 'Tyre-spiking "stinger" stops forecourt fuel thieves in their tracks', *The Times*, 22 May 2008, available from <http://www.timesonline.co.uk/tol/driving/article3981110.ece>, accessed 22 June 2009

Notes

1 Home Office, 'Statistics on the number of police officers assaulted on duty from 2005/06 to 2007/08 in England and Wales' (2008),

available at <http://www.homeoffice.gov.uk/rds/pdfs08/hosb0808 supptab1.pdf>, accessed 5 October 2009.

2 Home Office, 'Statistics on the number of police officers assaulted on duty for 2008/09 in England and Wales' (2009), available at <http://www.homeoffice.gov.uk/rds/pdfs09/hosb1309supp.pdf>, accessed 5 October 2009.

3 Bryant, R and Bryant, S (eds.) and Caless, B, Lawton-Barrett, K, Underwood, R, and Wood, D, *Blackstone's Student Police Officer Handbook*, 4th edn. (2010, Oxford: Oxford University Press).

4 See <http://www.independent.co.uk/news/uk/crime/police-criticise -safety-agency-over-failed-case-against-met-chiefs-542152.html> accessed 1 March 2010.

5 Adapted from Caless (2010: p 430); BEWARE has now been widely adopted in risk assessment, so you may already have met it, along with SPRAIN. The two together are comprehensive in guiding you to the best possible risk assessment in policing circumstances.

6 National Policing Improvement Agency, *Practice Advice on the Management and Use of Automatic Number Plate Recognition*, (2009, London: NPIA).

7 *Ibid.*

8 PA Consulting Group (2004b), *Driving Crime Down: Denying criminals the use of the road* (London: The Stationery Office).

9 National Policing Improvement Agency (2009b), *IMPACT Programme: Police National Database—Privacy Impact Assessment Report*, April 2009.

10 PA Consulting Group (2004b).

11 National Policing Improvement Agency (2009b).

12 *Ibid.*

13 PA Consulting Group (2004b).

14 Corbett, C, *Car Crime* (2003, Devon: Willan Publications); PA Consulting Group 2004b.

15 *Victim's Code*, 2006, replacing the *Victim's Charter*, details available from: <http://www.cjsonline.gov.uk/the_cjs/whats_new/news-3232. html>, accessed 1 March 2010.

16 *Trauma* is Greek for 'wound' and, whilst it is still used by specialist medical personnel to refer to particularly serious kinds of wounding, it has also come to mean *mental wound* in the sense of a horrific experience relived. The German word for 'dream' or nightmare is *traum* and the term has come to us largely through the domination of German psychologists and psychotherapists early in the field of recognizing and labelling mental disturbance.

17 Nicola and Keith Guy are directors and cofounders of The Red Poppy Company, researching trauma and alleviations of it. Keith is an expert witness in psychological trauma; more detail is available from their website: <http://www.theredpoppycompany.co.uk>.

18 Mcleod, J, 'Research into the effectiveness of workplace counselling: new directions', *Counselling at Work*, 2008, Winter, pp 7–8.

19 See, for example, Centurion Risk Assessment Services Ltd, available from: <http://www.centurionsafety.net/Corporate/Trauma_Risk_ management.html>, accessed 15 September 2009.

Chapter 7

Partnerships and Neighbourhood Policing

7.1 **Neighbourhoods and Communities**

In late 2008, a talented musician and conductor named Gareth Malone went to South Oxhey, near Harpenden in Hertfordshire, to try to create a 'community choir'. His persistent efforts were filmed by the BBC, as he recruited singers, staged concerts, and created a large choir containing all ages, including children from five primary schools and a men's chorus from local pubs. All parts of the town, a run-down urban landscape, came together to sing, in a symbolic unification as well as a musical one. People talked to one another again, friendships were formed, people began to recognize each other in the streets, and the sense of belonging to something bigger was voiced by many of those taking part. In other words, Gareth Malone's mission created afresh, a sense of community which had been lacking.[1]

7.1.1 **What is the difference between 'neighbourhood' and 'community'?**

In a report on progress in establishing Neighbourhood Policing, the Home Office wrote this:

> A 'neighbourhood' to an inner-city resident is very different from someone living in a rural area. For the former, their neighbourhood could be a few streets or the estate where they live; for the person in the country, it could be their village, or group of villages, or parish. Local communities, police forces, police authorities and partners are deciding what neighbourhoods mean—rather than being told by the Government—but typically, we would expect it to cover one or two local authority wards.

(Baggott and Wallace, 2006)

Neighbourhood, then, is about **place**, the physical location where people live, and consists of buildings: houses, flats, streets, shops, and other kinds of physical dwelling. It is tactile and dimensional. You can touch it, see it, and it remains more or less constant, though the human inhabitants of the neighbourhood may move in and move out regularly. People who live in a neighbourhood might actually have very little or nothing in common, even supposing that they know each other.

'**Community**', by contrast, is more about **combinations of things which people have in common**. It is a much vaguer, looser term altogether because we can be members of several communities simultaneously, so that a member of Gareth Malone's choir may have singing in common with the other members of the choir, but equally might be a member of a social club, have work, occupation, or other shared interests in common with some choir members, or have originally joined the choir with a group of friends, and others still might have 'community' with the choir because their siblings, older relatives, or children have become members. These 'social networks' may extend into considerable complexity and some, of course, will have nothing to do with belonging to a choir.

Task

Write down how many different communities you belong to.

Your list may have included some or all (and more) of the following:

Communities

Work (community of occupation)

Profession, skills, or knowledge (medicine, the law, retail, teaching, the military, building trades, maintenance, IT, civil engineer, commerce, and so on)

Professional or work associations (other members of the extended policing family, law enforcement agencies, professional institutions, trades unions, trade/skills 'guilds' or organizations, membership of professional bodies such as Chartered Management Institute, Institute of Electrical Engineers, British Forensic Association)

7.4 **Crime and Disorder Reduction Partnerships (CDRPs)**

The emphasis in both Neighbourhood Policing and Citizen Focus on establishing local partnerships and producing multi-agency responses to locally identified problems, takes place through the **Crime and Disorder Reduction Partnership (CDRP)**, sometimes called, particularly in Wales, the **Community Safety Partnership (CSP)** (the terms are interchangeable). This body *coordinates the public sector response to crime and disorder in an area* as it is now well established that such problems are not solely within the care of the police. This approach led to legislation to obligate local authorities and others to cooperate in producing solutions as part of their everyday activity. Section 17 of the 1998 Crime & Disorder Act imposed a duty on every local authority:

> [w]ithout prejudice to any other obligation imposed on it—[to] exercise its function with due regard to the need to do all it reasonably can to prevent crime and disorder in its area.
>
> (Crime & Disorder Act, 1998, section 17)

7.4.1 Membership of a CDRP

Five bodies have statutory responsibility for attending the CDRP and working towards its objectives—the police, the police authority, the fire and rescue service, the local authority, and the area primary health care trust. Not all problems relating to crime and disorder can be solved by these five organizations alone, so other organizations can be brought into the CDRP orbit, either as permanent or ad hoc members.

Task

Are there any other organizations you would want to work on a CDRP/CSP?

Consider what each could bring 'to the table' and what effect they could have on reducing crime and disorder in your area.

The lifeblood of the CDRPs is the flow of information about crime and disorder from *all* the partnerships as we demonstrate in the schematic diagram below. It is equally pertinent to suggest that in the same way that information flows into the CDRP so actions flow back out:

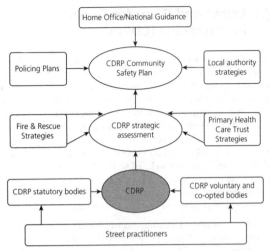

Figure 7.1: CDRP relationships

Task: turning the priorities into actions

Consider how *you* would use a CDRP to deal with a particular problem: under-age drinking. You must include roles for all the statutory CDRP bodies and include any other partners you feel could help.

Our suggestions are set out below:

Dealing with underage drinking

Information suggests that the problem of under-age drinking is becoming a real ASB nuisance within your area. The local media have run some stories and have alleged that little is being done to combat the nuisance.

Under-age drinking—CDRP partnership approach

The CDRP start the process by collecting the data and intelligence available to them, as well as highlighting those areas where information is sparse.

The following actions are then tasked to the five statutory CDRP agencies:

Police—provide an enforcement response to the problem by taking youths found drinking home to their parents; enforce any designated no-drinking zones allocated by the local authority; use intelligence sources to identify retail premises that may be selling alcohol to under-age persons.

Police Authority—monitor the activity of the police and link in with other partners to assist in the process.

Local Authority—consider implementing designated no-drinking areas; use licensing and trading standards officers to enforce legislation prohibiting sale of alcohol to those who are under age; use cleaning services to remove debris left behind by those drinking; instal CCTV if appropriate.

Fire & Rescue—start an education programme on the dangers of drink-driving; look at problem of under-age drinking and fire starting and enforce accordingly.

Primary Care Trust—provide education and literature to children and young people and their parents of the dangers of under-age drinking.

The following partners were then engaged under the aegis of the CDRP to add the following:

Local drug and alcohol charities to provide appropriate support and guidance to those affected by these problems.

Youth offending teams to provide positive support to young people, including diversionary activities.

Public Prosecution Service to ensure that convictions are sought for those found to be selling to under-age drinkers.

Voluntary community groups to enforce this message and to engage with communities to help provide solutions to the problems this can cause.

There is no one answer to the problem and our suggestions are merely illustrative of the approach a CDRP may take.

7.4.2 Some observations about CDRPs

Whilst it is well established that a multi-agency approach is one that works well with minor crime and disorder reduction, there are still many problems associated with CDRPs/CSPs. The practical nature of partnership work can be very difficult, especially if one agency seeks to dominate or another seeks to abrogate its responsibilities. The mechanics of getting all agencies on board and working towards specific problems can be very time-consuming. Rogers & Prosser (2006: p 12), for example, tell us that '[d]eep structural conflicts exist between the parties that sit down together in partnerships', which can make the whole process very frustrating. This is even without considering the potentially corrosive elements of politics, and the even more damaging atmosphere created by a perceived imbalance in resource allocation.

7.5 Partners and Communities Together (PACT)

Partners and Communities Together (PACT; sometimes confusingly but erroneously referred to as *Police* and Communities Together) is a part of neighbourhood policing in some police forces. It is impossible to provide a generic description of PACT because it functions differently in each force. This is not a sign of a lack of standardization, rather that neighbourhood policing *should* vary across the country, for without this variation how can the police properly respond to local concerns? The concerns and preoccupations of every neighbourhood will be different; it follows that the partnership arrangements to meet local needs in that locality will be different too.

7.5.1 What is PACT?

PACT is a *process*, not a series of fixed and timed events. *It is reflective of the attempts made by the police and partnership agencies in any given community to seek to understand the priorities that exist in that area.* This is the key point—PACT provides a series of opportunities for forces to understand what problems the local residents want the authorities to solve.

7.5.2 How does it work?

One illustrative example of the PACT process is provided by Devon and Cornwall Police (see Further Reading and references) which explains to the public what elements can be used in a PACT:

- **PACT Environmental Visual Audit (EVA)**—checking the locality for signs of deterioration
- **PACT Surgeries**—these are drop-in surgeries at advertised locations and times where members of the public can [. . .] speak to a police or local authority representative. Some [BCUs] use mobile police stations so that they can capture priorities from areas with a high 'footfall'
- **PACT Panel Meetings**—often follow a public meeting at which local residents [identify] the three top priorities for their community.

The panel is made up of representatives from the community and partnership agencies [see 7.7 for further details] and allocates these tasks accordingly

- **PACT Surveys**—can be door-to-door or [used] in areas where lots of people will be, and [can] capture local concerns but without the formality of a public meeting
- **PACT Postcards**—allow residents who cannot, or do not, attend meetings and surgeries to identify their concerns; instead post them in boxes that are then collected by the neighbourhood policing team (NPT)
- **PACT Response Mailing**—similar to the postcards but with prepaid envelopes that can be sent direct to the appropriate NPT.

This spread of projects for PACT is not unique to Devon and Cornwall, of course, (though it is a good example) and we know that such methods are replicated across England and Wales to a greater or lesser degree, with many forces showing considerable ingenuity in seeking to capture information on community priorities. Furthermore, in some forces there may already be mechanisms that can be utilized for identifying PACT priorities.

7.5.3 Problems with PACT

There are problems that can bedevil such a process. Not all are insurmountable, but they do represent a challenge to the NPTs, which are often charged with other busy tasks and which cannot devote all their time to PACT matters:

Possible problems with PACT
- Public meetings can be very time-consuming to manage, requiring as they do a chairperson, an agenda, a venue, publicity, quorate membership, resolutions, and actions
- Public meetings do not appeal to all sections of the community. Such events tend to favour those who are comfortable with public speaking and with formal discussions
- Public meetings can be hijacked by groups which have a single issue or political agenda that does not fully represent the views of the community, but about which they are vociferous (for example, by-pass roads and environmental concerns)
- Public apathy—meetings and surgeries can be sparsely attended (which lets the 'single-issue zealots' exercise disproportionate influence sometimes)

- Partnership non-attendance—the police is often the organization with the dedicated resources for the locality and it often falls on them to persuade other partners to attend; even the local authority can drag its feet
- How representative can PACT be? Does a public meeting of 25 people identifying local priorities reflect the will of the whole community?
- Costs—there may be costs associated with postcards, surveys, prepaid envelopes, etc
- It must be a problem-solving process not a 'talking shop'
- How is feedback provided to the residents of the locality? [Feedback is crucial as it can demonstrate success and may drum up further support]
- Will PACT always focus on the low-level problems?

These are by no means the only problems with PACT but they do demonstrate some of the potential pitfalls that need to be considered throughout the process. More positively, many police forces are establishing 'social identity PACTs' in order to capture the priorities of diverse and minority groups, as this example from Lancashire shows:

> What we're finding is that, as we develop PACT, the specific communities with specific issues are also coming under the PACT umbrella. . . we have a very active lesbian and gay PACT in Blackpool which talks about the issues that community are facing. We've recently initiated deaf PACT meetings for the deaf community. . .
>
> (ACC Cunningham, Lancashire Police quoted in *Police Professional*, 2006: p 24)

7.6 'Watch' Systems

The majority of 'Watch' systems in use in both rural and urban localities derive from the basis of the **Neighbourhood Watch** scheme. The concept is familiar to us from the history of the Special Constable (see 1.5) where even ancient communities banded together watchfully for their own protection and security. The Watch was a citizens' regular night patrol of the town or city, armed with staves and sticks, which bodily apprehended felons or wrongdoers (or people just out and about) for the parish or town constable to deal with in the 'lock-up' the next day. In more modern times, neighbourhoods realize that some local crime problems, such as casual or opportunistic burglary, are enabled because no one is watching—or seen to be watching.

By banding together in organized groups, Neighbourhood Watch aims to deflect or displace the intention to commit crime. Suspicious behaviour can be reported, vehicle registrations noted, and the early signs of anti-social behaviour, such as breaking windows, can be reported and dealt with. Occupants of houses put stickers in their downstairs windows, advertising or warning that Neighbourhood Watch is in operation. Similar notices can be placed on lamp-posts and telephone poles.

There is a downside to Neighbourhood Watch. It can be dominated by the middle-class, home-owning retired, with time on their hands and an inexhaustible nosiness about their neighbours' affairs. That said, Neighbourhood Watch (and in some areas Home Watch) has grown to a nominal 10 million members involving nearly 4 million households throughout England and Wales.[6] And yet this apparently enormous figure leads us back to the heart of an unease in policing about Neighbourhood Watch: in 1992, figures suggested that 70 per cent of Neighbourhood Watch schemes were in low crime-risk areas, where there was relative affluence. The highest-crime areas, described by HMIC as 'the poorest council estates, multi-racial areas and some inner city areas' had the fewest Neighbourhood Watch schemes. Indeed, only those city areas which had been 'gentrified' had schemes at all.[7]

This should not be surprising. NPTs or CDRPs find residents in high-crime areas the most difficult of all to persuade to take some measure of control of their own lives and surroundings, and in such places Neighbourhood Watch has few fertile patches in which to grow and develop. For all that, some schemes have shown development in spite of their unpromising environment. In Greater Manchester, a scheme involving long-term commitment by Special Constables has resulted in more crime being reported, whilst on a difficult housing estate in South Yorkshire, Special Constables work alongside other agencies such as housing and social services jointly to solve some of the locality's crime and disorder.[8]

7.6.1 Other kinds of watch scheme

There are many other kinds of watch scheme operating in England and Wales, of which the most prominent (and often most successful) are Shop Watch in shopping districts—using radio links between security patrols and stewards to monitor activity by the suspicious or anti-social—and, in the countryside, Horse Watch. The latter's most spectacular success to date occurred in 2007, when a man who had been systematically wounding horses by cutting their leg muscles with a scalpel was caught in the act and sentenced to a prison term for cruelty.

Here is a brief list of Watch derivatives:

Other kinds of Watch scheme
Boat Watch (Hampshire)
House Watch
Home Watch (Surrey)
Saddle Watch
Business Watch
Taxi Watch
Sheep Watch (North Wales)
Pony Watch
Pub Watch
Trailer Watch
Caravan Watch (Devon & Cornwall)
Tent Watch (Dorset)
Cattle Watch (Derbyshire)

(source: HMIC 1998)

7.7 Neighbourhood Policing Teams (NPTs)

Neighbourhood Policing is predicated upon responses to local issues and identifying local solutions for the priorities of residents in a given neighbourhood. Neighbourhood Policing should not only be different in Manchester and Harwich, *it should be different in differing neighbourhoods in the same town or police BCU*. It follows that the teams which deliver neighbourhood policing in all these localities should match the needs of the locality, not conform to any generic model.

7.7.1 The role of Neighbourhood Policing Teams

That said, there will be a common theme running through the work of most NPTs and this has been articulated by the Home Office as follows:

What does a Local NPT do?

Neighbourhood policing teams are involved in proactive or preventative work to tackle low-level crime and anti-social behaviour that may be a persistent issue or concern in the local community.

- communities can now expect to see increased numbers of PCSOs patrolling their streets, addressing anti-social behaviour issues and building relationships with local people
- communities should also have information about how their local force will be policing the local community, and have a point of contact for their neighbourhood team
- local people will have the opportunity to tell the police about the issues which are causing them concern and help shape the response to those issues.

(Home Office, <http://police.homeoffice.gov.uk/community-policing/neighbourhood-policing>, accessed 25 October 2009)

There are some key themes that inform the activities of an NPT and will determine their composition:

- **Work is both proactive and preventative**—an NPT requires an enforcement capacity but also focuses on crime reduction/prevention
- **Tackling anti-social behaviour**—partnership needed with local authorities as they have the lead responsibilities on many of the issues that ASB encompasses, such as noise, litter, dog fouling
- **PCSOs**—any NPT must embrace the extended policing family as part of its remit; PCSOs have effective powers to deal with low-level nuisance
- **Local people/local community**—the priorities of local people are paramount and therefore partnership must involve the community, not only in identifying problems but also in implementing long-term solutions.

7.7.2 The importance of visibility

A key aspect for any NPT is ensuring that the public is aware of what it does and who the individual team members are. Police forces have published details of who patrols which neighbourhood, with photographs of NP officers and PCSOs as well as their official contact details (force email address and force mobile phone numbers). Many police forces have functions on their websites that allow access to details of the local NPT. This service is also available via Directgov—a website that puts access to all public services in one place: see <http://www.direct.gov.uk>. This accessibility is also linked to the tasking of NPTs to undertake patrols in their areas/neighbourhoods:

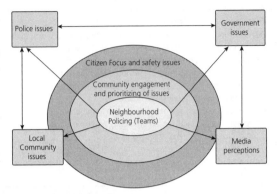

Figure 7.2: The NPT 'Square'

(Adapted from 'The Components of Community Engagement'

7.7.3 Composition of a NPT

The diagram below describes those generic factors that may appear in an NPT :

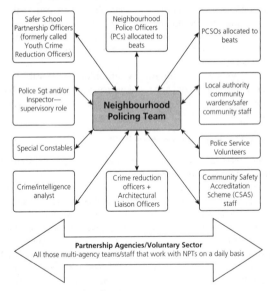

Figure 7.3: Components of NPTs

The composition of the NPTs will not necessarily fit into this neat, nicely delineated model, proud though we are of it. The local truth for your NPT will be more complex and will often be based on changing priorities. However, the essence in our model is crucial: the composition of an NPT must involve more than the police, and whilst partnership agencies and the voluntary sector are not formal members, they are important partners, without whom community engagement could not be achieved.

7.7.4 Success factors for an NPT

The composition of an NPT is only one factor. Getting the right blend of partners and an environment in which community engagement can flourish are factors that turn a good idea into an achievable event. Communities do not necessarily care about the foundation or rationale for neighbourhood policing, they simply want to see results. A recent academic study highlighted what those success factors are:

- An organization-wide community policing ethos
- Decentralized decision making
- Locale-based accountability
- The involvement of auxiliaries
- Proactive tactics oriented to crime prevention
- A problem-solving approach, and
- Sincere engagement in interagency partnerships and public involvement.

(Fielding, 2009, p 9)

Task

Consider each of the success factors outlined above.

How will you as a Special Constable ensure that you can contribute to each of these?

What can you bring to the role that will benefit community engagement for your force?

We believe that, if you examine your motivations for being a Special Constable (whether it involves making a difference, or performing some form of public service, or even in eventually becoming a regular officer), then you will fit into this community engagement rationale.

7.7.5 The Special Constable and Neighbourhood Policing

As both our model and our task have illustrated, there is a pivotal role for the Special Constable within Neighbourhood Policing, and in particular in community engagement. After all, what are these other than listening to the community and responding to their needs? The role of the Special Constable was highlighted in the **Special Constabulary National Strategy** as fundamentally within community engagement (see Introduction, where the *seven key areas of policing* were identified—which we used as the basis for this *Handbook*). If the Special Constabulary is to deliver all it can to policing, then it must enthusiastically embrace neighbourhood policing. Indeed, Peter Fahy, ACPO Lead for the Special Constabulary, suggests that Special Constables are uniquely placed to do so:

> The neighbourhood teams are all about building confidence and developing active communities. What better way to achieve this than by recruiting Specials who are citizens first and foremost and have those community links? And because Specials are flexible, committed, high-quality individuals, they are in great demand by the neighbourhood teams.

(Chief Constable Peter Fahy, *Specials*, April 2009, p 11)

7.8 The Special Constable and Neighbourhood Policing— Case Studies

Case Study No 1—ROC Cafe, Dinnington, South Yorkshire
This is a project designed to provide young people with a place of their own to meet in, and was established by a partnership involving the Special Constabulary, the Safer Neighbourhood Team, the local community, local churches, and the young people themselves. The ROC (Redeeming Our Communities) Cafe was opened and provided a diversionary activity for those people previously engaged in ASB. On the nights it is open there has been an 85 per cent decrease in reported ASB.

(*Specials*, August 2008c, p 16)

This example shows that, as a significant member of a neighbourhood team, the Special Constabulary has contributed to a reduction in ASB and subsequently provided reassurance to a community. This is hard-edged reality, because a reduction in crime and providing a sense of safety for residents is at the heart of what neighbourhood policing is.

Case Study 2: Neighbourhood Task Teams (NTT) and Specials in Kent

Neighbourhood Task Teams (NTTs) are a comparatively new addition to police resources in Kent and are intended to tackle crime, disorder, and the anti-social behaviour issues that adversely affect local communities, together with improving levels of confidence and satisfaction in the police service (see 10.2). NTTs were first implemented by Kent Police in September 2008 after a series of successful pilots. The teams tackle those issues and problems identified by the public that cause them most concern, or which negatively affect their quality of life, and which require immediate, comprehensive, and decisive intervention by a dedicated unit that can exercise full police powers.

NTTs are essentially proactive, tactical, neighbourhood policing support units that supplement the capacity of local NPTs, strengthening the number of staff available to combat and resolve local community issues, and providing an immediate response capability. The teams usually include five experienced regular police constables with a background in neighbourhood or enforcement-based policing, led by a police sergeant. The teams are specifically tasked to deal with and concentrate effort on addressing the most significant issues that affect local communities, such as anti-social behaviour by people both on foot and driving motor vehicles, vandalism, petty offending, disorder and nuisance issues, joyriding, littering, kerb crawling, prostitution, drug dealing, and illegal drug abuse. The NTT core role is to support the NPTs dedicated to a specific geographical area.

NTTs operate in crime 'hot spots', and in other areas that suffer from severe disorder problems, or persistent and recurrent anti-social behaviour. The teams respond either to a specific issue, such as vandalism, littering, or alcohol-related disorder fuelled by the night-time economy, or to a longer-term or more deeply rooted local neighbourhood problem such as drug dealing or prostitution.

In direct response to local community concerns about the anti-social behaviour issues created by a prolific reoffending gang of youths aged between 14 and 18, Medway BCU's NTT launched an intervention against the group, resulting in their arrests. The team was actively supported by the local community and was able to secure sufficient evidence to convince magistrates to impose strict bail conditions on each of the offenders. The youths now each have a curfew to remain indoors between 2100 and 0600 hours (when most of their offending behaviour had previously occurred); not to contact their co-defendants either directly or indirectly; not to contact or interfere with any witnesses; and not to enter specified streets or locations.

NTTs have also been used to reinforce and supplement the policing and enforcement of the 'alcohol control zone' in Gillingham BCU. The teams had measurable success in preventing, or rapidly responding to, alcohol-related disorder in the local town centre, particularly in the evenings and at weekends.

To tackle the problem of anti-social use of motor vehicles in central Tonbridge, and the associated issues of erratic, careless, inconsiderate, and dangerous driving, an NTT was tasked with conducting regular high-profile road-safety operations throughout the autumn and winter evenings. These operations provide the NTT with an opportunity to improve road safety within the locality and to tackle road-traffic-related offending, through issuing warnings to individuals, or prosecuting them where necessary. But it is important to note that the road safety operations are far more than simply enforcement-driven activities. They also allow officers the chance to interact and engage with road users and educate them about the safety implications of their offending behaviour or vehicle defects, emphasizing the drivers' own welfare, that of their passengers, and of other road users.

Special NTTs
Encouraged by the successes and positive impacts the NTTs have had on improving public confidence and satisfaction, in 2009 Kent Police actively engaged the Special Constabulary to enhance the capacity of the task teams to deal with local community concerns. In parts of Kent, Special NTTs

effect, where offenders simply move elsewhere, giving some other part of the area the headache of dealing with them) is another criticism, as is the 'fortress mentality' adopted by gated communities which exacerbates the inhabitants' already high fear of crime, both of which can dominate the crime prevention tactics used by local authorities and the Special Constabulary.

Social crime prevention, usually working in parallel with situational crime prevention, addresses the long-term motivation of the offender, often on the basis that early intervention may help to deflect potential offenders away from crimes, or that combined agency and partnership working, for example the Special Constabulary with social services, may offer alternatives to offending and role models other than criminals for younger people to emulate. Factors such as child abuse, neglect, poor or absent parenting, health, education, and aspirational issues may be taken into account, and alternatives offered, to reduce the risk of later offending.

If crime prevention is a series of measures, situational and social, designed to reduce offending, then **crime reduction** is the term given to all such strategies and methods, based on 'what works' in reducing crime. Needless to say, this is a huge area of academic research and applied thinking, best accessed through the Home Office Crime Reduction website <http://www.crimereduction.homeoffice.gov.uk>.

Crime prevention and crime reduction have become big business in the United Kingdom, not surprisingly since the cost of crime itself in 2009 was estimated to be **£78 billion** (Chambers *et al*, 2009). However, it is not just private companies, local authorities, and concerned citizens who have an interest in crime prevention; there is an obvious incentive for the government to reduce the cost of crime (particularly in the current economic climate and especially with the 2011 public sector spending review on the horizon). This central governmental concern permeates policing as well as local authorities, and has real resonance for the Special Constabulary.

7.9.1 Areas for crime reduction/prevention

Table 7.2 details those types of crime, crime audit, and local amenity for which the Home Office has published practical crime reduction advice ('toolkits') that are accessible to the public.

Any one of these areas has ramifications, since they are all areas in which Special Constables operate. Crime reduction/prevention should be at the heart of policing and it is one area in which

Table 7.2: Crime Reduction—Areas of Concern

Vehicle crime	Street crime and robbery
Domestic burglary	Repeat victimization
Using intelligence and information sharing	Alcohol-related crime
Anti-social behaviour	Rural crime
Motor salvage operators regulations	Public transport
Racial crime and harassment	Communities against drugs
Mentally disordered offenders	Trafficking in people
Fear of crime	Business and retail crime
Arson	Safer schools and hospitals

(From <http://www.crimereduction.homeoffice.gov.uk/toolkits/index.htm>, accessed 11 October 2009)

Special Constables need to be competent, not least because the public will expect them to have specialist levels of knowledge, or be able to direct them to access that knowledge.

7.9.2 Crime prevention products

There are Home Office-sponsored sites dispensing crime reduction advice (go to <http://www.crimereduction.homeoffice.gov.uk>, and scroll through the sections). Furthermore, many local authorities will have sector or charitable schemes that can assist with crime prevention. Forces too will distribute free products such as shed alarms or purse chains at community safety events, so it is worth Special Constables becoming familiar with the initiatives and resources on offer:

Table 7.3: Crime Prevention Products

Alarms	CCTV	Property marking (UV/SmartWater)
Security guards	Lighting	Signage
Door and window security	Layout design	Access control
Stop locks	Fake storage tins	Purse chains
Shredders	Safes	Gates
Barriers	Hedges	Intercoms
Identification badges	Vehicle tracking equipment such as 'Tracker' beacons	Nominated neighbour schemes

(See the 'Crime Matters' website for further details: <http://www.crimematters.org.uk>)

However, technical knowledge alone is not enough in crime prevention and the risk factors that lead to criminality must also be explored, assessed, and actions taken to address them.

7.9.3 Risk factors for criminality

The following diagram highlights some of the risk factors involved in criminality, whilst the circles identify possible preventative measures:

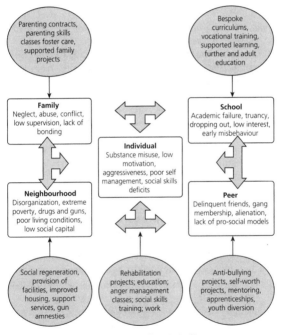

Figure 7.4: Risk factors and solutions for criminality

7.9.4 Youth crime prevention

Much of the above involves reducing or preventing crime amongst young people. This is often for self-evident economic reasons—if you can stop the criminality at a young age, the costs associated with its detection, prevention, and reduction are correspondingly reduced. The following is an example of attempts to provide young people with an alternative to crime:

Charlton Athletic Social Inclusion Programme

This scheme won the South East region award for the prestigious Tilley Awards in 2009 and is a partnership between Charlton Athletic FC and Kent Police.

The project engages children at risk of exclusion from school and [who are] becoming involved with anti-social behaviour and youth crime. With the help of coaches from the League One football club, coaching sessions were set up in areas around Kent and soon developed into wider community projects which engaged 2,000 young people.

The areas where the projects were set up saw a 25 per cent drop in reports of anti-social behaviour and reduced the exclusion rates amongst participants.

There can be considerable criticism of youth diversion programmes, coupled with tabloid accusations of rewarding poor behaviour, but in this case the drop in ASB and exclusion rates has obvious and positive ramifications for the participants, the police, and the community. This seems to us something to be applauded rather than criticized; but if the scheme persists, it will justify itself without either external support or detraction.

7.9.5 Crime prevention/reduction and the Special Constabulary

Special Constables have active roles within the crime prevention/reduction framework. The Special Constabulary National Strategy (2008) indicates that crime reduction is one of the four main areas where the Specials can make a real difference:

The National Strategy work was driven by the need to define a specific role for the Special Constabulary, a key purpose being to identify tasks that would make a real difference to community safety. These tasks had to play to the strengths of the Specials and recognize the limitations on the demands that can be placed on volunteers. The Special Constabulary was shown to have a key role to play in:
- *Crime reduction/detection*
- Incident response
- Neighbourhood Policing
- Protective Services.

(NPIA, 2008, 6.1.1, our italics)

7.9.6 Special Constables and crime prevention: cases in point

The following examples show the Special Constabulary participating, in a genuine operational sense, in crime prevention initiatives:

Operation Bond—Merseyside Police

In Liverpool, Special Constables contributed to an operation run by the Proactive Licensing Team designed to ensure the safety of people in the night-time economy. The operation included the use of 'sniffer dogs' to detect drugs, as well as plain-clothes Special Constables deployed to spot suspicious behaviour. The Operation ensures that around the clubs and bars there is a visible uniformed presence and is designed to deter ASB, violence and drug use.

(Specials, April 2009, pp 14–16)

Operation Scott—Gloucestershire Police

In Gloucestershire, 18 Special Constables have joined forces with the Roads Policing Unit to check speeding motorists and issue advice on the A46. This was intended to be an educative exercise and was named after a local boy who had died on that road. The operation was designed to check speeding but other offences were detected and dealt with.

(Specials, Summer 2009, p 5)

Crime prevention is as integral a part of policing as investigation of, or response to, criminal acts, even if society still has no objective correlative through which the effect of crime prevention can be quantified (not being able to 'count' it perpetuates its 'Cinderella' status).

7.10 Environmental Visual Audits (EVA) and Neighbourhood Concerns

One of the activities undertaken by neighbourhood Special Constables and PCSOs is that of the Environmental Visual Audit (EVA) and

> [it] is the insight that to an extent public anxiety and confidence reflects the nature of the physical environment they inhabit. The method of

environmental audit is an attempt to capture the central features of
the policed environment to which the law-abiding public responds.

(Fielding *et al*, 2002, p 6)

This makes EVA a powerful tool, particularly when many of
the problems identified might not previously have found their
way on to the police neighbourhood 'radar', either because the
problems were deemed to be not important enough, or because
they were seen as 'belonging' to the council or to someone else.
Thus, an EVA provides a window on to a community and in doing
so provides a more holistic problem-solving approach because
the problems identified are those that cause people the greatest
concern:

What to the police may seem low-level, trivial and routine behaviours
or disrepair can to the public represent serious threats to their sense
of comfort and well-being. The method of environmental audit is an
attempt to gauge the public's sensitivities and to provide an information base with which to accommodate these in partnership interventions whose outcome the public will regard as effective.

(Fielding *et al*, 2002, p 7)

7.10.1 Signal crimes perspective

In 2002, Dr Martin Innes (from the University of Surrey, working
alongside Surrey Police) developed the concept of a 'signal crimes
perspective' which sought to demonstrate that *some crimes and
acts of anti-social behaviour make people feel disproportionately unsafe
within their community*. These 'signal' crimes act as a social barom-
eter for feelings of safety. The kinds of activity we are talking
about are often low-level, even trivial in police terms, but Innes's
work demonstrated that dealing with these lower-level issues was
crucial to improving public perceptions of safety. Examples of
signal crimes include:

- Litter
- Dog fouling
- Nuisance noise
- Signs of criminal damage/vandalism
- Young people congregating (as perceived by others)
- Graffiti, and
- Abandoned cars.

The 'signal' is not a simple equation where **act + unease =
police intervention**. The psychological processes involved are

actually rather complex, and this is reflected in the complexity of the signal itself. Innes identified four elements to the signal crimes perspective—the *expression*, the *content*, the *effect* and the *control signal*:

The Signal Crimes Perspective—the constituent parts

Expression—the act of disorder or crime that gives concern for the person seeing it, or hearing about it.

Content—how it made that person feel about safety in his/her community.

Effect—what happened as a result of this incident.

Control Signal—what the authorities did to deal with this issue (or, in not doing something, what have they signalled to the community?)

An example

When I leave my house in the morning to walk to work I often have to walk past the empty alcohol cans and bottles left by the groups who gather to drink at night nearby (the *expression*). In the winter when I return, I worry that they may be gathered in the street and I worry about how they will react when I go by (the *content*). When I saw these groups, I often walked home a longer way round so as to avoid them (the *effect*). When this was highlighted by me and others at a public meeting, the police increased their patrols and the local authority made the vicinity a designated 'no-drinking area' (the *control signals*).

7.10.2 Signal crimes and Neighbourhood Policing

The relevance of the signal crimes perspective to neighbourhood policing is obvious, given that it deals with people's perceptions of safety, and this has been recognized by many police forces, which are alerted to act when examples are brought to their attention. This approach has been recognized as being complementary to the aims and objectives of Neighbourhood Policing:

> The Signal Crimes Perspective is equally valid in neighbourhood policing. The primary focus of the SCP is that some incidents of crime and disorder can act as warning signs to the public about the distribution of risks to their security in everyday life. Some crimes and disorderly behaviours will, therefore, have a disproportionate impact on public perception of risk.
>
> (ACPO/NPIA, 2006, p 6)

Signal crimes—an example

In Lambeth, south-west London, Clapham Park was chosen as a New Deal for Communities (NDC) regeneration project. Part of the problem was that the benches in housing blocks, which [originally] had been provided for elderly people, were used by drug dealers, drug takers, prostitutes, and those drinking alcohol. The debris [left by] these activities, and [concerns about the people] using the area, had made the benches a no-go area for the elderly residents. The way the benches were being used became the signal crime. When removed, the criminal and anti-social activity stopped and the complaints stopped. This was the control signal the community needed.

(Police Professional, 2009, p16; our explanatory additions in square brackets)

7.10.3 What will be on an EVA?

Each EVA will reflect a different set of individual, local, or parochial concerns but there may be similarities and overlaps in some areas: for example, many urban centres will highlight problems with graffiti or criminal damage. In terms of EVAs, geography matters:

Members of a community frame their sense of neighbourhood using geographic markers such as streets, buildings or natural land formations as boundaries. . . this proximity connects community members to the same experiences—good or bad. . .

(Wilson & Brown, 2009, p 30)

The actual capture of the issues is only one part of the overall strategy of engagement. The following table highlights many of the issues that could feature on a 'typical' EVA; many of these issues are signal crimes:

Table 7.4: Environmental issues that could feature on an EVA

Graffiti	Boarded-up premises	Abandoned premises
Heavy security shutters	Lots of CCTV	Overgrown gardens
Rubbish outside houses	Broken windows	Poor street lighting
Used condoms	Evidence of public urination	Loud music/noise
Homeless people	Begging	Congregations of large groups of people

Litter	Drugs paraphernalia	Broken bottles
Speeding cars	Illegal parking	Dog fouling
Stray dogs	Unlit alleyways	Signs of vandalism/criminal damage

7.10.4 Engaging with young people

The shaded example below shows an innovative way to engage with young people. Including them (and their families) in consultation on what problems may exist in a community is an excellent way to reach consensus solutions, as well as community ownership of those solutions:

Community Involvement in an EVA

An example of community involvement in an EVA is provided by Thames Valley Police:

Katesgrove neighbourhood policing team will be conducting an Environmental Visual Audit (EVA) around Katesgrove Primary School with children from the school.

The EVA, which aims to identify issues that impact on the quality of life of local residents such as graffiti and fly-tipping, will be carried out in partnership with Reading Borough Council and the local community.

This is a follow-up to an earlier EVA conducted in September 2008 with children from the school, which was considered very successful in identifying a number of issues.

(Thames Valley Police, 15 June 2009)

7.10.5 Conclusion

In its more formal adoption, the EVA is clearly a useful tool within Neighbourhood Policing itself, but its central tenets have applicability to the wider Special Constable role. If you understand the signal crimes perspective and realize that certain issues/disorders have a disproportionate effect on individual and communal perspectives of safety, then you understand why community engagement is central. Furthermore, in understanding this approach, you can begin to become part of the solution. After all, what better control signal is there than the Special Constabulary volunteers who wish to make a difference in their community?

In time, we envisage that the corollary to Martin Innes's signal crime will be the Special Constabulary's **'signal solution'**.

Further Reading

ACPO/NPIA, *Practice Advice on Professionalising the Business of Neighbourhood Policing* (2006, Wyboston, Lincolnshire: National Centre for Policing Excellence, part of NPIA), available from: <http://www.neighbourhoodpolicing.co.uk/doclib/doclib_view.asp?ID=528>, accessed 12 October 2009

ACPO, *Citizen Focus Hallmarks Summary*, (2008, NPIA) available from <http://www.npia.police.uk/en/docs/citizen_focus_hallmarks_summary_document.pdf>, accessed 12 November 2009

Baggott, M and Wallace, M, *Neighbourhood Policing Progress Report*, (May 2006, Home Office, Crown copyright)

BBC, *'Smith sorry over knife crime data'* 15 December 2008, available from <http://news.bbc.co.uk/1/hi/uk_politics/7784094.stm>, accessed 11 October 2009

Bottoms, A., Mawby, R, and Xanthos, P, 'A tale of two estates' in Downes, D. (ed.), *Crime & the City* (1989, London: Macmillan)

Bottoms, A and Wiles, P, 'Environmental Criminology', Chapter 18 of Maguire, M (ed.), *The Oxford Handbook of Criminology* (2002, Oxford: Oxford University Press)

Brand, S and Price, R, *The economic and social costs of crime*, Home Office Research Study 217 (2005, London: Home Office)

Brantingham P and Faust F, 'A conceptual model of crime prevention' in *Crime and Delinquency*, (1976) 22, pp. 284–98

Brogden, M and Nijhar, P, *Community Policing: national and international models and approaches* (2005, Devon: Willan Publishing)

Byrne, S and Pease, K, 'Crime reduction and community safety' in Newburn, T (ed.), *Handbook of Policing* (2003, Devon: Willan Publishing) Part III, pp 286–310

Caless, B (ed.), with Bryant, R, Spruce, B, and Underwood, R, *Blackstone's Police Community Support Officer's Handbook*, 2nd edn. (2010, Oxford: Oxford University Press)

Casey, L, 'Engaging Communities in Fighting Crime', (2008) *Cabinet Office Crime and Communities Review*, Crown copyright; available from: <http://www.cabinetoffice.gov.uk/newsroom/news_releases/2008/080618_fighting_crime.aspx>, accessed 1 March 2010

Chambers, M, Ullmann, Waller, I and Lockhart, G, *'Less Crime, Lower Costs. Implementing effective early crime reduction programmes in England & Wales'* (2009, Policy Exchange report for Devon & Cornwall Constabulary) available at <http://neighbourhoodpolicing.devon-cornwall.police.uk/PACT/Pages/default.aspx>, accessed 12 October 2009

Community Safety Advisory Service (CSAS), 'The role of CDRPs' available from <http://www.csas.org.uk/cdrp>, accessed 14 November 2009

Ditton, J, 'Fear of Crime' in Newburn, T and Neyroud, P (eds.), *Dictionary of Policing* (2008, Cullompton, Devon: Willan Publishing), pp 105–6

Farrell, S, *Experience and Expression in the Fear of Crime* (2007, Economic and Social Research Council (ESRC))

Feilzer, M, 'Not fit for purpose! The (Ab-)Use of the British Crime Survey as a Performance Measure for Individual Police Forces', *Policing* (2009) Vol. 3, No. 2, pp 200–211

Felson, M and Clarke, R, *Opportunity makes the Thief: Practical Theory for Crime Prevention*, Police Research Series, Paper 98 (1998, Home Office, Crown copyright)

Fielding, N, *'Getting the best out of Community Policing'* (2009) The Police Foundation, Paper 3, May 2009

HMIC, *A Special Relationship: Police Forces, the Special Constabulary and Neighbourhood Watch*, HMIC report 1996/97/98, (1998, Horn Ltd), Crown copyright

HMIC, *Serving Neighbourhoods & Individuals: A thematic report on Neighbourhood Policing and Developing Citizen Focus Policing* (2008) available from < http://www.hmic.gov.uk/SiteCollectionDocuments/Thematics/THM_20081101.pdf>, accessed 12 November 2009

Holloway, K, Bennett, T, and Farrington, D, *Does Neighbourhood Watch Reduce Crime?* (2008, Crime Prevention Research Review, Home Office, Crown copyright)

Home Office White Paper, *Building Communities, Beating Crime* (2004) available from: < http://police.homeoffice.gov.uk/publications/police-reform/wp04_complete.html>, accessed April 2008

Home Office (2005b),*'What the public can expect to see from local neighbourhood policing team'* available from <http://police.homeoffice.gov.uk/community-policing/neighbourhood-policing>, accessed 25 October 2009

Home Office (2006b), *Citizen Focus: Good Practice Guide* available from <http://police.homeoffice.gov.uk/publications/community-policing/citizen-focus-guide/>, accessed 12 November 2009

Home Office report (2006c) *British Crime Survey: Measuring crime for 25 years* available from <http://www.homeoffice.gov.uk/rds/pdfs07/bcs25.pdf>, accessed 11 October 2009

Home Office Green Paper, *From the neighbourhood to the national: policing our communities together*, Cm 7448 (2008, London: TSO), available from: <http://police.homeoffice.gov.uk/publications/police-reform/Policing_GP/>, accessed 11 June 2009

Home Office Crime Reduction website: <http://www.crimereduction.homeoffice.gov.uk>, accessed 11 October 2009

Innes, M, Fielding, N, and Langan, S, *Signal Crimes & Control Signals: Towards an Evidence-Based Conceptual Framework for Reassurance Policing. A report for Surrey Police*, (2002, University of Surrey)

———, 'What's your problem? Signal crimes and citizen-focused problem-solving', *Criminology and Public Policy* (2005) Vol 4, No 2, pp 187–200

Kent News, 'Police launch new Neighbourhood Task Teams' (2009) available at <http://www.kentnews.co.uk/kent-news/Police-launch-new-Neighbourhood-Task-Teams-newsinkent27634.aspx?news=local>, accessed 3 October 2009

Lee, M, *Inventing Fear of Crime: Criminology and the politics of anxiety* (2007, Devon: Willan Publishing)

Newcastle Evening Chronicle, 'Cheap booze removed from shelves in crackdown' (2008) available from < http://www.chroniclelive.co.uk/north-east-news/todays-evening-chronicle/2008/07/23/cheap-booze-removed-from-shelves-in-crackdown-72703-21389632/>, accessed 12 November 2009

NPIA (2008b) *Special Constabulary National Strategy Implementation Advice*

O'Connor, D, HMIC, *Closing the Gap: a Review of the fitness for purpose of the current structure of policing in England and Wales*, September 2005, HM Inspectorate of Constabulary (London: Home Office)

Police Professional, 'Community themes', 7 September 2006

Police Professional, 'Delivering change in the neighbourhood', No 175, August 2009, pp 15–18.

Reiner, R, *Law and Order: an honest citizen's guide to Crime and Control* (2007, London: Polity Press)

Rogers, C and Prosser, K, *Crime Reduction Partnerships* (2006, Oxford: Oxford University Press)

Slatter, R, *Measuring Neighbourhood Watch—Views of Effectiveness*, May 2009

Specials (2008b), 'The National Strategy for Specials', NPIA, March 2008

Specials (2008c), 'Cafe Culture Combats Crime', NPIA, August 2008

Specials (2009a), 'A vision for the next 12 months', NPIA, April 2009

Specials (2009b), April 2009, NPIA

Specials (2009c), Summer 2009, NPIA

Thames Valley Police, 'Katesgrove Environmental Visual Audit' (2009) available at <http://www.thamesvalley.police.uk/yournh-tvp-pol-area-read-newsitem?id=90173>, accessed 9 November 2009

Tilley, N (ed.), *Handbook of Crime Prevention and Community Safety* (2005, Devon: Willan Publishing)

Tonry, M and Farrington, D, *Building a Safer Society: Crime and Justice, a review of research*, Vol 19 (1995, Chicago: University of Chicago Press)

Wilson J and Kelling G, 'Broken Windows', *Atlantic Monthly* (1982) 249, pp 29–36

Notes

1 The programmes which detailed Gareth Malone's creations of a 'community choir' in South Oxhey, were called *The Choir: Unsung Town*, and shown on BBC2 during September 2009: see <http://www.bbc.co.uk/sing/choir/index.shtml>.

2 Neighbourhood policing is largely the brainchild of Denis O'Connor, ex-Chief Constable of Surrey and an HMI, and currently (2010) HM Chief Inspector of Constabulary. In the late 1990s he identified a gap between the public and the police, which the latter seemed unable to bridge. The concept of neighbourhood policing was designed to bring the police and the public closer together. Indeed, his HMI report [O'Connor, D, HMIC, *Closing the Gap: a Review of the fitness for purpose of the current structure of policing in England and Wales*, September 2005,

HM Inspectorate of Constabulary (London: Home Office)] addressed this very issue, but he notes that neighbourhood policing is only what cops used to do well before cars. (Conversation with the Editor, 4 December 2009.)

3 See for example Purves, L, 'If we can't have more police, have less tolerance', *The Times*, 21 September 2009, p 24 and the letter to the Editor from Dale Baker (a serving police officer) on the police response to Fiona Pilkington and her family, *The Times*, 21 September 2009. Original reports in the media on the inquest into the death of Mrs Pilkington and her daughter appeared on 18 September 2009.

4 It is worth noting that the police have been collating statistics on crime since 1857. The practice continues and is published by the Home Office annually as *Criminal Statistics: England and Wales*: see Hough, M (2008) 'Crime Statistics' in Newburn, T and Neyroud, P, *Dictionary of Policing*, (2008, Devon: Willan Publishing).

5 The example continues to state that only **5.5** of these offences are 'cleared up'; **3.0** offences result in caution or conviction, and in fact only **2.2** result in conviction, whilst **0.3** offenders receive a custodial sentence (Reiner, 2007, pp 57–8, based on work done by Barclay and Tavares in 1999). Whilst there may be about 85,000 people in prison currently, if they represent only 0.3 per cent of perpetrators of crime, then there are huge amounts of crime in the population at large which the police know nothing of. The classic instance of this is in domestic violence, where a victim averagely suffers 27 assaults before reporting the assailant to the police. That said, the 'attrition' between the 24.3 recorded crimes and the 5.5 cleared up is a pretty damning indictment of current police practices and of the ineptitude and sloth which characterizes the criminal justice system.

6 Home Office figures for 'Neighbourhood Watch Week' launched in Leeds in June 2009. Data is available on the home office website: <http://press.homeoffice.gov.uk/press-releases/launch-neighbourhood-watch-week>, accessed 21 September 2009, and on <http://www.mynhw.co.uk>, which is the Neighbourhood Watch website, also accessed on 21 September 2009. Figures are for 2008 and further data may be accessed periodically from <http://www.homeoffice.gov.uk/rds>.

7 HMIC 1998, *ibid*.

8 *Ibid*.

Chapter 8

Crime Scene Management

8.1 The Golden Hour: Priorities at a Crime Scene

Many of you will be familiar with the 'Golden Hour' of investigative opportunity. It is then that physical evidence is at its freshest (even fragile or evanescent evidence may be recovered), when eye-witnesses' and victims' memories are at their sharpest, and suspects least prepared with explanations or excuses for what has happened.

We go into more detail in the pages that follow, taking you from the common approach path (CAP) through to the current debate about criminal databases and personal privacy. First, though, we are going to describe a crime scene and summarize the things you should do and not do when you are the first law officer (**First Officer Attending** or FOA) entering a place where a crime has been reported or where it is suspected:

A Crime Scene

A crime scene can be:

The suspect (weapons, DNA, fingerprints, traces, body fluids, fibres, footprints)

The place (where the crime took place: a building, a vehicle, a structure, a site, a geographical location, a map reference)

The victim, *but do not describe the victim in this way* (may bear traces of an assault, or attack, or ordeal; of an assailant; may recall vividly, may know offender).

There are two priorities at a crime scene:

> **do** preserve important evidence, and
> **don't** contaminate the scene.

Crime scene indicators

The scene may show evidence of:

unauthorized entry (broken windows, forced locks)

physical assault (blood spatter on walls, stains on carpets, handfuls of hair)

searches for money or things to steal (ransacked cupboards, clothing strewn about, opened drawers)

vandalism (graffiti on walls or mirrors, destruction of items)

seizure of a weapon (knives missing from racks, evidence of a bottle having been broken for use as a weapon)

a struggle, or fight (overturned furniture, broken crockery and glass, damaged pictures, photographs, and so on)

anything taken away (victim may identify (or you may see) things like open or emptied handbags, open and discarded cash or jewellery boxes, open safes, broken cabinets containing objects)

anything left behind (such as items used to effect entry, discarded weapons, discharge from a firearm)

If you are the first on the scene, you need to build a picture of what has happened. A report of an abduction of a child or young person might produce evidence and physical traces of what occurred. You must be alert to possibilities of evidence recovery and aware of what kinds of evidence are important to establish which kinds of crime: such as empty containers and forced entry for burglary, blood from an assault, body fluids from a sex attack, and so on. The views of witnesses and victims are important in any context to establish what went on and whether a crime has been committed. Suspects, even if absent from the scene, can be put in the frame by witnesses and victims.

It follows from this, again, that you must have an understanding of the investigative process, which includes an understanding and appreciation of forensic evidence, where it might be found and what it might tell the investigators. A common example, in the aftermath of a sexual attack during which the victim might have fought off the attacker, is that the victim wants to wash. This is a normal response to a traumatic event, but there might be important physical evidence on, say, the victim's hands and face which should be recovered, so you would have to gently insist that things are left as they are until specialists arrive. Fortunately, many people (well versed in crime fiction) will understand this, but you should be prepared to explain how important it is that nothing is touched, rearranged, or restored until it has been examined and, if it is evidence, photographed or recovered.

8.1.1 Crime in progress?

We have so far been assuming that any offenders have left the crime scene, but it might be the case that you have to detain suspects (in which case the same principles about preserving evidence pertain as for the victim: don't allow a suspect to wash, discard clothing, or conceal anything). It might even happen that, if you arrived on the scene quietly and without lights and strobes (perhaps because a caller had reported a 'crime in progress'), that the crime itself, or other crimes, *are still being committed* at the scene.

If you arrive at a location where you suspect a crime to be continuing, you must proceed with great caution, aware of the need to protect your own and your colleagues' safety, consistent with saving life and protecting anyone who is being or has been attacked. If the discharge of a firearm has been reported, for instance, and you happen to be closest to the scene and therefore arrive before any armed police can get there, you will need to be very careful indeed that you do not 'spook' an offender into firing at you or anyone else. As a priority, you need to get other people out of the line of fire, and establish a cordon to keep the public, yourself, and your colleagues at a safe distance. Entering a strange building in pursuit of someone armed with a firearm is brave but foolhardy; it could also be fatal for you and your colleagues. The same applies to a building on fire, or a building or scene in the aftermath of an explosion.

We discuss later on what to do in establishing a cordon and outer perimeter around the crime scene; all those things can be done once you have ascertained that there is no further risk of injury to anyone in the vicinity of the crime scene. You and your colleagues must take immediate steps to isolate the largest practicable area around the 'seat' of the crime, so that evidence is preserved and contamination is kept to the barest minimum. If anyone points out the alleged offender or a suspect, that offender or suspect person must be detained, and ideally, isolated from others.

8.1.2 Aggravating factors

There might be aggravating factors which may make a crime scene even more important:

Aggravating or complicating factors at a crime scene

- The crime seems to be part of a significant series (such as the third reported attack on an elderly person, or the sixth example of a break-in on a lone female at home at night)
- The crime scene is in a place which is a 'hot spot' or where there is a local priority issue agreed with residents
- A weapon has been used, such as a firearm
- A weapon has been used but not recovered from the scene (so the assailant could strike again)
- The **victim** was in a position of trust (schoolteacher or nurse, for example)
- The **suspect** was in a position of trust (a solicitor or warden of a hostel, for example)
- The offence had a sexual motive
- The offence showed evidence of hate crime (such as the expression of racism or homophobia)
- A victim's injuries turn out to be worse than first thought (such as evidence of serious internal or tissue injury)
- A known serious offender has been detained or is identified as having taken part, particularly if being managed under Multi-Agency Public Protection Arrangements (MAPPA)
- The victim is a vulnerable child or adult.

8.1.3 Summary

Actions at a crime scene may be summarized in order like this:

- *Your first and absolute duty is the preservation of life.* Get people away immediately from any source or seat of danger
- If that means you have to let an armed offender escape, then so be it, but note and report what will be needed to pursue any offender (description, build, clothing, apparent weapons, vehicle registration, type, appearance)
- If a crime has occurred, you need to know what it was, take steps to detect what has happened (or is still happening), and minimize any further offending
- You must give time and thought to identifying and dealing with victims, witnesses, and suspects. You must be reassuring

and gentle with victims, who may be traumatized (deeply upset and disturbed)

- You must **secure** and **preserve** all available evidence, and
  a) prevent any further crimes where possible
  b) ensure that you, and others, **avoid contamination** of the crime scene
  c) be alert to the offender's route into and away from the crime scene
  d) consider and implement a cordon
  e) consider whether there might be **aggravating factors**
  f) if you are not sure whether or not you are dealing with a crime, err on the side of caution and assume that you are
  g) retain **witnesses** and, when time permits, record details and anything material to the offence
  h) keep your PNB up to date
  i) keep Control informed, and
  j) assume that you are in charge until someone with authority tells you otherwise (this is to avoid you going off shift without 'handing over' the case to another investigator or officer).

8.2 **Common Approach Paths (CAP)**

A cardinal rule to be observed at any crime scene is the establishment of a CAP. The purpose of this is to ensure that there is only one 'official' route into and out of the crime scene itself so that the chance of accidental contamination of the scene by visitors is reduced to the minimum.

Even if you are gloved before you go into the crime scene, it is unlikely that you will also be gowned and booted in protective clothing—that tends to be the apparel of those who come after you. In other words, because you are a Special Constable entering a crime scene not knowing what you will find, you may have to touch things (to move them out of the way so as to gain access to any injured parties, or to make closer inspection of a person or thing). There may be times when you have to move injured people—perhaps to get access to them for emergency life support or resuscitation—and thereby run the risk of contaminating the crime scene. Your first duty, to preserve life, overrides any other consideration, which is why the CAP is so important. If everyone who comes after you (paramedics, pathologist, Crime Scene

Investigator(s), sundry other Special Constables and police regulars, doctors, coroner's officers, and others) all choose their own way in, any forensic evidence at the site is likely to be irretrievably compromised.

8.2.1 Establishing a CAP

Choose a logical route: preferably one which is direct and which can handle human traffic: hard-standing tarmac is preferable to grass or a muddy track (as well as avoiding the risk of introducing material from outside the crime scene to the inside). *If possible, choose a route that is unlikely to have been used by either the victim or the offender.*

Obstacles must be avoided, such as trees, vehicles, smashed lights, broken doors, overturned furniture, and so on, since the positioning and condition of such items may furnish important indications of what happened in the crime. Do not tie tape to convenient objects—such as trees and lamp posts—which you would actually prefer to be *within* your crime scene.

A very important point: you *should not attempt to cover evidence, or close doors and windows at any major scenes*, but you can do so at a volume-crime scene, or at the scene of an assault, if the CSI is likely to be delayed getting there. Having said that, if rain, snow, or wind is getting into the crime scene you should consider closing doors or windows: but you should make sure that you do not wipe prints or blood off the surfaces you touch, and:

- always wear protective (surgical-type) gloves
- always make a PNB entry
- always inform the CSI, and
- do **not** use 'Police do not cross' tape inside a premises except, say, a block of flats—tape is best employed in making a cordon outside the crime scene itself.

If there is a body or bodies at the scene, you are obliged to look persistently for signs of life and to take remedial action if you find any such signs, but if you cannot detect a pulse or breathing, and you judge that you cannot resuscitate the victim(s), you should not move them more than necessary.

If you observe footprints or bloodstains (inside or outside), placing a box over them until the CSI arrives is probably enough. This is vital if it is raining, as any temporary cover is better than none at all. Remember, though, to draw the CSI's attention to what you have done.

Think of the CAP as the most sensible route to the scene which does not gratuitously contaminate evidence, even if this means a detour. In some instances, it might be better to offer authorized visitors to the crime scene an exit from it by a different route, if a particularly narrow route (a cliff path, say, or a canal towpath) might mean those returning along it cause difficulties or delay for those newly arriving at the scene.

A final point to be made about CAP is that it is important to exclude from the crime scene the morbidly curious, the onlooker, and the journalist. Help will arrive to support you, but it takes time. In addition to creating the CAP itself, you might have to arrange a rendezvous point (RV) or vehicle parking area for those attending the crime scene. Extend the cordon around the crime scene as far out as is practicable, to keep sightseers and sensation seekers at bay. The outer cordon can always be brought in later if need be, but if it is too restricted to begin with, important evidence might be overlooked or compromised, and people might be able to get too close to the crime scene for their own safety, or begin to hamper the investigation.

The simplest way to think of the crime scene is in concentric circles, like this:

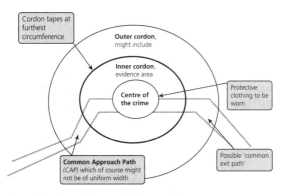

Figure 8.1: Schematic for routes into or out of a crime scene

8.3 **Forensic Science in Police Investigations**

The investigation of crime scenes using forensic science cannot be assessed in isolation.[1] Although it is an integral element in most police investigations (some would argue that it is seminal to successful prosecutions), forensic work must be put into a larger context. For example, at a crime scene a Crime Scene Investigator (CSI) might recover excellent fingerprint samples or substantial DNA,[2] but this work might be wasted unless the police officer in charge of the investigation can, at least, detect the crime, or, at most, produce a successful case which leads to conviction of the offender. In other words, forensic investigation cannot, of itself, produce a criminal prosecution. It is the investigating police officer, Special or regular, who does that, in conjunction with all the other apparatus of criminal justice.

Police officers generally have a very sketchy or imperfect understanding of forensic science and therefore of its potential benefit in crime scene analysis and the investigation of evidence at the scene. In its report in 2002 (*Under the Microscope Refocused*), HMIC deplored the general lack of understanding at all levels in policing, which meant that valuable opportunities were being missed, a point echoed by David Barclay (2009). What this means is that it is incumbent on all Special Constables to try to understand at least the outlines and potential for forensic science in aiding police investigations. We cannot hope to do the subject justice in this *Handbook*, which is focused on the whole Special Constabulary remit, but there are good references in the Further Reading section at the end of this chapter. You do not need to be a scientist to understand forensic science but if you persist in finding it an opaque subject, talk to a friendly CSI and ask for a 'walk through, talk through', which most would be very happy to provide. A Special Constable with the necessary grasp of what to do at a crime scene and how forensic science can aid an investigation is a boon to a CSI, so most will see a percentage in helping you.

8.3.1 Types of forensic evidence

8.3.1.1 *DNA*

DNA is an abbreviation for **deoxyribonucleic acid**, a chemical found in all the cells in our bodies which have a nucleus. The chemical carries information about us in the form of a chemical

The scientific laboratory uses an automated ('robotic') profiling system in five stages (followed by an interpretation stage), which consists of techniques to separate and identify the DNA 'fragments', amplifying them into specific areas noted above. A laser beam then converts the DNA fragments into mathematical data for interpretation. The interpretation stage uses specialist computer software which assigns numbers to the fragments of DNA. It is this combination of the sizes of fragments across the sites of interest which produces a unique string of numbers. The numbers are then loaded into the NDNAD and the result is fed back to the originating police force.

8.3.1.5 *Fingerprints*

Compared with the relatively recent developments in genetics, which followed the discovery of DNA, the science behind fingerprint identification is now some 100 years old, and has been tested on innumerable occasions in courts as well as in scientific laboratories across the world.[6] Indeed, so venerable is the fingerprint system in British jurisprudence that it is in danger of being slighted merely because it is so familiar as a forensic technique. You might have thought that there was little left in fingerprinting to discover, and that all criminals would habitually use gloves rather than run the risk of being identified through their 'dabs'. In reality, processes for fingerprinting are being developed all the time (the growth of 'palm-print' technology, which we look at below, is a case in point), and criminals remain peculiarly indifferent to the likelihood of being identified through their 'prints' at a crime scene.

Fingerprints may be taken in a number of ways. At a crime scene, they can be detected by 'dusting' reflective or polished surfaces, and 'lifting' the prints on to tape, or they can be detected and photographed through a series of chemical and physical treatments. Occasionally, prints can be obtained on an object taken from a crime scene which is then subjected to fluoroscopic techniques. In practice, photography is used only when the prints would otherwise be damaged by 'lifting'.

The process for taking prints from suspects in custody or at the scene of a crime is entirely electronic. This involves a suspect's fingers being pressed on to a glass platen, where his or her 'prints' are scanned electronically. The resultant digital data are sent electronically to **IDENT1**, a UK-wide automated analysis system which, in 2005 replaced the National Automated Fingerprint Identification System (NAFIS). IDENT1, which includes palm-prints in its databases, can record, analyse, and compare digital information and make 'matches' quite quickly.

8.3.1.6 *What is the science of fingerprinting?*

The hand (palm), toes, and fingers are covered with tiny ridges of skin called 'papillary ridges' (also known as 'friction ridges') which are separated by depressions called 'furrows'. The combinations of ridges and furrows (subclassified further into 'whorls', 'arches', and 'loops') on the soft pads of the fingertips and toes (and palms), are unique to each individual. No one human has a combination which is the same as any other, or at least, no match has ever been made between two humans. The characteristic 'print' remains the same throughout an individual's lifetime.[7]

There are three types of fingerprint: **latent prints**, which are invisible, generally, to the naked eye, are made by transferring drops of perspiration and natural oils from the skin ridges to another surface; **visible prints**, which are made through the contact of the skin ridges with a coloured material (such as soot, blood, or dust) prior to leaving the print on another surface; and **plastic prints**, which are the impressions of prints left on a 'malleable' surface, such as wet clay, fresh putty, or soap. Plastic prints can be transferred, of course, to other surfaces, like visible prints, if quantities of the malleable substance adhere to the fingertips. This is why the average bathroom contains hundreds of fingerprints: the users of the bathroom are in perpetual contact with 'malleable' surfaces, from skin cream to shampoo.

The second and third classes of fingerprint are relatively easy to find; 'latent prints' are much more difficult to detect and require special techniques to make them both visible and 'liftable'. When it comes to the technique of comparing prints, the individuality of a fingerprint is determined by examination of its ridge characteristics, called '*minutiae*'.[8] There are probably as many as 150 classifiable *minutiae* in any single fingerprint.

8.3.1.7 *Ultra-violet photography*

This is a forensic investigation technique which requires specialist training and equipment. The layers of human skin (the 'dermis') contain, in their base, a substance called melanin, a dark pigment which absorbs ultra-violet radiation from the sun.[9] When the body sustains an injury, cells called melanocytes (containing melanin) migrate to the wound during the healing process. This leaves an area which is 'depigmented', or without colour, surrounded by a heavily-pigmented area which delineates the shape of the object which produced the trauma. Whilst this may not be visible to the human eye, it can be photographed using ultra-violet light. This is of forensic use when considering injuries such as bite-marks, kicks (the imprint of a shoe), burns, and other latent injury marks, but is of especial value in revealing long-term abuse injuries which are no longer apparent from normal physical examination.

8.3.1.8 *Shoemarks*

The footprint, beloved of detective fiction of a certain vintage, has been given a new lease of life since a 'shoemark' at the scene of a crime can be forensically matched, in some instances, with the footwear of a suspect. In the event of a match, as with DNA and fingerprints, physical proof shows that the suspect was present at the crime scene (at some point), and therefore has an explanation to give. What has changed is the creation of a shoemark database, by means of which comparisons may be made with some accuracy, and thus there is a searchable repository to which Special Constables may have recourse. What happens normally is that CSIs will take photographs and 'lifts' of shoemarks at the scene of a crime. If there is a suspect in custody, his or her footwear will be taken and scanned. Both sets are then sent to a specialist database for a comparative study to be made. Should there not be a suspect in custody, the print recovered from the crime scene will be sent alone, and matches will be sought from the database.[10]

8.3.1.9 *Summary*

So integral is forensic science to successful preparation of cases against accused persons that it is difficult to imagine a major case succeeding without some aspect of science placing an offender in a place at a time. Some 'cold' cases (and some miscarriages of justice) have been resolved through advances in DNA analysis, and through the matching of DNA with new samples, often long after the event. Forensic science is almost always objective, detached, factual, and persuasive. Offenders, confronted with irrefutable evidence, often plead guilty—saving the courts and the Special Constabulary valuable time. There seems to be no limit to the ways in which all aspects of scientific research can be pressed into the service of justice—though specialist commentators have noted the occasionally sharp dislocation between the 'rules' of science and the rule of law.[11]

8.4 **Preserving Physical Evidence**

Physical evidence may take many forms at a crime scene. Here are a few of them:

Crime scenes: physical evidence

Location where the crime(s) took place

Body or part of a body (the body itself is a crime scene within a larger context)

Any place where the body has lain or from where it has been moved

Anywhere there is a physical trace such as tyre marks, footprints, broken glass from a window or a bottle, location of an object that might have been a weapon

A victim (injured party) whose body, like a murder victim, could be a crime scene (bruises in domestic violence, broken bones, cuts, or wounds)

Any witnesses

An attack site

Means of transporting a body or injured party (such as a car, van, quad bike, and the like)

Clothing connected to victim or offender

Material on which victim may have been laid or in which wrapped

Access or escape routes for offender or victim

Premises connected to the victim or to a suspect (remember evidence might have been removed from the crime scene and placed or secreted elsewhere)

Articles or objects brought in or used by victim or offender

Be aware of the potential for multiple crime scenes

(adapted from Roycroft, 2007)

It is important for the Special Constable attending a crime scene to be aware that the scene itself may only be part of where the crime occurred. There may be secondary and tertiary sites. In kidnap cases, for example, the seizure part of the crime, the transportation of the victim, the holding of the victim, and his/her subsequent release, or the collection of any ransom, may all be crime scenes, whilst the equipment used by the kidnappers, from vehicles to secure holding area to communications equipment, may all be important sources of physical evidence.

A further dimension to the usefulness of physical evidence is that it can be used to corroborate (or deny) the statements of witnesses, victim(s), or offender(s). This will assist in the (not necessarily actual) reconstruction of the crime and the sequence of events involved. Eyewitnesses can be mistaken (as any experienced Special Constable will confirm), confused as to the logic of events, or still in a state of shock. Those bank or building society staff who witness a violent armed robbery, for example, may take some time to be able to piece together a coherent account of what took place. If witnesses say that the robbers fired a sawn-off shotgun into the ceiling of the bank, and the CSI recovers a single spent round from a rifle in a wall, there might be difficulties in reconciling the two accounts of what took place. Physical evidence is not suggestible and cannot be influenced, even subliminally, as witnesses sometimes are.

The final point to make is that Special Constables must pay particular attention to the **continuity of evidence**. This sequence ensures the integrity of physical evidence recovered from a crime scene. As we have noted in other sections, the defence counsel team for an accused person will seek faults in the process by which the case against their client was assembled and conducted. Gaps in the continuity of evidence may be opportunities to suggest or allude to contamination of the evidence. Being able to account for every step of identifying, 'bagging and tagging', and then identifying and retaining physical evidence, is an essential part of modern police professionalism. Yet, every year, cases are lost because simple continuity of evidence rules were not observed.

8.5 **Contamination**

In 2003, an experiment was carried out in the UK to try to ascertain what contamination of DNA at a crime scene could occur, simply by other people (CSIs, Special Constables) being on the scene. The researchers devised four 'treatment conditions':

> *No movement*
> *Movement*
> *Coughing*
> *Talking*

which were all things which would happen through normal access by the police to a crime scene. In each test, the actions of a CSI or Special Constable were copied, such as movements to collect evidence or turning the head to look at something. Each experiment was repeated a number of times, both kneeling and standing, in protective clothing or not, using a face mask or not.

The results of the experiment showed, unsurprisingly, that there was no appreciable contamination when there was no movement. But that is impractical at a crime scene. When normal movement on a crime scene occurred, and no protective clothing was worn, *the contamination was enough to produce a full DNA profile of the person moving*. In other words, the contamination caused simply by moving across a crime scene unprotected was significant. Contamination increased still further with unmasked coughing and talking.

When those on the crime scene wore protective clothing, including gloves and masks, there was still some DNA contamination, but it was greatly reduced. This suggested two things:

- no one should enter a crime scene unless properly clothed, and
- movement and number of persons at a crime scene should be kept to the minimum.

(adapted from Page, 2004)

This is pretty much an ideal prescription since Special Constables and others on patrol or answering an emergency call do not routinely carry protective clothing, though they should have surgical or protective gloves with them. Perhaps Special Constables should also routinely carry face masks, as these are small, light, and easily pocketed. The point is nonetheless well made: the FOA a crime scene should do only what is necessary to save life and preserve the scene: otherwise there could be contamination of existing evidence of the crime which as a consequence might be damaged or compromised beyond practical use. No one expects sterile laboratory conditions at a crime scene—they are messy, untidy, bespattered, and dishevelled places—and only a defence lawyer could seriously expect there to be no contamination of evidence at all. However, that is not the same as letting people trample about.

The ACPO has been so concerned about the needless and avoidable contamination of crime scenes that its Crime Committee made the following point in written evidence to a House of Lords Select Committee on Science and Technology:

[Paragraph 24] Because of the enormous advances in the science of DNA within recent years, the risk of cross contamination at a crime scene has increased significantly. A stray hair, [a] sneeze, other body fluid or fingerprint, all potentially prejudice a crime scene by the cross-contamination of a DNA exhibit. Single cell analysis and vastly improved methods of collecting DNA from a crime scene exacerbate the risk.

(ACPO, 2000)

As a consequence of this concern, ACPO added a **Police Elimination Database** to the NDNAD so that front-line police staff can be eliminated from the crime scene, thereby reducing potential and actual contamination. It is now routine for new entrants to a police force, including all Special Constables and PCSOs, as well as new CSIs and regular officers, to have both their fingerprints and DNA recorded so that they can be eliminated from crime enquiries.

Contamination of a crime scene can occur, of course, before a Special Constable arrives. Consider a stabbing on a street in daylight. By the time a Special Constable has got to the scene, it is possible that anything between 5 and 25 people will have passed by, some of whom might be public-spirited enough or sufficiently experienced to render first aid or comfort to the victim. Inevitably there will have been considerable contamination of the crime scene by the public, from the best of motives, and part of the follow-up work at any crime scene will be the interviewing of witnesses and, if necessary, taking their prints and DNA samples to eliminate them from the physical evidence recovered from the scene.

8.6 Locard's Principle of Exchange: 'Evidence that does not Forget'

Max Houck, foremost among modern analysts of trace evidence, describes the process like this (Houck, 2009):

Trace evidence is a category of evidence that is characterized by the analysis of materials that, because of their size or texture, are easily transferred from one location to another.

It is testimony to the accuracy of the forensic science that the nature of this transfer 'from one location to another' is still potent in crime scene investigation, since Edmund Locard (1877–1966) advocated the application of scientific methods and logic to criminal investigation and first described the nature of criminal traces, which he observed in his science laboratory in Lyon, France, in the period around the First World War (1914–1918).

Nearly a hundred years after Locard's birth, a major US commentator on forensic science, Paul Kirk, Professor of 'Criminalistics' at the University of California, Berkeley, wrote this:

> Wherever he steps, whatever he touches, whatever he leaves, even unconsciously, will serve as a silent witness against him. Not only his fingerprints or his footprints, but his hair, the fibers [US spelling] from his clothes, the glass he breaks, the tool mark he leaves, the paint he scratches, the blood or semen he deposits or collects. All of these and more, bear mute witness against him. This is evidence that does not forget. It is not confused by the excitement of the moment. It is not absent because human witnesses are. It is factual evidence. Physical evidence cannot be wrong, it cannot perjure itself, it cannot be wholly absent.
>
> (quoted in Thornton and Kirk, 1974)

Kirk went on to observe that:

> the utilization of physical evidence is critical to the solution of most crime[s]. No longer may the police depend upon the confession, as they have done to a large extent in the past. The eyewitness has never been dependable, as any experienced investigator or attorney knows quite well. Only physical evidence is infallible, and then only when it is properly recognized, studied, and interpreted.
>
> (Ibid.)

These comments from eminent forensic scientists should reinforce for you, the Special Constable and probably FOA, *the importance of managing the integrity of a crime scene*. We're sorry if we seem to be labouring this point, but any CSI will tell you that a clumsy, over-hasty (if well-meaning) Special Constable, who is FOA at a crime scene, can ruin vital evidence. Conversely, a careful, thoughtful Special Constable arriving at a crime scene can preserve and sustain such evidence until it can be safely collected.

The principle of the exchange is that *when two things come into contact, information is exchanged by the transfer of trace material*. It occurs even if the results are not visible (Houck 2009, p 167). Ever since Locard's observation, forensic scientists and crime scene investigators have used this 'exchange principle':

> **Transfer of evidence**
> **Pressure applied during contact** (the greater the pressure, the more items are transferred)
> **The number of contacts** (again, the greater the contact the more will transfer)
> **How easily the item transfers material** (mud transfers more easily than concrete)
> **The form of the evidence** (solid/particulate, liquid or gas/aerosol)
> **How much of the item is involved** in the contact (1 sq cm transfers less than 1 sq m).

(adapted from Houck, 2009, pp 167–8)

But it is not just the nature of the transfer that is important, it is the nature of the thing itself, where it is, and how long it will endure:

> **The persistence of evidence**
> **The kind of evidence** (hairs, glass, blood)
> **The location of the evidence** (indoors or outdoors, protected or unprotected)
> **The environment around the evidence** (raining, dry, permeable, impermeable—hard or soft surfaces)
> **Time from transfer to collection** (generally, the shorter the time elapsed, the better the condition of the evidence)
> **Activity on or around the site of the evidence** (the lower the amount of activity, the better the chance of collection and the lower the chance of contamination)

(adapted from Houck, 2009, p 169)

The final importance of trace evidence may be in indicating 'association in criminal activity' (Houck, 2009, p 194). Although DNA analysis can often tell crime investigators 'who', it cannot tell 'what', where', 'when', or 'how'. Trace evidence can, but only if the FOA is alive to the possibilities of evidence recovery from the moment of his or her arrival at the crime scene.

Further Reading

Association of Chief Police Officers, Written submission on DNA evidence to House of Lords, 2000, available from <http://www.publications.parliament.uk/pa/ld199900/ldselect/ldsctech/115/115we05.htm>, accessed 1 March 2010

Barclay, D, 'Using forensic science in major crime inquiries', Chapter 13 in Fraser and Williams (eds.), *Handbook of Forensic Science* (2009—see below)

Becker, R, *Criminal Investigation*, 2nd edn. (2005, Sudbury, Mass: Jones & Bartlett Publishers), especially Chapter 3 'The Crime Scene'

Blackledge R (ed.), *Forensic Analysis on the cutting edge: new methods for trace evidence analysis* (2007, Hoboken, New Jersey: John Wiley & Sons)

Broeders, A, 'Principles of forensic identification science', in Newburn, T, Williamson, T, and Wright, A, *Handbook of Criminal Investigation* (2007, Devon: Willan Publishing), Chapter 12, particularly the subset 'All evidence is probabilistic', pp 316–18

Chisum, WJ and Turvey, B, 'Evidence Dynamics: Locard's Exchange Principle & Crime Reconstruction', *Journal of Behavioral Profiling*, (2000) Vol 1, No 1, available from: <http://www.profiling.org/journal/vol1_no1/jbp_toc_january2000_1-1_pub.html>, accessed 26 September 2009

Coleman, D, *DNA Best Practice Manual* (2003, ACPO)

Cooper, A and Mason, L, 'Forensic Resources and Criminal Investigations', in Fraser and Williams (eds.), *Handbook of Forensic Science* (2009—see below), Chapter 11

Fraser J and Williams R (eds.), *Handbook of Forensic Science* (2009, Devon: Willan Publishing)

Green, R, 'Forensic Investigation in the UK', in Newburn, Williamson, and Wright (eds.), *A Handbook of Criminal Investigation*, (2007—see above)

Hansard, ACPO (Crime Committee) *Written Evidence to the House of Lords Select Committee on Science and Technology*, 2000, available from: <http://www.parliament.uk/pa/ld199900/ldselect/ldsctech/115/115we05.htm>, accessed 27 September 2009

HMIC, *Under the Microscope Refocused: a revisit to the thematic inspection report on scientific and technical support* (2002, London: Home Office)

Houck, M, *Mute Witness: Trace Evidence Analysis* (2001, London: Academic Press)

Houck, M, 'Trace Evidence' in Fraser J and Williams, R, (eds.), *Handbook of Forensic Science* (2009—see above) Chapter 7, pp 166–95

NPIA (2007b), *Practical Advice on critical Incident Management*, available from <http://www.acpo.police.uk/asp/policies/Data/critical_incident_management_17x08x07.pdf>, accessed 1 March 2010

Tendler, S, 'British Police are taught to act fast and use the "golden hour" ', *The Times* 9 May 2007, available from: <http://www.timesonline.co.uk/tol/news/world/europe/article1764005.ece>, accessed 18 November 2009

Thornton, J (ed.) and Kirk, P, *Crime Investigation*, 2nd Edn., (1974, New York: Wiley & Sons)

Notes

1 Whilst we normally use the term 'forensic' to refer to *scientific evidence* (that is, evidence supported, explained, or detected using scientific methods), the word 'forensic' simply means 'of, or in connection with, a court of law' (*Oxford English Dictionary*: the word comes from the Latin *forum*, meaning a meeting place or gathering, which was originally where a court of law was held). So, strictly, forensic

evidence means 'legal evidence', but it is not used in that exact sense now. Forensic evidence, like any other, serves to explain to the investigator what has happened, and, eventually, helps a court to determine whether or not the person accused of a crime committed it.

2 CSIs in most police forces are now specialist police staff. The role used to be called 'Scenes of Crime Officer' or SOCO, and was often the province of a police officer. It was determined by most forces in the last ten years or so that possession of a warrant was not a necessary qualification for those employed to gather forensic science evidence from a crime scene and consequently the job could be done by (highly-trained) 'civilians', but increasingly Chief Constables of forces have had to 'license' CSIs to seize evidence through the granting of limited delegated powers. See the discussion in Fraser, J and Williams, R, *Handbook of Forensic Science* (2009; chapter 1 'The Contemporary Landscape of Forensic Science', especially pp 4–6).

3 The gist of this description of DNA is taken from the Forensic Science Service (FSS) (2002) *What is DNA?*; other texts are listed in the Further Reading above. The Forensic Science Service, a government company, maintains the National DNA Database (NDNAD) under Home Office auspices. Other service providers have to send data to NDNAD.

4 Based on Coleman, D, (2003): see Further Reading above.

5 The mitochondria are substances ('organelles') found in 'eukaryotic' (chromosomatic) cells, which contain enzymes for energy production and respiration.

6 It may be of interest that the first conviction for murder following identification using fingerprints was that of the Stratton brothers in 1905. The first *conviction* using fingerprints was in 1902 when a burglar, Harry Jackson, was found guilty. By contrast, the first 'palm prints' were not offered in evidence until 1931 at the Old Bailey. Details may be obtained of these cases from: <http://www.met.police.uk/history/fingerprint.htm>, accessed 25 September 2009. The pioneer of fingerprint evidence in Britain was Sir Edward Henry, who later became a Commissioner of the Metropolitan Police.

7 A very good study of the contemporary science of fingerprinting is in Champod, C and Chamberlain, P, 'Fingerprints' in Fraser and Williams, *Handbook of Forensic Science* (2009—see above), Chapter 3. Fingerprints are 'fixed' in a foetus at 25 weeks in the womb and will survive until the body decays, often some time after death. To date, the 'uniqueness' of fingerprints has not been successfully challenged in court (though lawyers have tried in the United States), and practitioners themselves tend to talk about 'reliability' of evidence from fingerprint comparison, rather than uniqueness—but this could be careful hedging of bets. See also Russ, J, *Forensic Uses of Digital Imaging* (2001, Boca Raton, Florida: CRC Press).

8 Latin, meaning 'small parts', hence 'minute,' meaning 'tiny'.

9 Melanin (from the Greek *melas* meaning 'black') is the substance which is responsible for the tanning of the skin when exposed to sunlight; hence 'melanoma', a usually malignant tumour of melanin-forming

cells, often called 'tanning cancer'. Melanin is also present in hair and in the iris of the eye.

10 Terence Napier, something of a pioneer in the scientific techniques of footwear comparison, has written a cogent account of what is involved (principally microscopy and photography) in 'Marks', his chapter (No 8) in Fraser and Williams' *Handbook of Forensic Science* (2009—see above).

11 See for example, 'The contemporary landscape of forensic science' by Fraser, J and Williams, R, in their *Handbook of Forensic Science*, (2009—see above), Chapter 1, and the excellent 'Crime Scene and Forensic Investigation' (principally written by Lawton-Barrett, K), Chapter 13 in Bryant, R and Bryant, S, (eds.), *Blackstone's Student Police Officer Handbook*, 4th Edn.(2010, Oxford: Oxford University Press).

Chapter 9

The Criminal Justice System

9.1 **The Criminal Justice System**

It is often said that the police stand as the 'gateway' to the criminal justice system, since no one will enter the criminal justice process unless investigated and charged with an offence by the police or another law enforcement agency such as Revenue and Customs. It is now time to consider what makes up the criminal justice system (CJS) in England and Wales. At its very simplest, the process looks like this:

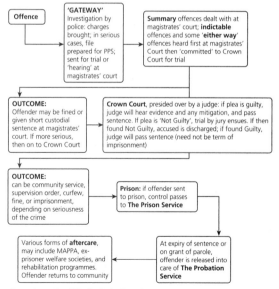

Figure 9.1: Simplified Criminal Justice route

The experienced Special Constable will note that there are some gaps in the way we have depicted the criminal justice process in this diagram (such as habeas corpus, procedure in the event of a suspicious death, the role of the defence team, and the time which elapses between indictment and hearing); but the basic system follows this route, or part of it, no matter what the court or crime. Offences in criminal law are classified in terms of their severity and their impact on people or communities. The following are the standard categories of offence:

Key Definitions: Offences

Summary: minor acts of disorder, road safety breaches, some forms of theft, possession of Class C drugs, and so on; these are tried at the magistrates' court and are likely to attract a fine or community service order. It is still fairly unusual for magistrates to give a custodial sentence.

'Either way': These are offences with a bigger impact than summary offences. For example, theft of a relatively small amount of money might be tried at a magistrates' court whilst a substantial theft might require trial at Crown Court. Depending on their seriousness, offences that can be tried 'either way' include fraud and burglary.

Indictable only: these are the most serious offences, such as murder or rape, which can only be tried on **indictment** (a document accusing a named person of an offence) at a Crown Court before a judge.

Indictable offences: a further 'greyish area' of offences, including arrest by someone other than a police officer. This group may include both 'either-way' and 'indictable-only' offences.

In this survey of the criminal justice system, it is helpful to consider briefly the kinds of court which examine actual or potential criminal charges. We examine the criminal courts in more detail in the sections which follow, but here is a summary:

Types of Criminal Court[1]

Magistrates' court: an 'inferior' (lower) criminal court presided over by two or more 'lay' (unpaid) magistrates, the more experienced among whom will be titled Justices of the Peace (JP). Alternatively, courts may be served by a District Judge sitting alone (District Judges used to be called Stipendiary (paid) Magistrates), and appointed from practising lawyers (barristers or solicitors). See 9.2 below.

Juvenile Court: now more often called a **Youth Court**, it is a magistrates' court which has jurisdiction over crimes committed by young

---

people aged under 18 years. The court is not normally open to the public. See 9.3 below.

Coroner's court: a court convened to investigate deaths suspected of being unnatural or violent, and presided over by a coroner (who may be a medical practitioner or a barrister or solicitor 'with five years' standing'). If an *autopsy* (medical investigation of a corpse) does not show death by 'natural causes', the coroner may conduct an *inquest* (an enquiry), with a jury. An inquest is not a criminal trial, but if unlawful homicide is suspected, the coroner will adjourn (postpone) the inquest until the outcome of any criminal trial. See 9.4 below.

Crown Court: A 'higher' court created by the Courts Act 1971 to take over the jurisdiction served by the old assizes and quarter sessions. The Crown Court has unlimited jurisdiction over all criminal cases tried on indictment, and also hears appeals from decisions in magistrates' courts. See 9.5 below.

There is a system for allocating cases between Crown Court centres, as follows:

First Tier: deals with both criminal and 'High Court' civil cases, served by *puisne* ('ordinary') judges, by *circuit* (experienced, including High Court) judges, and *Recorders* (part-time judges).

Second Tier: deals only with criminal cases, but any of the three kinds of judge noted in First Tier may serve here.

Third Tier: only deals with criminal cases: served by circuit judges and Recorders only.

Finally, in this section we need to present an overview of the whole process of criminal justice in England and Wales (Scotland and Northern Ireland have different laws and processes). The nature of appeal needs to be considered, since it often plays a large part in the outcome of criminal cases. Defence teams which are not satisfied with the verdict against a client by a jury or judge in a Crown Court may appeal against the sentence (or verdict), and carry the appeal forward—if there are substantial legal grounds—as far as the newly created Supreme Court.[2] There are a number of intermediate steps. Again, the simplest and most direct way of showing this is by means of a schematic, starting with the actions of the police following an offence and the arrest of the alleged offender:

Figure 9.2: The charge, conviction, and appeals route

9.2 **Magistrates' Courts**

Magistrates hear criminal cases, administer oaths of public office (such as a Special Constable's attestation), and sign search warrants. They have a limited jurisdiction in some civil matters, such as debt and 'family proceedings' (divorce, adoption, and so on).

The Courts Act 2003 gives magistrates national legal jurisdiction, but in practice all magistrates are assigned to a specific 'local justice area', usually reasonably close to where the magistrates themselves live.

Magistrates' courts are presided over either by:

> **Lay** (unpaid) **magistrates**, trained in the administration of justice, questions of law, practice and procedure, and in sentencing in line with legislation. They sit in 'panels', usually of three, one of whom—usually the most experienced—acts as the Chair, and who addresses the court and the accused.
>
> Magistrates appointed as **JPs** are advised on matters of law by a *Justices' Clerk,* who is always a qualified lawyer.

or by

> A **District Judge**, who is a paid, professional lawyer trained to administer the law both in magistrates' courts and in some Crown Courts. District Judges sit alone and tend to be used in complex or difficult cases.

Magistrates' powers to hear and pass sentence are derived from the Magistrates' Courts Act 1980 but, as we noted in the History of the Special Constabulary (1.5, above), JPs have been around since the fourteenth century and the relationship between JPs (the magistracy) and the police—particularly the Special or Parish Constable—is the oldest continuous local law-enforcement relationship in British legal history.[3] Like Special Constables, lay magistrates (JPs) are volunteers, drawn from the local communities, and often they have a very good knowledge of local situations and problems.

Discussion Point

Is it better to have amateurs or paid professionals judging a community's offences?

Which of magistrates and District Judges are more likely to understand why offences are committed?

The principle guiding which court hears which case is that the place where either the alleged offence was committed, or the person charged with the offence lives, or has his or her 'principal place of business', is within the court's **jurisdiction**. Magistrates' courts can only hear trials and pass sentence on adults for offences for which *the maximum penalty is six months in prison*. Accused people under the age of 18 are normally tried at a **Youth Court** (see 9.3 below), unless being tried with an adult.

The offences for which a magistrates' court passes sentence are called **summary offences**, and technically a magistrates' court sits as *a court of summary jurisdiction*—that is, a criminal court that tries without a jury, in which JPs decide all questions of law (assisted, as we noted above, by a Clerk to the Justices). The District Judge has the same powers and remit, though of course s/he sits alone and makes his or her own decisions. Summary offences constitute 95 per cent of all offences tried at court: it follows that very few of the total number of offences are tried at Crown Courts; but these, of course, are the more serious ones.

A crime may be classified as '**triable either way**' (see Chapter 5) which usually depends on the severity of the offence or, for example, the amount involved in a theft. If an offence is classed as 'summary' then a magistrates' court will hear it. Such offences include burglary, fraud, theft, and some instances of sexual assault. If an offence does not fall entirely within the 'summary' limitations, a magistrates' court will decide, on a preliminary hearing of the case with the outline evidence, whether the case should be *tried on indictment*: that is, at a Crown Court. An example might be in causing criminal damage: if the amount involved in the offence is £5,000 or less, it would probably be heard at a magistrates' court and tried summarily. If the amount is above £5,000, magistrates might decide to remit the case to the Crown Court (this is called 'referral'). Any *aggravating factor*, such as the use of violence or if the offence endangered life, means the case is more likely to go to the Crown Court for trial.

Straightforward **indictable offences**, such as murder and assault occasioning grievous bodily harm (GBH), are formally heard first at magistrates' courts, which may decide on questions of **bail**, or **remand in custody**, prior to committing the case to the Crown Court. All criminal cases in England and Wales, therefore, come first before magistrates' courts, whatever the severity or enormity of the crime. This is as true of mass acts of terrorism as it is of individual crimes of violence.

Task

Give examples of two offences under common law and two under statute law.

9.3 **Youth Courts**

Youth Courts used to be called Juvenile Courts (on the legal basis that anyone under the voting age of 18 was a 'juvenile'), but increasingly the criminological tendency to describe 'youth crime' and 'youth offences' meant that the term 'Youth Courts' gained ascendancy. The Youth Court is actually a section of the magistrates' court and is often sited in the same building complex. Youth Courts deal with nearly all cases involving people under the age of 18. Alleged offenders appear before specially trained youth panel magistrates or District Judges, either of whom have the power to give Detention or Training Orders lasting up to 24 months, as well as a range of sentences in the community.

The Youth Courts are much less formal than the standard magistrates' court and there is a deliberate attempt to engage with both the alleged offender and his or her family. Victims of the alleged crimes have the opportunity to attend a hearing or trial, although members of the public are usually excluded. However, victims have to apply to the Court for permission to attend, which has been the focus of some robust criticism in recent years.

Discussion Point

Why do you think this should be?

Do victims have the right to attend in other courts?

Is it insulting, as some have said, that the victim has to apply to attend the court in which the person who allegedly did wrong to that victim is tried?

9.4 **Coroners' Courts**

Originating in the 12th century, the office of **coroner** (the word derives from holding office under the Crown) was to lead an enquiry into 'unnatural' deaths, (murder or suicide—suicide was a crime until the beginning of the last century), and to investigate deaths which had occurred in unusual or perhaps suspicious circumstances. The coroner is usually a trained lawyer, but can be a medical doctor with forensic (legal) training. In the case of suspected murder, or unexplained but suspicious death, a coroner sits with a jury of between seven and eleven people. This will also be the case for manslaughter, infanticide, suicide, poisoning, and road accidents. A coroner can summon and examine on oath any person who is believed to have knowledge of the circumstances of the death. A verdict on the cause of death is delivered by the jury, or by the coroner if sitting without a jury.

If the cause of death cannot be fully established, an 'open' verdict is returned. If the verdict (from jury or coroner) is murder or manslaughter by someone who can be fully identified, a warrant for that person's arrest is issued and the normal criminal legal process is followed, including magistrates' court committal to the Crown Court. The coroner must adjourn the inquest if, before its conclusion:

- the clerk of a magistrates' court tells the coroner that someone has been charged with murder, manslaughter, or infanticide of the deceased, or of causing death by reckless driving, or of 'aiding, abetting, counselling or procuring the death of the deceased', or
- the Director of Public Prosecutions tells the coroner that someone has been charged with an offence committed in circumstances connected with the death of the deceased.

After the conclusion of any criminal trial, the coroner may resume the adjourned inquest if there is sufficient reason to do so, but this is can be a mere formality, since in law the coroner's findings cannot depart from the outcome of the criminal proceedings. One outcome of an inquest into the violent death of someone whose assailant is not identified, is the often-reported verdict of 'murder (or manslaughter) *by person or persons unknown*'.

9.5 **Crown Court**

9.5.1 **Layout of a typical Crown Court**

A typical Crown Court, hearing serious or complex criminal cases, will have most of the following physical features, though not necessarily in the layout given here. We present this outline as the most typical of Crown Court designs:

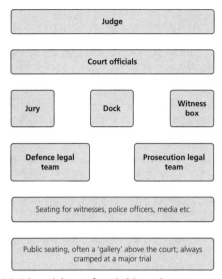

Figure 9.3: Schematic layout of a typical Crown Court

It can be seen from this outline that there are set 'spaces' in a courtroom for the various participants, and in a diagram, everything can look neat and orderly. In fact, courtrooms can be crowded, noisy places, where people are often much closer to each other than our typical layout might suggest. For example, the jury 'box' is often close enough to both the witness box and the dock for members of the jury to 'read' the expressions of the accused and of witnesses, to see complexions, perspiration, and hand movements quite clearly. This proximity can sometimes be oppressive, nowhere more so than when victims have to give evidence close to the person alleged to have carried out the offence(s).

9.5.2 The role of the judge

The Judge presides in a Crown Court, listening to all the evidence, and s/he will summarize the evidence for and against the accused, for the jury. The judge passes sentence in findings of guilt (or Guilty pleas, which earn a 30 per cent reduction in penalty, or prison sentence) and is responsible for keeping order in the courtroom, which includes curtailing the excesses of lawyers for either side, such as asking the accused leading questions. Judges will have been appointed after long experience of the legal profession, in which they could have been a defence lawyer, a lawyer in the Public Prosecution Service, or both; and most have practised as barristers rather than solicitors, though one or two serving judges were not 'called to the Bar' (to practise as barristers). Judges begin as Recorders (some of whom are part-time) before going on to become *puisne* or ordinary judges, becoming circuit judges as they gain experience. The usual pinnacle of a judge's career is to become a High Court judge, specializing in particular areas of the law, but some go further, to appointment as a judge in the Court of Appeal (usually entailing ennoblement in the House of Lords) or even, rarely, high judicial office as a Lord Justice in appointment to the Supreme Court.

For all the majesty of their office, and the sometimes gloomy splendour which surrounds them, Crown Court judges are not unchallenged. Defence teams can appeal against a judge's sentence if they see it as as too severe, or think that the jury was 'misdirected' by the judge, and judges' decisions can be overturned by the Court of Appeal, or the Supreme Court. This has some dangers, since sentences can also now be appealed (by the Attorney General on behalf of the PPS) as too lenient. Some recent cases, in which judges' sentences were indeed perceived as too lenient (one in a prominent rape case, and another in the trial of a paedophile), resulted, after appeal, in increased prison terms for the offenders. The media may be seen to play a part in orchestrating calls for tougher sentences, particularly for 'dramatic' crimes such as child murder or abuse.

9.6 The Public Prosecution Service (PPS)

Until comparatively recently (1986), the police would retain a solicitor or sometimes themselves present the 'prosecution case' at a magistrates' court. Now, both at magistrates' and Crown courts, the prosecution case is presented by lawyers retained by the government's Public Prosecution Service. Increasingly, the PPS's own lawyers are presenting cases at both courts, if qualified to do so.

The PPS was the Crown Prosecution Service (CPS) until 2009. The Prosecution of Offences Act 1985 established the CPS to prosecute criminal offences which had been investigated previously by the police forces of England and Wales, as well as by a number of specialist law enforcement agencies, such as Customs and Excise, as it then was (now an investigative arm in the Serious and Organized Crime Agency, SOCA). In simplified form, the context of the PPS in the criminal justice system looks like this:

(such as 'decoding' digital images). Examples would include *direct testimony* ('he shouted at me to lie down') and *direct experience* ('she threw the glass at me from a metre away'). This is distinct from a category of evidence often regarded as more uncertain or ambiguous: **hearsay evidence**, which consists in *'second-hand' evidence, of what someone else actually or implicitly said* (verbally, in writing, or by conduct, such as nodding or shaking the head). A Special Constable's PNB containing a statement in which an accused person admitted guilt to a crime, is actually hearsay evidence, though it would be admitted in a court. Not all hearsay is so reliable: recording in a PNB that Ms X said that Mr Y told her that he had stolen Mrs C's watch, is not very convincing and could be ambiguous.

Hearsay evidence usually requires corroborative or supporting evidence to be believable; but exceptions are made for deathbed confessions and the like.

These two explanations have been adapted from English and Card, 2009, Jefferson, 2007, and Martin and Turner, 2004.

9.8.2 *Actus reus* and *mens rea*

The Latin phrase *actus reus* can be translated as 'a guilty act'.[5] The *mens rea* is the second part of the 'equation'—the 'guilty mind' which accompanies the 'guilty act'—the act must be done knowing it to be against the law.[6] This is why, in English and Welsh law (and most other legal systems), a child under the age of ten years cannot be convicted of a crime, since the law presumes that the child cannot yet tell the difference between right and wrong and therefore cannot have a 'guilty mind'.

The two parts do not exist separately: the *mens rea* qualifies the *actus reus* (Jefferson, 2007, p 43), so in a rape the offender must recklessly intend sexual intercourse or oral sex, *and* know that the victim does not consent. Thus, all the elements here—'offender', 'victim', 'sexual intercourse or oral sex', and 'consent'—are the *actus reus*. The rapist's 'reckless intent' to commit the offence is the *mens rea* (Jefferson, 2007, pp 43–4). The 'equation' between the two 'elements' can be expressed like this:

Figure 9.5: *Actus reus* and *mens rea*

(adapted from Martin and Turner, 2004, p 5)[7]

Actus reus is not entirely expressed or defined as an act, because sometimes the *omission of action or the failure to do something* may result in a crime—such as letting someone starve to death, or failing to report a road accident. In one case, (*DPP v Santana-Bermudez*, 2003), the accused did not tell a police officer intending to search him that he had a hypodermic needle in a pocket. This omission amounted to *actus reus* (assault causing actual bodily harm or ABH) when the officer was injured by the needle (Martin and Turner, 2004, p 10).

9.8.3 Bad character evidence

On a similar basis, the rule used to be that a court could not consider the accused's character, but the Criminal Justice Act of 2003 abolished that exemption. The Act provides that evidence of the accused's bad character is admissible in criminal proceedings subject to the following conditions:

Evidence of bad character admissible only if:

- all parties agree to its being admissible
- 'it is evidence adduced by the accused [. . .] or is given in answer to a question asked by [him or her] during cross-examination . . . '
- it is important explanatory evidence
- it is relevant to an important matter in issue between the accused and the prosecution
- 'it has substantial probative [evidential] value in relation to [. . . an] issue between the accused and a co-accused'
- it is evidence to correct a false impression given by the accused, or
- the accused has made an attack on another person's character.

(summarized from English and Card, 2009, p 249)

9.9 The 'Virtual Court'

Discussions about a court which exists only in cyberspace have been around since the creation of the world-wide web in the last century and several schemes have been piloted (mostly with indifferent success) in Europe. Discussions remained at the theoretical level in England and Wales until a prototype 'virtual court' was attempted at Camberwell Green Magistrates' Court in London in July 2007. It ran for twelve weeks; the court was equipped with video-conferencing equipment, linked to four 'charging sites' at local police stations in Lambeth and Southwark (the districts bordering the magistrates' court). Essentially, interview rooms in the respective police custody suites were wired for video-conferencing, and the links enabled the defendants and legal representatives to be 'seen' in court whilst physically located in the police station. In diagrammatic form it looks something like this:

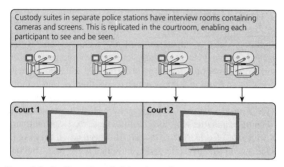

Figure 9.6: Configuration of a 'virtual court'

This is not a virtual court in the cyberspace sense, since two locations physically exist (a police station and a court). All that the technology does is link them, allowing participants in both places to see and be seen. The aim in all of this is to speed up the CJ process, not by cutting any corners in the *process*, but to get around the waiting time and the need to carry case papers from once place to another. In the virtual court, once a defendant has been charged with an offence, the papers for the case are uploaded into a 'collaboration space' *document management system* to which the police, the courts, the PPS, and the Probation Service all have access. This enables in turn the swift preparation of 'Advance Information' packs for the prosecution and defence, so that the case can proceed, almost without interruption.

During a hearing at the virtual court, the defendant can look at the court, the judge, or the magistrates' bench, the PPS lawyer, and the public gallery in the courtroom, on a screen in the custody suite interview room (see Figure 9.6 above). If the defendant pleads Guilty, the aim is to sentence at this first hearing or shortly afterwards if the Probation Service can submit a report on the defendant that day. What this means in effect is that a case can be prepared, heard, and sentence passed in short order, without the defendant or his/her legal team having to go to court physically. If the judge or magistrates' bench feels at any point that the process is unsuitable or unfair to the defendant, proceedings can be halted and the case referred for a conventional hearing in slower time. The pilot has been extended, but we do not expect its widespread adoption in the English and Welsh magistrates' courts until 2012–13 and beyond.

9.10 Going to Court

If you are called to appear in court (the technical term is '*summonsed*') to give evidence in a case, you need to be prepared properly and professionally for the experience. That said, following Lord Justice Auld's reforms in 2001 by which many offences were removed from magistrates' courts and punished with a fixed penalty notice (FPN) instead, whereas previously many Special Constables attended court as a matter almost of routine, these days, *Special Constables are much less likely to go to court*. However, when they do, the offences will tend to greater seriousness than in the past. The corollary is that, as a Special Constable, you are far more likely to issue a FPN. This has annoyed the magistracy a little, because they see their role being undermined by instant fines on the streets instead of the steady process of law, added to which, more than 50 per cent of fines remain unpaid—so defaulters end up in court anyway.[8]

The advent of the virtual court may well make a physical appearance in court a fairly unusual event altogether, but for the rest of this short section, we are going to assume that you are a Special Constable who has to appear in a physical court and give evidence, on oath, in the witness box. It does not signify whether the evidence is given at a magistrates' court, a Youth Court, a coroner's court, or the Crown Court; the processes are common to all places. Only the trappings and the nature or process of cross-examination (challenges to your evidence) will vary. In a magistrates' court, it might be a District Judge or a defence 'duty' solicitor who asks you to explain some point or to clarify your actions, whilst in a Crown Court this may done by the barrister 'lead' for the defendant's defence team.

9.10.1 Making an impression

In these days of relaxed dress codes and relaxed manners, it sometimes causes concern when Special Constables are told to look smart for court. But, if you think about it, courts are formal places with a serious purpose and it is insulting to everyone there if you do not make an effort to look well presented and smart. This has two distinct purposes, to do with making the right impression. Firstly, *it shows respect to the court*. You would not (we presume) turn up to a job interview wearing your gym kit or nightwear, because that is not the place for such clothing. The same applies to appearing in court. You are a Special Constable and should be in uniform and looking the business. This leads to the second point: *you will be judged on your appearance*. However compelling your evidence is, and however clearly recorded and articulated, however modulated your voice and arrestingly brilliant your brain, most people will make judgements about you by looking at you.

9.10.2 In the building

When you get to court (and we assume that you will have attended one before to familiarize yourself during your training, if not regularly since) you wait to be called into the courtroom. There might be a considerable wait, the claims for speeded-up criminal justice processes notwithstanding, and you may not speak to other witnesses while you wait your turn. There may be a reserved place for witnesses, or you might have to mill about with everyone else, also waiting to be called. Hanging about for an hour beyond the time given on your formal notice to attend court is about par. *Always be prepared for delay*, postponement, or recess because others have not turned up, or because the defence or prosecution wants a delay for some reason. When finally called by name (usually by a court usher, distinguishable in black clothing or black robes), you enter the court and go to the witness box.

9.10.3 Taking the oath

The first thing that you will be asked to do is to take the oath or make an affirmation. All this means is that *you promise to tell the truth*. The *oath* is for people who have a religious faith or belief system, and is invariably accompanied by some symbol or expression of that faith or belief. For Muslims, for example, it is the Holy Koran; for Hindus it is the Holy Gita, for Christians it is the Holy Bible (sometimes the New Testament only), whilst for Jews it may be the Scroll or Torah, or the Holy Bible (Old Testament only), and Sikhs swear by the Guru Nanak. Some faiths require a ritual or symbolic purification, such as washing the mouth or the lighting of a candle, whilst others require an image or picture to be present when they take the oath. All non-believers, some Quakers, Buddhists, Jehovah's Witnesses, Mormons, and others will make an *affirmation*, the wording of which is '*I do solemnly, sincerely and truly declare and affirm . . .*'

All will promise, by whatever they cherish most as their faith or their reason, to *tell the truth, the whole truth and nothing but the truth*. It is a solemn moment in a solemn undertaking, and reminds everyone that evidence is not to be given or taken lightly. The law is very clear: there are heavy penalties for committing perjury (telling lies on oath), as well as showing 'contempt of court', or 'perverting the course of justice'.

9.10.4 Giving evidence

9.10.4.1 *Not an expert*

The first thing to establish is that you are not an 'expert witness'. The term is much misused and usually refers to someone with specialist knowledge, like a forensic scientist or a pathologist, who is experienced in giving evidence in court. But defence teams often challenge expert testimony with experts of their own, directly exploiting the propensity of experts to disagree, and in some cases, to be mistaken in their conclusions.[9] You are a witness like everyone else in the case and you have no special status or privileges, though it is likely that your evidence will be given some weight because you are a police officer. As far as any defence counsel is concerned, this may also mean that you are fair game for a blunt onslaught, where your professionalism can be impugned and your objectivity challenged. That is more likely in a Crown Court as a tactic, but it is not unknown in a magistrates' court, particularly when a defence solicitor wants to attack the prosecution case and cast doubt on police procedures. Some solicitors make a good living from challenging police processes in magistrates' courts, particularly in trials for dangerous or reckless driving, where the letter of the law appears to matter less than the *minutiae* of process.

In a magistrates' court, you will begin by saying who you are:

> Melissa Emily van den Linden, Special Constable 162534 of Lanchester Police, currently stationed at Manor Park Police Station, Rochdale, your worship(s).

You would follow this with a statement, based either on your duty statement or on your PNB or both:

> At 0005 hours on Friday 30th March, I was on mobile/foot patrol (stationary/standing and location), when I saw a man who I now know to be *Antony Blair Wendell*, being ejected

from the Happy Banker Night Club. He was swearing and aggressive, and appeared to be intoxicated. As I moved towards him, he turned on the door steward who had put him outside, and lashed out with his right hand. I saw the glint of metal by the streetlight, and heard the door steward cry out and stagger backwards, bleeding from a cut or slash to his face.

Wendell attempted to run past me, but I stopped him, held him, and removed a thin-bladed knife from his right hand. The edges of his forefinger, thumb, and part of his wrist were wet with blood. I cautioned him, but he swung at me with his other hand. I then arrested him, but had to subdue him further with PAVA spray, as he continued to offer violence to me and to my police colleagues. Eventually he stopped struggling and was helped to sit up. As I instructed him how to cope with the aftermath of the spray, he said to me by his own free will without any prompting or questioning, 'It's my knife. I slashed the doorman 'cause he chucked me out.'

I placed Wendell into a police vehicle and he was taken to Manor Park Police Station where he was introduced to the custody officer, Sergeant Odinga.

Note that Wendell would not be charged until he had been interviewed and evidence gathered from a medical practitioner regarding the injuries of the doorman; in which case Wendell is likely to have been bailed to return to the police station for charging at a later date. *We have truncated some elements in the CJS to get everything into our story.*

What is notable here, apart from Special Constable van den Linden's calm professionalism, was the use of her senses to show the direct witness experience. She *saw* the glint of the knife blade, she *heard* the accused swearing, she *physically intercepted* and subdued him, disarming him as she did so, and *registering* the blood on his forefinger and thumb from where he had gripped the knife. She also *noted* (and presumably recorded in her PNB) what the accused had said as he was recovering from the effects of the PAVA spray.

If there is a defence solicitor present in the magistrates' court, the Special Constable might be questioned about her PNB which, of course, forms part of the evidence. The solicitor might ask her when the record in her PNB was made. It may have been made at the time (*contemporaneous*) and this will be proven by subsequent entries which post-date the entry on the incident. Alternatively, her PNB could have been written up, or additional notes made (as above) after the excitement had subsided and Wendell was in the cells. The point we should like to make here is that this small delay is perfectly acceptable, but the PNB really does need to be written up before going off duty. Any further delay would look slapdash and unprofessional and, if completion had been the following day or the day after, the evidence itself might be called into question by a defence solicitor.

We shall assume that our resourceful Special Constable did not write up her PNB later, but instead and properly made a persuasive contemporaneous account. It might still be the case in the magistrates' court that either the JPs on the bench or the District Judge (whoever is presiding) would have questions for the Special Constable about the police action in restraining and arresting Mr Wendell, particularly if there are any allegations of excessive use of force. This might be in addition to any questions about the evidence which the defence solicitor may want to ask. In this case, the doorman received a small cut above his left ear and hairline. As a consequence the PPS charging standards for 'minor, but not merely superficial, cuts of a sort probably requiring medical treatment (eg stitches)' clearly state that the most appropriate charge is one of assault occasioning ABH, contrary to section 47 Offences Against the Person Act 1861.[10] Even so, this offence is triable either way and therefore could be heard in a Crown Court should Wendell elect for such a hearing, or should the magistrates consider the possibility of a very heavy prison sentence if Wendell were to be found guilty.

Our purpose here is not to turn the process of evidence giving into a species of prolonged and minute dissection, but rather to show you that questioning in court can elicit more detail about the state of the accused and the facts of what happened. Although the defence solicitor (if present) will try to mitigate things for his or her client, it might well be the chairing magistrate (the centre of the bench of three) or the presiding District Judge who takes the lead in questioning witnesses. Alternatively, it might be the prosecuting counsel from the PPS who asks for more detail.

And you can understand why. The purpose of the hearing is to ascertain what the quality of the evidence is against Mr Wendell, so that the case may be either committed to the Crown Court or dismissed at this point. The seriousness of the charges faced by Mr Wendell might well hang on the nature of the arresting officer's evidence. Special Constable van den Linden saw the whole episode, and so her 'eyewitness testimony' is crucial to the charges—as would be the witness evidence and the injuries of the door steward whom Mr Wendell allegedly attacked with a knife. The knife, recovered from the crime scene and forensically tested, would also be 'exhibited' in evidence. Proof (from forensic science and testimony) that it was Mr Wendell's knife and that he used it against the door steward would be crucial evidential matters in the case proceeding to Crown Court.

9.10.4.2 *Giving evidence at Crown Court*

It is worth reminding you at this point that only about 5 per cent of criminal cases go to the Crown Court, as we have seen previously, but those cases will be the serious ones. The first thing that will happen in a Crown Court is that the charge against the accused will be read out. In our case, the charge read out by the Clerk of the Court against Antony Blair Wendell is this:

> You are charged under section 47 of the Offences against the Person Act of 1861 in that you did assault Dwayne Marshall Harris, door steward of the Happy Banker Dance Club and Bar, thereby occasioning actual bodily harm.
> How do you plead, Guilty or Not Guilty?

If Wendell pleads Guilty, the jury will not be required and matters will proceed swiftly to sentencing. Should Wendell plead Not Guilty, there would be a full trial. We shall assume that Wendell's defence case was that he was depressed and resentful and that he lashed out in anger at the door steward, forgetting that he had a knife in his hand at the time . . . Yes, we know, but unlikelier defences are mounted all the time. The point is that the Special Constable's evidence now becomes pivotal to the prosecution case.

Rather than make a statement, as in the magistrates' court, the officer's evidence is now brought out by the prosecuting counsel through a series of questions. The same needs exist for accuracy and calm professionalism, and the questioning will seek to make the case against the accused:

> **Prosecuting Counsel** You describe the accused's behaviour as he was ejected from the club as 'swearing and aggressive' and you noted in your Pocket Notebook that you thought him intoxicated. Why was that?
> **Special Constable van den Linden** His speech was slurred and he seemed to exaggerate his gestures. Once I had restrained him, I could smell the alcohol on his breath. The

club barman said to me afterwards that the accused had
drunk four double whiskies in the course of an hour or so.

PC How would you describe his demeanour?

SCvdL Aggressive frustration. He seemed to me to be ready
to lash out at anyone in his way. He told me later that he
had been ejected because he had climbed on to the bar at
the edge of the dance floor and challenged any man in the
place to fight him.

PC Indeed so, and we have the testimony of those in the bar
at the time who can confirm this. Why did you have to
restrain him?

and so on. Again, note that the Special Constable is careful not
to give an opinion, but to present evidence which she experienced directly, either by what she saw, smelled, heard, or felt, or
had herself taken in evidence (from the barman), and also what
Wendell had told her in his post-arrest statement.

The defence rises to cross-examine when the witness has finished
giving evidence. Remember what the defence role is: accused people are presumed *innocent until proven guilty*, and the defence team
will try to show that its client did not commit the offence with
which s/he is charged. Or, if the charge is irrefutable, the attempt
will be to mitigate the charge, either by suggesting that the assault
was in self-defence, or that the accused was in fear of his or her life
and that is why he lashed out. A secondary tactic would be to try
to shake or cast in doubt the reliability of witness testimony. This
is done by trying to spot anomalies, inconsistencies, or contradic-
tions in the evidence, by provoking the witness, or by confusing
and bewildering the witness. It's important to realize that these
are tactics to suggest innocence or mitigation of the accused, just
as the prosecution uses tactics to reinforce the accused's guilt. You
will often be told that such ploys are business, there's nothing personal in it. Yet that is hard to believe if someone has deliberately
suggested that you are hard of hearing, short-sighted, incompe-
tent, not much cop, a control freak, an officious busybody, or just
someone hiding his or her inadequacy behind a uniform.

Police officers have tactics themselves to deal with this approach
to their evidence. Some count silently to three before replying to
the question. Some do not respond unless a specific question is
asked. Others play each question with a 'dead bat', saying as little as possible. All remain calm and refuse to rise to the dangled
bait. They do not lose their tempers or fall into the trap of trying

to justify themselves. Be careful though—any attempt to score off the defence counsel may harm your professional image, or look like contempt of court—and you might not succeed anyway. We're sorry, but insults are a one-way traffic in a courtroom, and that's towards you, not from you. Let's go back to the impressions that you create in court. How would you view the Special Constable at the end of this exchange?

> **Defence Counsel** Officer, were you ever in fear for your own safety when restraining the accused?
>
> **SC van den Linden** No sir, I was not.
>
> **DC:** Yet you describe your actions as 'proportionate'. How can it be proportionate to use a pepper spray containing a volatile solvent on a man who is a registered asthmatic?
>
> **SCvdL** I was not aware at the time that the accused was an asthmatic, sir.
>
> **DC:** So why didn't you use a simple arm lock, or verbal persuasion? Why did you have to assault the accused in this unprovoked and extreme way?
>
> **SCvdL** I do not consider that my actions were either unprovoked or extreme, sir. In my judgement, an arm lock would not have been sufficient. The accused would not respond to spoken instructions.
>
> **DC:** You are a Special Constable, are you not?
>
> **SCvdl** I am, sir.
>
> **DC** A part-time police officer?
>
> **SCvdL** Yes, sir.
>
> **DC** (sneering) A 'hobby bobby', I believe you are called?

The abrupt change of tack is a common device, designed to disrupt the witness's concentration, and you can see that the questions are becoming personal. The defence counsel is using a risky strategy here, as insulting the police, especially the volunteer, unpaid police, might backfire. The Special Constable responds calmly to the deliberate insult:

> **SCvdL** That term is not a valid description of the Special Constabulary, sir.
>
> **DC** Tell me, officer, why do you do it?
>
> **SCvdL** Do what, sir?

DC: Do this volunteering to be a police officer. Like the uniform, do you? Like the power, hm?

SCvdL I see the volunteering as part of my civic duty, sir. I do not get paid because I am a volunteer. I have no opinion of the uniform: it was not part of my reason for volunteering.

DC Isn't it the case, officer, that you saw the chance to give a man a real hiding that night, while no one else was around, and you gave him the pepper spray because, well, you just don't like men, do you?

Prosecuting Counsel My Lord!

Judge Quite so, Miss Liebowitz. Mr Barter-Tuck, this will not do. You are simply insulting the officer and I do not see where this is going.

DC I apologize my Lord, but I simply seek to show that this officer reacted disproportionately and attacked the accused.

Judge I grow tired of this. Have you no real questions for this witness?

DC Yes I have, my Lord. Tell me, officer, what is your real job? What do you do when you are not dressing up as a police officer?

SCvdL I lecture in Law and Criminal Justice Studies, at the Reiner Centre, University of Oldham, sir.

DC Oh, I see. Well, um, no more questions, my Lord.

Judge: Well that's something. Officer, if Miss Liebowitz has no more questions for you, you may stand down.

The defence's risk has not paid off. The judge has made it clear that this is a pointless and time-wasting line of questioning and his intervention underlines the thinness of the defence case, where the provocation tactics have been too blatant. (Of course, we have exaggerated a little, but only a little.) The defence will try, if it suits their strategy, to provoke you, make you lose your temper, or make you out to be a fool, in order to discredit your evidence or to throw doubt on your actions. But it can have the reverse effect, as here. It is the Special Constable who stays calm, rational, and in control. It is the defence that looks increasingly desperate and devoid of purpose and direction. The jury will be impressed by this officer's evidence, as well as her demeanour, and the calm way she dealt with the histrionic questioning. It will also serve to underline the resolute and dispassionate way that she dealt with Wendell's provocation during the incident itself, so her response to the hostile questions actually reinforces her credibility as a witness.

You can see what was at the back of the defence's rather clumsy attempt to make her angry. If she had snapped back at the defence counsel, responded to the deliberate insults, or lost her temper with him (which is surprisingly common among witnesses in court under cross-questioning), then the jury could reasonably have wondered whether her evidence was indeed 'the whole truth'. Maybe someone so easily provoked in a courtroom *had* over-reacted to a bumbling drunk that night? If that happens, her testimony will begin to look shaky and correspondingly, Special Constable van den Linden's credibility as a witness will be impaired.

All the exchanges were heightened in this episode for effect, and to give you something of interest to read, but such tactics are common in real life. Many Special Constables with experience of going to court will describe the tactics used variously to disrupt, dismay, or discomfit an officer's testimony. The golden rule is *never to lose your temper*; always to remain calm and controlled, professional and detached, whatever the provocation. After all, it's what you do all the time on the job, isn't it?

9.11 **The Prison Service and the Probation Service**

The Prison Service, an executive agency of the Ministry of Justice, is at the later end of the criminal justice system and deals with those who are convicted of their crimes and sentenced to a term of imprisonment by the courts, for that period of imprisonment only. Once an individual leaves the prison system, s/he ceases to be of concern to the Prison Service (see The Probation Service: both organizations share the National Offender Management Service (NOMS)).

Currently, there are over 139 designated prisons in England and Wales (HM Prison Service, 2008a).[11] These establishments are intended to provide safe and secure accommodation for the current prisoner population which, at the time of writing, is in excess of 83,600,[12] and of whom approximately 95 per cent are male (National Offender Management Service, 2009):[13]

> **Types of prison**
> **high-security prisons** [for prisoners posing a high risk]
> **secure training establishments** [where prisoners obtain education and skills]
> **resettlement centres** [for prisoners about to be released]
> **local prisons** [accommodating low-risk prisoners]
> **open prisons** [low-security prisons for non-risk prisoners]
> **remand centres** [custody for those whose cases have not yet come to court]
> **immigration detention and removal centres**
> **young offenders' institutions** [for those under 18 found guilty of offences with a custodial sentence: some of these used to be called 'Borstals' after the first such institution for young offenders]

(HM Prison Service, 2008a)

Eleven prisons have been contracted out to the **private security industry** since the early 1990s, based on evidence that they can operate at lower running costs than public sector prisons (Joyce, 2006). These 'private sector prisons' tend to be low-security establishments, requiring minimal security and supervision.

The National Probation Service for England and Wales, part of the Justice Ministry too, is the law enforcement agency responsible for the supervision and management of offenders who:

- have been convicted at court and given a community sentence;
- have been released from prison on licence, usually after serving a minimum of two-thirds of their sentence and are now subject to a community order in lieu of additional gaol time;
- have been released from prison early following an assessment by the Parole Board.

(Directgov, 2009)

Customarily, it has been the aim of probation officers to befriend convicted criminals and to develop close, trusting relationships with them, characterized as '*caring for offenders and controlling their criminal behaviour*' (Worrall, 1997, cited in Joyce, 2006, p 397). Probation officers, using their experience, knowledge, and professional training, can offer advice, guidance, support, and counsel to offenders on a variety of personal and social issues, including relationships, accommodation, and employment problems, in the hope that their positive interaction with offenders and practical support will help to reform and rehabilitate them and prevent further reoffending (Worrall & Hoy, 2005).

Probation officers are also responsible for writing **Pre-Sentence Reports** for the courts, of which 250,000 are prepared annually (NOMS, 2006).[14] These reports are designed to provide magistrates or judges with more information about the offender in order that the former can make an informed decision when imposing a sentence. In addition, the Probation Service also operates a **Bail Information Scheme** that is designed to assist the PPS in reaching a decision as to whether or not to ask the court to remand a suspect in custody pending trial, or bail the person to attend court on the dates of the hearing (Joyce, 2006). The Probation Service recommends any restrictions that should be considered when contemplating granting a suspect bail: for example, requiring them to reside at a probation hostel (called Approved Premises) where they can be supervised 24 hours a day by probation staff, or having to report to their local police station each day at a specified time.

The Prison and Probation Services' headquarters were amalgamated in 2005 to form NOMS, an executive agency of the Ministry of Justice. NOMS aims to enhance the efficiency and effectiveness of the correctional agencies in England and Wales by exercising managerial control and oversight over each service, and by providing continuity in direction and leadership (Ministry of Justice, 2008a; 2008b).

9.11.1 Community sentences

Community sentences are becoming an increasingly popular means of punishing offenders found guilty by the courts in cases where the crimes committed are not severe enough to warrant imprisonment (Ministry of Justice, 2008c). Community penalties are advantageous in that they not only serve to divert offenders away from prisons ('universities of crime' said to reinforce and harden criminality rather than address it), but they also assist in alleviating the problems of overcrowding in prisons, thus reserving places for the most dangerous, intractable, or prolific offenders, in turn reducing strain on the Prison Service (Joyce, 2006; Ministry of Justice, 2008c). Evidence compiled by the Ministry of Justice suggests that community sentences are also more effective than imprisonment in preventing reoffending, but only for some kinds of crime (Ministry of Justice, 2008c).

The Criminal Justice Act 2003 consolidated and transformed the way community sentencing within England and Wales operated. It created a single **community order** that could be imposed on any person aged 16 years or over who is convicted of a crime and for whom prison was deemed an unsuitable penalty (Elliot and Quinn, 2006).[15] 'Community orders' may have various requirements or conditions attached to them for a specified period of time, with which the offender must comply. The conditions imposed are decided and set by the court when passing sentence and may include:

- **Unpaid work requirement** (to be carried out in the community, and provide a benefit to local residents) eg conservation work, graffiti removal, litter picking, commonly referred to as '**community payback**' schemes, or 'justice seen, justice done'
- **Activity requirement**, eg providing reparations to a victim of crime, taking part in an educational course, discussing relationship, employment, or offending problems in a peer group, or with a counsellor
- **Programme requirement**, eg attending anger management classes, drink-impaired driving courses, or domestic abuse workshops
- **Prohibited activity requirement**, eg visiting certain people, taking part in certain activities such as drinking alcohol in public, attending football matches, or possessing, using, or carrying a firearm
- **Curfew requirement** supported by electronic monitoring (tagging)
- **Exclusion requirement** (an order to stay away from specified locations, often used in cases of harassment to ensure an offender does not attempt to contact the victim)
- **Residence requirement** (an order to reside at a specific location; police officers are sometimes involved in checking these addresses to ensure compliance)
- **Mental health treatment requirement**
- **Drug rehabilitation requirement**
- **Alcohol treatment requirement**
- **Supervision requirement**, where an offender is placed under the supervision of a probation officer for a specified period of time and must attend all scheduled meetings with them. Work takes place to help the offender change their offending habits and attitudes
- **Attendance centre requirement** (much the same as a supervision requirement, but aimed at 18–24 year-olds).

(adapted from: Elliot & Quinn, 2006, and NOMS, 2006)

9.12 Restorative Justice (RJ)

The Home Office defines RJ in the following terms:

Restorative justice brings victims, offenders and communities together to decide on a response to a particular crime. It's about putting victims' needs at the centre of the criminal justice system and finding positive solutions to crime by encouraging offenders to face up to their actions.

(Home Office website)

The rationale behind RJ is that it can help victims deal with the stress of being a victim by providing them with options, as opposed to being merely one small and apparently insignificant part of a giant justice system, within which victims quickly feel they have no power. By contrast, RJ can empower victims to find (excuse the cliché) 'closure' of what happened to them, or at least acceptance that it has gone as far as is practicable. Justice becomes something that they are part of, not something done (or not done) to them by some unseen arcane process. The victim has a voice. RJ can also turn around offender behaviour by bringing the perpetrators, in some cases, face to face with the victims whose lives they have blighted, and by showing that their crimes or anti-social behaviour do affect real people. (If you think about it, is there really anything that can be called a 'victimless' crime?) Offenders are shown the repercussions of their actions, the responsibility they bear for their decisions. This can make it a very powerful tool to redirect those who might otherwise embark on a life of ASB or crime, provided always that the effect on the offender is as profound and as intense as is supposed from appearance (Crawford and Newburn, 2003).

9.13 **Reoffending/Recidivism**

The subject of reoffending and rehabilitation is one which is central in the criminal justice world and it is sensible to look at the offender's behavioural pattern, lest the chain of causality that can lead some people to becoming permanent fixtures in police stations and courts is not broken. One term you may hear in relation to this subject is **recidivism**, which means the same as reoffending. Given that the costs associated with the criminal justice system are enormous (think about police, courts, probation, prison, etc), it makes sound fiscal sense to try to stop people from becoming repeat offenders.

9.13.1 **Diagram of criminal behaviour**

Consider this diagram of criminal behaviour in relation to reoffending:

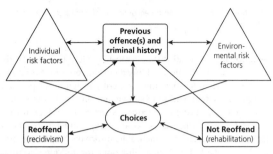

Figure 9.7: The cycle of reoffending

This demonstrates the **cyclical** or **iterative** [repeated] **pattern** inherent in repeated criminal behaviour. Crime is not committed in a vacuum nor can it be explained solely in terms of the morality of the individual. There are factors at play that can influence an individual's propensity to take decisions that result in criminal outcomes.

9.13.2 Risk factors involved in reoffending/recidivism

In his work on recidivism among adults with psychotic disorders, JS Lamberti (2007) identified eight major risk factors that contribute to reoffending.

(NB this does *not* mean that we think all criminals have psychotic disorders, rather that the research helps identify risk factors that may have an impact on your role as a Special Constable).

These eight factors are:

- History of anti-social behaviour
- Anti-social personality
- Anti-social cognition
- Anti-social attitudes
- Family and/or marital circumstances
- School and/or work circumstances
- Leisure and recreation activities, and
- Substance abuse.

9.14 **Rehabilitation**

Rehabilitation is a concept much debated in criminal justice and political circles, offering as it does the tantalizing opportunity to make considerable savings within the law-and-order budget in most countries. However, it is perhaps a concept that is not much understood, since many people in the CJS seem to search for a 'one size fits all' solution. *The Oxford English Dictionary* defines 'rehabilitate' as:

> **Verb 1** restore to health or normal life by training and therapy after imprisonment, addiction, or illness. **2** restore the standing or reputation of. **3** restore to a former condition.

Therefore, in terms of criminal rehabilitation, the many agencies that work within the CJS, either explicitly or at the periphery, must consider rehabilitation as a key aim *because it restores offenders to their previous non-offending status*. Of course the police should *prevent* crime but equally they should prevent reoffending; however, they cannot do everything alone.

9.14.1 **Rehabilitation of Offenders Act 1974**

One of the key pieces of legislation in this area is the 1974 Rehabilitation of Offenders Act (ROA) which allows ex-offenders at least the chance to gain employment and start making a difference to those individual and environmental risk factors we explored earlier. The ROA does not apply to those offences where a custodial sentence of 2½ years (or longer) has been passed, nor where applicants are applying for jobs that involve working with children and/or vulnerable adults, where national security is an issue, nor for certain legal professions, nursing, or accountancy.

9.14.2 **Conclusion**

No exploration of the criminal justice system would be complete without considering the issues of reoffending and rehabilitation. The key to breaking the negative cycle that some people find themselves in does not just lie with the police and requires a multiagency approach to a complex problem. However, since you are a Special Constable, it is important that you consider the issues because you might well deal with the same people again and again and it would be easy to become complacent and prejudiced.

There are many reasons why people reoffend and no single definitive route to rehabilitation, but you should at least try to understand what is involved; the alternative is that you will become cynical or embittered and eventually fixated purely on enforcement.

Further Reading

Almandras, S, 'Special Constables', Standard Note SNHA/1154 (31 October 2008, House of Commons Library)

Auld, Lord Justice, *A Review of the Criminal Courts of England and Wales* (2001, London: The Stationery Office, Crown copyright)

Bullock, S and Gunning, N, *Police Service Strength*, Home Office Statistical Bulletin 13/07, (2007, London: Home Office, Crown copyright)

Cape, E, 'Defence Lawyers' in Newburn, T and Neyroud, P, *Dictionary of Policing* (2008, Devon: Willan Publishing)

Crawford, A and Newburn, T, *Youth Offending and Restorative Justice: implementing reform in youth justice* (2003, Devon: Willan Publishing)

Directgov, 'Probation and the National Probation Service' (2009) available at <http://www.direct.gov.uk/en/CrimeJusticeAndTheLaw/PrisonAndProbation/DG_181731>

Doak, J and McGourlay, C, *Criminal Evidence in Context* (2009, Routledge-Cavendish)

Dorries, C, *Coroners' Courts: a guide to law and practice* (2004, Oxford: Oxford University Press)

English, J and Card, R, *Police Law*, 11th edn. (2009, Oxford: Oxford University Press), especially Chapter 7, 'The Law of Evidence'

Fitzpatrick, B, Menzies, C, and Hunter, R, *Going to Court* (2006, Oxford: Oxford University Press)

Jewkes, Y, *Handbook on Prisons* (2007, Devon: Willan Publications)

Johnstone, G and Van Ness, D (eds.), 2007, *Handbook of Restorative Justice* (2007, Devon: Willan Publications), especially Chapter 16, Hoyle, C, 'Policing and Restorative Justice', pp 292–311

McCold, P, 'What is the role of community in restorative justice theory and practice?' in Zehr and Toews (eds.), *Critical Issues in Restorative Justice*, (see below) Ch. 13, pp 155–72

Ministry of Justice (2008a), 'National Offender Management Service' available at <http://www.justice.gov.uk/about/noms.htm>

Ministry of Justice (2008b), 'About NOMS: How NOMS works' available at <http://noms.justice.gov.uk/about-us/how-noms-works/>

Ministry of Justice (2008c), *Community Sentencing—Reducing reoffending, changing lives* (London: Ministry of Justice)

Moore, T, and Wilkinson, T, *Youth Court Guide* (2009, Haywards Heath, W Sussex: Tottel Publishing)

Mulchandani, R and Sigurdsson, J, *Police Service Strength: England and Wales*, Home Office Statistical Bulletin 13/09 (2009, London: Home Office, Crown copyright)

HM Prison Service (2008a), 'Prison Estate Map', available at <http://www.hmprisonservice.gov.uk/resourcecentre/estate_map/>.

Sherman, LW and Strang, H, 'Restorative Justice: the evidence' (2007, London: The Smith Institute)

Starmer, K, *The Public Prosecution Service: Setting the Standard* (2009, London: OPSI, Crown copyright)

Tapper, C, *Cross and Tapper on Evidence*, 11th edn. (2007, Oxford: Oxford University Press)

Youth Justice, 2009, detail available from <http://www.yjb.gov.uk/en-gb/yjs/Courts/YouthCourt.htm>, accessed 14 July 2009

Zehr, H and Toews, B (eds.), *Critical Issues in Restorative Justice* (2004, Monsey, New York: Criminal Justice Press)

Notes

1 Courts martial, which exist to try offences committed by members of the Armed Forces, are not considered here. A good description of the difference between a court martial and a civil criminal trial is in Gooch and Williams (2007, p 91). The European Court of Justice is also outside the remit of this *Handbook*. For all practical purposes, the new Supreme Court is the final court of appeal in criminal cases in the UK (see footnote 2 below).

2 The old House of Lords Appellate Court of Law Lords was abolished in July 2009, and a Supreme Court instituted. This may sound like a borrowing from the American system, but is in fact a renaming of the old process. The Supreme Court consists of Law Lords, just as the previous system did. The change, then, is largely political and probably has more to do with sending a signal to Brussels and the EU than to any fundamental changes in the judiciary of England and Wales.

3 The Justices of the Peace Act of 1361, which subordinated constables to the magistracy: see 1.5, A Short but Exciting History of the Special Constabulary.

4 Keir Starmer, the Director of Public Prosecutions, wrote an article for *The Times*, entitled 'Criminal Justice must break free from the past', 23 July 2009 from which these extracts are taken. His main document, also published on 23 July, is titled *The Public Prosecution Service: Setting the Standard* (2009, OPSI, Crown copyright). Note that the DPP refers to the 'Public Prosecution Service': the change from Crown Prosecution Service was announced in 2008, but is taking time to gain acceptance.

5 It comes from a whole Latin phrase *actus non facit reum nisi mens sit rea*, which we may translate as 'the act itself is not evidence of guilt unless it is accompanied by a guilty mind'.

6 Though of course, ignorance of the law is no defence. It is a neat paradox that, under the law, you must know the law, yet may defend your action if done without 'guilty knowledge'.

7 Martin and Turner (2004, p 5) note that *actus reus* and *mens rea* are not wholly satisfactory terms, since their translations can be ambiguous. Lord Diplock (in 1983) preferred 'prohibited conduct' for *actus reus*, whilst the Law Commission (in 1989) used 'external element'. On *mens rea*, the Law Commission in 1989 used the term 'fault element'. None is much of an improvement.

8 Gibb, F, 'En garde! Magistrates ready for battle over punishments', *The Times*, 26 February 2009, available from <http://business.timesonline.co.uk/tol/business/law/article5802325.ece>, accessed 27 February 2009 and Gibb, F, 'On-the-spot fines mean justice is not seen to be done, say critics', *The Times*, 5 May 2009, available from <http://www.timesonline.co.uk/tol/news/uk/article6222312.ece>, accessed 5 May 2009.

9 The example of Professor Sir Roy Meadow comes to mind. A paediatrician and expert witness of many years' standing, Professor Meadow opined in court on misleading or misinterpreted statistics that cot deaths were far more rare than is the case, which led to an unsafe conviction against a mother, Sally Clark, two of whose children had suffered cot deaths. Mrs Clark was convicted of killing both her baby sons and served three years in prison before she was freed and her conviction quashed in 2003 after a second appeal (*British Medical Journal* (2003) 326, p 304). Professor Meadow was struck off the Medical Register in 2005: see an article by Dyer, C in *British Medical Journal* (2005) 331(7510), p 177, 23 July 2005. Details of the Sally Clark case are available from Batt, J, *Stolen Innocence, A Mother's Fight For Justice, The Authorised Story of Sally Clark* (2004, London: Ebury Press).

10 The PPS offers guidance concerning cases of offences against the person through the use of what are commonly known as 'charging standards'. These standards are designed to assist prosecutors in selecting the most appropriate charge. The decision to charge is based upon the severity of the injury sustained by the victim. However, the guidance is quite clear that the standards should never be used to make any investigatory decision, such as making an arrest. The PPS charging standards can be found at <http://www.cps.gov.uk/legal/l _to_o/offences_against_the_person/#P48_1458>, accessed 2 November 2009.

11 HM Prison Service (2008a), 'Prison Estate Map', available at <http://www.hmprisonservice.gov.uk/resourcecentre/estate_map/>.

12 Ministry of Justice, National Offender Management Service Population Strategy (2009), 'Prison Population & Accommodation Briefing for 03rd July 2009', available at <http://www.hmprisonservice.gov.uk/assets/documents/100047CC03072009_web_report.doc>.

13 *Ibid*.

14 National Offender Management Service (2006), 'The National Probation Service for England and Wales', available at <http://www.probation.homeoffice.gov.uk/files/pdf/The%20National%20Probation%20Service%20for%20England%20and%20Wales%20Leaflet.pdf>.

15 Elliot, C and Quinn, F (2006).

Chapter 10

Futures

10.1 Introduction

This is a dangerous chapter to write. The reason is that it is very easy for writers to get carried away when they study a particular organization in some detail, and constantly hunt up references about it and look at plans being made for it. They are apt to assume that the future as mapped must happen as fact. The Special Constabulary is no exception to this general observation. In the course of more than a year's work of studying, interviewing, questioning, researching, and reading, the authors of this *Handbook* have been involved in detailed and occasionally impassioned debates about the future of the Special Constabulary, the future of public policing more generally, the role of police in society, and the resource pressures that will affect all parts of the public service over at least the next five years.

10.2 The Policing Pledge

The Policing Pledge was launched at the very end of 2008, becoming part of standard police performance measurement during 2009. It replaces all the previous performance measures for community policing with one measure. Home Office figures published in March 2009 showed that confidence levels currently vary across England and Wales, with the national average at 46 per cent. The national target is 60 per cent by 2012. This means that on average, the gap between current performance and the 60 per cent target has to be closed progressively, averaging 5 per cent improvement per year, and totalling 15 per cent or thereabouts. The single national target is just one part of the **Policing Green Paper** published in 2008,[1] which signalled a fundamental shift in police accountability and reporting. Local people are telling the police what service they need and holding them to account via the Policing Pledge. Instead of many measures, there is now one.

10.2.1 Monitoring and evaluating

The Home Office report *Delivering the Policing Pledge: Early Findings* notes that:

> The main national target concerns confidence. However, forces [. . .] need a monitoring regime to understand business delivery and progress against their Pledge. [. . .] Each police force, working closely with key local partners, will be expected to increase [its] own confidence rating by at least 12 percentage points from its current level *to reach the national 60% target by 2012*—those forces with the lowest level of confidence will be expected to make the greatest improvement.
>
> (full text available from Home Office website: <http://www.hmic.gov.uk/ SiteCollectionDocuments/Policing%20Pledge%20Inspections/policing-pledge-early-finds.pdf>, accessed 5 August 2009)

Nearly all forces have published the Policing Pledge text in full. We shall do the same for reference in the following pages, but will add commentary on what we think each section of the Pledge entails. You will see from what we discuss below that quantitative measurement is alive and well, but that the **single confidence measure**, whilst essentially numeric (at 15 per cent over three years at 5 per cent per year), nonetheless is also a *qualitative* measure, because it is concerned with perceptions of service: in this case the public satisfaction with what the police have done locally.

The Pledge begins with this strong preamble:

THE POLICE SERVICE IN ENGLAND AND WALES WILL SUPPORT LAW ABIDING CITIZENS AND PURSUE CRIMINALS RELENTLESSLY TO KEEP YOU AND YOUR NEIGHBOURHOOD SAFE FROM HARM.

[Note: Capital letters are used in the original, which gives the statement a strident touch; the whole text is available from <http://police.homeoffice.gov.uk/publications/police-reform/ Policing_Pledge.html>.]

It goes on:

WE WILL:

1. Always treat you fairly with dignity and respect ensuring you have fair access to our services at a time that is reasonable and suitable for you.

Commentary: This is the main indication that all citizens are to be treated well ('without fear or favour') and that the police will try to accommodate the needs of the citizen. This is a major move away from policing being done *to* people, towards policing being done *on behalf of* people. In other words, the police no longer claim to know best and to decide what is wanted in any given situation. Instead, the citizen's viewpoint will be listened to and police officers will respond to diversity with respect and understanding. This is a significant part of a journey from requiring *compliance* to engaging in *consensus*.

2. Provide you with information so you know who your dedicated Neighbourhood Policing Team is, where they are based, how to contact them and how to work with them.

Commentary: A perennial complaint about the formation of any police team which has extensive interaction with the public, is that membership of the team fluctuates excessively. No sooner is one officer known by name than s/he is posted elsewhere. This was acknowledged from the outset in the *Ten Principles of Neighbourhood Policing*,[2] and this part of the Pledge aims to reassure people that the teams who respond to community needs will, as far as is reasonable, remain consistent, become familiar, and enable relationships to develop over time.

3. Ensure your Neighbourhood Policing Team and other police patrols are visible and on your patch at times when they will be most effective and when you tell us you most need them. We will ensure your team are not taken away from neighbourhood business more than is absolutely necessary. They will spend at least 80% of their time visibly working in your neighbourhood, tackling your priorities. Staff turnover will be minimised.

Commentary: This is also in part a response to a perennial complaint that there is not enough of a visible police deterrent to anti-social behaviour and minor crime, and links with principle 2 above in keeping members of a team together for as long as possible. One of the reasons that PCSOs have proved so popular with the public is that they are visible, they are in uniform, and they stay with their 'patch' for a long time.[3] Patrolling in response to requests from communities is a further innovation and one which suggests that the citizen may genuinely be able to take some ownership of local security.

4. Respond to every message directed to your Neighbourhood Policing Team within 24 hours and, where necessary, provide a more detailed response as soon as we can.

Commentary: This is a combination of quality and quantity measurement but its main message is reassurance that people who report things to their NPT are taken seriously and that something is being done about those things. Of course, it is generally implicit that a consensus opinion about what needs to be done locally is the basis for action, rather than the problem experienced by a single individual, though there will be occasions when police deploy in support of a single person or family. There is no definition of what constitutes a 'response' here, but presumably it would be more than a mere acknowledgement.

> 5. Aim to answer 999 calls within 10 seconds, deploying to emergencies immediately giving an estimated time of arrival, getting to you safely, and as quickly as possible. In urban areas, we will aim to get to you within 15 minutes and in rural areas within 20 minutes.

Commentary: This is a policing performance measure incorporated wholesale from an earlier performance regime. It is true that, as perceived by the public, slow response times, or the failure to provide 'someone real' to talk to, are persistent shortcomings of the police. However, whilst the rapid response times can be met and counted relatively straightforwardly, there is no measure of the quality of what officers do once they have arrived at the emergency or crime scene. This suggests to us that the short-term expediency of finding a quantitative response is preferred to the longer-term, harder-edged qualitative assessment of police action once at the scene. Yet the Pledge aspires to be a qualitative measure; this is evidence of the assessment methodology not having been properly thought through.

> 6. Answer all non-emergency calls promptly. If attendance is needed, send a patrol giving you an estimated time of arrival, and:
> • If you are vulnerable or upset aim to be with you within 60 minutes.
> • If you are calling about an issue that we have agreed with your community will be a neighbourhood priority [. . .] and attendance is required, we will aim to be with you within 60 minutes.
> • Alternatively, if appropriate, we will make an appointment to see you at a time that fits in with your life and within 48 hours.
> • If agreed that attendance is not necessary we will give you advice, answer your questions and/or put you in touch with someone who can help.

Commentary: This is about appropriate and proportionate action in non-emergencies. It will not always be necessary for Special Constables to attend in person when an incident is reported, and it might be enough to pass advice to the caller on the phone. On other occasions, if it is an agreed NPT or local BCU priority (such as graffitists in the act of vandalizing), or if the caller is frightened (such as threatening behaviour outside someone's house), then attendance might be preferable. This measure places the citizen at the centre of the police response and answers an often-stated objection to the impersonal nature of police responses and the lack of follow-up visits. However, there are so many possible permutations of 'action in response' here that it will be difficult to evaluate or to find a meaningful comparator. Certainly, public satisfaction measures might be confused by such a range of options and possibly valid responses.

> 7. Arrange regular public meetings to agree your priorities, at least once a month, giving you a chance to meet your local team with other members of your community. These will include opportunities such as surgeries, street briefings and mobile police station visits, which will be arranged to meet local needs and requirements.

Commentary: There are good practical reasons for public meetings involving NPTs and members of the various communities which make up that neighbourhood. In the first place it is a good investment of police time to meet a range of people at one time and in one place. There is also a sense in which the members of the communities might draw strength and purpose from being part of a larger gathering. This shared purpose may directly contribute to PACT and to the participation of other partners. Finally, there is the comfort of the interaction and the fears/concerns of the communities being taken seriously by the police—which is a large reassurance measure. The flexibility of the police response is also encouraging, but sometimes public meetings can be hijacked by 'splinter' opinions or by strident voices, and it might be that the people who ought to be there are not, because they are fearful, or cannot express themselves in public, or have other inhibitions about joining larger groups.

> 8. Provide monthly updates on progress, and on local crime and policing issues. This will include the provision of crime maps, information on specific crimes and what happened to those brought to justice, details of what action we and our partners are taking to make your neighbourhood safer and information on how your force is performing.

Commentary: This is primarily a reassurance measure. A common complaint from communities is that the police do not routinely inform them of progress or action on a range of issues which are local concerns. For example, people might want to know how measures to curb joyriding are working, or what is being done to improve lighting, or how quickly the local authority will send a team to clean up graffiti. The police are likely to be in the best position to provide information about progress on such issues.

9. If you have been a victim of crime agree with you how often you would like to be kept informed of progress in your case and for how long. You have the right to be kept informed at least every month if you wish and for as long as is reasonable.

Commentary: It is a recurrent feature of the annual British Crime Surveys that victims feel abandoned and left out of the 'information loop' when a crime is investigated by the police and a case is prepared for prosecution. People may not understand the length of time it takes from a crime being committed to a case coming before the courts. It is not unusual for a case to take a year or more to come to Crown Court (via committal proceedings in a magistrates' court), and victims say that they often feel completely left out of the criminal justice system if no one takes the trouble to let them know what is happening. There is a balance to be struck: police officers have other jobs to do and cannot give progress reports off the cuff. There is no objective test for what is 'reasonable', and every victim will be different, but a Special Constable given the victim liaison task should expect monthly contact for a year or so if a case is going to the Crown Court. It is unlikely to drag on for more than 18 months. S/he should explain to the victim at the outset that criminal prosecutions (if they go ahead at all) take time and that there may be no custodial outcome at the end of the process.

10. Acknowledge any dissatisfaction with the service you have received within 24 hours of reporting it to us. To help us fully resolve the matter, discuss with you how it will be handled, give you an opportunity to talk in person to someone about your concerns and agree with you what will be done about them and how quickly.

Commentary: This is a proactive response to complaint. Although this final part of the Pledge is poorly written and lacking in coherence, what it tries to convey is that a person's dissatisfaction with the police response will be dealt with. The mere 'acknowledgement' of dissatisfaction is not enough: the police must meet the individual and work out a way to satisfy the complainant's concerns. Special Constables should take seriously anyone who tells them that they are not happy with what

Importantly, the development of community policing in the last five years is a defining moment: it takes us further along the road of enabling the citizen to have a say in managing his or her life.

The police response to the concerns of the public, through the BCS, CDRPs, PACT arrangements, NPTs, and a strong emphasis on engaging with local communities, has resulted in a slowly increased public satisfaction with the police and clearer perceptions of community safety.[7] The complete trust that 'enabling' requires is not yet there, nor is there much evidence to support claims that the police are reaching effectively into hostile, marginal, or indifferent groups in society. Violence continues to rise, fuelled (evidently) by the constant availability of cheap alcohol. There are still hugely lucrative criminal 'businesses' ranging from identity theft to people and commodity trafficking, and there is clear evidence that the police are losing the war against drugs.[8]

So the picture is by no means perfect, but a start has been made. The creation of NPTs to respond both to crime and to anti-social behaviour at a local level was a step change for the police, as was the idea that they should respond to what most disturbs the law-abiding resident, whether based in minor crime or in intimidating behaviour, rather than to what the police themselves defined as worthy of their engagement (which meant, in effect, dealing with crimes only). Overall, crime continues to decline steadily (we are back to 1982 levels at the time of writing), but this does not mean that the police can ignore people's fear of crime, *which may increase as a perception.*

10.4 Changes to Laws and Police Powers/Actions in Prospect and in Flux

At the time of writing, the Government has set out proposals to make changes to police powers and procedures within the PACE Act 1984. We do not have a crystal ball and cannot determine in advance what will be put into a 'new' PACE Act, nor do we yet know precisely what will be taken out. In the same way, whilst we know that there are proposals in various stages of discussion to abridge, revise, and amalgamate some of the NOS, we don't yet know exactly what will stay and what will go. This is a risk inherent in any *Handbook* which attempts to be as up-to-date as possible and we are, of course, constrained by the finality of publishing deadlines.

That said, in this section we want to look at the possible changes to the PACE Act and also to glance ahead at other legal reforms in prospect (including restrictions on the use of the caution and FPN) to give you some idea of the flux which surrounds contemporary policing. To the best of our knowledge and belief, the following is an accurate summary of the proposals for change most relevant to the operational duties of a Special Constable.

10.4.1 Proposals for change summarized

10.4.1.1 *Stop and search*

Replace the requirement to provide a written record, with a simple receipt; so long as the police officer making the search is using mobile technology with direct input into a force computer system.

10.4.1.2 *Arrest*

Add to existing police powers of entry, to enable premises to be entered in order to arrest for any offence, subject to necessity.

Remove the requirement that you must be in 'immediate pursuit' to enter premises and arrest a person who is unlawfully at large.

Remove the requirement for officers to be in uniform when entering premises for the purpose of making an arrest.

Clarify the status of voluntary interviews at the police station.

10.4.1.3 *Entry, search, and seizure*

Combine sections 18 and 32 of the PACE Act 1984, giving police officers the power to enter premises after arrest to search for evidence of an offence.

Enable an Inspector to authorize entry and search of a suspect's premises where grounds for arrest exist but no arrest has taken place.

Provide a power to enter premises to search for missing persons or any information or material that could assist in locating the person.

Clarify the existing common law powers on seizure and removal of vehicles and 'entire premises'.

10.4.1.4 *Search warrants*

Replace all powers relating to the issue of a warrant to search for evidence, with a single PACE Act power based on necessity.

However, this 'one-size-fits-all' warrant will still require application to, agreement of, and issue by, the judiciary (see 4.4.4.2).

10.4.1.5 *Bail*

Create two new offences of failing to comply with conditions attached to bail issued on the street or issued pre-charge at the police station.

Provide the power to enter premises in any circumstance where reasonable suspicion exists and this is necessary for the enforcement of bail or conditions of bail.

Provide a new power to arrest, when it is anticipated that the suspect will fail to answer police bail to attend a police station, or will breach any conditions of that bail.

Provide the opportunity to use the postal charging process to cancel police bail and, where necessary, replace it with bail to attend court.

Extend the discretionary power to attach conditions to police bail before charge.

10.4.1.6 *Drink-driving hospital procedure*

Provide the opportunity for a registered healthcare professional to take evidential blood specimens at a hospital.

10.4.1.7 *Appropriate adult and parent/guardian involvement in custody procedures*

Extend the access to an appropriate adult for persons in custody from those under 17 to those under 18.

Limit the role of the appropriate adult to those who have received adequate training.

Invite parents, guardians, or other relatives or friends of the suspect to attend the police station but allow the investigation to proceed in their absence.

Provide access to an appropriate adult during voluntary interviews.

10.4.1.8 *Post-charge questioning*

Amend the 'now' caution after charge to state that inferences will be allowed to be drawn.

Allow questioning after referring a case to the PPS (see 9.6) for a decision on charging.

Raise the period of detention for the purpose of questioning to a maximum of 24 hours, subject to authorization by an Inspector or above; and thereafter, on application to a magistrate.

Introduce a condition applying to police bail which enables a requirement to return to the police station for further questioning following a decision to refer the case to the PPS for a charging decision.[9]

10.4.2 Proposed clarification of the police caution and the use of fines and penalties

In early November 2009, the Director of Public Prosecutions (DPP) drew attention to anomalies both in the use of police cautions and in the use of fixed penalties. Cautions, particularly, had been introduced to deal with minor offences, such as shoplifting, aiming to reduce the expense of the legal process engaging with trivial crimes and freeing court time to take on more serious crimes. The DPP noted that 'there was a proper place' for trivial offences to be dealt with outside the courts through FPNs, 'simple' cautions, and 'conditional' cautions,[10] but that the development and exponential increase in the use of these measures has been unsystematic and 'incoherent'. He noted, for example, that 40,000 assaults each year are dealt with ('brought to justice') by on-the-spot cautions. The DPP has issued guidance to the PPS that 'violent offences—those above common assault—should go before the courts'.

Since 2005 Public Prosecutors have had powers to issue 'conditional' cautions, which are similar to a suspended sentence and can include time allocated for community service.[11] Over the same period, the PPS has issued nearly 20,000 such conditional cautions. In 2008–9 the rate was between 600 and 700 conditional cautions per month, or about 8,000 a year.[12] The police, as we saw in 4.5.1, can give 'simple' cautions and FPNs (usually the £80 fine: see 5.3.3), and the Home Office, acting on behalf of the Policing Minister, is seeking to extend the range of offences that can be dealt with by the police in this way.

Nearly half of all crimes, about 700,000 offences each year, are handled outside the courts, including shoplifting, burglary, and assault. It is the last of these particularly which has caused adverse comment, notably from the Lord Chief Justice, the aptly-named Lord Judge, who deplored the use of cautions for 'any crime of violence'.[13] This outcry has led the DPP to consider revision of the existing system. One instance quoted in a BBC *Panorama* interview with the DPP, screened on 9 November 2009, was that of a boy aged 15 cautioned for rape, and another example was when a pub landlady was attacked by having a beer glass smashed into her face. The assailant received a caution because the police adjudged that the landlady's injuries were minor. The use of cautions varies, inevitably, from police force to police force, some using them more than others.

The DPP and the PPS will issue guidelines to the police, and hence to Special Constables, on what actions are appropriate to caution, for what offences to issue a FPN, and what offences should be automatically referred to the courts. This comes at a time and in a context when magistrates are uneasy about the number of offences dealt with by the police that do not come to court, and they note that in more than half of all cases (53 per cent) the fine is not paid and the offender then has to go to court anyway. The Commissioner of the Metropolitan Police joined the debate and was concerned that the increasing police issuing of on-the-spot penalties was undermining the magistrates' court system. He commented that:

> [This] puts the police in the correctional business instead of what we should be in, the law-and-order business, preventing and detecting crime. We've ended up cautioning far too many people.[14]

Our suggestion to summarize this complex issue, then, is that *the review will recommend a reduction in the number of opportunities to levy a fixed penalty or to issue a police caution*, and that these will be for defined minor offences. Physical violence more serious than 'common assault' will be an offence (see 5.1.1) which must be referred to the court system. This will undoubtedly impact upon Special Constables' activities on the streets and in their dealing with incidents.

10.5 Special Constabulary—A 'Mainstream Profession'?

In 2006, on the 175th anniversary of the 'establishment of the Special Constabulary',[15] it was announced that a national strategy for the Special Constabulary was being proposed, following consultation with a working group comprising of HMIC, ACPO, APA, and others. We looked at the National Strategy in detail in the Introduction. What is clear from the National Strategy, and all the initiatives flowing from it (many of which we have covered in the preceding pages), is that the future of the SC is inextricably linked to the future of policing in its much wider sense. In addition to those things which we have looked at already in this chapter, like the Policing Pledge, the future of the PACE Act, the NOS, the use of cautions and the FPN, the following are areas in which we feel the future may contain some substantial developments.

10.5.1 Neighbourhood Policing morphing into neighbourhood management?

Special Constables are certainly embracing the movement of policing into community-based activity and in many forces have contributed to the successful embedding of this new (since 2005) focus. Special Constables can often bridge any perceived gaps between community and the police as they have 'a foot in both camps', coming as they do from the voluntary sector.

However, the next transition is likely to be in terms of making a move towards **neighbourhood management**. This philosophy embraces the partnership approach in community activity, emphasizing that local changes in the socio-economic conditions within neighbourhoods can make ripples at a societal level. The focus will be increasingly on environmental issues affecting people where they live, allied to attempts through partnerships to provide a more holistic approach. Policing is an integral part of this process because environmental conditions affect the way in which law and order are viewed (as we saw with Signal Crimes in 7.10). Policing therefore will form a cornerstone of neighbourhood management:

> This may be why crime and policing are so salient in the public mind: they reveal, specifically, the condition of the community and, generally, the state of society . . . concerns about crime and police effectiveness may thus serve as a lay seismograph of social cohesion and moral consensus.
>
> (Jackson & Bradford, 2009, p 514)

How the Special Constabulary responds to the challenge of neighbourhood management is a key question and the future may lie in Special Constables becoming more embedded and allied to Neighbourhood Police Teams. That too will bring difficulties in its train, as not all Special Constables are enamoured of Neighbourhood Policing, and in some forces we know of strong resistance to what seems to some to be a force's 'default option'. Indeed, we have shown in many examples, how Special Constables prefer to embrace the whole range of policing activities, not a restricted part of them. The police service must tread carefully here: Special Constables will not be retained if they feel strait-jacketed by NPTs, any more than they relished defaulting to car-parking at village fetes some 40 years ago.

10.5.2 The future of volunteering in the police

The introduction of Police Service Volunteers in many forces has already produced a challenge to the Special Constabulary's dominance in police volunteering. Now people can 'volunteer for the police' by helping out on front counters, populating telephone contact bureaus, washing police cars, or 'working' in local neighbourhood teams (see 1.4). Indeed, the parameters for police volunteering are only constrained by how imaginatively each force approaches the offers of help. It is therefore possible for people to see the SC as being merely one option among several when it comes to volunteering for the police.

This presents the SC with a challenge, one which needs to be embraced—how can the SC provide a distinctive volunteering opportunity that differs from that for the PSV? The answer may lie in emphasizing the variety of roles *as police officers* that the Special Constables can undertake, as well as highlighting the opportunities for a fulfilling volunteer experience. Applicants will still join the SC to get a grounding in policing before making their application to join the regulars, but how do forces attract and retain the 'career Special Constable'?

10.5.3 Conclusion

The Special Constabulary, it seems to us, cannot continue to rely only upon its traditional appeal to those wishing to join the regulars, nor upon those for whom policing was always one desire among others. It must reach out to the wider volunteering community at a time when there has never been such choice available to the would-be volunteer. In short, the SC needs to sell itself, and in doing so must consider its 'brand', its 'unique selling point', and how comprehensively it wishes to be part of modern policing.

10.6 Chapter Summary

In some ways, this chapter summary is also a summary of this *Handbook*, closing as it does with a consideration of what the Special Constabulary is and the nature of volunteering.

We remarked earlier in the *Handbook* that some regular police officers are amazed by the vocational spirit of Special Constables, and nonplussed why someone would voluntarily engage in the complex business of policing without any remuneration, even though, from time to time, the question of paying Special Constables has arisen.[16] We hope that, in response to this amazement, we have shown the uniqueness of the Special Constabulary within policing, at the same time as explaining the many parts of policing which go to make up the fabric and texture of the volunteering job itself.

Management in the police is often equated with being economical with resources, but that is only part of the issue. Management is also about ensuring that Special Constables are properly equipped, adequately trained, well supported, fully briefed, and comprehensively assessed. Meeting performance targets goes with the territory in any public service these days, and the Special Constabulary is no exception: indeed, some Special Constables will remember the heady days of the late 1980s when measurement in policing seemed to consist merely of counting arrests. The convulsions of the 1990s and the early years of this century, which marked the importing into the public services of private sector business assessments left many feeling that management was the only thing that mattered, and that leadership, initiative, and discretion were of secondary importance. Simultaneously, with the move from mere managerialism to performance measurement came a steady recognition of the needs of the public.

The citizen focus of successive administrations from 2002 onwards has become central to policing and finds its most appropriate (if not always its clearest) expression in the Policing Pledge. Even here, we have noted that not all police forces have embraced the Pledge with wholeheartedness and some are clearly marking time with it. The purpose of the Pledge seems serious, and given HMIC's interest, it is likely to endure, but (since this is a chapter about futures) perhaps not in its current 'Ten Commandments' form. Reassuringly, the nature of police leadership and police discretion are being revisited too, with a corresponding weight being given to less tangible things that police officers do. *We may even have left behind at least some of the dreary emphasis on quantitative measurement which made the performance indicator regimen so sterile and unrewarding.*

The acknowledgement that policing actually has to move in concert with developments in society at large has given rise to another image in our crystal ball, that of a journey from compliance to consensus. The service is migrating tangibly and in proportion from doing policing *to* people to doing policing *with* people, and we generally applaud such a development whilst remaining conscious that contemporary society continues to be violent and often feckless. There will always be a need to ensure or enforce compliance with the law.

Mechanical factors, such as legislation and assessment structures, analysis of competences, and so on are all in the same restless state of flux that characterizes both society and 'late-modern' policing. If you have come with us all the way from the beginning, you will now know, we hope, a lot more than you did. This is not a handbook simply for the person thinking of volunteering to become a Special Constable. It is not solely for the new joiner. It is not aimed exclusively at the seasoned and experienced Special Constable on independent patrol. *It is intended for all of you,* because what we hope we have done is to provide you with two things: firstly; a clear explanation of the factors, content, tolerances, and essence that policing involves and the complexities of that interaction with all parts of society, and secondly, a context and a meaning to the often arcane or obscure things that police officers are expected to do.

Understanding, we think, is a key to knowledge, and that is the gateway to advancing and developing skills, attitudes, and behaviours. It was our pleasure to try to lay out here some ways to understand that unique, elusive, multi-faceted, and universal person: the *Special Constable.*

Further Reading

Ainsworth, D, 'Spectrum of transition from compliance to cooperation', Kent Police, reproduced in Caless, B (ed.), *Blackstone's PCSO Handbook,* 2nd edn. (2010, Oxford: Oxford University Press), p 508

Arnstein, S, 'A Ladder of Citizen Participation', *Journal of the American Planning Association* (1969) 35[4], pp 216–24, reprinted in Gates, R and Stout, F (eds.), *The City Reader,* 2nd edn. (1996, London: Routledge Press)

British Crime Survey in *Economic and Data Service* 22 July 2008, SN5755, available from <http://www.esds.ac.uk/findingData/snDescription.asp?sn=5755>

Byrne, S and Pease, K, 'Crime Reduction and Community Safety' in Newburn, T (ed.), *Handbook of Policing* (2003, Cullompton, Devon: Willan Publishing), Chapter 12, pp 286–310

Caless, B and Spruce, B, 'Problem-Solving', in Harfield, C (ed.), *Blackstone's Police Procedural Handbook* (2009, Oxford: Oxford University Press), Part 3: Neighbourhood Policing, Chapter 3.7

Farrell, G and Pease, K, 'Crime in England and Wales: more violence and more chronic victims', *Civitas review* (2007) Vol 4, Issue 2, June

Flannery, K, HMIC, 'Police Performance Indicators', in Newburn, T and Neyroud, P (eds.), *Dictionary of Policing* (2008, Devon: Willan Publishing), pp 209–10

Home Office, *Managing Police Performance: A Practical Guide to Performance Management* (2004, London: TSO)

Home Office, *Review of the Partnership Provisions of the Crime and Disorder Act 1998—Report of Findings* (2006, London: Home Office, Crown copyright)

Home Office, *National Community Safety Plan 2008–2011* (2008, London: Home Office, Crown copyright)

Innes, M, 'What's your problem? Signal crimes and citizen-focused problem-solving', *Criminology and Public Policy* (2005) Vol 4, No 2, pp 187–200

Jackson, J and Bradford, B, 'Crime, policing and social order: on the expressive nature of public confidence in policing' *The British Journal of Sociology* (2009) Vol 60, Issue 3, pp 493–521

Laycock, G, 'Crime Prevention (Situational and Social)' in Newburn and Neyroud, (eds.), *Dictionary of Policing* (2008, see above), pp 59–61

Mistry, D, *Community Engagement: practical lessons from a pilot project*, Home Office Development and Practice Report No. 48 (2007, London: TSO, Crown copyright)

PricewaterhouseCoopers, *ACPO Neighbourhood Policing Survey* (2006, ACPO)

Rogers, C and Prosser, K, *Crime Reduction Partnerships* (2006, Oxford: Oxford University Press), p.12

Stichbury, J, *Delivering the Policing Pledge: early findings* (2009, HMIC), also available from <http://www.hmic.gov.uk/SiteCollectionDocuments/Policing%20Pledge%20Inspections/policing-pledge-early-finds.pdf>, accessed 12 November 2009

Tilley, N (ed.), *Handbook of Crime Prevention and Community Safety* (2005, Cullompton, Devon: Willan Publishing)

Wright, A, *Policing: an introduction to concepts and practice* (2002, Devon: Willan Publishing), particularly Chapter 5, 'Policing as the management of risk' and Chapter 7, 'The politics of policing', 'New public management: modernity's finest hour?' (pp 160–6), and 'Policing futures' (pp 166–9)

On BCS and crime data, see Hough, M and Maxfield, M (eds.), *Surveying Crime in the 21st Century* (2008, Cullompton, Devon: Willan Publishing)

Notes

1 A Green Paper is a government discussion paper, which may or may not lead to legislation. Some things in the 2008 Green Paper on Policing were clear enough signals of Government intent, such as the assertion that there is a single route into policing, at constable level, which effectively ends, at least for now, the discussion about

multiple entry to the police. A White Paper is an announcement of forthcoming legislation.

2 See ACPO, *Practice Advice on Professionalising the Business of Neighbourhood Policing*, produced in 2006 for ACPO by the National Centre for Policing Excellence on behalf of the NPIA. It is available at <http://www.neighbourhoodpolicing.co.uk/doclib/doclib_view. asp?ID=528>, accessed 6 January 2009.

3 See Caless, B (ed.) *et al*, *Blackstone's PCSO Handbook*, 2nd edn. (2010, Oxford: Oxford University Press).

4 Jane Stichbury, former Chief Constable of Dorset and an HMIC of some seniority, reported in October 2009 after a website exami- nation of all forces in England and Wales and direct visits to a selection of forces, to ascertain progress in public confidence in the police responses. She concluded that forces had some way to go to embed the Pledge properly, and a similar distance to engage adequately with communities. Her report is available from <http://www.hmic.gov.uk/SiteCollectionDocuments/Policing Pledge Inspections/policing-pledge-early-finds.pdf>, accessed 12 November 2009.

5 Reported as the ACPO response by the Centre for Public Scrutiny, October 2009. CC Spence was one of the originators of the Policing Pledge during 2008, and worked hard to ensure the insertion of the final *caveat* (personal communication with the editor, July 2009).

6 Wright's book is well worth reading. He is a challenging and knowl- edgeable writer, and his short piece on Policing Futures in his Chapter 7 ('The Politics of Policing'), pp 166–9 is masterly, as he shows how the police have not yet developed 'suitable adaptive mechanisms' to enable them to survive rapidly changing conditions.

7 See *British Crime Survey 2007–2008* (financial year), published by the Home Office, July 2008, in which public satisfaction with the police rose by two percentage points between 2006–2007 (51 per cent) and 2007–2008 (53 per cent). Of course, there is still a very long way to go before we can say with confidence that the public trusts the police and is satisfied with what the police do.

8 See, for example, the report from the UK Drugs Commission of July 2008 in which UKDC commented: 'despite significant drug and asset seizures and convictions of traffickers and dealers, drugs markets have proven to be extremely resilient. They are highly fluid and adapt effectively to government and law enforcement interventions.' Street prices for heroin, cocaine, cannabis resin, and Ecstasy have fallen steadily since 2004, suggesting that seizures are having little effect on the quantity imported. Indeed, the Cabinet Office estimated in 2009 that there would have to be sustained seizure rates of between 60 and 80 per cent to put major traffickers out of business, something never before achieved (see UK Drug Policy Commission report 2008).

A number of prominent chief police officers, among them Richard Brunstrom, previously Chief Constable of North Wales, have consist- ently called for the legalization or 'decriminalization' of drugs so that obtaining, smuggling, and trading in drugs would cease to attract criminals.

9 The foregoing has been adapted from the document 'PACE Review, Government proposals in response to the Review of the Police and Criminal Evidence Act 1984', Policing Powers and Protection Unit, Home Office, August 2008, available at: <http://www.homeoffice. gov.uk/documents/cons-2008-pace-review/cons-2008-pace-review-pdf2835.pdf?view=Binary>, accessed 5 November 2009. We must emphasize again that none of the changes envisaged has yet been ratified or promulgated. You should check the current status of the changes with your force.

10 The DPP was speaking on a BBC *Panorama* programme, broadcast at 2030 hours on 9 November 2009 (see note 12 below), and was reported in an interview with Frances Gibbs, Legal Editor of *The Times*, published on the morning of 9 November 2009, ahead of the TV broadcast that evening.

11 See 4.5.1 for the police caution. According to the Home Office 'Ask the Police' website (see note 12 below), an adult offender can be given a 'simple caution' or a 'conditional caution'; both require the offender to admit the crime but the 'conditional' caution also demands that the offender pay for damage caused and/or to enter a rehabilitation process (see 9.14). Neither caution gives the offender a conviction, but the offence prompting the issue of the caution will be recorded on police databases. Cautions incurred may be disclosed by the police to a potential employer. 'Punitive measures' in conditional cautions can include paying a fine, performing unpaid work for not more than 20 hours, or attending a specific place for not more than 20 hours. Unsurprisingly, many criminals opt for a caution rather than a court appearance plus a possible custodial sentence or larger fine. Between 2000 and 2008 2,200,000 people received cautions: of those, 550,000 received two or more, and 51,000 were cautioned four times or more.

See also 'Guilt without a conviction' by Gibb, F, *The Times*, 9 November 2009.

12 *The Times*, *ibid*, and Home Office, <https://www.askthe.police. uk/default.mth>, accessed 9 November 2009. The issue was aired on BBC Radio 4 *The World At One*, and then on BBC TV *Panorama*: see <http://news.bbc.co.uk/panorama/hi/front_page/newsid_8341000/8341162.stm>, programme by Shelley Jofre entitled 'Do cautions "deny victims justice" ', screened on 9 November 2009.

13 The Lord Chief Justice was cited on the BBC Radio 4 *World At One* programme on 9 November 2009, and other judges were quick to join in the chorus of disapproval, among whom Judge Keith Cutler, a senior Circuit judge, believes that a caution for assault 'will one day be followed by murder'. His comments were reported by Gibb, F in an article titled 'Caution for assault "will one day be followed by murder"' in *The Times*, 9 November 2009.

14 Sir Paul Stephenson in an interview with *The Sunday Times*, 8 November 2009.

15 Dating from the 1831 Special Constables Act. In fact, as we demonstrate in 1.5, the history of the Special Constable goes back, in generic terms anyway, to the relationship between the parish constable and

the Justice of the Peace. Strict historians would say that the Statute of Winchester in 1285 is a better date from which to trace the origins and history of Special Constables (making 2010 the 725th anniversary); we are studiedly neutral on the matter.

16 . . . and it actually happened in Derbyshire Police in 2008.

Bibliography and Further Reading

[NB: Place of publication is London, unless otherwise indicated. The date of a publication followed by 'a' or 'b' denotes that the author or originator of the publication produced two or more publications in the same year.]

ACPO/NPIA, *Practice Advice on Professionalising the Business of Neighbourhood Policing* (2006, Wyboston, Lincolnshire: National Centre for Policing Excellence, part of NPIA), available from: <http://www.neighbourhoodpolicing.co.uk/doclib/doclib_view.asp?ID=528>; accessed 11 November 2009

——, *Guidance on the Use of Incapacitant Spray* (2006, Association of Chief Police Officers)

——, (2007a), *Police Health and Safety: a Management Benchmarking Standard* (2007, Association of Chief Police Officers)

——, (2007b), *Strategy for a healthy police service* (2007, Association of Chief Police Officers)

——, *Citizen Focus Hallmarks Summary*, (2008, NPIA) available from <http://www.npia.police.uk/en/docs/citizen_focus_hallmarks_summary_document.pdf>, accessed 12 November 2009

——, *Guidance on the Use of Handcuffs* (2009, Association of Chief Police Officers)

Ainsworth, J, 'The Black & Tans and Auxiliaries in Ireland, 1920–1921: Their Origins, Roles and Legacy', a paper presented to the Annual Conference of the Queensland History Teachers' Association in Brisbane, 12 May 2001, available from <http://eprints.qut.edu.au/9/1/Ainsworth_Black_conf.PDF>, accessed 2 June 2009

Alderson, J, *Policing Freedom* (1979, Plymouth: McDonald and Evans)

——, *Law and Order* (1984, Hamish Hamilton)

——, and Stead, P (eds.), *The Police We Deserve* (1973, Wolfe Publishing)

Alexander, J, *Investigation into premature wastage of Special Constables* (2000, Home Office Police and Reducing Crime Unit)

Almandras, S, 'Special Constables', Standard Note SNHA/1154 (31 October 2008, House of Commons Library)

Amey, P, Hale, C, and Uglow, S, *Development and Evaluation of a Crime Management Model*, Police Research Series, Paper 18 (1996, Home Office, Crown copyright)

Anon [unidentified author], *Metropolitan Special Constabulary: an illustrated history from 1831 to today* (1989, Metropolitan Police)

Anon [no by-line], 'Making Specials Count', *Police Professional*, No 102, 13 March, pp 18–21

Arnstein, S, 'A Ladder of Citizen Participation' in *Journal of the American Planning Association* (1969) 35(4), pp 216–24; reprinted in R Gates and F Stout (eds.), *The City Reader*, 2nd edn. (1996, Routledge Press)

Ascoli, D, *The Queen's Peace: the origins and development of the Metropolitan Police, 1829–1979* (1979, Hamish Hamilton)

Bibliography and Further Reading

Audit Commission, *Hearts and Minds: Commissioning from the Voluntary Sector* (2007, Audit Commission)

Aynsley-Green, A, Towler, K, Marshall, K, and Lewsley, P, *United Nations Report on Britain's Youth Justice System*, reported as Bennett, R 'Law creates underclass of child criminals' in *The Times*, 9 June 2008, available at <http://www.timesonline.co.uk/news>, accessed 9 June 2008

Baggott, M and Wallace, M, *Neighbourhood Policing Progress Report* (May 2006, Home Office, Crown copyright)

Barclay, D, 'Using forensic science in major crime inquiries', Chapter 13 in Fraser and Williams (eds.), *Handbook of Forensic Science* (2009—see below)

Barron, T, *The Special Constable's Manual* (1994, London: Police Review Publishing); a 1999 reprint may be more available: (1999, York: New Police Bookshop)

Baxter, I, 'The Royal Ulster Constabulary Reserve', *Police* (1988) 24[4] (December)

Beaufort-Moore D, *Crime Scene Management*, Blackstone's Practical Policing (2009, Oxford: Oxford University Press)

Bebbington, S, 'Vanishing vandals: a dedicated unit to tackle teenage troublemakers', *Police Review* (2008) 11 January, pp 22–3

Becker, R, *Criminal Investigation*, 2nd edn. (2005, Sudbury, Mass: Jones & Bartlett Publishers), especially Chapters 3, 4 and 5 on crime scenes

Blackledge R (ed.), *Forensic Analysis on the cutting edge: new methods for trace evidence analysis* (2007, Hoboken, New Jersey: John Wiley & Sons)

Bland, N and Read, T, *Policing Anti-Social Behaviour* Police Research Series Paper 123 (2003, Crown copyright)

Bloom, B and Krathwohl, D, *Taxonomy of Educational Objectives: The Classification of Educational Goals, by a committee of college and university examiners. Handbook I: Cognitive Domain* (1956, New York, Longmans, Green), and others in the series to 1964

Brand, S and Price, R, *The economic and social costs of crime*, Home Office Research Study 217 (2005, London: Home Office)

Bratby, L, 'Looking up: innovative partnership scheme in Taunton', *Special Beat* (2004) Summer, pp 24–5

Broeders, A, 'Principles of forensic identification science', in Newburn, T, Williamson, T, and Wright, A, *Handbook of Criminal Investigation* (2007, Devon: Willan Publishing), Chapter 12, particularly the subset 'All evidence is probabilistic', pp 316–18

Brogden, M and Nijhar, P, *Community Policing: national and international models and approaches* (2005, Devon: Willan Publishing)

Brown, B, *Assaults on Police Officers: an examination of the circumstances in which such incidents occur*, Police Research Series, Paper 10 (1994, Home Office, Crown copyright)

Bryant, R and Bryant, S (eds.), *Blackstone's Student Police Officer Handbook*, 4th edn. (2010, Oxford: Oxford University Press)

Busuttil, W, 'Some veterans have trauma from four conflicts', *The Independent*, 28 February 2009

Button, M, *Private Policing* (2002, Devon: Willan Publishing)

Byrne, E, 'Auxiliary Police Officers', *Law and Order* (1980) September

Byrne, S and Pease, K, 'Crime reduction and community safety' in Newburn, T (ed.), *Handbook of Policing* (2003, Devon: Willan Publishing) Part III, pp 286–310

Caless, B, *Best Value Review of Targeted Policing* (2005, Kent Police)

——, 'Numties in yellow jackets', *Policing, A Journal of Policy and Practice*, 1[2] (August 2007, Oxford: Oxford University Press)

——, (ed.), with Bryant, R, (Morgan, D), Spruce, B, and Underwood, R, *Blackstone's Police Community Support Officer's Handbook* 2nd edn. (2010, Oxford: Oxford University Press)

Calligan, S, *Taking Statements*, 6th edn. (2007, Goole, East Yorkshire: The New Police Bookshop)

Carlisle, P and Loveday, B, 'Performance Management and the Demise of Leadership', *The International Journal of Leadership in Public Services* (2007) 3(2), July, pp 18–26

Carrabine, E, *Crime, Culture and the Media* (2008, Cambridge: Polity Press)

Carter, P (Lord Justice), *Managing Offenders, Reducing Crime: A New Approach* (2003, HMSO (now The Stationery Office))

Carter-Wood, J, *Violence and Crime in Nineteenth-Century England: The Shadow of our Refinement* (2004, Routledge)

Casey, C and Dean, J, 'Rural Blues: Parish Constables', *Special Beat* (2000) 10[4], Winter, pp 8–11

Casey, L, 'Engaging Communities in Fighting Crime', (2008) *Cabinet Office Crime and Communities Review*, Crown copyright; available from: <http://www.cabinetoffice.gov.uk/newsroom/news_releases/2008/080618_fighting_crime.aspx>, accessed 1 March 2010

Chisum, WJ and Turvey, B, 'Evidence Dynamics: Locard's Exchange Principle & Crime Reconstruction', *Journal of Behavioral Profiling* (2000) 1[1], available from: <http://www.profiling.org/journal/v011_n01/jbp_toc_january2000_1–1_pub.html>, accessed 26 September 2009

Christmann, K, Rogerson, M, and Walters, D (2003), 'New Deal for Communities: the National Evaluation', Research Paper 14, *Fear of Crime and Insecurity in New Deal Communities Partnerships*, Sheffield Hallam University

Clark, D, 'Life and Limb: the enforcement of health and safety law on the police service', *Police Professional,* No 61, 21 September 2006, pp 50–52

Clarke, C, 'Hot Products: Understanding, Anticipating and Reducing Demand for Stolen Goods', Police Research Series, Paper 112 (1999, Home Office, Crown copyright)

Cohen, L and Felson, M (1979), 'Social Change and crime rate trends: a routine activity approach'; reprinted in Part XI, 'Environmental Criminology', in Cullen, F and Agnew, R (eds.) *Criminological Theory* (2007—see below)

Coleman, D, *DNA Best Practice Manual* (2003, ACPO)

Coleman, K, *Homicides, firearms offences and intimate violence 2005/2006: supplementary volume 1 to Crime in England and Wales 2005/2006*, Research and Statistics Directorate (2007, The Home Office)

Community Safety Advisory Service (CSAS), 'The role of CDRPs' available from <http://www.csas.org.uk/cdrp>, accessed 14 November 2009

Cook, T and Tattersall, A, *Blackstone's Senior Investigating Officers' Handbook* (2008, Oxford: Oxford University Press)

Bibliography and Further Reading

Cooper, A and Mason, L, 'Forensic Resources and Criminal Investigations', in Fraser and Williams (eds.) *Handbook of Forensic Science* (2009—see below), Chapter 11

Corbett, C, *Car Crime* (2003, Devon: Willan Publications)

Crawford, A, 'The pattern of policing in the UK: policing beyond the police' in Newburn, T (ed.), *Handbook of Policing* (2003, Devon: Willan Publishing), Chapter 7

Crawford, A and Newburn, T, *Youth Offending and Restorative Justice: implementing reform in youth justice* (2003, Devon: Willan Publishing)

Crawford, A and Lister, S, 'Extended police family: visible patrols in residential areas', (2004, York: Joseph Rowntree Foundation)

Critchley, T, *The Conquest of Violence: Order and Liberty in Britain* (1970, Constable) (mostly on England and Wales)

——, *The History of Police in England and Wales* (1978, Constable)

Crowe, T, *Crime Prevention Through Environmental Design*, 2nd edn. (2000, Elsevier Butterworth-Heinemann)

Crown Prosecution Service, *Prosecution Team Manual of Guidance*, 2004 edn. [online] available at: <http://police.homeoffice.gov.uk/publications/prosecution/prosecution-team-manual/indexbafb.html?view=Standard&pubID=656164>

Cullen, F and Agnew, R (eds.), *Criminological Theory: Past to Present, essential readings* (2007, Oxford: Oxford University Press)

Cushway, B, *Employer's Handbook 2009–2010: an essential guide to employment law, personnel policies and procedures*, 6th edn. (2009, Kogan Page)

Dale, W and Becker, W, *The Crime Scene: how forensic science works* (2007, New York: Kaplan)

Davis Smith, J and Rankin, M, *Attracting Employer Support for the Special Constabulary*, Home Office Policing and Reducing Crime Unit Occasional Paper (1999, Home Office, Crown copyright)

Dean, J, 'Role of special constables: a case study,' *Police Journal* (1997) 70[1], January, pp. 45–8

Dixon, B, *Very Special Force: 175th Anniversary of Hampshire Special Constabulary* (2006, Winchester: Hampshire Constabulary)

Dixon, D, 'Beyond Zero Tolerance' in T Newburn (ed.), (2005) *Policing: Key Readings* (1999, Devon: Willan Publishing), pp 483–507

Dorries, C, *Coroners' Courts: a guide to law and practice* (2004, Oxford: Oxford University Press)

Drake, D, Muncie, J, and Westmarland, L (eds.), *Criminal Justice; Local and Global* (2009, Devon: Willan Publishing)

DTI, *Business and Society: corporate social responsibility* [CSR] *report* (2002, Department of Trade and Industry)

Eames, B, Hooke, A, and Portas, D, *Court Attendance by Police Officers*, Police Research Series, Paper 9 (1994, Home Office, Crown copyright)

Eck, J and Spelman, W, 'Who ya gonna call? The police as problem-busters', *Crime and Delinquency* (1988) 33, January, pp 31–52

Edwards, C, *Changing Police Theories for 21st Century Societies* (2005, Leichhardt, New South Wales: The Federation Press), particularly Chapter 14 'Control of Policing', and the sections 'Police and Privatisation', pp 311–13, and 'Private Security as Private Police', pp 314–16

Ekblom, P, *Foundations: Issues in Crime Prevention, Crime Reduction and Community Safety* (2000, cited in Byrne and Pease, 2003—see above, pp 296–7)

Elliot, C and Quinn, F, *English Legal System,* 7th edn. (2006, Essex: Pearson Longman), especially Chapter 20 'Sentencing'

Emmott, J, 'Managing a Police Welfare Function', *Executive Development* (1994) 7[3], MCB UP Ltd, pp 13–15

Emsley, C, *Policing and its Context 1750–1870* (1983, Macmillan)

——, *The English Police: A Political and Social History,* 2nd edn. (1996, Longman)

——, *Crime and Society in England 1750–1900,* 3rd edn. (2004, Longman)

——, *Hard Men: the English and Violence since 1750* (2005, London: Hambledon and London) (also published with the title *Hard Men: Violence in England since 1750*)

——, *Crime, Police and Penal Policy: European Experiences 1750–1940* (2007, Oxford: Oxford University Press)

——, and Shpayer-Makov, H (eds.), *Police Detectives in History 1759–1950* (2006, Aldershot: Ashgate)

English, J and Card, R, *Police Law,* 11th edn. (2009, Oxford: Oxford University Press), especially Chapter 7, 'The Law of Evidence'

Epstein, J and Thompson, D (eds.), *The Chartist Experience: Studies in Working-Class Radicalism and Culture, 1830–1860* (1982, Basingstoke: Macmillan)

Fahy, P *et al* (Strategy working group members), *National Strategy for the Special Constabulary* (2007, Working Group on Strategy, NPIA Conference, 3 December), also available from <http://www.npia.police.uk/en/9353.htm>, accessed 2 July 2008

Farrell, S, *Experience and Expression in the Fear of Crime* (2007, Economic and Social Research Council (ESRC))

Felson, M and Clarke, R, *Opportunity makes the thief: Practical Theory for Crime Prevention* Police Research Series Paper 98 (1998, Home Office, Crown copyright)

Fielding, N, *Community Policing*, (1995, reprinted 2002, Oxford: Clarendon Press)

——, *Getting the best out of Community Policing,* The Police Foundation, Paper 3, May 2009

Fielding, N, Innes, M, and Fielding, J, *Reassurance Policing & the Visual Environmental Audit in Surrey Police: A Report* (2002, University of Surrey)

Feilzer, M, 'Not fit for purpose! The (Ab-)Use of the British Crime Survey as a Performance Measure for Individual Police Forces', *Policing* (2009) 3[2], pp 200–211

Fisher, B, *Techniques of Crime Investigation* (2004, Boca Raton, Florida: CRC Press)

Fitzpatrick, B, Menzies, C, and Hunter, R, *Going to Court,* Blackstone's Practical Policing, (2006, Oxford: Oxford University Press)

Flanagan, Sir R, *Modernising the police service: a thematic inspection of work-force modernisation: the role, management and deployment of police staff in the police service of England and Wales* (2004, Her Majesty's Inspectorate of Constabulary (HMIC), Home Office, Crown copyright)

Bibliography and Further Reading

——, *The Review of Policing: Final Report* (2008) available at: <http://police. homeoffice.gov.uk/publications/police-reform/Review_of_policing_ final_report/>, accessed 8 June 2008

Flett, K, *Chartism after 1848: The Working Class and the Politics of Radical Education* (2006, Merlin Press)

Forrest, S, Myhill, A, and Tilley, N, *Practical Lessons for Involving the Community in Crime and Disorder Problem-Solving*, HO Development and Practice Report 43 (2005, Home Office, Crown copyright)

Fraser J and Williams R (eds.), *Handbook of Forensic Science* (2009, Devon: Willan Publishing)

Gardner, R, *Practical Crime Scene Processing and Investigation* (2004, Boca Raton, Florida: CRC Ltd)

Gaston, K and Alexander, J, 'Effective organisation and management of public sector volunteer workers: Police Special Constables', *The International Journal of Public Sector Management* (2001) 14[1], pp 59–74

Gatrell, V, Lenman, L, and Parker, G (eds.), *Crime and the Law: The Social History of Crime in Western Europe since 1500* (1980, Europa Press)

Geary, R, *Policing Industrial Disputes 1893–1985* (1985, Cambridge: Cambridge University Press)

Gersons B, Carlier I, Lamberts R, and van der Kolk, B, 'Randomised clinic trial of brief eclectic psychotherapy for police officers with post-traumatic stress disorder', *Journal of Traumatic Stress* (2000) 13, pp 333–47

Gibson, B, *The Magistrates' Court* (2009, Waterside Press)

——, and Cavadino, P, *The Criminal Justice System; an introduction* (2008, Waterside Press)

Gilbertson, D, 'Plastic policemen: introduction of community support officers', *Police Review*, 21 February 2003, pp 28–9

Gill, M and Mawby, RI, *A Special Constable: A Study of the Police Reserve* (1990, Aldershot: Avebury (Gower Publishing Co Ltd))

——, *Volunteers in the Criminal Justice System: A Comparative Study of Probation, Police* [Special Constables] *and Victim Support* (1990, Open University Press)

Gilling, D, 'Partnership and Crime Prevention' in N Tilley (ed.), *Handbook of Crime Prevention and Community Safety* (2005, Devon: Willan Publishing)

——, *Crime Reduction and Community Safety: Labour and the politics of local crime control* (2007, Devon: Willan Publishing)

Godfrey, B and Lawrence, P, *Crime and Justice, 1750–1950* (2005, Devon: Willan Publishing)

Goldstein, H, 'Improving policing: a problem-oriented approach', *Crime and Delinquents* (1979) 25, April, pp 236–58

Gooch, G and Williams, M, *Oxford Dictionary of Law Enforcement* (2007, Oxford: Oxford University Press)

Goodey, JK, *Victims and Victimology* (2005, Harlow, Essex: Longman)

Graham, K and Homel, R, *Raising the Bar: preventing aggression in and around bars, pubs and clubs* (2008, Devon: Willan Publishing)

Greater Manchester Police, 'Counselling for volunteers helping the police' (1999), available from: <http://www.gmp.police.uk/mainsite/ 0/921EC2E1E03A467F802571040047E594/$file/Counselling for vol-unteers Helping the police.pdf>, accessed 15 September 2009

Green, R, 'Forensic Investigation in the UK', in Newburn, Williamson, and Wright (eds.), *A Handbook of Criminal Investigation* (2007—see below)

Greenbery, N, Langston, V, and Jones, N, 'Trauma Risk Management (TRiM) in the UK Armed Forces', *Journal of the Royal Army Medical Corps* (2008) 154(2), pp 123–6; available from: <http://www.kcl.ac.uk/kcmhr/information/publications/articles/screening/123TraumaRisk.pdf>, accessed 15 September 2009

Greenbery, N, Langston, V, and Scott, R, *How to TRiM away at post Traumatic Stress Reactions: Traumatic Risk Management- Now and in the Future* (2006, King's Centre for Military Health Research), available from <http://www.stormingmedia.us/67/6772/A677274.html>, accessed 15 September 2009

Grover, C, *Crime and Inequality* (2008, Devon: Willan Publishing)

Guy, K and Guy, N, 'Psychological Trauma', *Counselling at Work* (2009) Spring, pp 19–22

Hadfield, P, *Bar Wars: contesting the night in contemporary British cities* (2006, Oxford: Oxford University Press)

Hall, J, 'Trauma and Stress in high-demand conflict and emergency settings', *Counselling at Work* (2006) Autumn, pp 2–4

Hancock, J, 'Special Delivery', *Police Review*, 15 June 2001, pp 18–19 [argues for paying SC]

Hansard, ACPO (Crime Committee) *Written Evidence to the House of Lords Select Committee on Science and Technology* (2000) available from: <http://www.publications.parliament.uk/pa/ld199900/ldselect/ldsctech/115/115we05.htm>, accessed 1 March 2010

Harfield, C (ed.), *Blackstone's Police Operational Handbook: Practice and Procedure*, (2009, Oxford: Oxford University Press)

Harron, M and Mawby, RI, 'Special Constabulary', in Newburn, T and Neyroud, P (eds.), *Dictionary of Policing* (2008, Devon: Willan Publishing), pp 263–4

Hedges, A, *Attracting and Keeping Special Constables*, HO Report on qualitative research (2000)

Hezlet, Sir A, *The 'B' Specials: a History of the Ulster Special Constabulary* (1972, Stacey Publishing)

Hitchen, P, *A Brief History of Crime: The Decline of Order, Justice and Liberty in England* (2003, Atlantic Books)

Her Majesty's Courts' Service, *Definitions of vulnerable and intimidated witnesses*, 2006, available from <http://www.hmcourtsservice.gov.uk/infoabout/attend/witness/special-measures.htm>, accessed 1 March 2010

Her Majesty's Inspectorate of Constabulary (HMIC), *Leading from the frontline—thematic inspection* (2008, Home Office, Crown copyright), available from: <http://www.hmic.gov.uk/SiteCollectionDocuments/Thematics/THM_20080531.pdf>, accessed 11 June 2009

——, *Under the Microscope Refocused: a revisit to the thematic inspection report on scientific and technical support* (2002, Home Office)

——, *Serving Neighbourhoods & Individuals: A thematic report on Neighbourhood Policing and Developing Citizen Focus Policing* (2008) available from <http://www.hmic.gov.uk/SiteCollectionDocuments/Thematics/THM_20081101.pdf>, accessed 12 November 2009

Bibliography and Further Reading

Home Office, Circular 60/1990 (revised 19/2000)

——, *Report of the Working Group on the Special Constabulary in England and Wales, 1995–1996* (1997, Home Office Communications Directorate)

——, *Policing a new century: a blueprint for reform*, Cm 5326, (2001, TSO, Crown copyright), and available from <http://library.npia.police.uk/docs/homeoffice/policing_survey.pdf>, accessed 13 June 2009

—— (2003a), *Public Perceptions of Police Accountability and Decision-Making* (TSO, Crown copyright), and available at <http://www.homeoffice.gov.uk/rds/pdfs2/rdsolr3803.pdf>, accessed 2 July 2008

—— (2003b), *Safety and Justice: Domestic violence consultation paper* (London: HMSO, Crown copyright)

—— (2004a), White Paper, *Building Communities, Beating Crime* available from <http://police.homeoffice.gov.uk/publications/police-reform/wp04_complete.html>, accessed April 2008

—— (2004b), *Violent Crime Unit, Domestic Violence Strategies: A guide for partnerships* (London: TSO, Crown copyright)

—— (2005a), *Community Policing: The Neighbourhood Policing Programme*, available at <http://police.homeoffice.gov.uk/community-policing/neighbourhood-policing>, accessed 29 April 2009

—— (2005b), 'What the public can expect to see from local neighbourhood policing team' available from <http://police.homeoffice.gov.uk/community-policing/neighbourhood-policing>, accessed 25 October 2009

—— (2006a), *Special Constabulary: clarification of review of allowances*, HO Police Human Resources Unit, HO Circular 12/2006; available from <http://www.homeoffice.gov.uk/about-us/publications/home-office-circulars/circulars-2006/012-2006/index.html>, accessed 1 March 2010

—— (2006b) *Citizen Focus: Good Practice Guide* available at <http://police.homeoffice.gov.uk/publications/community-policing/citizen-focus-guide/>, accessed 2 July 2008

—— (2006c) *British Crime Survey: Measuring crime for 25 years* report available from <http://www.homeoffice.gov.uk/rds/pdfs07/bcs25.pdf>, accessed 11 October 2009

—— (2007a), *National Community Safety Plan 2008–2011* (2008) Crown copyright, available at <http://www.crimereduction.homeoffice.gov.uk/communitysafety01.htm?fp>, accessed 22 September 2008

—— (2007b), *Citizen Focus: A Practical Guide to Improving Police Follow-Up with Victims and Witnesses* available at <http://police.homeoffice.gov.uk/publications/police-reform/CF-victimsandwitnesses.html>, accessed 2 July 2008

—— (2007c), *Police and Justice Act 2006*, Home Office, Police Reform Unit, HO Circular 21/2007

—— (2007d), *Amendments to HO health and safety guidance for police officers and police staff*, Home Office Circular 23/2007

—— Green Paper, *From the neighbourhood to the national: policing our communities together*, Cm 7448 (2008, TSO), available from: <http://police.homeoffice.gov.uk/publications/police-reform/Policing_GP/>, accessed 11 June 2009

——, policing web pages for Special Constabulary <http://specials.homeoffice.gov.uk>, accessed June 2009

——, White Paper: *Protecting The Public: supporting the police to succeed,* December 2009 (The Stationery Office, Crown copyright), available from: <http://police.homeoffice.gov.uk/publications/police-reform/protecting-the-public.html>, accessed 3 December 2009

Hostettler, J, *A History of Criminal Justice in England and Wales* (2009, Waterside Press)

Houck, M, *Mute Witness: Trace Evidence Analysis* (2001, Academic Press)

——, 'Trace Evidence' in Fraser J and Williams, R (eds.), *Handbook of Forensic Science* ((2009, Devon: Willan Publishing) Chapter 7, pp 166–95

Hough, M and Maxfield, M, *Surveying Crime in the Twenty-first Century* (2007, Devon: Willan Publishing)

HSE, *Striking a balance between operational and health & safety duties in the police service* (2009, Health & Safety Executive)

Hughes, G, *The Politics of Crime and Community* (2007, Palgrave Macmillan)

——, and Edwards, A, *Crime Control and Community; the new politics of public safety* (2002, Devon: Willan Publishing)

——, McLaughlin, E, and Muncie, J, *Crime Prevention and Community Safety: New Directions* (2002, Open University/Sage Publications)

Humphries, S, *Hooligans or Rebels? An Oral History of Working Class Childhood and Youth, 1889–1939* (1981, Oxford: Basil Blackwell)

Hurd, D, *Sir Robert Peel: a biography* (2007, Weidenfeld & Nicolson)

Ilston, G, 'Database report condemned as "inconsistent and inaccurate"', *Police Professional*, 26 March 2009

Innes, M, *Investigating Murder* (2003, Oxford: Oxford University Press)

——, Abbott, L, Lowe, T, and Roberts, C, 'Seeing like a citizen: field experiments in "community intelligence-led policing"', *Police Practice and Research* (2009) 10[2], April, pp 99–114

——, Fielding, N, and Langan, S, *Signal Crimes and Control Signs: Towards an Evidence-Based Conceptual Framework for Reassurance Policing, A report for Surrey Police* (2002, University of Surrey)

Institute of Directors (IoD)/Health and Safety Commission, *Leading health and safety at work* (2007, Sudbury, HSE) (full text available from <http://www.hse.gov.uk/pubns/indg417.pdf>)

Ipos MORI, *Closing the Gaps. Crime and Public Perceptions* (2008) report available at <http://www.ipsos-mori.com/researchpublications/publications/publication.aspx?oItemId=11>, accessed 2 July 2008

Jackson A and Jackson J, *Forensic Science* (2004, Harlow, Essex: Pearson Prentice Hall)

Jason-Lloyd, L, '"Special" change in police powers', *Justice of the Peace* (2007) 171[8], 5 May, pp 316–7 [on paras 21–3, Schedule 2 of Police and Justice Act 2006, allowing SC to exercise powers anywhere in England and Wales]

Jefferson, M, *Criminal Law*, 8th edn. (2007, Pearson Longman)

Jefferson, T and Grimshaw, R, *Controlling the Constable* (1984, Frederick Muller)

Jewkes, Y, *Handbook on Prisons* (2007, Devon: Willan Publications)

Jeynes, J, *Managing health and safety: learning made simple* (2007, Oxford: Elsevier Butterworth-Heinemann)

Bibliography and Further Reading

Johnston, L, *The Rebirth of Private Policing* (1992, London: Routledge)

Johnstone, G, *Restorative Justice: ideas, values, debates* (2002, Devon: Willan Publications)

——, (ed.), *A Restorative Justice Reader* (2003, Devon: Willan Publishing)

——, and Van Ness, D (eds.), *Handbook of Restorative Justice* (2007, Devon: Willan Publications), especially Chapter 16, Hoyle, C, 'Policing and Restorative Justice', pp 292–311

Jones, T and Newburn, T, *Private Security and Public Policing* (1998, Oxford: Clarendon Press)

——, *Widening Access: improving police relations with hard to reach groups*, Police Research Series, Paper 138, (2001, Home Office, Crown copyright)

——, *Plural Policing: a comparative perspective* (2006, Routledge)

Joyce, P, *Criminal Justice: an introduction to crime and the criminal justice system* (2006, Devon: Willan Publishing)

Kappeler, V and Gaines, L, *Community Policing: a contemporary perspective* (1990 and 2005, Cincinnati, Ohio: Tin Box Studio Inc)

Karagiozis, M and Sgaglio, R, *Forensic Investigation Handbook* (2005, Springfield, Ohio: Charles C Thomas Publisher)

Kelling, GL and Wilson, JQ, 'The police & neighbourhood safety' (1982), available at <http://www.theatlantic.com/doc/198203/broken -windows>, accessed 8 June 2008

Kent, J, *English Village Constable 1580–1642; a social and administrative study* (1986, Oxford: Clarendon Press)

Kent Police, *Policy N11: Crime Scene Management* (2009), available from <http://www.kent.police.uk/About%20Kent%20Police/policies/n/n011.html>, accessed 27 September 2009

Kent, S, *Making Peace: The Reconstruction of Gender in Interwar Britain* (1993, Princeton, NJ: Princeton University Press)

Kershaw, C, Nicholas, S, and Walker, A, *Crime in England and Wales 2007–2008* (2008, Home Office, Crown copyright)

Kimmet, J, 2005, 'Towards common goals and standards: a consideration of the training and operational development of the West Midlands Police Special Constabulary at local level, and how this can contribute to the provision of a more effective community service', author's unpublished text [Bramshill Police Staff College Library, NPIA, ref.: 3FW KIM O/S, C15762]

Kolb, D, *Experiential Learning, experience as a source of learning and development* (1984, New Jersey: Prentice Hall)

Lamberti, JS, 'Understanding and Preventing Criminal Recidivism Among Adults with Psychotic Disorders', *Psychiatric Services* (2007) 58, pp 773–81, June 2007

Landau, N, *The Justices of the Peace, 1679–1760* (1984, Berkeley, CA: University of California Press)

—— (ed.), *Law, Crime and English Society, 1660–1830* (2002, Cambridge: Cambridge University Press)

Larcombe, M, 'Counselling isn't for the completely bonkers!' *Counselling at Work* (2007) February, pp 16–7

Laycock, G and Tilley, N *Policing and Neighbourhood Watch: Strategic Issues*, Crime Detection and Prevention Series, Paper 60 (1995, Home Office, Crown copyright)

Lee, H, Palmbach, T, and Miller, M, *Henry Lee's Crime Scene Handbook* (2001, Elsevier Academic Press)

Lee, M, *Inventing Fear of Crime: Criminology and the politics of anxiety* (2007, Devon: Willan Publishing)

Leon, C, 'The mythical history of the "specials"', (1989) *Liverpool Law Journal* 11[2], pp 187–97, available at <http://www.springerlink.com/content/104947/>, accessed 2 June 2009

Levine, Sir M and Pyke, J, *Levine on Coroners' Courts* (1998, Sweet and Maxwell Publishing)

Liebling, A, assisted by Arnold, H, *Prisons and their Moral Performance: a Study of Values, Quality and Prison Life* (2004, Oxford: Clarendon Press)

Lilley, D & Hinduja, S, 'Police Officer Performance Appraisal & Overall Satisfaction', (2007) *Journal of Criminal Justice*, 35, pp 137–50

Lukka, P, *Employee-Volunteering: a Literature Review* (2000, Institute of Volunteering Research)

Lund, S, 2003, 'Special forces: Thames Valley Police campaign to boost the number of Specials', *Police Review*, 17 January 2003, p 25 [TVP has joined with Buckinghamshire Chilterns University to encourage students on 3yr policing degree to become Specials]

Lurigio, A, Skogan, W, and David, R (eds.), *Victims of Crime: problems, policies and programs* (1990, Thousand Oaks, California: Sage Publications)

Lustgarten, L, *The Governance of the Police* (1986, Sweet and Maxwell)

Macquillan, I, 'Duty in civvies', *Special Beat* (1995) 5[2], Summer, pp 10–13 [Bramshill reference: C24941; on detective roles taken by SC and other undercover work]

Macpherson, Sir W, *The Stephen Lawrence Inquiry: Report of an Inquiry by Sir William Macpherson of Cluny*, Cm 4262 (1999, TSO, Crown copyright), Chapter 10, 'First Aid'; also available from <http://www.archive.official-documents.co.uk/document/cm42/4262/4262.htm>

Mannheim, H, *Social Aspects of Crime in England between the Wars* (1940, George Allen & Unwin)

Mark, Sir R, *In the Office of Constable* (1978, Collins)

Marshall, G, *Police and Government* (1965, Methuen)

Marshall, TF, 'Restorative Justice. An Overview' Home Office Research Paper (1999)

Martin J and Turner C, *Criminal Law*, 2nd edn. (2004, London: Hodder Arnold)

Marx, G, 'The New Surveillance' in Newburn, T (ed.), *Policing: Key Readings* (2005, Devon: Willan Publishing), Chapter 43, pp 761–6

Masini, R, 'The Metropolitan Police strike of 1918 and 1919: a case study of police trade unionism 1912–1919', unpublished MA thesis, 1992, Brunel University [Bramshill reference: 3B42.1 MAS O/S]

Mason, G, 'Where have all the Specials gone?' *Police Review*, 19 January 2001, pp 18–20

——, 'Special concern: dwindling numbers of Special constables', *Police Review*, 22 March 2002, pp 22–3

Mason, M, *Findings from the second year of the national Neighbourhood Policing Programme evaluation*, Home Office RDS, (2009) available from <http://www.homeoffice.gov.uk/rds/pfds09/horr14a.pdf>, accessed 11 June 2009

Bibliography and Further Reading

Mason, P, 'Lancashire Special Constabulary: the way forward', unpublished MBA thesis, 1993, University of Central Lancashire [Bramshill reference: 3WF MAS O/S]

Mather, F, *Public Order in the Age of the Chartists* (1959, Manchester: Manchester University Press)

Maunga, M, 'The Changing Role of the Special Constabulary in England and Wales', unpublished MA thesis, 1994, University of Exeter [Bramshill reference: 3FW MAU O/S, C42932]

Mawby, RI, *Policing Across the World: Issues for the Twenty-First Century* (1999, Routledge)

McBain, C and Machon, J, *Caring Companies: Engagement in employer-supported volunteering* (2009, London: Institute for Volunteering Research)

McCold, P, 'What is the role of community in restorative justice theory and practice?' in Zehr and Toews (eds.), *Critical Issues in Restorative Justice*, (see below) Ch. 13, pp 155–72

McLaughlin, E, *The New Policing* (2007, Sage Publishing)

Mcleod, J, 'Research into the effectiveness of workplace counselling: new directions', *Counselling at Work*, 2008, Winter, pp 7–8

Miller, M, 'Eyewitnesses, Physical Evidence, and Forensic Science: A Case Study of *State of North Carolina v. James Alan Gell*' in *Victims and Offenders Journal* (2008) 3[2 & 3] April, Routledge Taylor and Francis Group, pp 142–9

Millie, A and Jacobson, J, *Employee Volunteering and the Special Constabulary: a review of employer policies* (2002, Police Foundation)

Ministry of Justice (2008a), 'National Offender Management Service' available at <http://www.justice.gov.uk/about/noms.htm>

—— (2008b), 'About NOMS: How NOMS works' available at <http://noms.justice.gov.uk/about-us/how-noms-works/>

—— (2008c), *Community Sentencing—Reducing reoffending, changing lives* (Ministry of Justice)

Moon, D, Walker, A (eds.), Murphy, R, Flatley, J, Parfrement-Hopkins, J, and Hall, P, *Perceptions of crime and anti-social behaviour: findings from the 2008/09 British Crime Survey Supplementary Volume 1 to Crime in England and Wales 2008/09*; November 2009, Home Office RDS

Moon, J, *Reflection in Learning and Professional Development Theory and Practice* (1999, London: Kogan Page)

Moore, T, and Wilkinson, T, *Youth Court Guide* (2009, Hayward's Heath, W Sussex: Tottel Publishing)

Moore T, and Lakha, R (eds.), *Tolley's Handbook of disaster and emergency management* (2006, Oxford: Newnes)

Morgan, J, 'Safer Communities: the local delivery of crime prevention through the partnership approach', [The Morgan Report], (1991, The Home Office Standing Conference on Crime Prevention), August, available from <http://www.mhbuk.com/reports.aspx?sm=c_b>, accessed 7 June 2009; additional material relating to the Morgan Report and the Crime and Disorder Act 1998 is available from: <http://www.crimereduction.homeoffice.gov.uk/toolkits/p010301.htm>, accessed 7 June 2009

Morgan, J, *Conflict and Order: The Police and Labour Disputes in England and Wales, 1900–1939* (1987, Oxford: Clarendon Press)

Mould, P, 'Voluntary service: the introduction of payment for Specials', *Police Review*, 9 February 2001, pp 19–20

Muir, R and Lodge, G, *A New Beat: Options for More Accountable Policing* (2008, Institute for Public Policy Research), available at <http://www.ippr.org>, accessed 20 June 2008

Mulchandani, R and Sigurdsson, J, *Police Service Strength: England and Wales*, Home Office Statistical Bulletin 13/09 (2009, Home Office, Crown copyright)

Mullins, LJ, *Management & Organisational Behaviour*, 7th edn. (2005, Harlow: FT Prentice Hall)

Muncie, J, *Youth and Crime*, 2nd edn. (2004, Sage)

——, Hughes, G, and McLaughlin, E, *Youth Justice: Critical Readings* (2002 (reprinted 2006), Thousand Oaks, California: Sage Publications in association with the Open University)

Myhill, A, *Community Engagement in Policing: lessons from the literature*, Home Office Report 47 (2006), available at <http://www.crimereduction.gov.uk/policing18.htm>, accessed 17 February 2009

Neuberger, J (Chair), *Report of the Commission on the Future of Volunteering and Manifesto for Change* (2008, available from <www.volunteering.org.uk/NR/rdonlyres/0B8EC40C-C9C5-454B-B212-C8918EF543F0/0/Manifesto_final.pdf>, accessed 7 July 2009)

——, *Volunteering across the criminal justice system*, Cabinet Office/Third Sector Report, March 2009, Crown copyright, available from: <http://www.cabinetoffice.gov.uk/third_sector/news/news_stories/090303_neuberger.aspx>

Newburn, T and Stanko, E (eds.), *Just Boys Doing Business? Men, masculinities and crime* (1994, Routledge)

Newburn, T and Jones, T, *Consultation by Crime and Disorder Partnerships*, Police Research Series, Paper 148 (2002, Home Office, Crown copyright)

Newburn, T, Williamson, T, and Wright, A, *A Handbook of Criminal Investigation* (2007, Devon: Willan Publishing)

Neyroud, P, *Public Participation in Policing*, Institute for Public Policy Research (2001, Criminal Justice Forum)

Nolan, Lord, *First Report of the Committee on Standards in Public Life*, Cm 2850–I (1995, The Stationery Office)

NPIA (2007a), 'Special Constables: eligibility for recruitment', (National Policing Improvement Agency) [cancels HO Circular 12/2000]

—— (2007b), NPIA, *Practical Advice on critical Incident Management*, available from <http://www.acpo.police.uk/asp/policies/Data/critical_incident_management_17x08x07.pdf>, accessed 1 March 2010

—— (2008a), *A National Strategy for the Special Constabulary* (2008, Strong Worldwide on behalf of the National Policing Improvement Agency), available from <http://www.npia.police.uk/en/11813.htm>, accessed 10 March 2009

—— (2008b), *Special Constabulary National Strategy Implementation Advice*

—— (2009a), *Special Constabulary*, Police Recruitment and *Specials* Magazine, available from <http://www.npia.police.uk/en/10040.htm>, accessed 9 June 2009

Bibliography and Further Reading

—— (2009b), *IMPACT Programme: Police National Database—Privacy Impact Assessment Report*, April 2009, National Policing Improvement Agency

O'Connor, D, HMIC, *Closing the Gap: a Review of the fitness for purpose of the current structure of policing in England and Wales*, September 2005, HM Inspectorate of Constabulary (Home Office)

——, *Adapting to Protest*, HMIC's Report on policing the G20 protests, (2009, Home Office, Crown copyright)

Omand, Sir D, 'National Security Strategy', (2009, Institute of Public Policy Research Paper)

Orr-Munro, T, 'Something Special: Special Constables', *Police* (2006) 38[3], March, pp 22–3 [proposals to allow SC to join Police Federation]

Page, D, 'Scene of the Grime', *Law Enforcement Technology*, (2004) 31[3], pp 108, 110, 112–13

Parris, H, 'The Home Office and the provincial police in England and Wales—1856–1870', *Public Law* (1961) pp. 230–55

Paterson, T and Axworthy R (1983), 'Extra-Specials: Proposals to strengthen the Special Constabulary', *A Bow Paper*, [Bramshill Police Staff College Library, Bramshill, Hook, Hants., (NPIA)]

Pepper, I, *Crime Scene Investigation: methods and procedures* (2005, Maidenhead: Open University Press)

—— and Pepper, H, *Keywords in Policing* (2009, Milton Keynes: Open University)

Phillips, C, Jacobson, J, Prime, R, Carter, M, and Considine, M (2002), *Crime and Disorder Reduction Partnerships: Round One Progress*, Police Research Series Paper 151, Home Office, Crown Copyright; available at <http://www.crimereduction.homeoffice.gov.uk/publications8.htm>, accessed 6 August 2008

Phillips, D, *Crime and Authority in Victorian England* (1977, Croom Helm)

Phillips, Sir D, Caless B, and Bryant, R, 'Intelligence and its Application to Contemporary Policing', *Policing: a Journal of Policy and Practice* (2007) 1[4], pp 438–46, Oxford: Oxford University Press

Pohl, M, *Learning to Think, Thinking to Learn: Models and Strategies to Develop a Classroom Culture of Thinking* (2000, Cheltenham, Victoria, Australia: Hawker Brownlow)

Police (Conduct) Regulations, Statutory Instrument 2864, detail available from: <http://www.opsi.gov.uk/si/si2008/plain/uksi_20082864_en_1>, accessed 30 July 2009

Police National Legal Database, *Blackstone's Police Operational Handbook: Law*, Bridges, I and Sampson, F (eds.) (2010, Oxford: Oxford University Press)

Policing Pledge, Home Office 2009, available from: <http://www.direct.gov.uk/en/CrimeJusticeAndTheLaw/ThePolice/DG_181995>, accessed 1 May 2009

Police Professional, 'In sickness and in health: the way the service manages sickness absence', *Police Professional*, No. 76, 3 May 2007, pp 38–41

—— 2008a, 'Making Specials count', *Police Professional*, No. 102, 13 March, pp 18–21

—— (2008b) 'Breaking the Mould,' 11 September

——, 'Delivering change in the neighbourhood', No 175, August 2009, pp 15–18

Police Review, 'Met health and safety trial', *Police Review*, 9 November 2007, pp 4–6 [on the guilty verdict under the Health and Safety at Work Act 1974, against the MPS in relation to the operation at Stockwell Underground Station in July 2005 when J-C de Menezes was shot dead in error]

Police Service Recruitment, *Could You?—Special Constables*, available from <http://www.policecouldyou.co.uk/specials/overview.html>, accessed 1 June 2009

Povey, D and Smith, K (eds.), with Hand, T and Dodd, L, *Police Powers and Procedures: England and Wales 2007/08*, 07/09 (2009: Home Office, Research and Development Studies Directorate (RDSD), 30 April, also available from the Research Development Statistics website: <http://www.homeoffice.gov.uk/rds/index.html>, accessed 1 May 2009)

Povey, D, (ed.), Coleman, K, Kaiza, P, and Roe, S, *Homicides, Firearm Offences and Intimate Violence 2007/08* (Supplementary Volume 2 to *Crime in England and Wales 2007/08*), 02/09, January 2009

Povey, K, *Open all hours: a thematic inspection report on the role of police visibility and accessibility in public reassurance* (2001, HMIC, Home Office, Crown copyright)

Prenzler, T and Ransley J (eds.), *Police Reform: building integrity* (2002, Leichhardt, New South Wales: Hawkins Press (a division of Federation Press))

Prime, D, Zimmeck, M, and Zurawan, A, *Active Communities: Initial findings from the 2001 Home Office Citizenship Survey* (2002, Home Office)

Prissell, M, 'Federation predicts PCSOs will become PCs', *Police Review*, 9 October 2009, p 11

Quattrucci, B, 'Citizens on patrol: an investigation into the training and deployment of the Special Constabulary on 4 Area (South East) of the Metropolitan Police', unpublished MSc thesis, 1996, University of Leicester [Bramshill reference: 3FW QUA O/S, C9987]

Quinton, P, and Morris, J, *Neighbourhood policing: the impact of piloting and early national implementation*. Home Office Online Report 01/08 (2008), available from: <http://www.homeoffice.gov.uk/rds/pdfs08/rdsolr0108.pdf>, accessed 11 June 2009

Radzinowicz, L, *A History of English Criminal Law and its administration from 1750*, Vol. 1: *The movement for reform* (1948, Stevens and Sons Publishing)

—— (1956a), *A History of English Criminal Law and its administration from 1750*, Vol 2: *The clash between private initiative and public interest in the enforcement of law* (1956, Stevens and Sons Publishing)

—— (1956b), *A History of English Criminal Law and its administration from 1750*, Vol 3: *Cross-currents in the movement for reform of the police* (1956, Stevens and Sons Publishing)

Rawlings, P, *Policing: A Short History* (2000, Devon: Willan Publishing)

——, 'The Idea of Policing: A History', *Policing and Society* (1995) 5[2], pp 129–49

Redmayne, M, 'Evidence', in T Newburn and P Neyroud (eds.) *Dictionary of Policing* (2008, Devon: Willan Publishing)

Reiner, R, *The Blue-Coated Worker* (1978, Cambridge: Cambridge University Press)

Bibliography and Further Reading

——, 'Who Are the Police?', *Political Quarterly* (1982) 53[2]

——, *The Politics of the Police* (1985, Brighton: Wheatsheaf Press), and 3rd edn. (2000, Oxford: Oxford University Press)

——, *Chief Constables, Bosses, Bobbies or Bureaucrats?* (1991, Oxford: Oxford University Press)

——, 'Policing and the Police' (1997) in Maguire, M, Morgan, R, and Reiner, R (eds.), *The Oxford Handbook of Criminology* 2nd edn. (2002, Oxford: Oxford University Press)

——, *Law and Order: an honest citizen's guide to Crime and Control* (2007, Polity Press)

Riley, J, Cassidy, D, and Becker, J, *Statistics on race and the criminal justice system 2007–8* (2009, Ministry of Justice)

Rivers, K, 'Traumatic Stress: An Occupational Hazard', *Journal of Workplace Learning* (1993) 5(1), MCB UP Ltd, pp 4–6

Robertson, B and Vignaux, G, *Interpreting Evidence: Evaluating Forensic Science in the Court Room* (1995, Chancery Law Publishing)

Roberts, S, *The Chartist Movement 1838—1848* (2002, BBC, available from <http://www.bbc.co.uk/history/british/victorians/chartist_01.shtml>, accessed 8 June 2009

Robinson, T, 'Cashing in on Specials: how can the recruitment and retention of Specials be improved?' *Police Review*, 2 March 2001, pp 28–9 [on payments for SC]

Roche, D, 'Retribution and Restorative Justice', Johnstone and Van Ness, *Handbook of Restorative Justice* (2007—see above), Part 1, Chapter 5, pp 75–90

Rogers, C, 'Team talk: an integrated model of policing crime and disorder', *Community Safety Journal* (2005) 4[3], July, pp 29–34

—— and Prosser, K, *Crime Reduction Partnerships* (2006, Oxford: Oxford University Press)

Rowntree, Joseph (Foundation), *Database State*, March 2009, The Joseph Rowntree Foundation

Roycroft, M, 'What Solves Hard to Solve Murders', *Journal of Homicide and Major Incident Investigation*, (2007) 3[1], NPIA

Sanders, A and Young, R, *Criminal Justice*, 3rd edn. (2007, Oxford: Oxford University Press) [first published in 2000]

Segrave, K, *Policewomen: a history* (1995, McFarland) [largely based on USA]

Seth, R, *The Specials* (1961, Victor Gollancz)

Scottish Government, *The Police (Scotland) (Special Constable) Regulations and Determinations* (2006), available from <http://www.scotland.gov.uk/Publications/2006/01/19102939/0>, accessed 1 March 2010

Sherman, LW and Strang, H, 'Restorative Justice: the evidence' (2007, The Smith Institute)

Simpson, K and Rogers, 'Take on trained recruits: a joint venture between South Wales Police and University of Glamorgan', *Constabulary* (2007) September, pp 6–7

Skills for Justice, *A Guide to the Development of Education and Training Using the National Occupational Standards* (2006, Sheffield: Skills for Justice)

SMART Company, *The Changing Nature of Corporate Responsibility: what role for corporate foundations?* A Report for Corporate Citizenship by The SMART Company, (2007), available from <http://journals. cambridge.org/spd/action/digest?type=null&category=Voluntary activity and civil society&topic=Business and social responsibility>, accessed 1 March 2010

Smith, A, *Crime Statistics: An Independent Review, Carried out by the Crime Statistics Review Group for the Secretary of State for the Home Department* (2006, Home Office), available from <http://www.homeoffice. gov.uk/rds/pdfs06/crime-statistics-independent-review-06.pdf>, accessed 21 October 2009

Smith, J and Rankin, M, *Attracting Employer Support for the Special Constabulary*, Home Office Police and Reducing Crime Unit, Report No. 141 (1999, Crown copyright), available from <http://www.home-office.gov.uk/rds/pdfs2/ah141.pdf>, accessed 1 December 2008

Smith, M, 'Office of Special Constable', *Police* (1998) 30[9], September, pp 32–3 [The author is a solicitor and special constable serving at West Hampstead]

——, 'Life in the Met,' *Police* (2001) 33[2], February, pp 22–3 and 25

Smith, N and Vallejo, J, 'Contamination', *Counsel Magazine* (2006) December, British Forensic Services

Southgate, P, Buck, T, and Byron, C, *Parish Special Constables Scheme*, Home Office Research Study 143 (1995, Home Office, Research and Planning Unit) [Bramshill reference: 3FV SOU, 1858934583]

Special Beat, 'Exit poll: Hertfordshire Special Constabulary has gained a valuable insight into what motivates its voluntary officers by conduct-ing a survey of those who leave', *Special Beat* (1998) 8[2], Summer, pp 16–17

—— (2003a), 'Creating a special role: the Special Constabulary needs to have a distinctive role based in community policing', *Special Beat*, (2003) September–October, pp 8–10 [interview with Peter Fahy]

—— (2003b), 'International perspective: additional policing in other European countries,' *Special Beat* (2003) September–October, pp 16–17 [compares Finland, Germany, The Netherlands, and Scotland as differ-ent kinds of Special]

Special Constabulary website: <http://www.policespecials.com>, accessed June 2009

Specials, 'One Hundred and Seventy-Five: this year is a landmark anniver-sary for the Special Constabulary', *Specials* (2006, NPIA), Autumn, pp 6–9 [Act to establish SC was passed on 15 October 1831]

—— (2008a), 'Employer-supported policing in forces around the country', *Specials* (2008, NPIA), January, pp 9–11 [on retail employees becoming Specials in West Midlands, Merseyside, Suffolk, for example]

—— (2008b), 'The National Strategy for Specials', *Specials* (2008, NPIA), March

—— (2008c), 'Cafe Culture Combats Crime', *Specials* (2008, NPIA), August

—— (2008d), 'Watershed for Specials: the first national strategy for the Special Constabulary', *Specials* (2008, NPIA), August

——, 'A vision for the next 12 months', *Specials* (2009, NPIA, April

Squires, P, Grimshaw, R, and Solomon, E, *Gun Crime: a Review of Evidence and Policy* (2008, Centre for Crime and Justice Studies)

Bibliography and Further Reading

Stanley, N, 'Common goal: police reform', *Special Beat* (2004, Autumn), pp 8–10

Starmer, K, *The Public Prosecution Service: Setting the Standard* (2009, OPSI, Crown copyright)

Stead, P, *The Police of France* (1983, Macmillan)

——, *The Police of Britain* (1985, Macmillan)

Steedman, C, *Policing the Victorian Community: The Formation of English Provincial Police Forces, 1856–1880* (1984, Routledge)

Stichbury, J, (HM Inspector of Constabulary), *Responsive Policing: delivering the Policing Pledge* (2009, HMIC, Crown copyright)

——, *Delivering the Policing Pledge: early findings* (2009, HMIC), also available from <http://www.hmic.gov.uk/SiteCollectionDocuments/Policing Pledge Inspections/policing-pledge-early-finds.pdf>, accessed 12 November 2009

Stranks, J, *Health and Safety at Work: an Essential Guide for Managers*, 8th edn, revised (2008, Kogan Page)

Tapper, C, *Cross and Tapper on Evidence*, 11th edn. (2007, Oxford: Oxford University Press), Chapter 1, particularly Section 3 'Purposes and categories of judicial evidence', part 4 'Things or Real Evidence'

Tarlow, P, *Event Risk Management and Safety* (2002, New York: John Wiley and Sons)

Thames Valley Police, 'Katesgrove Environmental Visual Audit' (2009), available from <http://www.thamesvalley.police.uk/yournh-tvp-pol-area-read-newsitem?id=90173>, accessed 9 November 2009

Thomas, L, Straw, A, and Friedman, D, *Inquests: a practitioner's guide*, 2nd edn. (2008, Legal Action Group)

Thornton, J, (ed.) and Kirk, P, *Crime Investigation*, 2nd edn. (1974, New York: Wiley & Sons)

Tilley, N, 'Crime Prevention in Britain 1975–2010', in Hughes, G, McLaughlin, E, and Muncie, J, *Crime Prevention and Community Safety* (2002—see above), Chapter 2

——, 'Community Policing, problem-oriented policing and intelligence-led policing', Chapter 13 in T Newburn (ed.), *Handbook of Policing* (2003, Devon: Willan Publishing, pp 311–39)

—— (ed.), *Handbook of Crime Prevention and Community Safety* (2005, Devon: Willan Publishing)

Townsend, C, 'Special staff: Special constables', *Police Review*, 21 March 2008, pp 32–3

Travis, A, 'Morality of mining for data in a world where nothing is sacred' (on Omand's report, cited above), *The Guardian*, 25 February 2009; available from <http://www.guardian.co.uk/uk/2009/feb/25/database-state-ippr-paper>, accessed 2 October 2009

Tuffin, R, Morris, J, and Poole, A, *An Evaluation of the Impact of the National Reassurance Policing Programme* (2006, Home Office Research Study 296), available from <http://www.homeoffice.gov.uk/rds/pdfs06/hors296.pdf>, accessed 12 June 2009

Tuffrey, M, 'Getting the measure of community involvement', *The Guide to UK Company Giving* (1999, Directory of Social Change), available from <http://www.corporate-citizenship.co.uk>, accessed 28 May 2009

——, *Employees and the community: how successful companies meet human resource needs through community involvement* (1995, Prima Europe Ltd)

UK Drug Policy Commission Report 2008, available from <http://www.ukdpc.org.uk/reports.shtml>, accessed 1 March 2010

Umbreit, M, *The Handbook of Victim–Offender Mediation* (2001, San Francisco: Jossey-Bass Inc., Publishers)

University of Central Lancashire with Lancashire Police, 'Learning policing by degrees', *Police Professional* (2007) No 80, 28th June, pp 28–32 [students on foundation policing degrees given opportunity to become Specials]

Waddington, P, 'Time to own up and accept blame', *Police Review* (2007) 25 May, quoting contributions to *Community Engagement, Criminal Justice Matters* No 64, Summer 2006, published by the Centre for Crime and Justice Studies at King's College, London

——, 'Local standards in a global world', [on community policing], *Police Review* (2008) 26 September, pp 16–17, available at <http://www.policereview.com>, accessed 20 October 2008

Walker, P, *Pulling the Devil's Kingdom Down: the Salvation Army in Victorian Britain* (2001, Berkeley, CA: University of California Press)

Warrington, D, 'Who says you can't do that? Crime Scene Contamination', *Forensic Magazine* (2005), April/May issue

Watkins, M and Johnson D, *Youth Justice and the Youth Court; An Introduction* (2009, Waterside Press)

Weinberger, B, *Keeping the Peace? Policing Strikes in Britain 1906–1926* (1991, New York and Oxford: Berg Publishing)

Weiner, M, *Reconstructing the Criminal: Culture, Law and Policy in England, 1830–1914* (1990, Cambridge: Cambridge University Press)

——, *Men of Blood: Violence, Manliness and Criminal Justice in Victorian England* (2004, Cambridge: Cambridge University Press)

White, P (ed.), *Crime Scene to Court: the essentials of forensic science* (2004, Cambridge: Royal Society of Chemistry)

Whitehead, P, 'Restructuring NOMS and reducing cultural divides between prisons and probation: a cautionary note', *cjm* (*Criminal Justice Matters*) (2009) Issue 77, September, pp 8–9

——, *Exploring Modern Probation: Social Theory and Organizational Complexity* (2010, Bristol: The Policy Press)

—— and Statham, R, *The History of Probation: Politics, Power and Cultural Change 1876–2005* (2006, Crayford: Shaw and Sons)

Whittle, B and Ritchie, J, *Prescription for Murder: the true story of mass murderer Dr Harold Frederick Shipman* (2000, Warner Books)

Wilcox, D, *The Guide to Effective Participation* (1995) Joseph Rowntree Foundation, also available from <http://www.partnerships.org.uk/guide/index.htm>, accessed 5 June 2008

Willett, T and Chitty, P, 'Auxiliary Police in Canada—An Overview', *Canadian Police College Journal* (1982) 6[3]

Williams, A, 'Special volunteers: perceptions of an Area Special Constabulary', unpublished MSc thesis, 1999, University of Middlesex [Bramshill reference: 3FW WIL O/S, C14675]

Wilson, A, *Is business missing a trick in its support for the voluntary sector?* Leadership development across the sectors (2009, Corporate

Citizenship), available from <http://www.corporate-citizenship.com/>, accessed 28 May 2009

Wilson, D, Ashton, J, and Sharp, D, *What Everyone in Britain Should Know About the Police* (2001, Oxford: Blackstone Press)

Wilson, RE and Brown, TH, 'Preventing Neighborhood Crime: Geography Matters', *National Institute of Justice Journal* (2009) No 263, June, pp 30–35

Worrall, A and Hoy, C, *Punishment in the Community: managing offenders, making choices* (2005, Devon: Willan Publishing)

Wright, A, *Policing: an introduction to concepts and practice* (2002, Devon: Willan Publishing)

Zedner, L, *Criminal Justice*, Clarendon Law Series (2004, Oxford: Oxford University Press)

Zehr, H and Toews, B (eds.), *Critical Issues in Restorative Justice* (2004, Monsey, New York: Criminal Justice Press)

Index

Index

Index

Index

Index

Index

Index

Index

Index